A Friend Among the Senecas

THE QUAKER MISSION TO CORNPLANTER'S PEOPLE

David Swatzler

STACKPOLE
BOOKS

Published by
STACKPOLE BOOKS
5067 Ritter Road
Mechanicsburg, PA 17055
www.stackpolebooks.com

Printed in the United States of America

10 9 8 7 6 5 4 3 2 1

FIRST EDITION

Library of Congress Cataloging-in-Publication Data

Swatzler, David.
    A Friend among the Senecas : the Quaker mission to Cornplanter's people / David Swatzler.—1st ed.
        p.   cm.
    Includes bibliographical references and index.
    ISBN 0–8117–0671–0
    1. Seneca Indians—History.   2. Seneca Indians—Social life and customs.   3. Seneca Indians—Missions.   4. Society of Friends—Missions—Pennsylvania—History.   5. Cornplanter, Seneca chief, 1732?–1836.   6. Simmons, Henry, fl. 1798–1799.   I. Simmons, Henry, fl. 1798–1799.   II. Title.

E78.S3 S93   2000
974.7004'9755—dc21   00–041058

In memory of
Elizabeth J. Ahearn Marsteller (1936–1966)
Jacqueline O. Fuhrmann (1941–1971)
and Ruben T. Timones (1952–1991)

CONTENTS

PREFACE

At the heart of this book is the 1799 journal of Quaker missionary Henry Simmons. For the most part, the book is structured to follow the chronology of the Simmons narrative. Many topics encountered in the narrative, however, required treatment outside the journal's bounds of time and place. The story of how the Senecas lost almost all of their land during the later part of the eighteenth century also required a departure from the journal, and consideration of the cultural conflicts engendered by the mission necessitated a review of events surrounding the mission during the first two decades of the nineteenth century.

An edited version of the Simmons 1799 journal is quoted in this book. Both the original and edited versions are presented in the Appendix. For granting me permission to publish the 1799 journal of Henry Simmons I acknowledge the Quaker Collection of Haverford College. I would also like to express my gratitude to the following institutions for access to their collections of microfilm, manuscripts, and rare books: the Quaker Collection, Friends Historical Library of Swarthmore College, the Darlington Library of the University of Pittsburgh, the Reed Library of the State University of New York at Fredonia, and the Library of the American Philosophical Society, Philadelphia.

I want to thank my editor, Kyle Weaver, for giving such a rare opportunity to a first-time author, and Amy Cooper, for attending to a daunting mass of details, including the final copyediting. I also thank my sister, Valerie, for her encouragement and advice.

David Swatzler
2000

MAPS

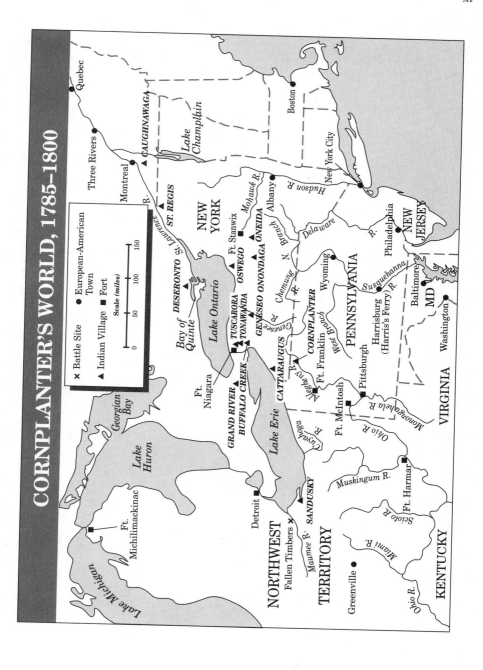

CORNPLANTER'S WORLD, 1785–1800

Battle Site ✕ European-American Town ●

Indian Village ▲ Fort ■

Scale (miles)

0   50   100   150

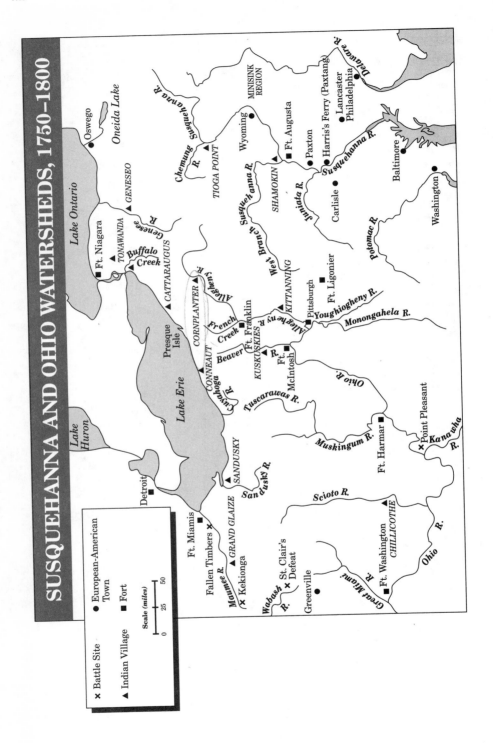

SUSQUEHANNA AND OHIO WATERSHEDS, 1750–1800

● European-American Town
■ Fort
✕ Battle Site
▲ Indian Village

Scale (miles)
0   25   50

Oswego

Lake Ontario

Oneida Lake

Lake Huron

Lake Erie

Detroit

Ft. Niagara

TONAWANDA

Buffalo Creek

▲ GENESEO

Genesee R.

▲ CATTARAUGUS

Presque Isle

CONNEAUT

Cuyahoga R.

CORNPLANTER ▲

Allegheny R.

French Creek

Ft. Franklin

KUSKUSKIES

Beaver R.

Ft. McIntosh

Chemung R.

Susquehanna R.

TIOGA POINT

MINISINK REGION

Wyoming

Ft. Augusta

Paxton

SHAMOKIN

West Branch *Susquehanna R.*

KITTANNING

Pittsburgh

Ft. Ligonier

Youghiogheny R.

Allegheny R.

Monongahela R.

Delaware R.

Harris's Ferry (Paxtang)

Lancaster
Philadelphia

Susquehanna R.

Juniata R.

Carlisle

Baltimore

Potomac R.

Washington

Ohio R.

Tuscarawas R.

Muskingum R.

Ft. Harmar

✕ Point Pleasant

Kanawha R.

SANDUSKY

Sandusky R.

Ft. Miamis ✕

Fallen Timbers ✕

Maumee R.

▲ GRAND GLAIZE

Kekionga

Wabash R.

St. Clair's Defeat ✕

Greenville ●

Great Miami R.

Ft. Washington

CHILLICOTHE ▲

Scioto R.

Ohio R.

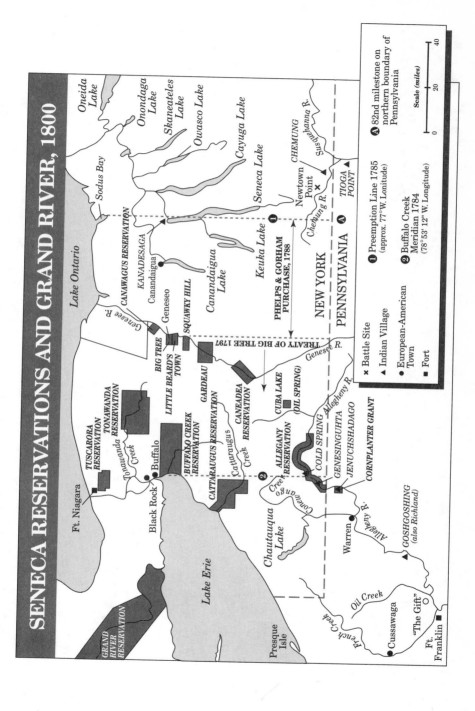

SENECA RESERVATIONS AND GRAND RIVER, 1800

Scale (miles)

0   20   40

Ⓐ 82nd milestone on northern boundary of Pennsylvania

❶ Preemption Line 1785 (approx. 77° W. Lonitude)

❷ Buffalo Creek Meridian 1784 (78° 53' 12" W. Longitude)

× Battle Site
▲ Indian Village
● European-American Town
■ Fort

NEW YORK
PENNSYLVANIA

Oneida Lake
Onondaga Lake
Skaneateles Lake
Owasco Lake
Cayuga Lake
Seneca Lake
Sodus Bay
Lake Ontario
CHEMUNG
Newtown Point ×
Chemung R.
Susquehanna R.
TIOGA POINT ▲
Keuka Lake
❶
CANAWAGUS RESERVATION
KANADESAGA
Canandaigua
Canandaigua Lake
PHELPS & GORHAM PURCHASE, 1788
Genesee R.
Geneseo
SQUAWKY HILL
BIG TREE
LITTLE BEARD'S TOWN
TREATY OF BIG TREE 1797
GARDEAU
Genesee R.
CANEADEA RESERVATION
CUBA LAKE (OIL SPRING)
TUSCARORA RESERVATION
TONAWANDA RESERVATION
Tonawanda Creek
Buffalo
Black Rock
Ft. Niagara
BUFFALO CREEK RESERVATION
CATTARAUGUS RESERVATION
Cattaraugus Creek
❷
ALLEGANY RESERVATION
COLD SPRING
GENESINGUHTA
JENUCHSHADAGO
CORNPLANTER GRANT
Allegheny R.
Conewango Creek
Chautauqua Lake
Warren ●
Allegheny R.
GOSHGOSHING (also Richland) ▲
Lake Erie
GRAND RIVER RESERVATION
Presque Isle
Oil Creek
French Creek
"The Gift" ○
Cussawaga ●
Ft. Franklin ■

IROQUOIS HOMELANDS BEFORE THE AMERICAN REVOLUTION (EXCEPT SENECA)

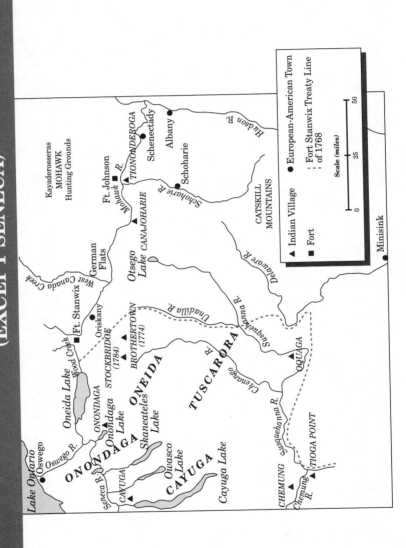

Kayaderosseras
MOHAWK
Hunting Grounds

Ft. Johnson

German Flats

West Canada Creek

Ft. Stanwix

Wood Creek

Oriskany

STOCKBRIDGE (1784)

BROTHERTOWN (1774)

Oneida Lake

ONONDAGA

Onondaga Lake

ONEIDA

Skaneateles Lake

TUSCARORA

Lake Ontario

Oswego

Oswego R.

Seneca R.

CAYUGA

Owasco Lake

CAYUGA

Cayuga Lake

Chenango R.

Susquehanna R.

OQUAGA

CHEMUNG

Chemung R.

TIOGA POINT

TIONADEROGA

Schenectady

Albany

Schoharie

Schoharie R.

Mohawk R.

CANAJOHARIE

Otsego Lake

Unadilla R.

Susquehanna R.

Delaware R.

Hudson R.

CATSKILL MOUNTAINS

Minisink

▲ Indian Village   ● European-American Town
■ Fort   ┊ Fort Stanwix Treaty Line of 1768

Scale *(miles)*

0   25   50

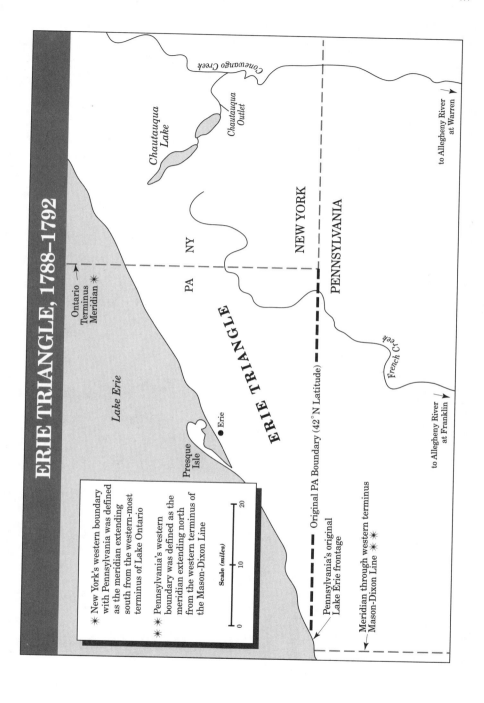

ERIE TRIANGLE, 1788–1792

Lake Erie

Chautauqua Lake

Chautauqua Outlet

Conewango Creek

Ontario Terminus Meridian

PA
NY

NEW YORK

PENNSYLVANIA

French Cr.

ERIE TRIANGLE

Presque Isle

● Erie

to Allegheny River at Franklin

to Allegheny River at Warren

— Original PA Boundary (42° N Latitude)

← Pennsylvania's original Lake Erie frontage

Meridian through western terminus Mason-Dixon Line

✳ New York's western boundary with Pennsylvania was defined as the meridian extending south from the western-most terminus of Lake Ontario

✳ Pennsylvania's western boundary was defined as the meridian extending north from the western terminus of the Mason-Dixon Line

Scale (miles)

0   10   20

Strawberry Time on the Upper Allegheny, 1799

In mid-June 1799 the Allegany Senecas living in Chief Cornplanter's village along the upper Allegheny River in northwestern Pennsylvania were finishing their spring planting.[1] The month that we call June was to them the Berry Moon, and they were preparing to celebrate their annual Strawberry Festival.

On the morning of June 15, while the dew was still drying, Handsome Lake, a 64-year-old Seneca, who had been gravely ill for several weeks, thought he heard someone calling him from outside.[2] Hoarsely, he shouted, "So be it." Then, summoning all his remaining strength, he rose from his sickbed and staggered out of his daughter's house to embrace his fate. His daughter and her husband, who were in the front shed preparing beans for planting, had left the door open so they could hear the sick man if he called for assistance. They heard him shout and stir within the house and then saw him tottering through the doorway. The daughter rushed to her father's side, catching him in her arms just as he collapsed. Handsome Lake had fallen into a state of unconsciousness so deep that his daughter and son-in-law thought he was at the very point of expiring.[3]

The son-in-law, Hatgwiyot, ran to fetch Handsome Lake's nephew, Blacksnake, who also lived in Cornplanter's village. Upon receiving the news of his uncle's dire condition, Blacksnake directed Hatgwiyot to carry the news on to Cornplanter, the village headman, while Blacksnake hurried directly to his failing uncle's side. Cornplanter was Handsome Lake's half brother and also Blacksnake's uncle.

Upon reaching the scene, Blacksnake checked his uncle for signs of life, but detected no pulse or respiration. The body was already cool to the touch. With the help of others present, Blacksnake began moving the body back into the house, where it could be prepared for burial.[4] While handling the body, Blacksnake discovered a warm spot on Handsome Lake's chest. By the time Cornplanter arrived, Handsome Lake had been returned to the sickbed, around which family members and neighbors had gathered. Cornplanter could find no pulse or perceptible breathing, but he verified the existence of the persistent warm spot. So everyone just waited. When the warm spot disappeared, Handsome Lake's death would be confirmed.

But the warm spot did not disappear. It began to grow, and gradually the warmth spread throughout Handsome Lake's body. By noon Blacksnake could feel a pulse, and shortly thereafter Handsome Lake's breathing became perceptible. Finally, some two and a half hours after lapsing into unconsciousness, Handsome Lake opened his eyes. At first he could make no sounds, but soon he found his voice and began to speak. He related a religious vision that came to him during his comatose state. That vision, the first of a series, marked the beginning of a sixteen-year ministry that focused on themes of spiritual renewal, religious reformation, and social morality.

Through his ministry, Handsome Lake redeemed his own heretofore dissolute life, reclaimed for his people much of their traditional religion, and proclaimed a new covenant between the Creator and his Indian children. He restored the spiritual integrity of religious feasts, revived ancient rituals to mark the new covenant, and preached a moral code that equipped the Senecas to cope with the difficult transition to reservation life and to resist the relentless onslaught of European-American culture. He so inspired his followers that a new religion emerged, based on his sermons. Unlike many other native religious revitalization movements, the Longhouse religion survives to this day as a non-Christian alternative for Iroquois believers.

As of that mid-June morning, however, when Handsome Lake stumbled out of his daughter's house, no one could have guessed that such a human derelict would become an important American Indian prophet. The name by which we know him was actually a title, not his given name. According to tradition *The Handsome Lake,* also translated as *The Beautiful Lake* or *The Good Lake,* was the name of one of the original fifty peace chiefs, or sachems, of the Iroquois League. When a league sachem died, a condolence ceremony was conducted to mourn his passing, expunge hostile impulses born of grief, and requicken the name of the deceased in a living member of the same clan. A succession of these ceremonies had been performed through countless generations until the title alighted on an obscure member of the wolf clan, so anonymous that his given name is now unknown. The man who wore the title The Handsome Lake during the close of the eighteenth century had by 1799 become an utter reprobate, given to drinking and brawling.

Late in the previous autumn he had led a party of hunters and their families out of Cornplanter's village for a winter-long hunting trip down the Allegheny River. They moved in canoes as the weather and the river ice permitted, living in a series of temporary camps, staying in each until they had hunted out the local game, and then pushing down river to fresh hunting grounds.

Early in the next spring, the men in Handsome Lake's band temporarily left their families in an encampment, while they floated their winter's accumulation of pelts, hides, and dried meat down the Allegheny to Pittsburgh, where they bartered them, mostly for whiskey. For the return trip, they lashed their canoes together, side by side, to form a raft, with the whiskey kegs in the center. As they paddled up the river, they began consuming the whiskey. By the time they reached the camp where they had left their women and children, some of the men were so drunk they "yelled and sang like demented people" and had to be kept within the inner canoes, lest they fall into the water.[5] With men who were a little more sober paddling in the outer canoes, the families embarked on the tipsy flotilla, which then returned to Cornplanter's village, sometime during the first part of May, just when the planting season was getting into full swing.

Handsome Lake's drunken band burst upon the village and literally raised hell. Many of the other villagers, including women, joined in the drinking. The quarreling and brawling that ensued became so intolerable that sober persons, in fear for their safety and that of their families, abandoned their houses in the village and hid in the surrounding woods. All the fires in the village went out and no meals were prepared. The debauchers did not bother to do such chores as gathering firewood, hauling water, or cooking food, and very likely they did not eat much during their alcoholic binge. The drunken rampage went on for at least a week, until the whiskey finally ran out. When the madness ended, all the houses in the village had been ransacked, and several people lay dead from wounds sustained in the brawling, acute alcohol poisoning, or exposure and hypothermia.

Years later, Handsome Lake recalled the despair and terror of this unhappy episode. "Now the drunken men run yelling through the village and there is no one there except the drunken men. Now they are beast-like and run without clothing and all have weapons to injure those whom they meet. Now there are no doors left in the houses for they have all been kicked off."[6] His recollection is confirmed by Henry Simmons, a young Quaker missionary—or "Friend," as members of the Religious Society of Friends called themselves—who was living in Cornplanter's village at the time:

> A party of Cornplanter's Indians returned from Pittsburgh with a quantity of whiskey that caused much drunkenness among them, which lasted for several weeks and was the means of some of their deaths. One old woman perished outdoors in the night season with a bottle at her side. Numbers of them would go about the village, from morning till evening and from evening until morning, in a noisy distracted condition, sometimes fighting each other. They would enter other people's houses in a detestable manner, ready to pull others out of their beds. They even did so in the very house where I myself lodged—and in the dead of the night too![7]

Late in November 1798, at about the same time Handsome Lake's party had departed for their winter hunt, Henry Simmons had moved into Cornplanter's village to conduct school for the Indian children. The rampant disorder that started in mid-May when Handsome Lake's party returned made it impossible for Simmons to hold classes. This was doubly unfortunate because at that particular time most of the families, having been away for lengthy periods earlier in the year while hunting, maple sugaring, and fowling, were back in the village, where the children could once again attend Simmons's school.

Soon after the disturbance subsided, Simmons, deeply concerned about the threat to Indian well-being posed by alcohol, asked Cornplanter to allow him to address a general council of the village inhabitants. Simmons wanted an opportunity to exhort the villagers to temperance. Cornplanter, always sober himself, was only too happy to oblige the young Friend.

The chief and numerous other native leaders had tried for years to stem the alcohol trade and dissuade their people from drinking "ardent spirits." European Americans plied Indians with alcohol in many different ways, but one of the most insidious practices was that of the itinerant traders who traveled to the Indian country with nothing but alcohol to offer in return for pelts and hides. These traders left no room for Indians to avoid the occasion of sin, transporting the liquor to the very doorsteps of many who would otherwise have remained sober. Cornplanter wanted to see this trade regulated, with the federal government issuing licenses only to reputable traders, who would supply goods that the Indians needed, such as blankets, clothing, rifles, ammunition, and a wide variety of other manufactured articles ranging from hand axes to sewing needles. In a written address to George Washington delivered in Philadelphia in 1791, Cornplanter expressed his gratitude to the president for his efforts to regulate the Indian trade. "And we thank you for the care you have taken to prevent bad men coming to trade among us; if any come without your license, we will turn them back; and we hope our nation will determine to spill all the rum which shall, hereafter, be brought to our towns."[8]

When federal authorities failed, in Cornplanter's view, to live up to their responsibilities by acquiescing to excessive alcohol use among Indians, he did not hesitate to protest and to chide them. In March 1799 for example, Cornplanter, who could not read or write, asked Simmons to take down a letter for him to Israel Chapin, the federal Indian agent stationed at Canandaigua, New York. In the letter, Simmons informed Chapin of Cornplanter's refusal to attend a council scheduled to be held at the Buffalo Creek Reservation because "he knows there will be much drunkenness among them, as it has hitherto been the case, which he does not want to see. And [he] rather censures thee on that account, for not using thy power . . . to suppress that evil habit among them."[9]

The chaos precipitated by the return of Handsome Lake's drunken band had thoroughly disrupted the planting season. Cornplanter, who bore ultimate responsibility for the welfare of his people, was desperate to preserve them from such debauchery. But, on the subject of temperance, many of the villagers had stopped listening to him. He might have hoped that some frank words from an outsider like Simmons would galvanize his people into finally doing something to curb drunken excesses.

Within days of Simmons's request, the Allegany Senecas met in general council with Simmons and two of his fellow Quaker missionaries, who lived on and operated a model, or demonstration, farm about ten miles up the Allegheny River from Cornplanter's village. Simmons enumerated the benefits that flowed from temperance and expounded on the destructive results of drunkenness. In light of recent events, the audience probably received his message with approval, at least insofar as his last point was concerned.[10]

The council adjourned at the conclusion of Simmons's address, his Quaker companions returned to their farm, and the villagers deliberated among themselves. These discussions went on for several days, after which the villagers summoned Simmons to hear their decision. They would not "suffer any more whiskey to be brought amongst them," and they appointed two abstemious warriors to enforce the ban. The drunken rioting during the first half of May had brought the Allegany Senecas to the collective decision that the entire community must swear off alcohol altogether and establish temperance as a community standard.

Handsome Lake, incapacitated by the debilitating effects of chronic alcohol abuse and binge drinking, did not participate in the temperance council or the subsequent deliberations. He lay on his sickbed in his daughter's house, suffering from withdrawal symptoms, enervation, and depression. He was wasting away and he knew it. He experienced a dark night of the soul, regretting the way he had squandered his life and feeling he must be "evil and loathsome . . . before the Great Ruler." He grew morose and despondent.

Then, one morning he noticed the sunshine pouring through the smokehole in the roof of the house. He longed to walk in the sunshine again and thanked the Creator for allowing him just to see it once more. Handsome Lake prayed that he might live until nightfall so that he could watch the stars moving across the smokehole. When he saw the stars passing overhead that night, he gave thanks to the Creator.

And so Handsome Lake went on, surviving from dawn to dusk and dusk to dawn, still fearful and remorseful, but with a growing sense of hope. With each sunny morning and each starry night he was allowed to witness, Handsome Lake became more confident of the Creator's love and care. By the morning of June 15 he had the faith and courage to rise from his sickbed and answer the call.

Upon emerging from the house, Handsome Lake found three spirits, or angels, waiting for him. To help him recover from his illness, they fed him berries and promised to instruct the foremost herbalists in Cornplanter's village—a husband-and-wife team—to prepare a medicine that would restore his ailing health. The angels approved the villagers' plans to celebrate the Strawberry Festival the next day in traditional fashion by performing sacred dances, feasting on freshly picked strawberries—the first of the season—and imbibing strawberry juice mixed with maple sugar. They declared that the festival should be celebrated annually in similar manner, when the strawberries ripened.

The angels then turned Handsome Lake's attention to his own misdeeds, chief of which was his recurrent drunkenness. They told him he must repent and reform, and so must other Indians who were "too fond" of alcohol. "So now all must say, 'I will use it nevermore. As long as I live, as long as the number of my days is, I will never use it again. I stop now.' So must all say when they hear this message."[11] The angels went on to explain that the Creator had made whiskey exclusively for the "white man" to use as a medicine or a balm after hard labor. True, the Creator's white children abused alcohol as badly as, or worse than, his Indian children, but whiskey was never intended for the Indians, for whom it was "a great and monstrous evil" that had "reared a high mound of bones." Finally, the angels condemned witchcraft and denounced the use of "love charms" and abortion-inducing potions.

When Handsome Lake revived from his coma shortly after noon on June 15, he related this vision to those gathered around his sickbed, including Cornplanter. From that very instant, Cornplanter became one of Handsome Lake's most ardent supporters, wholeheartedly endorsing the new prophet's message of abstinence from alcohol. Handsome Lake, still too weak to address the entire village, asked Cornplanter to assemble all the people in general council and recount his vision. He also requested that once assembled, all the villagers eat whatever berries could be provided on such short notice, even dried berries from last season, as a sign that they accepted the message from the three angels.

Wasting no time, Cornplanter called a general council and invited Simmons and Joel Swayne to attend. Swayne, one of the Quakers operating the farm, happened to be in the village helping Simmons build a small schoolhouse. Cornplanter probably figured that Simmons had played a helpful role in forging the consensus to ban the importation of alcohol and that the young Quaker might lend some support to Handsome Lake, especially in light of the prophet's sudden conversion to abstinence from alcohol.

And, indeed, after Cornplanter related to the general council his half brother's vision and the community signified its acceptance by ritually consuming all the berries available in the village, Simmons did speak approvingly of Handsome Lake's message. Simmons was impressed by the promptness of the community in assembling for the council, by the seriousness and solemnity accorded the occasion, and by his own palpable sense of the Holy Spirit at work among the Indians. As he put it:

> I attended the council, for which a large number of them assembled with shorter notice than ever I had seen them before—men, women, and children—many of whom appeared solid and weighty. During the council I felt the love of God flowing powerfully among us. Near the close, I had to communicate some counsel to them, which was, I believe, well accepted. The old chief's sister came to us after the council was over, and thanked me for what I had said to them.[12]

In the months and years that followed, Cornplanter would continue to support his half brother, whose developing moral and social agenda would often coincide with his own. Henry Simmons and other Friends would also find much in Handsome Lake's message that they could endorse.

CHAPTER ONE

Friends Come to the
Upper Allegheny

Friends came among the Senecas on the upper Allegheny River because Chief Cornplanter wanted them there.

During the late autumn and early winter of 1790–91, Cornplanter and a few other Seneca chiefs had spent more than three months in Philadelphia pressing the state government of Pennsylvania to redress Seneca grievances, lobbying the newly formed federal establishment to provide aid, and soliciting the Quakers to educate Seneca youngsters.[1] Cornplanter had made several appeals directly to George Washington, including one in which he asked the president to send the Senecas smiths, millers, schoolteachers, and agricultural instructors.[2]

The fledgling federal government, impoverished and deeply in debt, possessed few resources for providing assistance in any effective way. Nevertheless, little more than a month after Cornplanter's departure from Philadelphia, Henry Knox, Washington's secretary of war, had dispatched Capt. Waterman Baldwin of the U.S. Army to Cornplanter's village, ostensibly to serve as a schoolteacher and agricultural instructor.[3] Baldwin, who had been Cornplanter's prisoner of war during the American Revolution, spoke the Seneca language.

The fact that the United States was still at war with the Indians of the Old Northwest Territory, with whom the Senecas still maintained close—if not always cordial—ties, probably explains the speed with which Baldwin was dispatched. His official mission as teacher and farming instructor seems to have been little more than a convenient cover for unofficial intelligence gathering. Most likely his real job was to alert Washington and Knox of any indication that the Senecas might be planning to renounce their peace treaty with the United States and enter the war on the side of the Northwest Indians. Baldwin's reports to Knox certainly contained a great deal of information on Indian politics and diplomacy. In any case, Baldwin's stay among the Senecas was intermittent and spanned a period of only the seven months between mid-April and mid-November 1791.[4]

Cornplanter obtained better results from Pennsylvania and the Quakers. The state government not only compensated the Senecas for their grievances, but did so very nearly in the amount sought by Cornplanter and the other chiefs.[5] Some Philadelphia Friends agreed to take two Seneca boys into their homes and educate them alongside their own children in a Quaker school.[6] No one, including the Quakers, however, was really ready to send the Senecas the kind of technical and educational assistance that Cornplanter was seeking. That could not happen until the war for the Old Northwest ended and peaceful relations between the United States and the Senecas were confirmed, neither of which occurred until 1794. Even then the federal government and the Quakers required a few more years to refine their policies and coordinate their efforts.

Not until 1798 did Friends first arrive upon the upper Allegheny. Although they came with their own motives and agendas, and as part of a federal government program to "civilize" the Indians, in the final analysis they were there because Cornplanter wanted them to be. They remained on the upper Allegheny for over 140 years, mostly because the majority of the Allegany Senecas wanted them there.[7]

Cornplanter's desire that Friends establish a mission among the Allegany Senecas cannot be understood apart from the preceding forty years of history between the Iroquois and European Americans. The Senecas had become vulnerable to European-American power in ways they had never experienced before. Political vulnerability led to the calamitous loss of Seneca land. Legal vulnerability manifested itself in the failure of the American justice system to protect the lives and property of Seneca persons. These vulnerabilities, combined with the long-term economic dislocations suffered during the American Revolution, contributed to a decline in the Seneca standard of living. Moreover, the legal system's failure to protect Seneca persons and property strained the peace between the United States and the Seneca nation and posed the threat, ultimately, of open warfare and the expulsion of the Senecas from their remaining ancestral lands. The Quakers figured prominently in Cornplanter's strategies to secure a land base for his people, to deflect those elements of European-American society inclined to prey upon and cheat Indians, and to open economic opportunities by which his people could recover their standard of living.

FORTY YEARS OF SETBACKS

Four decades of military and policital setbacks at the hands of first the British and then the Americans left the Senecas in a precarious position. The long string had begun with the French and Indian War of 1754 to 1763. Prior to the conflict, the Seneca nation together with the other Iroquois nations—the Cayuga, Onondaga, Oneida, Tuscarora and Mohawk—had been able to play the British and French colonial powers against one another. In the early 1700s, those two powers, engaged in a long rivalry for empire in America, had each come to perceive the Iroquois as being able to swing the balance of power to its rival. The Iroquois took advantage of this perception by maintaining an armed neutrality and by trading with both sides. To help ensure continued Iroquois neutrality, both sides periodically gave "presents" to the Iroquois—firearms, ammunition, alcohol, and a variety of other trade goods. For half a century, this strategy guaranteed the Iroquois territorial security and assisted in their political ascendancy over other American Indian nations.

During the French and Indian War, the Iroquois balance-of-power strategy collapsed, along with New France. After the war, the British had the upper hand in dealing with the Iroquois, who discovered a new parsimony in British gift-giving and found themselves trading on much less favorable terms. British forts surrounded the Iroquois homelands. In 1763, during the general Indian war known as Pontiac's Uprising, the Senecas and Western Indians from the Ohio River Valley and Great Lakes region tried to push the British back with military force. It did not work; the Iroquois were forced to further accommodate themselves to British policy.

But at least the Indians had gained the attention of the British, whose policy now turned toward stopping the further westward advance of the frontier that separated the American colonists from Indian tribes that were not yet subdued. That frontier coincided, more or less, with the crest of the Appalachian Mountain chain, which the British Proclamation of 1763 declared to be the official western limit for colonial settlement. The idea was to keep the settlers and natives apart until a more orderly and peaceful method of colonial expansion could be worked out. The British wanted to avoid any more Indian wars, which were very expensive and which the colonists were loath to help finance.

This policy, cut short by American independence, was probably doomed to failure anyway. Wealthy land speculators had the financial resources to compromise it, and poor frontier squatters simply ignored British colonial authorities and kept on pushing westward. The policy did, however, suggest to the Indians that the British might be their last bulwark against the land-hungry Americans.

It is not surprising that during the American Revolution, the Iroquois (except for the Oneidas and the Tuscaroras) joined forces with the British. But during the course of the war, the strategic situation deteriorated rapidly for the Iroquois. By 1779 they had lost almost all of their major towns. They had been forced to abandon some, but most, including the crops surrounding them and the provisions stored within, had been destroyed by raiding American armies. The soldiers in those armies were astounded at the evident prosperity and comparatively high standard of living of the Senecas. They found that the "Indians were living in a state of civilization equal to, and in some cases better than, that of the frontier whites."[8]

During September Gen. John Sullivan's 5,000-man army executed a massive and systematic raid against the Seneca and Cayuga homelands in present-day western New York State, destroying the towns and crops between Cayuga Lake and the Genesee River. In their diaries and journals, Sullivan's soldiers described Seneca prosperity in the western districts of the Finger Lakes region. Ironically, these glowing descriptions were written in terms of towns and crops destroyed. One of these towns was Kanadesaga, located near the outflow of Seneca Lake. "There were fifty well-built houses, apple, peach, and cherry orchards, and extensive fields of corn and other vegetables. The army spent September 7 and 8 destroying this settlement."[9]

Lt. John Jenkins, an officer in the Sullivan expedition, remarked on the bounty of the Seneca fields and orchards in the vicinity of Kanadesaga:

This is a very beautiful town, situate[d] on a rising piece of ground about one mile from the mouth of the lake. It contained about 60 houses and was surrounded with apple and peach trees. Our soldiers lived very bountifully on vegetables, etc., while here, as the enemy had plenty of such things for their own support, but being hurried off they left them behind.[10]

Lt. Col. Adam Hubley described what the troops did with the bounty that they could not consume: "There was in the neighborhood [of Kanadesaga] a great quantity of corn, beans, etc., which . . . we totally destroyed; burned the houses which were in number about fifty, and girdled the apple trees."[11]

The productivity and prosperity of the Genesee River valley can be inferred from the descriptions of the largest Seneca town on that river—the Genesee Castle, also known as Geneseo. In his official report, General Sullivan wrote that the Genesee Castle "consisted of 128 houses, mostly very large and elegant. The town was beautifully situated, almost encircled with a clear flat, which extended for a number of miles, where the most extensive fields of corn were, and every kind of vegetable that can be conceived."[12]

No less impressed than his commander about the Genesee Castle and its surrounding fields, Capt. David Livermore wrote that they were "the most beautiful flats I ever saw, being not less than 4 miles in width, and extending from right to left as far as can be seen; supposed to be 15,000 acres in one clear body . . . It consists of upwards of 100 houses. The fields of corn are beyond account, there being not less than 700 acres in the place."[13]

The Sullivan campaign was the most powerful of three strokes against the Seneca and other Iroquois nations in the late summer and early autumn. Gen. James Clinton and his brigade of 1,600 men descended the Susquehanna River from Otsego Lake, New York, to Tioga Point, present-day Athens, Pennsylvania, destroying five Indian towns before joining forces with Sullivan for the scorched-earth march through the Seneca and Cayuga country. In all, the Sullivan and Clinton expeditions destroyed forty towns and villages and "160,000 bushels of corn and a vast quantity of vegetables of every kind."[14]

At about the same time Sullivan was laying waste to the western Finger Lakes district and the Genesee Valley, Col. Daniel Brodhead and a force of 600 men ascended the Allegheny River from Pittsburgh and destroyed Seneca towns and villages on the upper Allegheny in present-day northwestern Pennsylvania and southwestern New York.

Like the soldiers in Sullivan's army, Brodhead and his troops were impressed with the degree to which the Seneca country was not only civilized but also prosperous. In his report to General Washington, Brodhead wrote: "The greatest part of the Indian houses were larger than common and built of square & round logs & frame work. . . . From the great quantity of corn in new ground and the number of new houses built & building, it appears that the whole Seneca and Muncy nations intend to collect to this settlement." Brodhead added that he had destroyed at least 500 acres of corn and vegetables.[15]

Sullivan's Campaign *by Ernest Smith. The Sullivan-Clinton military expedition of 1779 devastated the Iroquois country. Five thousand troops systematically burned some forty towns and villages, including the crops surrounding them and the provisions stored within. Over 160,000 bushels of corn were destroyed. The Senecas suffered the economic consequences of this blow for decades.* ROCHESTER MUSEUM & SCIENCE CENTER, ROCHESTER, NEW YORK.

Although the raids failed in their military objective, which was to knock the Iroquois nations out of the war, they did have disastrous economic consequences, from which the Senecas were decades in recovering. Among the Senecas, these raids earned George Washington, who had conceived, planned, and ordered them, the name of "Town Destroyer."

Many of the Senecas who were living along the Allegheny River when the Quakers arrived in 1798 had lived in the Genesee Valley prior to Sullivan's 1779 campaign and had relocated to the upper Allegheny during the early 1780s. Among these transplanted Genesee Senecas were Cornplanter and Handsome Lake. Cornplanter was drawn to the upper Allegheny by family connections. His uncle, Guyasuta, had been the most important Seneca chief in the region for several decades. When Cornplanter settled there, Guyasuta's health and powers were already in decline, and the nephew quickly succeeded to the uncle's former position.

The Iroquois were able to continue fighting effectively after 1779, but only by relying almost completely on the British for food and supplies, and in some cases, for shelter for their women and children. When the British gave up the fight, the Iroquois were left in a weakened condition to stand alone against the Americans.

The victorious Americans were not in a magnanimous mood. The United States claimed that, based on the "right of conquest," it could take land from the Indians without paying for it. The Iroquois were forced to accept a series of treaties that gobbled up even more of their territory.

Although armed resistance was no longer a real option for the Iroquois following the American Revolution, it was still a viable strategy for Indian tribes living in present-day Ohio, Indiana, and Michigan. These tribes—Shawnees, Delawares, Wyandots, Miamis, and Potawatomies—lived farther from the reach of American military power than did the Iroquois, located in western New York. For more than ten years, these tribes, known as the "Western Confederates," prevented the United States military from occupying the Northwest Territory.

The war for the Northwest Territory finally ended in 1794, when Anthony Wayne defeated the Western Confederates at the battle of Fallen Timbers, in Ohio. Though militarily defeated, the Indians had gained something as a result of their fight. In return for peace and the recognition of its political sovereignty, the United States dropped the "right of conquest" theory and recognized Indian rights to the soil. The Indians would have to be paid for their lands, and in principle, could not be forced to sell. In practice, however, they often had little choice but to sell, and they never received fair payment for their lands.

This was the fate of the Senecas, whose claim to 6,250 square miles in western New York had been recognized by the United States as late as 1794 in the Treaty of Canandaigua. But in September 1797, at the Treaty of Big Tree, the Senecas were finally maneuvered into selling the last of their ancestral lands, except for eleven reservations scattered throughout the western part of the state, which altogether totaled 311 square miles.[16]

One of these reservations, located along the upper Allegheny River, extending both above and below present-day Salamanca in southwestern New York, was designated for the Allegany Senecas, headed by Cornplanter. A ribbon of land, 1/2- to 1-mile wide on each side of the river, the Allegany Reservation stretched from the Pennsylvania–New York border upstream into New York for thirty-five miles.[17] The reservation land belonged to the Seneca nation as a whole, not to any individual or individuals.

CORNPLANTER'S ECONOMIC STRATEGY

Cornplanter's strategy for recovering the Allegany Seneca standard of living was flexible, pragmatic, and diversified. Only one part of it involved the adoption of farming in the European-American style of plow agriculture and animal husbandry. The previous economy of the Allegany Senecas had consisted of hunting to obtain meat and skins, conducted by the men, and hoe horticulture to raise subsistence crops, performed by the women. The men traded deerskins and other pelts for manufactured articles such as clothing, blankets, firearms, and tools, upon which, by the latter part of the 1700s, the Senecas and other American Indians had long been dependent. The women cultivated corn, beans, and squash to form the basis of a subsistence diet, supplemented by meat and fish provided by the men and by seasonal offerings of field and forest, such as berries, nuts, and maple syrup, collected by members of both sexes and all ages.

The Senecas had been agriculturists for centuries. Long before Columbus arrived in North America, Seneca men had been clearing fields, Seneca women had been planting and tending the crops, and both sexes had been harvesting the produce. The women used nothing but handheld implements to cultivate the crops; virtually no livestock was kept; meat came from hunting. Traditional Seneca horticultural methods were entirely adequate for subsistence farming. European-American methods were necessary only for growing a surplus that could be sold as a cash crop.

Cornplanter frequently referred to the need for his people to learn how to "till the ground with the plow, as the white people do" and to "plow and grind corn." But, just as often, he requested technical aid and sought assistance in building and equipping forges, sawmills, and gristmills.[18] Although these technologies could certainly be applied to European-American–style farming—in maintaining plows, farm tools, and saw irons; in building barns, stables, and fences; and in grinding grain—they could all be applied equally as well in other pursuits such as in hunting, to maintain rifles and traps; in lumbering, to fell trees and saw them into boards; and in hoe horticulture, to grind corn grown in the traditional way. The Allegany Senecas engaged in all of these pursuits during the 1790s and the early decades of the 1800s.

Long before the government or the Quakers raised the issue of the Senecas taking up plow agriculture, Cornplanter was making requests for blacksmith services. At the conclusion of the Treaty of Fort Harmar in January 1789, he added: "We shall want our hoes and other articles mended, and for that purpose we would wish to have a blacksmith settle amongst us."[19]

The fact that Cornplanter never contemplated exclusive reliance by his people on European-American–style farming is demonstrated by the pains he took during the 1780s, under the most unfavorable circumstances, to preserve hunting within the state of Pennsylvania as a viable economic option for the Allegany Senecas. In 1784, just after the close of the American Revolution during which four of the Six Nations had fought on the losing side, the Iroquois were forced to sell for a pittance the remainder of their lands within Pennsylvania to the state government. Although the state negotiators held the upper hand, Cornplanter insisted that his people retain their hunting privileges on the ceded lands. The state agreed that the Senecas would retain their hunting privileges until the lands were actually settled by European Americans.[20] Of course, when the lands became settled the viability of hunting as an economic alternative as well as the value of any residual Indian hunting rights would decline rapidly.

Although this was one of the few points on which Cornplanter was able to prevail during the negotiations with Pennsylvania, it was an important one because it bought the Allegany Senecas at least another thirty years of active and productive hunting, which would have been denied to them if their hunting rights had been restricted to land privately owned by individual Indians. After 1784 there were no

Indian-nation reservations left in Pennsylvania. In 1789 during the negotiations by which Pennsylvania acquired the Indian title to lands within the Erie triangle, which the federal government had recently sold to the state, Cornplanter again insisted that the Senecas and other Indians who had been living there be allowed to retain their hunting and fishing rights within the triangle.[21]

Similarly, in 1797 when the Senecas sold their lands, except for some reservations in western New York, they retained hunting rights on the lands sold.[22] Although the Allegany Senecas saw their land holdings shrink to the confines of their 42-square-mile reservation along the upper Allegheny River, this had no immediate effect on their ability to hunt and to trade pelts and hides for manufactured goods. Within the region inhabited by the Allegany Senecas, game animals were in no immediate danger of extirpation and remained abundant for at least the first decade and a half of the 1800s. The deer herd, in particular, was still quite robust, and Pittsburgh, about 207 miles downriver, or 150 miles overland, from Cornplanter's village, was the center of the deer hide trade at that time.[23]

One of the Quaker missionaries, reporting on the 1798–99 winter hunting season, wrote that "some of their best hunters killed near one hundred deer, . . . taking off the skins and leaving much of the meat scattered about in the woods." In another report he noted that "in the winter time, when they have great success in hunting, they leave much of the flesh in the woods, which is devoured by wolves and other animals of prey." As late as 1809, a visiting Canadian Mohawk observed that the forests along the upper Allegheny River constituted "the most valuable hunting ground of any possessed by the [Iroquois] Nations" and that the Allegany Senecas could "conveniently take skins, meat, and timber to Pittsburgh, where they generally get a good price for these articles."[24]

The land drained by the upper Allegheny was very slow to fill up with European-American settlers, mostly because of the mountainous terrain. Every summer hordes of settlers passed through the region, using the Allegheny as a waterway to the west. The high mountains on both sides of the river kept them on the water and moving downstream. The few who stopped to settle as farmers often became discouraged after a few years, pulled up stakes, and resumed their westward migration. Significant settlement did not occur until the 1820s, when a thriving lumber industry developed in the heavily forested region. Until then game was plentiful, and hunting for meat and hides remained a viable economic activity for Allegany Seneca men.[25]

The depletion of game was a prominent and repetitive theme in diplomatic exchanges between the government of the United States and the Senecas and in the correspondence between the Senecas and the Philadelphia Yearly Meeting (PYM) of the Religious Society of Friends. It was a government and Quaker mantra that the key to survival for the Senecas—as for other Indians under the political sovereignty of the United States—was for them to become a nation of farmers.[26] Government and PYM communications directed at Indians almost always hammered home the twin themes that the game was disappearing and that the Indians must take up farming in the European-American style, as if no other economic alternatives were available.

In the case of other Iroquois, such as the Oneidas and the Tuscaroras, located farther east near larger European-American populations and restricted to tiny reservations, there were few alternatives, though some of the Oneidas turned to making splint baskets, which they sold for cash.[27] For the Allegany Senecas, however, there were alternatives, and one of them was hunting, which remained viable until 1814 and perhaps even later.

Why then were communications flowing from Cornplanter to the government and the Quakers replete with references to dwindling game and the need to take up the "white people's way of raising corn"? Mostly because the game would eventually decline, and when it did, plow agriculture would provide an economic alternative to hunting.

Cornplanter was also telling the government and the Quakers what they wanted and expected to hear. He was not being deceitful, just diplomatic. A statesman must respect the views of the other side and consider its priorities. The transmission of European-American farming equipment and methods to the Senecas was a piece of common ground between Cornplanter and his European-American correspondents, who never failed to tell him just how important they thought it was. In December 1790 President Washington told Cornplanter and the other Seneca chiefs visiting Philadelphia that "tilling the ground" was "the only business which will add to your numbers and happiness." In January 1796 the Philadelphia Quakers wrote to the Six Nations asking if the Iroquois were "willing to be instructed in cultivating your land, and in the method which white people take to live plentifully." In February Secretary of War Timothy Pickering told the Six Nations that "by cultivating the ground as the white people do," the Iroquois could "get food and clothing without hunting" by raising wheat, with which they could "purchase all other necessaries."[28]

Cornplanter was quite capable of using this obsession about changing Seneca agricultural practices for his own purposes. In his address to Washington in December 1790, he recited the familiar European-American mantra: "The game which the Great Spirit sent into our country for us to eat is going from among us. We thought that he intended that we should till the ground with the plow, as the white people do, and we talked to one another about it." Having set the stage in this innocuous and even ingratiating way, Cornplanter went on to deliver a stinging rhetorical question, which made his real point: "But before we speak to you concerning this, we must know from you whether you mean to leave us and our children any land to till?"[29]

Sometimes Cornplanter's request that his people be instructed in plow agriculture was merely a preface to his main concern, which was a request for technical and educational assistance. And, on at least one occasion, Cornplanter paid due deference to the European-American priority for the Indians to take up plow agriculture by stating that "the sooner we do this the better for us."[30] To Cornplanter, the value of the Quaker mission consisted not just in the dissemination of farming equipment and techniques, but also in the access it afforded the Allegany Senecas to the smithing and milling technologies of the day, which in turn afforded a variety of economic opportunities to his people.

SENECA VULNERABILITIES

However important the Quakers may have been to Cornplanter's economic strategy, they were even more integral to his strategy for coping with Seneca political and legal vulnerabilities, which European Americans had been exploiting since the end of the Revolution. Political vulnerability had resulted in the steady erosion of the Seneca land base, and if past trends continued, the Senecas would soon be completely dispossessed of their national lands in New York, as they had already been dispossessed in Pennsylvania.

Politically Untenable Indian Landholding

The Iroquois and other Indians lost so much of their former territory partly because they were often lied to and deceived during treaty negotiations. The classic example of this is the infamous Walking Purchase of 1737, in which the Delaware Indians agreed to sell a tract of land along the west bank of the Delaware River to William Penn's sons, John and Thomas, who obviously did not share their father's view that honesty and justice should be scrupulously observed in all transactions with the Indians. Nor did the Penn brothers, who had long since left the Religious Society of Friends, uphold, as the Proprietors of Pennsylvania, the Quaker tradition of peaceable and amicable relations with the natives. The extent of the tract conveyed to the Penns was defined as the distance that a man could walk in a day and a half.[31] This was the customary Indian way of expressing distance and would generally be taken to mean about twenty-five to thirty miles. The Delawares assumed that "the man" would walk along the Delaware River or the Indian trail that skirted it, in either case following a somewhat meandering and circuitous route. In no case did they intend the transfer to include any land above Tohiccon Creek and its confluence with the Delaware.

When the day appointed for the walking came, however, the Delawares discovered that agents of the Proprietors had surveyed a nearly straight-line route through the forest and had cleared it of all tree branches and underbrush, and they had hired three of the swiftest runners in the province to "walk" off the tract by racing against each other. The athlete who went the farthest after a day and a half would be the "man" mentioned in the treaty. Employing three fit athletes not only introduced the element of competition but also helped to ensure that at least one "walker" would still be traveling at the end of the allotted time, not overtaken by mishap or exhaustion.

The walk started at sunrise on September 19, 1737, and continued until nightfall. Attendants traveling on horseback supplied the "walkers" with food and water throughout the marathon. The Indian observers assigned to witness the walk turned away in disgust, complaining that the three men were running. The walk resumed at dawn on the second day, and by noon only a single "walker" was still going. During eighteen hours of "walking," the lone finisher had covered 64 miles—a distance more than twice that intended by the Delawares. To complete the boundaries of the purchase, a line was to be drawn from the terminus of the walk back to the Delaware River. The Delawares intended that the line be drawn from the terminus to the nearest point of the river. The Proprietors arbitrarily drew the line way off to the northeast, to the mouth of Lackawaxen Creek, thereby encompassing an area the size of Rhode Island, approximately 1,200 square miles. The Delawares lost all their land south of the Kittatinny Mountains, including most of the Lehigh River Valley and their favorite Minisink hunting grounds.[32]

Members of the Religious Society of Friends in Philadelphia who had long been politically alienated from the Penns deplored their behavior, and not just because of their shabby treatment of the Indians. Until 1756 Quaker delegates held the majority of seats in the provincial legislature and used that majority to mount a determined political opposition to the Proprietary government.

The Quakers objected to paying taxes for military expenditures, preferring to see the money spent on gifts and presents to keep the Indians friendly. They chafed under a system in which revenues from the taxes they paid were used by the Propri-etary government to host lavish conferences and treaties with the Indians, at which the Proprietors exercised their exclusive right to purchase lands from the Indians. Funds from the public coffers thus subsidized the enlargement of the Proprietors' private estates. The Quakers resented this, and they detested the unethical practices used by the Proprietors to swindle the Indians, which in the Quaker view only served to estrange and antagonize the Indians. The Quakers blamed the outbreak of general Indian warfare within Pennsylvania in 1755 on the Proprietary government's mismanagement of Indian affairs.

The Quakers' pacifism during the French and Indian War cost them popular po-litical support, and they lost their legislative majority in the provincial elections of 1756. The Proprietary government seized upon the opportunity not only to fund full-scale war against the Indians but also to offer cash bounties for Indian scalps, in-cluding those of women and children. Several of the remaining Quaker legislators resigned in protest, ushering in a period of Quaker withdrawal from government.

To win back the confidence of the Indians, restore peace, and prevent outrages like the Walking Purchase from happening again, individual Philadelphia Quakers—prominent men of wealth and influence, many of them merchants—formed the Friendly Association in 1756. The Association was neither part of the provincial government nor part of the Philadelphia Yearly Meeting (PYM). Although the provincial government viewed the Friendly Association as a meddlesome pressure group, the PYM approved of its goals, one of which was to promote justice in the provincial government's land dealings with the Indians.[33]

To settle Indian land claims and other grievances, the Friendly Association arranged conferences between various Indian nations and the provincial government. Members of the Association acted as mediators at these conferences, dispensing both gifts and advice to the Indians. So successful was the Association in its early years that in 1757 the Delaware chief Teedyuscung refused to negotiate a treaty un-less Friends were present, and by 1758 Proprietary officials could not hold treaty ne-gotiations or conduct business with the Indians without Association members attending and moderating the proceedings. The Association continued to operate until 1764, though less effectively after 1758. Pontiac's Uprising of 1763 turned the Pennsylvania body politic firmly and finally away from Quaker pacifism.[34]

At the conclusion of the Revolution, the Philadelphia Friends once again started sending delegates to treaty negotiations—this time between the Indian nations and the national government of the United States. This time the delegates went under the auspices of the PYM as a corporate entity. Acting as observers and witnesses, these delegations advised the Indians and tried to ensure that they received fair treatment. At the invitation of Iroquois chiefs, delegations of Friends attended the treaty negotiations at Newtown in 1791, at Sandusky in 1793, and at Canandaigua in 1794.[35]

Cornplanter was not only impressed by the personal integrity of the Friends with whom he dealt directly, but also by the Quaker reputation among important European Americans for honesty, fairness, and dedication to principle. The Quakers were already becoming something of a moral force in the new United States, and they came highly recommended to the Senecas by the likes of George Washington, Henry Knox, and Timothy Pickering. Cornplanter almost certainly appreciated the efforts of Friends at treaty negotiations and he definitely thought they could be of help in defending the Seneca land base against the incessant machinations of speculators and land companies.

In June 1798 just after the first Quaker missionaries arrived at his village, Cornplanter pleaded with Quaker elders John Pierce and Joshua Sharpless to join him in attending an important council at Buffalo Creek, present-day Buffalo, New York. The council was to be held between the chiefs of the Seneca nation and Joseph Ellicott of the Holland Land Company, which had recently purchased the bulk of the Seneca homelands from Robert Morris, who in turn had acquired them from the Senecas at the Treaty of Big Tree in 1797. Ellicott had been appointed by the secretary of war to supervise the surveying of the boundaries for the Seneca reservations on Buffalo Creek, Tonawanda Creek, Cattaraugus Creek, and the Allegheny River. The general location and amount of acreage for each of these reservations had been agreed upon at the Treaty of Big Tree, but the specific tracts of land to be reserved and the actual boundaries were yet to be negotiated by the chiefs and Ellicott. The federal Indian agent for the Six Nations, Israel Chapin, Jr., would be present at the meeting too, ostensibly to safeguard the interests of the Seneca nation. But as Cornplanter well knew, Chapin was also a paid agent of the Holland Land Company—a definite conflict of interest.

Cornplanter may have thought that the mere presence of the Friends would not only deter Ellicott from any chicanery, such as shorting the Indians on maps or surveys, but would also make it difficult for him to refuse reasonable Seneca demands regarding the layout of the reservations. The presence of the Quaker elders might facilitate some dubious stratagems of Cornplanter's, as well as enhance his own standing among the other chiefs. Pierce and Sharpless agreed to attend, and they traveled to Buffalo Creek, arriving at the appointed time. But so delayed were Ellicott and Chapin in their journey to Buffalo Creek that the Quaker elders felt compelled to leave on their return trip to Philadelphia before either the land agent or the federal agent had even arrived. Pierce and Sharpless had come to the Seneca country only long enough to oversee the initial establishment of the Allegany mission. Three younger Friends, including Henry Simmons, remained on the upper Allegheny River to staff the mission.

In his showdown with Ellicott and Chapin, Cornplanter acquitted himself with distinction as a wily negotiator and a wearisome haggler, making effective use of the Quakers even in their absence. It was generally recognized that if the Quakers observed any European-American malfeasance toward the Indians, they would report it to the federal authorities in Philadelphia. Cornplanter realized that a Quaker presence among the Allegany Senecas would deter other European Americans, whether of high station or low, from trying to swindle the Indians in land transactions or in trade.

Intercultural Crime and the Risk of War

The failure of the American legal system to protect the Indians was not only a gross injustice to individual Senecas, but it also posed a threat to peace and, consequently, to the remaining Seneca land base. As the list of unpunished and uncompensated European-American crimes against Seneca persons and property grew longer, it became ever more difficult for chiefs like Cornplanter to restrain their people, especially their young men, from seeking revenge. Violent retaliation by disaffected Seneca individuals would almost certainly be indiscriminate, as would the ensuing counter-retaliation by European Americans. A cycle of spiraling violence could lead to war between the United States and the Seneca nation, in which case the Senecas would almost certainly be driven from their homes forever.

The American legal system left the Senecas vulnerable. When European Americans committed crimes, such as robbery or murder, against Senecas, they always went unpunished by the legal system. European-American perpetrators were seldom charged; if charged, they were rarely apprehended; if apprehended and tried, they were never convicted. Juries were composed exclusively of European Americans. During the decade and a half between the end of the Revolution and the arrival of the Quaker missionaries, no jury ever convicted a European American of a serious crime against a Seneca.[36]

When Indians committed crimes such as murder, robbery, or theft, an Indian or Indians were usually punished, even if the punishment was extrajudicial, or vigilante, and even if the ones punished were not the perpetrators. Allegany Senecas were frequently blamed for crimes committed by marauding bands of hostile Indians from present-day Ohio, Indiana, and Michigan.[37]

European-American merchants and traders routinely cheated Indians, who had no legal recourse for recovering their losses. Some traders came into the Seneca villages, selling only whiskey, but even those who peddled useful articles charged exorbitant prices. The only force that acted to curb the worst impulses of these itinerant traders was the overwhelming numerical superiority of the Indians, who might expel, beat, or kill a trader who gouged too much. The gouging was even worse when the Senecas traded away from home in Franklin[38] and Pittsburgh, where there were virtually no restraints on the greed of traders and merchants, except perhaps the fear that a defrauded Indian might resort to violence against his cheater, despite the suicidal implications of doing so.[39]

Aside from the denial of justice and the intolerable perpetuation of injury to the Senecas, the legal vulnerabilities were a serious threat to peace with the United

States. Traditional Seneca justice was dispensed by the kinsmen of the victims of murder and other violence. The Senecas had no courts or police. The family of a murder victim had the right to take the life of the killer or, in lieu of that, to accept some form of compensation put up by the murderer's family, which the bereaved family deemed to be adequate. In contrast to European-American notions of justice, Seneca notions focused more on compensation of the victim's survivors than on punishment of the offender. By the end of the 1790s, compensation was often paid in cash. In earlier times it had been paid in goods—guns, blankets, metal cooking pots, and hatchets—and in spiritually significant materials, such as wampum, tobacco, and copper gorgets. If the murderer's family did not provide compensation acceptable to the victim's family, the murderer's life was forfeit and any male blood relative of the victim had the right, indeed the duty, to kill him.

Federal officials, such as Secretary of War Henry Knox and his successor Timothy Pickering, frequently exerted themselves on behalf of aggrieved Senecas. They might have done so, in part, from a humanitarian desire for impartial and disinterested justice. But their main motive probably was to simplify the management of Indian affairs and, especially before General Wayne's victory in 1794, to avoid adding the Senecas to the country's long list of Indian enemies.

Most crimes against Seneca people were committed within the jurisdictions of Pennsylvania and New York, where the federal government had no authority over local matters. Indian wars were expensive and the governors and legislatures of these states were not insensible to the military, administrative, and fiscal expediency of satisfying Seneca demands for justice. But state authorities were unwilling to pay the political price for prosecuting European Americans charged with serious crimes against Senecas. They recognized and often shared the racial prejudices and cultural biases of their constituents.

Cornplanter understood that the presence of Friends among the Allegany Senecas could work—indirectly—to reduce the threat to peace posed by the failure of the legal system to protect the Senecas from crimes committed by European Americans. Aside from retaining legal counsel for Seneca defendants, neither the Senecas nor the Quakers had the capacity to influence the administration of European-American justice, let alone remedy its deficiencies. But the Quakers could help Cornplanter win compensation from federal and state governments. Receipt of compensation could, in the Seneca scheme of things, assuage painful wounds, blunt the impetus to vengeance, and preserve the peace.

With their reputation among higher-ranking federal and state officials for altruism and veracity, and with their close physical proximity to the federal and state establishments in Philadelphia, the Quakers were well placed to gain a sympathetic hearing for Seneca grievances. Other avenues, such as the federal Indian agent at Canandaigua and the United States military commandants at Franklin and Pittsburgh, led to the secretary of war and the president. Ties to county sheriffs, magistrates, and lieutenants of militia led to the state executive. But none of these could be relied upon to present the Seneca point of view with as much fidelity and empathy as could the Quakers.

ESTABLISHMENT OF THE QUAKER MISSION
TO THE ALLEGANY SENECAS

The government's prescription for the Indians was essentially one of radical accul-turation. Acculturation is the process by which one culturally distinct group takes on the cultural traits of another group.[40] Policy makers like Washington, Knox, and Pickering spoke in terms of "civilization," meaning they wanted the Indians to start living like white people.

The Quakers shared the government's belief in this prescription and volunteered to provide not only the equipment but also the technical instruction that the Senecas would need to embark upon an ambitious program of acculturation. The Quakers, furthermore, were prepared to bear much of the cost of such a program.[41]

In January 1796 the Indian Committee of the Philadelphia Yearly Meeting (PYMIC) sent a circular letter to the Six Nations of the Iroquois, offering to provide free technical and educational assistance.

> We have heard some of your chief men say that they believed the Good Spirit de-signed that you should not live much longer by hunting alone. The game is growing scarce. Yet, although your lands are much less than they once were, they are, with a small degree of industry, abundantly sufficient to supply all your needs.
>
> Now we desire to ask you a few questions. We hope you will answer us can-didly. . . . Are you willing to be instructed in cultivating your land, and in the method which white people take to live plentifully? . . . Do you desire to learn something of our useful trades, such as blacksmithing, wheelwrights, millwrights, and carpenters, that you may build houses and mills, and do other necessary things, to make you live more comfortable? . . . Would it be agreeable to you that your chil-dren should be taught to read and write?
>
> We desire none of your lands nor anything else that you have, but only to do you and your children good. Think well of what we now propose to you, and send us word as soon as you can.[42]

The following month Pickering wrote to the Six Nations recommending that they accept the Quaker plan for introducing plow agriculture and animal husbandry. He stated the problem as it was understood by the government and the Quakers:

> I have often shown you what good things the white people enjoy, and explained how you also might enjoy them. You have answered that what I told you was very good, and that you were willing to adopt the useful ways of the white people by de-grees, but that you could not lay aside your own customs all at once. This was a wise answer. It will be necessary for you to continue your hunting while the game is so plenty as to be worth pursuing. But you already know that the game is becoming scarce, and have reason to expect that in a few years more it will be gone. What then will you do to feed and clothe yourselves, your wives and children?
>
> Brothers, This is an important question. Think well upon it. The oldest hunters may perhaps find some game as long as they live, but before the young men grow old, all the game will be destroyed. The young men, then, and the boys should learn to get food and clothing without hunting. How are they to do this?

Pickering then proposed the solution as the government and the Quakers saw it:

> By cultivating the ground as the white people do. For with wheat grown out of the ground they can purchase all other necessaries. If you make fences to inclose many fields you can then securely raise corn, wheat and hay in abundance to feed your families, and as many cattle and hogs as you want, and the cattle and hogs will give you more meat than you could ever obtain by hunting even when game was plentiest.

Pickering finally endorsed the Quaker plan:

> Now, Brothers, I have the great pleasure to inform you that your good friends, the Quakers, have formed a wise plan, to show your young men and boys the most useful practices of the white people. They will chuse [sic] some prudent good men to instruct them. . . . The Quakers . . . will ask nothing from you, neither land nor money nor skins nor furs for all the good they will render to you. . . .
>
> If this first attempt succeeds the way will be opened in which your young people may learn other useful practices of the white people, so as to enable them to supply all their own wants. And such as chuse [sic] it may learn to read and write.[43]

The Oneida nation was the first and only one to respond to the Quakers' circular letter. During the summer of 1796 the Quakers established a mission among the Oneidas in central New York. Henry Simmons was one of the pioneer missionaries and served as the schoolteacher. He left Oneida in October 1797 to spend some time with his family in Middletown, in Bucks County, Pennsylvania.

The PYM's Oneida mission would close in 1799. The Oneidas grew suspicious of Quaker motives and feared that the missionaries would start charging for their services or make future claims on Oneida land or resources as payment for services already rendered. The Quakers decided the best thing to do in this circumstance was to withdraw to prove the Oneida fears unfounded. In keeping with a promise made at the inception of the mission, the Quakers left all of the tools and implements that had been stocked there to reassure other tribes about their motives. The New York Yearly Meeting of Friends, moreover, had become interested in the Oneida country as a potential field for missionary activity. The PYM looked upon this as an opportunity to devote its full attention to the newly established mission among the Allegany Senecas.[44]

The Oneida mission was still a going concern, however, when in March 1797 the PYMIC voted "to assist and encourage any suitable friends who may feel their mind drawn to go into this country . . . of the Seneca Nation of Indians . . . for the purpose of instructing them."[45] A full year passed before sufficient volunteers for staffing this additional mission presented themselves. In the spring of 1798 Henry Simmons, having spent the winter with his family, volunteered for the Seneca mission. Two other young men, Halliday Jackson and Joel Swayne, also offered their services.

Neither Jackson nor Swayne had any missionary experience, and Simmons's experience was limited to teaching school. Accordingly, the committee designated one of its own members, John Pierce, and an additional Quaker elder, Joshua Sharpless, to accompany the young missionaries on their trip to the Seneca country. Pierce and Sharpless arranged and managed the logistics of equipping and supplying the initial establishment of the mission, and they took the lead in negotiations with the Indians to set the ground rules for operating the mission on Seneca land.

In mid-May, when the five Quakers arrived in northwestern Pennsylvania, they found that almost all of the Allegany Seneca were living on Cornplanter's private property, instead of on the reservation in southwestern New York. The Cornplanter Grant consisted of 660 acres on the west bank of the Allegheny River, about four miles south of the Pennsylvania–New York border, plus some additional acreage on two nearby islands in the river.[46] The grant was transferred to Cornplanter personally, not to the Seneca nation, from the Commonwealth of Pennsylvania, in 1791, to reward Cornplanter for helping the state acquire the Indian titles to the Erie Triangle at the Treaty of Fort Harmar in 1789 and to "fix his attachment to the state."[47]

About 350 Indians resided in a single village, referred to herein as Cornplanter's village.[48] The actual Seneca name for the village was *Jenuchshadago,* meaning "there a house was burned."[49] A few Indians lived on the grant outside Jenuchshadago and fewer still lived at a place called *Genesinguhta,*[50] located about nine miles up the river from Cornplanter's village, in New York. Additionally, there was a third settlement about ten miles upriver from Genesinguhta, which the Quakers referred to simply as "the upper settlement."[51] All told, about 400 Allegany Senecas lived along a twenty-mile stretch of river, all of them under Cornplanter's supervision.[52]

The majority of the Allegany Senecas had taken up residence on the grant because the boundaries, unlike those of the reservation, had already been surveyed in July 1795. A land patent had been issued to Cornplanter in March 1796. The reservation boundaries were not surveyed until the autumn of 1798. In moving onto the grant, the Allegany Senecas could be certain that they were settling on a piece of property to which the Indian title was clear, even if held by only a single individual.[53]

Their former large village, moreover, had been recently evacuated after severe spring flooding and an early autumn frost combined to destroy the corn crop and create a food shortage. Cornplanter had personal resources, including private stores of flour, which he had prudently shipped up the river from Pittsburgh.[54] He was also in charge of the annuities paid to the Allegany Senecas by the federal government. As their foremost "headman," Cornplanter was bound by tradition and obliged by politics to use all the resources at his disposal, personal and national, to sustain his followers. The vast majority of the Allegany Senecas apparently decided that close physical proximity was the best assurance of a share in their chief's bounty.

One of the first things the Quakers did upon arriving in the Seneca country was to find a site for the model farm. They explained to Cornplanter and his people that the farm would give the Seneca men an opportunity to observe and practice "the works of the handy workman," which, in the Quaker view, were plowing, sowing, reaping, mowing, tree felling, rail splitting, fencing, carpentry, house and barn building, and so on. The Quakers also intended to eventually include women Friends in the missionary staff, who would teach the Seneca women domestic arts such as spinning and weaving.

The farm would also be the means by which the missionaries would support themselves while living in Seneca country. Initially dependent on the Indians for food, the Quakers were anxious to show that they would not be a drain on the local larder for long. It is doubtful that the Indians were too concerned, as the Quakers paid for everything in cash. The Quakers also informed the Indians that a boat slowly working its way up the Allegheny River from Pittsburgh contained not only all the equipment and tools needed for the farm, but also 120 pounds of bacon.

Regarding a site for the model farm, Cornplanter told the Quakers, "Brothers, . . . all our Land is before you. You may choose any place you like best."[55] It did not take the Quakers long to determine that the model farm should *not* be established on the Cornplanter Grant, although it would have been advantageous for several reasons. There was plenty of land available and the soil was fertile; it would be close to Cornplanter's village, where most of the population was concentrated; and a large number of young children lived in the village, making it a convenient location for a school. The grant, however, was quickly eliminated as a potential site for one fundamental reason. The land belonged to Cornplanter, not to the Allegany Senecas. Improvements made to the land by the Quakers and the tribe, such as clearing and fencing, would legally redound solely to the benefit of Cornplanter. Similarly, buildings such as the house and barn that were to be erected would belong to Cornplanter alone.

Thus, the Quakers scouted the reservation for a site. They found a suitable location at the nearly abandoned site of the old town of Genesinguhta, nine miles upriver from Cornplanter's village. The Senecas seemed fairly certain that when the boundary survey was complete, Genesinguhta would be on the reservation. As things turned out, it was. The farm with all its improvements would, therefore, be on land owned collectively by all the Allegany Senecas.

Genesinguhta possessed some intrinsic merits as a farm site. There was a flat of about 150 acres, mostly cleared of trees, and free of stones. The flat had a good southern exposure and was sheltered from the prevailing westerly winds by a large razorback hill. It was bordered by stands of white pine suitable as lumber for building and fencing. There were disadvantages, however. Some stretches of the flat were subject to flooding, which had forced the Indians out in the first place. Only three or four Indian families remained at Genesinguhta, meaning that virtually all of the Allegany Seneca would have to travel at least nine miles to receive instruction at the farm. The Quakers living on the farm would be somewhat isolated from the Allegany Seneca population. After weighing the pros and cons, and realizing that any other suitable site on the reservation would be even farther away from Cornplanter's village, the Quakers decided to build at Genesinguhta.

Within a week of first arriving in the Seneca country, the Quakers purchased an old Indian cabin at Genesinguhta. They immediately set to work, chinking up the cracks in the old cabin, digging and planting a vegetable garden, and preparing the ground for plowing. On the last day of May, a boat from Pittsburgh arrived carrying almost 5,000 pounds of food and other consumable supplies, plus tools and farming implements, including plow irons.[56] As the planting season had almost passed, a plow was put to work right away. To pull it, the Quakers used some of the horses they brought from their homes back east.

Late in May there was a major conference between the Quakers and the Senecas at Cornplanter's village. The elder Quakers outlined a series of cash incentives intended to encourage the Seneca men to raise field crops such as wheat, rye, hay, corn, and potatoes. Cash incentives were also offered to the Seneca women to spin and weave linen and wool. The Quakers specified that these last incentives would be paid "to the woman." Before any Indian could collect a cash incentive, two of the headmen would have to verify the amount of crop or cloth produced and certify that it had been produced by the Indian on his or her own property without the hired help of "white people." The headmen would also have to certify that the Indian had not been alcohol-intoxicated for a period of six months prior to application for the incentive.[57]

The Quakers offered to split the cost of constructing a gristmill. This offer was intended to get the Indians in the habit of applying a large portion of their yearly annuity money toward capital improvements. Construction was planned for the summer of 1799, provided that the Indians had by then raised sufficient grain to justify it.[58]

By the end of the first week of June, the Quaker elders could take some satisfaction at what had been accomplished in three weeks: a site for the farm had been selected, the Senecas had agreed to it, the supply boat had arrived with everything intact, plowing and planting were underway at the farm site, and the Senecas had listened to and taken under advisement the cash incentive offers. With relations off to a friendly start and their part of the mission accomplished, Pierce and Sharpless bid their three young Friends farewell on June 7 and began their journey home. Henry Simmons, Halliday Jackson, and Joel Swayne were on their own.

The three Friends finished plowing and planting. They then felled trees, split rails, and fenced their fields. Many of the Senecas did travel to Genesinguhta to observe the missionaries' activities. The Quakers encouraged attendance by giving small presents: needles, thread, scissors, combs, and spectacles. The Indians reciprocated by giving the Quakers fresh fruit, meat, and fish. One historian has interpreted these exchanges as a "lively barter."[59] The Senecas, however, might have viewed them not as barter, but as reciprocal gift giving, in which economic parity of the items exchanged was neither required nor sought. Whatever one might wish to call them, these exchanges did serve as an inducement for the Senecas to come to Genesinguhta and see what the Quakers were doing.

During the summer, the young missionaries helped the Senecas build several houses,[60] and later in the season, they built a small farmhouse for themselves at Genesinguhta.[61] It was "a comfortable two story hewed log house, 18 feet by 22, covered with white pine shingles and cellared underneath, with a chimney composed of stone and clay." They also "erected a good stable large enough to accommodate our horses and a cow."[62] The three Friends moved into their new house on October 6.[63]

Sometime between November 9 and 13, another council was held between the Senecas and the Quakers, at which Cornplanter renewed his request that the Quakers start teaching the children.[64] Simmons, the only missionary present with any experience at teaching Indian children, was the logical candidate for schoolteacher. Because virtually all of the school-age children lived in Cornplanter's village, nine miles downriver from Genesinguhta, Simmons decided to leave his comfortable new house and move into the village. On November 23 he began teaching school in Cornplanter's house in Jenuchshadago.[65]

In the latter part of January 1799, the three missionaries collaborated on one of their longer letters to the Indian Committee, which included a status report on the new school and a proposal to build a schoolhouse at Cornplanter's village during the upcoming summer.

> We have kept a school at Coniscotago in one of the Indians houses this winter, where from 12 to 25 children have attended who appear to make as much progress in learning as can reasonably be expected; and we have had in contemplation the propriety of erecting a school house at that place the ensuing summer, as the children are principally there we think it will be of the most general utility; which we submit to you.[66]

CHAPTER TWO

Henry Simmons
Among the Senecas

About two months after Henry Simmons moved into Cornplanter's village, he began to keep a journal. The first event that he recorded resembles an inquisition. On Sunday, February 2, 1799, a group of Allegany Seneca headmen summoned Simmons to Cornplanter's house. Present were Cornplanter, his eldest son Henry, and "about a dozen other Indians, some of them petty chiefs." Henry had received some education in Philadelphia and was the only bilingual person there. He had been serving as interpreter ever since the Quakers first arrived in May 1798. At first he was not too skillful, and the Quakers and Indians had difficulty understanding each other.[1] Over the intervening eight months, Henry had improved somewhat.

Through Henry, the Indians asked Simmons to "tell them how the world and things therein were created in the beginning." Simmons recognized the question as loaded. His immediate reaction was to pray for divine assistance in formulating an answer, which he then delivered to his inquisitors.

> I immediately applied my heart with fervent breathings to the Lord for his aid and support in this question. I found him to be a present help. Then, I told them it was a hard question, that I understood it better than I was able to explain it to them, but that I would endeavor to satisfy them. I told them there is a certain good book, called the Holy Scriptures. Very few people who can read will deny the truth of this book. It gives us an account of the world being made (and of all living creatures both in water and on land) by the Great Spirit, who also made the first man and woman from the dust of the earth, and breathed life into them. Thus, they became living souls. They had two sons; one was a good man; the other was wicked. The wicked son killed his brother, because he knew his brother was more righteous than himself. I asked them if they did not see it so nowadays—that wicked people envied good ones, and at times were ready to take their lives.

Here, Simmons tried to turn the tables on his inquisitors—the nativists who distrusted European-American culture—by implicating them in the practice of witchcraft. The wicked people, who envied good people and sometimes killed them, were witches. Many Senecas of that era feared witchcraft and suspected others of practicing it. They believed that witches were motivated by envy of the good fortune of others. Cornplanter was an obvious target for witchcraft because of his personal

27

wealth, prestige, and influence. Simmons implied that those who opposed Corn-planter did so out of envy and, therefore, might resort to witchcraft. He then went on to explain why the Christian Sabbath was kept to remember and worship the Creator.

> I told them the Great Spirit made all things in six days, and on the seventh day he rested from his labor. Accordingly, we now keep First Day, on which we rest from our labor, to serve and worship him. Because of this and because we worship him on an additional day during the week, he has blessed us and made us happy. He comforts our hearts, and preserves us in love and unity with one another. I told them I desired that the same might be the case with them.[2]

Simmons next bore eloquent witness to one of the most fundamental Quaker be-liefs. In addition to the revelation of holy scripture, every human soul was blessed with an "inner light" that, if followed, led to moral behavior and to God.

> I supposed some of them doubted the truth of the holy writings. So I told them how I know the Scriptures to be true, which is by reading them and by waiting on the Great Spirit to manifest their truth in the secret of my heart. The Great Spirit makes my heart sensible of their truth, even to the extent that, sometimes when I read the Scriptures, tears flow from my eyes. And I told them that this was also the only way I could tell whether I was doing right or wrong. That is, by strictly attending as the Great Spirit spoke to my heart. I asked them if this was not also the case with them, when they thought of doing something wrong. Did not they too feel something pricking at their hearts, and telling them not to do it?

Simmons's personal testimony struck a sympathetic chord among the chiefs.

> Several of the chiefs, including Cornplanter, confessed it was the very truth; they had experienced it so. I told them it is the Great Spirit who pricks our hearts and tells us not to do wrong. It is the devil who urges us to do wrong.

With sympathy resonating among the chiefs, Simmons seized the moment and plugged one of the main items of the Quaker agenda—the education of children and young people—as an avenue to spiritual enlightenment.

> I told them this was one of the advantages of their children learning to read. They would be able to read the good book for themselves. Then, as it pleased the Great Spirit to enlighten their understanding, they would sense the truth of the good book. Many other benefits would also derive from their children being educated.

Simmons finished delivering his answer and the Indians conferred among them-selves regarding its acceptability.[3] After the Indians reached a consensus, they in-vited Simmons back into their presence and informed him of their decision. Not only were they satisfied with his answer, but the chiefs encouraged Simmons to tell the villagers what he had told them as an antidote to the opposition of some to education for the children. The inquisition had backfired on the nativists. Cornplanter's faction handily won this round, thanks in part to Simmons's carefully calculated answer. Following the acquittal of Simmons, attendance at his school increased and even in-cluded some adults.

Later, after this meeting, my school was much larger than before, between twenty and thirty scholars, several of them grown men. Some of them are anxious to learn, though in many cases instructing them is very tedious. But this keeps me faithful in teaching them, so much so that at times I have been almost weary in well doing.

GENESIS REDACTED

Simmons's recounting of the story of Genesis is noteworthy because of the way he abridged it.

It gives us an account of the world being made (and of all living creatures both in water and on land) by the Great Spirit, who also made the first man and woman from the dust of the earth, and breathed life into them. Thus, they became living souls. They had two sons; one was a good man; the other was wicked. The wicked son killed his brother, because he knew his brother was more righteous than himself.

Simmons was apparently familiar with the ancient Iroquois creation story, a major portion of which occurs before the final creation and concerns the lives and adventures of several generations of supernatural beings, the last of which consisted of twin brothers.[4] The Good Twin, or Good Spirit, *Tarachiawagon,* was born first via the normal birth canal. The Evil Twin, *Tawiskaron,* burst out through his mother's side, killing her. The Good Twin was the creator, but the Evil Twin had a hand in the way the world turned out—as we shall see.

The ocean, the air, and their inhabitants were already here. The barren earth, which the animals of sea and air had piled up upon the back of the great mud turtle was ready for the hand of the Creator. The Good Twin's task was to make this protoworld ready for man. He created the sun and the moon, made the first man and woman from the dust of the earth, and breathed life into them. Next, he created the rivers, the corn, beans, and squash, and the game animals, like deer, bear, and beaver. His creation was perfect. The rivers ran straight and smooth, with the water on opposite sides flowing in opposite directions, so that men could always paddle their canoes downstream no matter which way they wanted to go.

The Evil Twin followed his brother around and spoiled creation as much as he could. He made the rivers twist and turn, broke them up into rapids, whirlpools, and waterfalls. And he made the water on both sides run in the same direction. He blighted the corn so that it was harder to grow, yielded less, and did not taste as good. He made worms and snakes. He brought sickness and death. Everything good came into the world through the Creator, and everything evil came through the spoiler.[5]

There was a contest between the twins, and the Creator won. He moved the mountains on the rocky rim of the world much farther than did the spoiler. The Evil Twin submitted and agreed to a covenant, under which he now acts as a benefactor of mankind. In return, men remember him by wearing false-face masks and offering him tobacco. The Good Twin was able to repair much of the damage done to creation by his brother, but not all of it.

Simmons skipped much of the creation story given in Genesis and proceeded quickly to the subject of Cain and Abel, who were similar to the Twins. Aside from the theme of two brothers, one associated with good and the other with evil, and the theme of man being made from the dust of the earth and given the breath of life by the Creator, there is little in common between the creation stories of Genesis and the Iroquois.

FACTIONS: PRAGMATIST VERSUS NATIVIST

The fundamental challenge facing the Seneca people in 1799 was cultural survival. Embedded in this challenge were questions of whether, of what, and of how to acculturate. After some 300 years of contact with European-American culture, American Indians had become dependent on manufactured products that could be obtained only by purchasing them from European Americans. Up to this point, they had traded beaver pelts and deerskins for manufactured goods. Now that they were dispossessed of most of their hunting territory, the day could be foreseen when the Allegany Senecas would need to find other ways of generating the cash needed to purchase manufactured goods. Some Allegany Senecas, such as Cornplanter, saw no point in waiting for the game animals to be eradicated before engaging in new economic activities. By 1795, he was deriving income from a sawmill he owned on the upper Allegheny River, near the state line between New York and Pennsylvania. By 1794 Allegany Seneca men were finding employment as pilots and pole men on cargo boats, barges, and rafts running the Allegheny River.[6]

The Senecas did not all see the issue of cultural survival in quite the same way. They had differing opinions about the extent to which they could take up some of the ways of the "white people" before they stopped being Indians. Consensus on this point could not be reached until there was broad agreement on the answer to an even more basic question: What did it mean at the beginning of the 1800s to be an Indian? What was at the core of Seneca cultural identity? As Handsome Lake was to show over the next decade and a half, this basic question could be answered only in terms of cultural values.

Pragmatists like Cornplanter were willing to try anything that might earn a living: timbering and lumber milling, river rafting and piloting, commercial planting, raising livestock to sell as meat on the hoof, raising horses, and even day laboring. To the extent that taking up such activities required cultural innovation, pragmatists were willing to accommodate change that helped keep their culture viable.

Cornplanter was pragmatic and eclectic in his approach to cultural issues. He was one of the foremost spokesmen for acculturation among not just the Allegany band but all of the Seneca nation. During the winter of 1790–91, he had headed a delegation of Seneca chiefs that traveled to Philadelphia, at that time the seat of the United States government, the state capital of Pennsylvania, and the foremost center of American Quakerism.[7] While there, he submitted to President Washington several written speeches, which he had composed through an interpreter, as he did not read, write, or speak English.[8]

You give us leave to speak our minds concerning the tilling of the ground. We ask you to teach us to plow and to grind corn; to assist us in building saw mills, and supply us with broad axes, saws, augers, and other tools, so that we may make our houses more comfortable and more durable; that you will send smiths among us, and above all that you will teach our children to read and write, and our women to spin and weave. The manner of your doing these things we leave to you, who understand them, but we assure you we will follow your advice as far as we are able.[9]

Cornplanter had long advocated education for Indian children and young people. While in Philadelphia, he requested of the Religious Society of Friends that some willing Quaker families be found to receive two Seneca boys into their homes and provide them with Quaker educations. In his words, "We cannot teach our children what we perceive their situation requires them to know, and we therefore ask you to instruct some of them—We wish them to be instructed to read and to write and such other things as you teach your own children."[10]

Sometime during 1791 or 1792 Cornplanter made arrangements for his eldest son, Henry, to be educated in the east under government auspices. Henry's academic career from 1792 to 1795 was somewhat erratic and certainly less than stellar. His sponsor, Timothy Pickering, reported that, after two years at the "school of the university" in Philadelphia, Henry had learned next to nothing. The school Pickering referred to was not an institution of higher learning, but the Academy and Charitable

Henry Abeel (1774–1832), son of Corn-planter. Portrait by John Bird King, 1827. THE NATIONAL MUSEUM OF DENMARK, DEPART-MENT OF ETHNOGRAPHY. LENNART LARSEN, PHOTOGRAPHER

School, which because of a loose association with the University of Pennsylvania was sometimes called "the University School." At the Academy, Henry had attended classes with "a multitude of small children." Pickering placed him in a New York academy, but after only a brief enrollment there, Henry was transferred to Dr. Hunter's School at Woodbury, New Jersey. In the autumn of 1795, Henry was returned to the West at government expense.[11]

The nativists tended to reject innovations on the basis of their association with white culture. Nativism, however, did not necessarily translate into an unconditional preference for perpetuating Seneca culture as it existed at the time. Though nativists did resist many forms of acculturation, their resistance was not based on an opposition to cultural change but rather to the source of those innovations—European-American culture. Nativist sentiment stemmed in part from a sense of bitter outrage over the accumulated injustices perpetrated on Indians by European Americans. As chief Red Jacket was to put it in 1805:

> There was a time when our forefathers owned this Island [the American continent]. Their seats extended from the rising to the setting of the sun. The Great Spirit had made it for the use of the Indians. He had created the buffalo, the deer and other animals for food. He made the bear and the beaver; their skins served us for clothing. He had scattered them over the country, and taught us how to take them. He had caused the earth to produce corn for bread. All this he had done for his red children because he loved them. If we had some disputes about hunting grounds, they were generally settled without the shedding of much blood.
>
> But an evil day came upon us. Your forefathers crossed the great water and landed on this Island. Their numbers were small; they found friends and not enemies. They told us they had fled from their own country for fear of wicked men, and had come here to enjoy their own religion.
>
> They asked for a small seat; we took pity on them and granted their request; and they sat down amongst us. We gave them corn and meat; they gave us poison [alcohol] in return.
>
> The white people had now found our country. Tidings were carried back; and more came amongst us. Yet we did not fear them; we took them to be friends; they called us brothers. We believed them and gave them a larger seat.
>
> At length their numbers had greatly increased; they wanted more lands; they wanted our Country. Our eyes were opened; our minds became uneasy. Wars took place; Indians were hired to fight against Indians; and many of our people were destroyed. They also brought strong liquor amongst us; it was strong and powerful and has slain thousands."[12]

The nativist reaction to the perceived threat to their identity was to encyst traditional Seneca values and norms.[13] The main areas of nativist concern were conservation of indigenous religion, preservation of the remaining Seneca land base, protection of communal property, continuation of the practice of reciprocity among Indians, and promotion of traditional gender-based economic roles. Nativists also had some serious misgivings about education, especially formal classroom education. They had no objection to the training of American Indians in crafts such as blacksmithing and carpentry.

Though present among the Allegany Senecas as a minority faction, the nativists looked to their strongest spokesman, Red Jacket, at the Buffalo Creek Reservation in western New York. In 1791 during treaty negotiations at Newtown Point, Red Jacket had declared that it would be a matter of "great time" before the Indians gave up their beloved ancient customs and became educated and civilized. In 1800 he told a missionary who was visiting the Buffalo Creek Reservation that he and Farmer's Brother, another headman at Buffalo, were of the opinion that learning would be of no service to the Indians. Farmer's Brother confirmed this opinion to the missionary by relating a story about one of his grandsons. Several years previously, the young man had been sent to Philadelphia to receive an education. An education he received, but not the kind his grandfather had in mind. On a visit to Philadelphia,

Farmer's Brother found his grandson successively in a tavern, a gambling den, and a brothel.[14]

SO MUCH NOISE ABOUT DREAMS

A week and two days after his first journal entry, Simmons wrote again. A little girl living on the Buffalo Creek Reservation, some eighty miles distant, had a dream. News of the dream was carried by express runner to Cornplanter's village where an urgent council was held on the subject of the dream. The next day, Cornplanter paid an early morning visit to Simmons to discuss the situation.

Regarding Seneca preoccupation with dreams, Simmons's journal entry suggests only the seed of an explanation: "[M]any of them put great confidence in their dreams." The Iroquois of that era believed that dreams were wishes of the soul that must be satisfied to preserve health and forestall misfortune. In some situations, dreams were messages from good spirits sent to warn of dire consequences that would flow from commission or omission of some particular deed.

Red Jacket (1758–1830), speaker for the Seneca nation. Portrait by Robert W. Weir, 1828. NEW-YORK HISTORICAL SOCIETY.

Early in the morning of Monday, February 11, 1799, Cornplanter and two of his sons came to the Indian house in which Simmons lodged.

> Cornplanter said they had come to talk about something in particular, which was as follows. They had lately received an express from the Buffalo Indians regarding a dream that one of their little girls had had. She had dreamed that the devil was in all white people alike, and that the Quakers were doing no good among them, but otherwise. She had also related that it was not right for the Indian children to learn to read and write. Cornplanter and his people had held a council yesterday on the subject. And many of his people were so foolish as to believe the dream was true, for many of them put great confidence in their dreams. But he did not believe it, and had got very tired of hearing so much noise about their dreams. He wished me not to be discouraged, for he intended to make his people do better.

Cornplanter obviously thought that the dream reported from Buffalo was false. Either someone had told the little girl to report this dream or the whole missive was entirely fabricated; Cornplanter characterized his people who believed it as "foolish." It is not just that he wished they were more discerning. Nativists among the Allegany Senecas had gladly seized upon the anti-Quaker content of the dream in an attempt to stir up trouble for Cornplanter and the Quakers, forcing the previous day's council. Cornplanter probably had a difficult time defusing the situation.

His remark that he was tired of hearing "so much noise about their dreams" does not mean that Cornplanter no longer held the traditional Iroquois beliefs regarding the spiritual significance of genuine dreams. It probably stemmed from the fact that many of his own people's dreams were false too—and very inconvenient for him. People sometimes fabricated false dreams to manipulate others into giving them something. No doubt Cornplanter's material and political resources were the frequent targets of such false dreams. Based on his later actions, Cornplanter evidently still held traditional Iroquois beliefs regarding both witchcraft and dreams.

Simmons's reaction to the dream and all the attention it had been getting was one of equanimity. He saw it as a maneuver on the part of nativist chiefs at Buffalo Creek who opposed the Quakers.

> I told him I did not feel at all uneasy about the dream because I thought I knew from whence it had originated. I knew that Farmer's Brother and others of the Buffalo Indians were much injured and set against the Quakers by the instigation of some bad white people at Buffalo. Cornplanter said that was very true.

Farmer's Brother, another of the headmen at the Buffalo Creek Reservation, was an ally of Red Jacket. The bad white people at Buffalo were Joseph Ellicott, chief surveyor and soon-to-be resident-agent of the Holland Land Company (HLC), and his associates.

The bad blood between the Quakers and some of the chiefs at Buffalo went back to the previous summer when the boundaries of the Allegany Reservation were being negotiated. The Quakers had urged Cornplanter, who actually needed no encouragement, to drive a hard bargain during negotiations over how much prime bottomland would be included in the reservation. Ellicott had wanted to minimize the amount of bottomland reserved to the Allegany Senecas, thereby maximizing the amount available for the Holland Land Company to sell. Ellicott had offered a bribe to Farmer's Brother, provided that the chief would persuade Cornplanter to compromise.[15]

It is possible that the amount of the bribe was contingent upon how much bottomland was finally excluded from the Allegany Reservation. Tying the amount of a bribe to the magnitude of its results was a favorite tactic of Holland Land Company agents. By autumn a compromise was reached in which Cornplanter gave very little ground. The Holland Land Company got very little bottomland.[16] Farmer's Brother probably collected only a fraction of what he could have received. Ellicott and Farmer's Brother blamed the Quakers for Cornplanter's intransigence.[17]

Simmons believed that Farmer's Brother invented the little girl's dream as a way of getting back at the Quakers. Personal motives, in this case nativist Farmer's Brother's desire for revenge both on the meddling Quakers and the unyielding Cornplanter, often blended with a chief's ideological affinities. Simmons furthermore believed that he and the other Quakers were doing God's work; and, therefore, he was content to leave the matter in God's hands.

I told him our work was certainly a very good work from the Great Spirit. Therefore I knew the devil would use his utmost endeavors to lay it waste. It had been my experience, from the time I was a very little boy, that he is always seeking and ready to destroy all that is good. But, as our work is a work from the Great Spirit, I believed he would support and carry it on to his own glory. . . . I told him I would continue teaching those who would come. And, as for the rest, we would let them quietly alone. Perhaps the Great Spirit would open their eyes and enlighten their understanding, so they might behold the nonsense of such dreams and stories. After all, the Great Spirit could, if he pleased, change their thoughts in an hour's time.

And, sure enough, school attendance dropped off for only one day and then reached a higher level than ever before.

Simmons's remark about Farmer's Brother and the "bad white people" reminded Cornplanter of the many land swindles that whites had perpetrated on Indians. He succinctly described a ploy often used to defraud Indian nations of their land.

Cornplanter said that some of the white people were as much to blame as the Indians for the devil's frequent interference. When these white people wanted to get Indian land, they would go to some of the most dissolute and disreputable Indian individuals, and make a bargain with them first, and afterwards apply to the chiefs to honor the deal. I believed that to be true.

Cult of Dreams

It would be difficult to overstate the importance of dreams to the Iroquois psyche. Embedded in ancient Iroquois religious beliefs and practices pertaining to dreams was a very sophisticated psychoanalysis that anticipated Freud by hundreds of years. The Iroquois looked to their dreams for guidance not only in their daily personal lives but also in matters of national importance. Dreams figure prominently in the Simmons journal, especially those of the Seneca prophet Handsome Lake, whose dreams or visions form the basis of the present-day Longhouse religion.

But there was another, sometimes humorous, side to this cultural phenomenon. Some individuals were not above falsely reporting manufactured dreams, the content of which they had specifically designed to manipulate their fellows in some particular way. Iroquois people, steeped in the dream culture, were generally quite adept at discriminating between reports of genuine and false dreams and at thwarting the intention of the manipulator. European Americans, however, often were not so adept. And many Iroquois could not pass up an opportunity to practice false dream reporting on unwary European Americans, especially on those who presumed to "understand Indian ways."

Iroquois dreams can be categorized as either visitation or nonvisitation. A visitation dream was one in which a supernatural being, or spirit, appeared. A nonvisitation dream was one devoid of any such apparition.

The Iroquois believed that a nonvisitation dream expressed a wish of the dreamer's own soul. If this message of the soul was not heeded and the wish not granted, the soul could revolt against the body, leading to mental or physical illness or even death. Even dreams about future misfortune, such as being captured and tortured by an enemy tribe, were viewed as a wish of the soul. Such wishes, although irrational and destructive to self, family, or friends, were seen as fateful. If an evil-fated dream could be acted out more or less literally or even symbolically, the soul's wish might be satisfied and the evil fate implied by the dream might be averted. *The Jesuit Relations,* a voluminous collection of letters and reports written by French Jesuit missionaries operating out of Canada during the 1600s and 1700s, are replete with accounts of Iroquoians trying to satisfy what they discerned as the soul's wish, expressed in a dream.[18]

> The Iroquois have, properly speaking, only a single Divinity—the dream. To it they render their submission, and follow all its orders with the utmost exactness. The Tsonnontouens [Senecas] are more attached to this superstition than any of the others; their Religion in this respect becomes even a matter of scruple: whatever it be that they think they have done in their dreams, they believe themselves absolutely obliged to execute at the earliest moment. . . . He who has dreamed during the night that he was bathing, runs immediately, as soon as he rises, all naked, to several cabins, in each of which he has a kettleful of water thrown over his body, however cold the weather may be. Another who has dreamed that he was taken prisoner and burned alive, has himself bound and burned like a captive on the next day, being persuaded that by thus satisfying his dream, this fidelity will avert from him the pain and infamy of captivity and death,—which, according to what he has learned from his Divinity [dream], he is otherwise bound to suffer among his enemies.[19]

The characterization of dreams as the Iroquois "Divinity" was not accurate. The Senecas believed in many spiritual beings, including one with higher rank than any other: Tarachiawagon, the Good Twin. He was their Divinity.

The Iroquois also believed that the true wish of the soul was sometimes hidden by the literal content of the dream, which was only symbolic of the true wish and therefore required interpretation. Some dreams remained unknown to the dreamer, who forgot them before or after waking. Additionally, the soul could have a secret wish that it would not reveal in any dream, not even symbolically. This was particularly troublesome in that an unfulfilled secret wish could lead to adverse consequences as bad as those of a dream-disclosed wish that remained unsatisfied. The Iroquois attributed much physical illness to dream-disclosed wishes that had yet to be remembered or correctly interpreted and fulfilled and to undisclosed wishes that remained a secret of the soul. In the ancient Iroquois view, disease or bodily infirmity, aside from injury sustained by accident or in battle, arose in one of two ways: from the malevolent spell of a hostile witch and from "the mind of the patient himself, which desires something, and will vex the body of the sick man until it possesses the thing required."

> For they think that there are in every man certain inborn desires, often unknown to themselves, upon which the happiness of individuals depends. For the purpose of ascertaining desires and innate appetites of this character, they summon soothsayers [shamans], who, as they think, have a divinely-imparted power to look into the inmost recesses of the mind. These men declare that whatever first occurs to them, or something from which they suspect some gain can be derived, is desired by the sick

person. Thereupon the parents, friends, and relatives of the patient do not hesitate to procure and lavish upon him whatever it may be, however expensive, a return of which is never thereafter to be sought.[20]

Shamans and clairvoyants were able to look into the dreams of others and discern the true wish hidden in the symbolism. They also were able to help others remember and interpret their forgotten dreams and even to uncover the soul's secret wishes that were never expressed in any dream, either literally or symbolically. The following passage from *The Jesuit Relations* was written about the Hurons, who like the Iroquois were obsessed with the cult of dreams.[21]

> The Hurons believe that there are certain persons, more enlightened than the common, whose sight penetrates, as it were, into the depths of the soul. These see the natural and hidden desires that it has, though the soul has declared nothing by dreams, or though he who may have had the dreams has completely forgotten them. It is thus that their medicine-men . . . acquire credit, and make the most of their art by saying that a child in the cradle, who has neither discernment nor knowledge, will have . . . a natural and hidden desire for such or such a thing; and that a sick person will have similar desires for various things of which he has never had any knowledge. . . . [T]he Hurons believe that one of the most efficacious remedies for rapidly restoring health is to grant the soul of the sick person these natural desires.[22]

A dreamer was not always able to interpret his own dream. This combined with the adverse consequences of failing to discover the soul's true wish ensured that a dream was always told, sometimes to many, in search of its true meaning. Each village had several clairvoyants, male and female, who could be consulted—for a fee. They used a form of free association to interpret the dream.[23] Sometimes a dreamer would take advantage of a public gathering to relate a particularly singular dream, or even have a village gathering called for the express purpose of relating a startling or perplexing dream. A significant portion of the Midwinter Rites were devoted to dream-guessing and to literal and symbolic wish fulfillment. Dreams were meant to be told and their meaning guessed, so that the soul's wish could be satisfied.

Regarding nonvisitation dreams, the Iroquois had intuitively attained considerable psychological insight, recognizing the conscious and unconscious parts of the mind, and developing a healthy respect for the power of unconscious desires. They understood that these desires, if repressed or frustrated, could lead to psychic or psychosomatic illness. They realized that these desires were often expressed symbolically in dreams, and that the dreamer could not always interpret the symbolism. They distinguished between the manifest and latent content of dreams, and used the technique of free association in dream-guessing rites to reveal the latent meaning. They believed that the best way to relieve psychic or psychosomatic distress was to satisfy the repressed or frustrated desire, either literally or symbolically.[24]

In visitation dreams, a supernatural being appeared who often delivered a message. Sometimes it was intended for a wider audience, such as the entire village or nation. In such cases, it was the responsibility of the dreamer to relay the message and the duty of the wider audience to heed it.

Visitation dreams were not rare. For example, teenage boys, undergoing rites of passage into manhood, actually sought out such dreams in hopes of finding a life-long guardian spirit. In these cases, the message was intended only for the boy and was usually a promise to protect him and to endow him with some special gift, such as prowess as hunter or warrior, skill as orator or herbalist, or power of clairvoyance or prophecy. Sick persons also often had visitation dreams involving supernatural protectors or persecutors. From the identity of the spirit, the medicine man or shaman would infer the appropriate content for a therapeutic ritual.[25]

A visitation dream could reveal the wishes not only of the dreamer's own soul, but also those of the spirit who appeared in the dream. To ignore the wishes of a su-pernatural being was to court disaster—perhaps death itself. If its message had been directed to a larger audience, a spirit dissatisfied with the response might destroy the entire village or even the whole world.

A community's willingness to act on a visitation dream experienced by one of its members hinged upon whether the dream was judged to be genuine. Signs that a dream was genuine varied. If the dreamer made a prediction that came to pass, had been in a coma at the time of the dream, or exhibited a radical and persistent trans-formation in personality or behavior, the dream could probably be trusted.

Assuming that a visitation dream with a message addressed to the entire nation was judged to be genuine, then the priority accorded the message and the urgency at-tached to heeding it depended upon the rank of the spirit who delivered it. A mes-sage from the Good Twin, delivered in a visitation dream, was a matter of the utmost importance to the dreamer, the village, and the nation.

Lighter Side of Dreams

Some individual Iroquois were not above reporting fabricated dreams intended to be-guile other Indians. There were some cultural checks, however, that restrained such manipulation. For many individuals, simple honesty was a significant barrier against making false reports about dreams. Then, too, the general perceptiveness of the Iro-quois regarding the truthfulness of reported dreams deterred would-be perjurers. When an individual was so brazen as to perpetrate a counterfeit dream, the Iroquois were not only quick to spot the forgery, but also quite adroit at putting themselves to very little trouble or expense in fulfilling the stipulations of the fraudulent dream—if they bothered to do so at all. Also, victims of exorbitantly demanding dreams could retaliate with counterdreams of their own.[26]

Most European Americans who had much direct contact with the Iroquois knew that they paid great attention to their dreams. And they were aware of the Iroquois belief that to leave a dream unfulfilled was to invite ill health or some other misfortune. They sometimes observed firsthand how Iroquois individuals went to great lengths to fulfill each other's dreams. Good manners required that these European Americans respect Iroquois beliefs regarding dreams and most were willing to do so.

This provided an opportunity ripe for exploitation by dream-kiting Iroquois. An Iroquois might tell his European-American companion or visitor of a dream in which the European American gave him something such as a shirt, a knife, or some food. It would then be incumbent upon the European American to make a present of the article featured in the dream, thereby fulfilling the dream. Otherwise, he would be responsible for any bad health or other bad luck that might befall the "dreamer."

No doubt many European Americans who had dealings with the Iroquois were stung at least once by scheming dreamers. But some, like John Adlum, were quick studies and soon mastered techniques for thwarting the unwelcome intent of contrived dreams. Adlum, a surveyor who hailed from York, Pennsylvania, first met Cornplanter and the Allegany Senecas in 1787 while executing a commission from the state of Pennsylvania to survey its northern boundary. He returned to northwestern Pennsylvania in 1789 to survey tracts reserved by the state as future town sites, and again in 1790 to survey river routes and portages. In 1792 he was appointed to a permanent position with the state as a deputy surveyor. All of these assignments brought him into repeated contact with Cornplanter and the Allegany Senecas.[27]

During the summer of 1794 Adlum was in northwestern Pennsylvania again, surveying a half-million acres on French Creek and the Allegheny River that had just been sold by James Wilson, a land speculator and associate justice of the United States Supreme Court, to a group of Dutch financiers who later incorporated as the Holland Land Company.

Tensions in the region were high at the time. A confederacy of Indians in Ohio, Indiana, and Michigan, headed by the Shawnees, had been at war with the United States for several years. Known as the Western Confederates, they had inflicted two stunning defeats on United States forces, including the Regular Army. The Allegany Senecas, disappointed at their treatment by the United States in a series of treaty negotiations during the 1780s and early 1790s, were by the summer of 1794 on the verge of entering the war on the side of the Western Confederates.

So Adlum's first order of business was to travel to Cornplanter's village to seek assurances of safe conduct for his survey teams. In late July Adlum arrived at Fort Franklin, present-day Franklin, Pennsylvania, located on the Allegheny River about eighty miles—by water—below Cornplanter's village. There he met a large party of Seneca hunters, who were on their way home, having just received runners with word from Cornplanter to return for an important council. Adlum knew some of the hunters and they agreed to take him along as they poled their way up the Allegheny River in canoes. They apparently had no objection to also transporting his not inconsiderable cargo of baggage.

The journey up the river was very pleasant. The Indians were expert at poling upstream and could do so without much exertion at this time of year when the river was low and the current more easily overcome.[28] The mood was lightened by the presence of some women and children who had accompanied their men folk on the hunting expedition, which was not unusual in the summer season when the women's workload was relatively light, it being well after the planting season and yet still before the harvest. Adlum describes a placid and languid ascent of the meandering river: "[W]here there was a current or a ripple [riffle] we had to use our poles, but sometimes where the water was still and deep, they used their paddles. . . . Some of the men and some of the women at times went on shore and walked along the path on the bottoms of the river—and they frequently changed situations."

On the second day of the river trip, the flotilla of canoes pulled ashore for a rest shortly before noon. The leader of the Seneca party was a headman named Half Town, the same who had accompanied Cornplanter to Philadelphia in 1790, and to whom on this current river journey, Adlum had playfully given the appellation of "commodore." When everyone had disembarked from the canoes, the "commodore" assembled them and made a little speech, which he concluded by thanking the Great Spirit for fine weather and a safe journey and by telling his listeners of a dream that had come to him during the previous night. In Half Town's dream, Adlum had given each of the men present a dram of whiskey at noon. Adlum's baggage cargo included a ten-gallon keg of whiskey and a five-gallon keg of wine—neither of which he had intended to broach until he got to Cornplanter's village. Once the "commodore" had recounted his potable dream, however, Adlum bowed to the inevitable and gave everyone a drink. But he conjectured "if I could not put a stop to it, that in future they would have more powerful dreams, and drain my kegs before I got to their towns."[29]

Adlum went to work that very afternoon on a stratagem that would put a cork in the dreaming-drinking-draining process. His artifice centered on a deceased Seneca chieftain, much renowned and greatly revered, named Guyasuta. Unknown to any of the Indians in the commodore's flotilla was the fact that Adlum had met Guyasuta in Pittsburgh in 1787 and remembered well what he looked like. Adlum also was aware that Guyasuta's first wife had died before her husband, that the chieftain had remarried, and that the second wife was still alive. Guyasuta's widow, in fact, was among the women on this very flotilla. During the afternoon journey, Adlum discretely prevailed upon one of his interpreters to provide a detailed description of Guyasuta's first wife and then swore the interpreter to secrecy regarding the subject of their afternoon discussion.

Adlum was ready to make his move. "I had therefore made up my mind to get the start of the dreamers—So just as the sun rose the next morning, I called all hands including the women and children to the front." Adlum made some preliminary remarks in which he urged all to give thanks to the Good Spirit for prospering their journey to this point and for giving them the promise of a fine new day to continue their travels.

> I had no doubt but that if we felt grateful for these favors, he would continue to bless us with fine weather, to the end of our journey—Here I made a pause and with great solemnity looked upwards—and resumed by saying—He [the Good Spirit] last night caused two persons to appear to me, and they told me that I had done very wrong, to broach the keg of whisky before I arrived at their town."

Adlum explained to his listeners that he had intended to use the whiskey to treat all of his friends at the town, not just the party in the flotilla. Therefore, the Spirit had told him, "every part that I used on the way was depriving those at the town of a part of their share . . . [A]nd that it was not then mine though it was in my possession—but it belonged to those I first intended it for." Adlum then described the deceased Guyasuta and his dead wife so convincingly that the older people present "immediately exclaimed that it was old Kyashota [Guyasuta] and his first wife that had appeared to me. His widow and even old Half Town were satisfied that I had seen them in a vision."

> And after some consultation among themselves, there was two young Indians appointed to carry the kegs into and out of my canoe, which they did with great ceremony and solemnity—and they were looked on as sacred articles—not to be touched by profane hands.

If any of the Allegany Senecas ever tried to foist a counterfeit dream on Simmons, he did not record it in his journal nor in any of his correspondence from Jenuchshadago, but it is doubtful that any of them did. Adlum was a friend to the Senecas on their own Indian terms. They were familiar with Adlum in ways that they were not familiar with Simmons, who was also their friend but on his own European-American, Quaker terms.

The Allegany Senecas certainly did not give the same kind of welcome to Simmons and the other Quakers when they arrived in May 1798 as they had given to Adlum when he arrived at Cornplanter's village in early August 1794. In Adlum's words: "[I]mmediately upon our arriving at the lower end of the town, the Cornplanter gave the word of command and a loud whoop, whoop, whoop, when they immediately commenced firing with ball, all of which passed between the young Indian in the head of my canoe and myself, many of them within less than a yard of me. . . . I counted eighty odd as we passed, those that fired first reloaded and fired a shot over our heads."

Cornplanter and his warriors were according Adlum an honor such as they would bestow on a well-respected Iroquois. Indeed, the closer the bullets came, the greater the honor.[30] The Senecas would not, however, greet Simmons or any other Quaker in similar fashion. Not that they held the Quakers in disrespect. Quite to the contrary, they simply understood the Quaker's aversion to violence and everything associated with it, including guns. The complex nuances of intercultural protocol were not lost on the Senecas.

DANCING FROLICS AND PROBING QUESTIONS

Simmons's next three journal entries fell on consecutive days: February 27 and 28 and March 1, 1799. At issue in the first two of these entries was what Simmons referred to as the Indians' "dancing frolics," which his Quaker sense of dignified decorum could not abide. The dances at issue appear to have been social occasions as opposed to religious exercises. The only religious festival on the Iroquois calendar for late February or early March was Thanks-to-the-Maple, a celebration of the requickening of the sap in maple trees, which the Senecas tapped for making sugar. Thanks-to-the-Maple was a one-day religious feast, not the weeks-long series of nighttime dances described by Simmons.[31] The dancing was performed only by the men and boys, the women attending but not dancing. At religious ceremonies, the women danced too, though there was never dancing between mixed couples. The purely social nature of these dances helps to explain a startling Seneca decision, announced at a formal council and recorded by Simmons.

On Wednesday, February 27, Simmons was teaching school in Cornplanter's house when his students suddenly became excited and then deserted him.

> This day proved a very trying and painful one to my soul, by reason of the prospect of an approaching dance and frolic among the Indians. I had beheld some of these before with great grief, though not to so great a degree as at this time. They had been having such frolics every two or three days or nights for many weeks back. I conduct the school in one half of Cornpanter's house, which is actually two houses, close-by each other, with the space in between them roofed over. In the other half of Cornplanter's house, two large kettles, each capable of holding near or quite a bar-rel apiece, were being prepared with provisions for the upcoming frolic. While I was helping one of the scholars, someone informed the others about the planned frolic. This put them in such a state of agitation that I was scarcely able to teach them at any rate. Some of them left the school and went home to prepare for the dance. This was the second time of my being so served.[32]
>
> After I let out school, I went into the woods and felled several large trees for the women to use as fire wood, which had been my frequent practice during the winter. By the time I returned to Cornplanter's house, they had got into the career of their folly, with a large concourse of men and boys dancing and shouting in an astonishing manner. Their musical instruments were large water turtles that had been dried after the entrails had been taken out and replaced with corn kernels. The neck was stretched to serve for a handle. Several women had collected, but ap-peared only as spectators.

Although it is not entirely clear from the Simmons account, the "dancing frolic" was probably held out of doors. The largest house in the village was Cornplanter's double structure, one "half" of which measured thirty feet by sixteen feet; the other, twenty-four feet by sixteen feet.[33] It seems doubtful that even the larger compartment could accommodate the "large concourse of men and boys dancing and shouting" in "the career of their folly" with "several women" gathered around as on-lookers.

> I entered the half of Cornplanter's house where he, his son Henry, and most of his family were sitting. I acquainted Cornplanter with the painful exercises under which I had labored at various times, on account of their many dancing frolics. I told him that it had appeared much more exercising to me that day than it had hitherto. I en-deavored to assert to him the evil of these dancing frolics, which were certainly the devil's works. Those who participated were serving the devil. I told him I thought every man had a right to be master of his own house, and before I would suffer such doings in mine, I would burn it to ashes and live in a cave. I hoped that I might never see any more of it among them. I further told him that what made it more painful to me was the fact that they collected the innocent children and were bring-ing them up in their footsteps, in doing that which was so very wicked, when it ought to be otherwise. And more I said to him, nearly to the same purport, in a very broken manner, to the amazement, I believe, of many of the spectators. He told me he could not say much about it at the present, but would converse on the subject the next day. I then retired to my house of lodging.

The "broken manner" that Simmons mentioned here probably referred to his becoming very emotional and perhaps crying.

> And on the morrow, I went as usual in order to teach school and found a large number of adult Indians collected in council in that half of Cornplanter's house that I used for the school. I entered into the other apartment and waited for them to call me to the council. As I sat there, the subject of poor Mordecai, sitting at the King's gate waiting to see how the matter would go, was vividly brought to my remembrance. After a while I was called in, and went with great willingness, though in much fear.
>
> Cornplanter informed me they had been discussing the subject that I had spoken about the evening before, and had concluded, although they did not all see alike, to quit such dancing frolics. Some of them thought it must be a wicked habit because they had learned it of white people, as well as that of drinking rum or whiskey and getting drunk, which they knew was evil. However, they had a hustling kind of play and dance too twice a year of their own production originally, which they thought to continue in the practice of.

Cornplanter referred to a difference of opinion among the Allegany Senecas on the issue of whether to discontinue the social dances, which Simmons found so abhorrent. This split may or may not have followed the contours of the nativist-versus-pragmatist division; it is not possible to know for sure one way or the other. It is conceivable that the nativists could have been on either side of the "frolics" issue. If these frolics were indeed a contamination of Indian practices by European-American–style reels and jigs, then it would be consistent for the nativists to have opposed them. So far as we know, however, they had not objected to these dances; it was Simmons not the nativists who brought the issue to the fore. And, it is entirely possible that the nativists were among those who wanted to retain the social dancing. Like all missionaries, Simmons condemned strong drink and "wild" dancing. In reaction to what they viewed as his presumptuous interference, the nativists might have called for retention of the social dancing, if not the drinking.

The "hustling kind of play," as Simmons described it, was a reference to either lacrosse or the bowl game. Most probably it was a reference to lacrosse, which was quite a rough-and-tumble game, as played by the Senecas of this period. And, even in the bowl game, participants and onlookers could become quite boisterous, which Simmons would find objectionable. But the Allegany Senecas were unwilling to part with either game. The Senecas used the opportunity afforded by the council to probe Simmons with some serious questions that mirrored concerns not only of the nativists but of the community at large.

> They asked me several questions. First, whether I thought it was right for Indians and white people to mix in marrying. I told them it was a bad question. It might be right for some to marry so, but thought it would not be right for me. Second, whether Indians and white people went together to the same place after death. I told them there were but two places, a place for the good and a place for the bad of all nations of people. Third, whether all would be of one language when in that place after death. I answered yes. They seemed satisfied.

Here the Senecas probed Simmons on the issue of race in two fundamental areas: marriage and religion. The first question was so telling and so direct that Simmons balked at it. He gave an answer, but to a degree sidestepped the question. He did not, as a general rule, disapprove of intermarriage, but acknowledged that he would not marry an Indian. And even on the question of such marriages as a general proposition, his answer—it might be right for some to marry so—was hardly an unqualified endorsement. It must be pointed out that Simmons, as a devout Quaker of the late 1700s, was obligated to marry none other than a Quaker in good standing. Given his personal piety, it is entirely possible that his response to the group's first question was not based on latent racism, but was made out of deference to Quaker marriage laws.

In putting this question to Simmons, the Senecas could have been coming from either of two directions. They might have intended it as a litmus test of Simmons's own personal racism or of his freedom from racism. If so, they certainly hit upon an acid test. The issue of "miscegenation" encapsulates questions pertaining to race, religion, and sex—always a volatile mixture. In this case, the honesty with which Simmons answered was probably more important than whether or not he wholeheartedly approved of mixed racial marriages. Then too, the Senecas themselves might have had some problems regarding intermarriage with whites.

On a practical level, the propensity of European-American males for forming sexual relationships with Indian females, fathering children, and then abandoning mother and children had created some problems for the Indians. From early contact times it had been common for a European-American man, such as a trader, on lengthy or frequent visits to the tribes to take an Indian woman as a temporary wife. When his business was done or his trade route changed, his Indian wife and children saw him no more. From the Indians' point of view, this was probably what Indian-white intermarriage had come to mean because it was virtually the only kind of intermarriage practiced.[34] The fact that the Senecas brought up this very point as the next topic of discussion tends to confirm that intermarriage—as it had actually been practiced—was as problematic for them as it was for Simmons.

The religious questions, which dealt with whether Indians and whites share the same afterworld as equals, were much less troublesome for Simmons. Based on his Quakerism, he answered these questions affirmatively and without reservation and reiterated the notion of heaven and hell. The Senecas moved on to the subject of white men who were delinquent fathers of mixed blood children.

> They informed me of one of their women who had a child by a white man who then resided at Pittsburgh, and never came to see anything about his child. They thought the Great Spirit intended that every man should care for and maintain his own children.

The Indians had not raised a frivolous concern here. In 1791 Cornplanter even complained of the problem in a letter to President Washington.

> Father, there are men who go from town to town and beget children and leave them to perish, or, except better men take care of them, to grow up without instruction.[35]

Of the Senecas present with Simmons that Thursday morning, at least one had been forsaken by his white father. Cornplanter's father was a white man named John Abeel, who would have nothing to do with his Indian son. Regarding his early life, Cornplanter wrote the following to the governor of Pennsylvania, Joseph Hiester, in 1822:

> When I was a child I played with the butterfly, the grasshopper, and the frogs; and as I grew up, I began to pay some attention and play with the Indian boys in the neighborhood; and they took notice of my skin being a different color from theirs, and spoke about it. I inquired of my mother the cause, and she told me that my father was a residenter in Albany. I still ate my victuals out of a bark dish. I grew up to be a young man, and married me a wife. I had no kettle or gun. I then knew where my father lived, and went to see him; and found he was a white man, and spoke the English language. He gave me victuals whilst I was at his house; but when I started to return home, he gave me no provisions to eat on the way. He gave me neither kettle nor gun.[36]

Simmons refused to be drawn into a discussion about the problems devolving from mixed marriages, preferring instead to excoriate the Indians for some of their customs, which he found offensive.

> I, along with the interpreter, arose and made a long speech to them, opening more clearly the evil of many customs prevailing among them, particularly that of dancing and shouting in such a hideous manner, which they are accustomed to. I did this because there were many then present who did not hear me the evening before. While thus engaged, I experienced the God of Israel to be my present help. He brought me into such a broken state that I believe some of them present were fully convinced and many of their dark hearts, more enlightened. The council continued until dark. I then returned to my house of lodging.

RESENTMENT RISING

Simmons's next journal entry was the final in a series of three for three consecutive days. The events of the two preceding days and his proclivity for criticizing Seneca behavior must have increased resentment against Simmons, certainly among the nativists and quite possibly among some of the pragmatists. Cornplanter apparently felt the need to reassure Simmons of his own personal support for the school and for ongoing Quaker involvement in Seneca affairs. But the chief was reluctant to do so publicly. On the morning of Friday, March 1, Cornplanter, two of his sons, and some of his most loyal followers called on Simmons before he had even left his lodgings to go teach school.

> Cornplanter informed me he had come for the express purpose of telling me something particular that he had not wanted to bring up the day before because some of his people did not see and think as he did. As for his own part, he had a great regard for the Quakers and could find no fault with me or my companions, but felt happy we were among them. He had several times before expressed his gladness at my being with him, and he hoped we might live a long while together. He also said that when he first saw us coming to his house, he was glad and thanked the Great Spirit at that time, whom he thought must have brought us thither.

Cornplanter clearly felt reticent, for the moment at least, about making a public declaration of his continued support for Simmons and the Quaker program. Cornplanter admitted there were things he had wanted to say to Simmons the day before but that he had felt too uncomfortable to do so "because some of his people did not see and think as he did." Yet tensions were so high that Cornplanter felt he must do something to reassure Simmons. Hence, the personal testimonial and the imminent award of special stewardship over some selected Indian children.

> He further said there was a number of boys and some girls, some of whom were then present, whom Cornplanter and his supporters intended should attend the school steadily. They would give up the boys into my care, for me to do by them as I would by my own son. He wished me to help them learn to work and to correct them as they deserved, including his own children.

The pragmatists were promising to ensure that their children would attend school more regularly. In light of Iroquois childrearing practices and the participation of children in the seasonal round of Iroquois life this was a significant commitment to what, in Iroquois eyes, was a daunting regimen for children.

> And, also, if I wanted any of the young men to go to Genesinguhta or do any business that I thought would be of advantage to them, I should command them. He mentioned one or two, who were then present, upon whom I could call when I needed them.

Halliday Jackson and Joel Swayne were living and working on the model farm at Genesinguhta, nine miles up the Allegheny River from Cornplanter's village. Simmons did have occasional need to reach them, both for his own purposes and to arrange assistance for Cornplanter and his people. Simmons was genuinely touched by Cornplanter's trust and confidence.

> Thus, he seemed, in a manner, willing to resign his own commission to me. I acknowledged his love and tender regard toward me. I felt truly thankful to the Lord for these favors.

After Cornplanter delivered his testimonial, a young Indian man related a dream that provided timely support for several of the key Quaker recommendations.

Seneca Factionalism
Conflict among the Senecas was nothing new in 1799. Differences of opinion had arisen before as to the best way to deal with the "white man." Factions had formed around a variety of issues, including religious affiliation.[37]

During the 1660s the admission of French Jesuit missionaries from Canada and the resulting conversion to Catholicism of about 20 percent of the Iroquois population gave rise to traditionalist versus Christian factions. The conflict became so intense that many of the Christian converts emigrated to Canada during the 1670s. The sudden exodus of several thousand pro-French Christian converts paved the way for the ascendancy of pro-British traditionalists during the 1680s. This faction led the Iroquois into a series of wars that eventually resulted in military disaster during the 1690s, when the French and their Indian allies devastated the homelands of the Mohawks, the Oneidas, and the Onondagas. By the 1690s a tripartite division had arisen: a pro-French faction eager to sue for peace and end the destructive war, a pro-British faction that relied on the colonial government of New York as a buttress against the French, and a neutralist faction that wanted to play the British and French against each other. In the end neutralist policies prevailed, and Iroquois fortunes improved greatly during the first half of the 1700s.[38]

During the French and Indian War, a pro-British faction among the Mohawks and a pro-French faction among the Senecas pursued diametrically opposite policies.[39] The Mohawks fought the French and the Senecas fought the British. The Mohawks and the Senecas fought on different fronts, however, and therefore did not fight each other.[40] This situation continued the neutralist strategy, and if the French had been able to hold on to Canada, the Iroquois position following the war would have been greatly strengthened. With French defeat and English control of Canada, however, the playoff game abruptly ended.[41]

Factionalism arose again at the outset of the American Revolution. The Oneidas and the Tuscaroras were pro-American, mainly because they were strongly influenced by the Presbyterian missionary, Samuel Kirkland.[42] The Mohawks were decidedly pro-British, perhaps hoping to eventually reinstate the play-off strategy, this time between the Americans and the British. The remaining Iroquois nations were internally divided between neutralist and pro-British factions. The neutralists eventually threw in their lot with the pro-British faction and went to war against the Americans, even though in the case of neutralist leaders like Cornplanter and Red Jacket, it was against their better judgment. Too many Iroquois had come to recognize the insatiable land greed of the Americans. Neutralist sentiment was overwhelmed by a desire to stop the Americans while there was still a chance. When neutralist leaders like Cornplanter did take up the tomahawk in 1777, they vigorously prosecuted the war against the Americans.[43]

By the late 1790s the issues before the Iroquois were radically altered. They had no significant military power. They had no European ally to reinforce them against the Americans. And they had no counterweight—such as a militant and expansionist Canada—with which to re-institute the play-off strategy. Confined to their reservations and dependent on annuities from the federal government, they had to recognize the political sovereignty of the United States. They were being engulfed by European-American culture; differences of opinion about how to proceed from this point on were at the root of the pragmatist-nativist factionalism.

In 1795 Cornplanter wrote to the army commander at Pittsburgh asking that inquiries be made in the east where his son Henry was being educated, explaining that he wished "to hear from my son and what progress he is making in his learning, and as soon as he is learned enough I want him at home to manage my business for me." The business Cornplanter referred to was his sawmill, which provides insight into Cornplanter's own personal acculturation.[44]

Built sometime between 1791 and 1795, Cornplanter's sawmill predated by at least five years any European-American–owned sawmills on the upper Allegheny River.[45] This was a genuine cultural innovation, independently initiated by Cornplanter. He employed European Americans to construct and operate the mill. He negotiated contracts for the sale of boards to the U.S. Army at Franklin and Pittsburgh, which took the mill's entire output for some time.[46] In 1796 the Holland Land Company's storehouse at Warren was constructed of boards purchased from Cornplanter's sawmill.[47] He had the mill reconstructed in 1806.

Cornplanter thus demonstrated not only that he had internalized some mercantile traits normally associated with European-American culture, but also that he had mastered facets of the roles of entrepreneur, capitalist, employer, and salesman sufficiently to make a commercial success of the enterprise. In Cornplanter's mind, traditionally "white" business ventures were not off limits to Indians, who were free to pursue them in their own way and for their own ends. The fact that Cornplanter had internalized some traits of the shrewd businessman does not mean that he had completely internalized the values typically held by a businessman. Cornplanter accumulated wealth, in large part, to be able to give it away.

As the foremost headman of his band, Cornplanter was expected by Iroquois cultural norms to be able to assist needy members of his band in a variety of ways. He could be called upon to provide food and clothing for destitute women and children in his band, to give cash for the purchase of a rifle or gunpowder to a hunter whose credit was overextended with European-American traders, and to arrange legal assistance and bail for Indians who ran afoul of the "white man's law" in Franklin or Pittsburgh. The income from his sawmill helped Cornplanter meet these obligations.

Cornplanter was also undoubtedly motivated by some desire to accumulate personal wealth. His keen sense of his own personal and private property was well-known to his European-American contemporaries. During the spring of 1798, for example, when the party of five Quakers were making their outbound journey to Cornplanter's village, they stopped in Pittsburgh for a few days to arrange for the shipping of supplies by boat up the Allegheny River. While there, they called upon General Wilkinson, commander of U.S. troops in the region, who at the conclusion of the meeting "gently insinuated a cautionary hint respecting the private character of Cornplanter; that he was sufficiently possessed of the idea of distinct private property, and pretty artful in adopting measures to his own interest."[48]

The historical record, nevertheless, shows many instances of Cornplanter providing the members of his band with exactly the kind of assistance traditionally expected of a headman. In May 1798 at the second general Seneca-Quaker council, Cornplanter was observed to give one of his men a public dressing-down. Extracting the man from the European-American justice system had just cost Cornplanter a small fortune.

> Cornplanter made a pretty lengthy speech. It did not appear to be directed to us but our interpreter informed, was for an Indian then in the house who had been charged with murdering a white man for which he had been in jail in Pittsburgh, and tried for his life, but being acquitted by the jury, he was now at liberty. The

trial and court expenses we understood, had cost Cornplanter more than 200 dollars. Though there was not evidence to support the charge yet there was cause to fear it was too true. The chief's speech appeared to be delivered with much earnest and serious expostulation."[49]

If Cornplanter had not provided assistance as expected, the Allegany Senecas would have turned to someone else to be their headman. The resources that he drew upon to provide such assistance did include annuity payments to the Allegany Seneca band, of which Cornplanter had charge. But they also included stores of cash, food, and goods that he amassed as a result of his personal income from the sawmill.

In a few cases, Cornplanter's pragmatism was revolutionary. He was willing to overthrow long-established Iroquois customs when he thought it was necessary to do so to cope effectively with European Americans. In 1794 he proposed overriding the veto that clan matrons could traditionally exercise over a decision by the warriors and chiefs to go to war. He was deterred from doing so, and from taking up the war hatchet against the United States, only by news of Gen. Anthony Wayne's victory at Fallen Timbers over the Shawnee-led confederacy of Indian tribes—the Western Confederates—inhabiting the Old Northwest Territory.[50]

Nativists opposed changes in the traditional sexual division of labor almost as much as they opposed religious acculturation. They opposed plow agriculture because it required men to become involved in cultivating the fields, which was considered to be women's work. Men's role in traditional agriculture had been limited to initially clearing the fields by removing trees and underbrush. Women did all the subsequent cultivation and planting, using hoes. Most Seneca men were probably reluctant to take up plow agriculture because it resembled hoe horticulture and might be perceived as "unmanly," and nativists agreed with the Oneida men who opined in 1796 that "squaws and hedgehogs are made to scratch on the ground."[51]

Nativists seem to have believed, however, that a man's strength was needed to handle a plow and its team of horses or oxen, which means that they tacitly recognized plowing as "men's work." In time, this perception together with the preachments of Handsome Lake and the ubiquitous example of European-American men plowing their fields rendered the prospect of an Iroquois man behind a plow much less odious to nativists.

In general, nativists did not oppose the changes in their material culture that had already occurred. Anthropologists have noted that "material culture forms are more amenable to change than are more purely symbolic forms."[52] Few nativists were willing to give up rifles, steel hatchets and knives, brass kettles, and woven clothes and blankets.

Indeed, it can be argued that prior to the late 1700s, the adoption of these products represented the assimilation of European-American cultural elements into the traditional Iroquois culture. By virtue of the ways in which they incorporated these items into existing and familiar patterns of artifact usage, the Iroquois did not become more "European American." Rather, the items became "Indian." Brass kettles, iron axes, iron-bladed hoes, and woolen blankets superseded ceramic pots, stone celts, wooden digging sticks, and animal skins. These manufactured imports were more efficient, but the underlying purposes for which they were used remained unchanged, as did the culture.[53]

All goods destined for the "Indian trade," including clothes, were thus tailored specifically to suit American Indian tastes. As early as the middle of the 1600s, a heavy thick-napped woolen cloth called "duffle" was a common material in the Dutch trade. Indians had begun to use duffel to make their clothes, in place of traditional deerskin leather. Later, after the English took over the trade, the equivalent blanketlike woolen cloth manufactured in Britain became known as "stroud." Indians preferred their duffel or stroud in precise hues of dark red, deep blue, or steel gray, cut into standard-sized bolts. Successful traders catered to their customers' tastes and preferences. Other trade items—shirts, hatchets, kettles—were similarly manufactured to Indian specifications. The Iroquois did not so much purchase "European-American goods" as "Indian goods" manufactured in Europe or by European Americans in North America.[54]

The fact that use of certain manufactured goods did not transform American Indians into European Americans, but, instead, allowed them to be "better Indians"—equipped with more efficient tools, more desirable clothes, warmer blankets, and so on—made these changes in material culture not only palatable but welcome to the nativists. The Iroquois attitude, nativist and pragmatist, toward the changes in material culture that had occurred from early contact times through the end of the 1700s was one of robust self-confidence and self-direction. A late-eighteenth-century Seneca man decked out in his finest regalia did not feel the least bit "contaminated" by his calico shirt, stroud breechcloth, or brightly colored leggings. His imported metal gorget, armband, and earrings, as well as his vermilion and verdigris face paint, were all personal adornments manufactured specifically for Indians and worn only by them. Armed with a steel knife, a steel hatchet, and a rifled gun, he considered himself no less an Indian than his great-great-grandfather, who had not carried such weapons only because they were not available. We must question whether it really makes sense to apply the term acculturation to such changes in material culture.[55]

On the question of additional technological innovation (such as saw- and gristmilling and blacksmithing, and with the exception of plow agriculture) even the nativists tended toward pragmatism. This was simply an extension of their attitude toward the changes in material culture that had occurred earlier in their history. And, unlike plow agriculture, innovations such as sawmilling, gristmilling, and blacksmithing did not upset the traditional sexual division of labor. The grinding of corn was traditionally a "female" task. Nativists apparently perceived gristmilling, however, as far enough removed from the manual, wooden mortar-and-pestle methods by which women had traditionally ground corn so as to render it inoffensive to manhood.

When it came to education, nativists tended to oppose "book learning," although they grudgingly admitted that a few individuals would have to learn to read and write to be able to deal with the surrounding European-American culture and prevent their fellow Indians from being cheated. Nativist objections to formal, academic education might have stemmed from concerns about overt, or even covert, religious indoctrination that could take place in the classroom. Nativists did not object to vocational-technical instruction, which presumably afforded little opportunity for cultural "subversion" or religious indoctrination.

PRECURSOR TO THE PROPHET

According to Simmons's journal entry for Friday, March 1, Cornplanter and some of his supporters visited Simmons privately at his lodgings and reassured him of their commitment to the Quaker plan. During the remainder of this council, a young man related a recent dream of his that featured astonishing visions of heaven and hell, including bizarre punishments for specific sins of which he himself was guilty. The young man was moved to personal repentance and reform. Simmons endorsed the dream, which was very timely in that it tended to buttress his position among the pragmatists.

In this council, a young man informed the company of a dream that he had a few nights before, when out in the woods hunting, in company with a lad. He thought an Indian struck him twice with a knife; he fell and thought he must die. But soon he appeared to ascend upwards, some distance along a narrow path, in which appeared many tracks of people, all going up, some barefoot and some not.

At length he came to a house and the door opened for him to go in, which he did. The most beautiful man whom ever he had seen in his life was seated inside. The man invited him to sit down and he endeavored to do so, but he could not sit down. He tried to stop moving and he tried to talk to the man. But, he could do neither. Unable to stop moving, he passed on and went out through a door, opposite to the one he had come in at. And so, he found that he had both come and gone before he could even utter a word to the beautiful man.

When outside again, he heard a great noise and, after traveling some distance, he came to another building which had an uncommon large door, like a barn door. Standing in the doorway to meet him, was a man who looked very dismal and whose mouth appeared to move in different shapes, from one side of his face to the other. This person conducted him inside where he beheld numbers of like Indians who seemed to be drunken and very noisy, and who looked very distressed. He knew some of them, but they had been dead several years.

Among them was one very old white-headed woman whom they told him was dying, and when she went, the world would go too. There appeared to be a fireplace on the ground, although he could not discern anything but smoke and ashes, with which the hair on their heads was covered. He soon found he could sit and talk fast enough in this house, which he could not do in the other.

The person who conducted him in, who appeared to be their official, gave him some stuff to drink, like melted pewter. He told the official that he could not take it down. But the official insisted he should, by telling him he could drink whiskey and get drunk, and that was no worse than to take this drink. He then took it, which he thought burned him very much.

The official then took a chain and bound it round him. He asked what that was for, and the official told him it was to prevent him from going after women and other men's wives. The official then told him to go strike a woman who was sitting there, which he attempted to do, but could not because he suddenly discovered that his arms were off. The official told him the reason he had lost his arms, which was because he had often been guilty of striking his wife. And, if he would entirely quit that practice, he should have his arms made whole again. And, if he forsook all other evil practices, which he had been guilty of, he should have a home in the first house he had entered.

He was then bade to go home. When he awoke he found himself crying. He could not tell his dream for some time afterward because he would cry so much and because he knew it was true. He confessed in the council that he had been guilty of all those actions above mentioned.

After I had considered the matter well, I told him I believed his dream was true and that I hoped he would remember it as long as he lived, etc. He said he intended to try to do better than he had done, and he intended to learn to read. Regarding the old gray-headed woman, I told them that I thought she was the mother of wickedness, and as they had been so long in a dark and evil state, I thought she must be white-headed. And I hoped that she was dying from among them because when she was dead, the worldly spirit would go too. Cornplanter said the devil would die if they tried to do good.

Clearly, the young man experienced a visitation dream, in which he saw two supernatural beings: the beautiful man in the first house and the "official" in the second. What is not clear from Simmons's account is that the Iroquois of that period believed that when a person dreamed of going to a place such as another village, a different country, the afterworld, one of his souls left the body and actually traveled there. The Iroquois of that time conceived of a person's soul as a plurality of souls. To simplify matters, here we will define two broad categories of "soul," body soul and free soul.

The body soul, which remained in the body and sustained life, was associated with the warmth and breath of the body, and also with emotion and irrationality. When a person died, his body soul retreated into his bones, causing the rest of the body to cease functioning. The free soul, which was free to leave the body and travel about, was associated with consciousness, intellect, reasoning, and rationality. It left the body during periods of unconsciousness, such as sleep, coma, trance, or drunkenness. Dreams were adventures of the free soul as it roamed outside the unconscious body, which was being kept alive, warm and breathing, by the body soul.[56]

According to Iroquois belief of that day, the young man's free soul had actually left his body, traveled "along a narrow path," to reach first heaven, where he manifestly did not fit in, and then hell, where he unhappily did fit in. It is from his description of hell that we know his free soul reached the afterworld: "[H]e beheld numbers of like Indians . . . who looked very distressed. He knew some of them, but they had been dead several years." He met their free souls, which had left their bodies permanently after these people had died.

The dream seems to have had a profound effect on the young man, rendering him tearful for days, forcing him to confront his personal vices of drunkenness, promiscuity, and wife beating, and moving him to confess and repent of his sins during the council at Simmons's lodgings. Given the Iroquois dream cult, it is easy to see how a dream like this could have life-changing effects. Doubtless the young

man's listeners waited and watched during the days, weeks, and months that followed to see if he actually mended his ways.

But regardless of whether he reformed his personal behavior or not, the young
man's dream is significant for the many ways in which it stands as a precursor to the
visions of Handsome Lake. During his second vision, Handsome Lake's free soul
left his body and traveled on a "sky journey," met supernatural beings and the free
souls of deceased persons, and saw heaven and hell. He too had a guide, although a
much more benevolent one than the young man's "official."

The enumeration of specific punishments fitted to particular sins was a prominent feature in Handsome Lake's early visions, which also sounded a strong apocalyptic theme in which the imminent end of the world was prophesied—unless the
Indians reformed their ways. The appearance of the "old white-headed woman,"
who when she died would take the world with her, injected a similarly apocalyptic
theme into the young man's dream. Also, Handsome Lake was shown the path to
salvation, as was the young man: "And, if he forsook all other evil practices which
he had been guilty of, he should have a home in the first house he had entered."

Simmons was certainly impressed by this strikingly singular and vivid dream,
otherwise he would not have recorded it in such length and detail. Simmons did not
record that the young man or any of the other Indians asked for his opinion about the
dream; but by telling the dream the young man had in effect invited Simmons's
comments. The Iroquois related their dreams to each other so that their meaning or
message could be interpreted. Simmons commented that the dream was "true" and
that the old white-headed woman was the "mother of wickedness."

Simmons's comment was not about the genuineness of the dream, that is,
whether or not the young man made it up. Rather, when Simmons said he believed
the dream to be "true," he meant that it contained a good message, as opposed to an
evil or deceitful one. An answer implies that there was a question—and in this case
the implied question was whether the content of this dream, or of any other dream
for that matter, was the prompting of a benevolent and trustworthy spirit or of a
malevolent and treacherous one. This question is similar to Hamlet's quandary over
whether the apparition he saw was really his father's ghost or the devil trying to
trick him into murder and damnation: "The spirit that I have seen may be a devil;
and the devil hath power t' assume a pleasing shape; yea, and perhaps out of my
weakness and my melancholy, as he is very potent with such spirits, abuses me to
damn me."[57]

This concern about the moral impetus behind dreams would be echoed in Handsome Lake's sky journey, during which the prophet was told by his guide that "the Indians dreamed a lot. And, sometimes their dreams were true, having come from the
Great Spirit. But, often, when a dream was true, the Indians would not believe that it
had come from the Great Spirit. Instead, they would think it had come from the devil.
And, when the devil told them something in a dream, they often believed that the
message had come from the Great Spirit."[58] Simmons's foreshadowing of Handsome
Lake's concern about the spiritual origin of dreams was probably coincidental.

Regarding the comment about the mother of wickedness, it seems likely that Simmons was trying to force his own interpretation on the Indians, which was that they were living in a "dark and evil state" and had been living so for a very long time. Simmons was stretching things here because the apocalyptic theme introduced by the dying, old woman seems straightforward enough. To the young man and the other Indians, she probably represented the apocalyptic notions that time is running out, the end of the world is coming soon as are judgment and punishment, and the time for repentance is now. Soon everyone will be in one of the two houses: the first one with the beautiful man or the second one full of smoke and ashes.

This dream was actually helpful to Simmons in that some of the practices against which he had been inveighing—especially drunkenness—were dramatically portrayed as evil and deserving of punishment in the next life. Although it is a fact that Simmons endorsed the young man's dream, it is perhaps more significant that the dream endorsed some of Simmons's preachments.

CHAPTER THREE

The Children of Onas

Henry Simmons was raised in the heartland of American Quakerdom, by solid Quaker parents, during a radical transformation within the Religious Society of Friends (RSF) in Pennsylvania. All these factors influenced his religious and spiritual formation.

So little is known about Simmons's life prior to his arrival at Cornplanter's village in May 1798 that our only avenue to understanding him and the other Quaker missionaries, aside from their letters and journals, is to examine the sectarian milieu that shaped them. The RSF exerted more influence on Simmons than anyone or anything else, except for his own parents and family. The nature of the RSF in the years during which Simmons grew up and matured into adulthood did much to determine his values, attitudes, and aspirations. The reasons that Simmons and the other Quakers engaged in the Allegany mission and the goals they hoped to advance cannot be understood apart from the RSF and the crises through which it passed during the second half of the eighteenth century.

Simmons and his contemporaries referred to the RSF, which played such an important role in determining the contours and direction of their lives, simply as "our Society" or "Friends." The Indians of Pennsylvania and New York frequently called the Quakers "our good Friends," but they also referred to them as "the children of Onas." *Onas* means "quill" or "feather" and was the name given by Iroquois counselors to William Penn, the Quaker founder and Proprietor of colonial Pennsylvania.[1] Henry Simmons's outlook on religion, education, and American Indians derived in many respects from the collective experience of the children of Onas during the latter half of the eighteenth century.

The reformation of American Quakerism began during the French and Indian War, about a decade and a half before Simmons was born, and it continued through the end of the American Revolution, about a decade and a half after he was born. During the nearly three decades between 1755 and 1783, the RSF in Pennsylvania underwent a radical transformation, wrought mostly through the efforts of zealous reformers working inside the Society. But the reformers could not have finished the job without the political tensions that led up to the American Revolution and without the political upheavals that accompanied it.[2] In fact, the reformation spread to other parts of American Quakerdom—New York and New England—only with the onset of emergencies posed by the American Revolution.[3]

Among the children of Onas, the reformation was so severe that it can be viewed as a purge, conducted from within. Over the almost thirty-year course of the reformation, the Philadelphia Yearly Meeting (PYM) "disowned," or expelled, more than 4,000 of its members for failing to live up to the Society's standards and refusing to submit to its "discipline."[4] During this period, the children of Onas never numbered more than about 13,000 persons. By one estimate, between 1760 and 1776, the PYM expelled 20 percent of its membership.[5] The reformers consciously decided to accept decreased membership as the price of purification.[6]

Peccant Friends were not "disowned" summarily. In each case, the Society scrupulously adhered to a disciplinary review procedure, which included an appeals process, and during which the delinquent Friend had ample opportunity to reform his or her behavior and make amends as necessary. Disownment followed only when the erring Friend refused to submit to the Society's discipline.[7]

Strict enforcement of the Society's standards and discipline meant that, by the end of the reformation, only the most fervent and dedicated of the children of Onas remained in the Society, and they were required to lead ever more sectarian lives, marked by increased asceticism. They had been sorely tried, even persecuted, by the revolutionary government of Pennsylvania. By 1783 the remnant Friends were willing to sacrifice and suffer for their convictions.

The details of the reformation and the Revolution, together with PYM records on membership, marriage, and discipline tell us much about the parents of Henry Simmons and about Simmons himself. We know that his parents married within the constraints of Quaker discipline, which meant that they withstood the Society's careful scrutiny of their worthiness and preparation for marriage. They lived under the watchful supervision of their local meeting, attended worship regularly, adhered to the Society's code of behavior, raised their children according to Quaker precepts, including a religious education "guarded" from vain, "soaring airy head knowledge."[8] There is only one record of either of them being disciplined. Henry's father was rebuked for accusing a woman of stealing when he did not have the evidence to prove it. He acknowledged "his impudent conduct," and that was the end of it.[9]

RELIGIOUS SOCIETY OF FRIENDS

The RSF was organized around "yearly meetings." Yearly referred not only to frequency of meeting, but also to position within the administrative hierarchy. The yearly meetings were the highest administrative units. In the late 1700s there were yearly meetings in Philadelphia, Baltimore, New York, New England, North Carolina, and Virginia—and, of course, in London and Dublin. The yearly meetings maintained communion with one another through correspondence and visits, and were, in theory, coequal with each other. Throughout the eighteenth century, however, yearly meetings all around the Atlantic basin deferred to the London Yearly Meeting as the first among equals.[10]

Within a yearly meeting, such as the Philadelphia Yearly Meeting (PYM), the organizational structure was that of a pyramid, with the "yearly meeting"—which indeed met once per year—at the apex. At the base of the pyramid were the weekly—actually semiweekly—meetings for worship, which had virtually no administrative function. Rather, the administrative affairs of several, nearby weekly meetings were combined into a monthly meeting for business and discipline, which was the basic unit of local Quaker administration.[11]

The monthly meeting was responsible for controlling membership, maintaining discipline, providing relief for needy Friends, placing older children as apprentices, administering a local school, placing orphans in suitable homes, and arbitrating business and other disputes between Friends. A treasurer managed its finances, which were funded by collections, subscriptions, and endowments. Trustees supervised church property, schools, and graveyards, and dispensed charity to needy Friends. The monthly meeting determined the places and times of worship, including the establishment of new meeting places. Marriages were made under the auspices of the monthly meeting.

As did all Quaker meetings of record, the monthly meeting had a clerk, who kept the minutes.[12] The clerk captured the "sense of the meeting," which was open to all members in good standing. A wide range of opinions might be expressed on some questions. After allowing what he or she judged to be sufficient discussion on a particular topic, the clerk stated a summary of the emergent consensus, enunciating the sense of the meeting as accurately and faithfully as possible. In articulating the sense of the meeting, clerks tended to give more weight to the views of ministers, elders, trustees, and disciplinary overseers than they did to those of ordinary members or infrequent attendees. If no one objected to the clerk's formulation, it was recorded in the minutes; if someone did object, further discussion ensued. The clerk steered the meeting toward consensus without resorting to votes or invoking majority rule.[13]

Reporting to each monthly meeting were several "preparative" meetings, which usually met weekly to carry forward on-going business between sittings of the monthly meeting. The preparative meetings also conducted active surveillance of Friends' comportment and initiated disciplinary cases as warranted. Any Friend who observed a fault in another was obligated to reprimand his wayward brother, reminding the straying Friend of the Society's code of behavior and standards of conduct and perhaps suggesting that they pray together for strength and guidance. If the violator failed to heed the friendly reproach, the admonishing Friend would inform the preparative meeting about the problem.

Each preparative meeting included "overseers," appointed by the monthly meeting, who were experienced in dealing with "stumbling" Friends. Adept at detecting and correcting misbehavior, the overseers themselves might initially discover the infraction. In either case, they rebuked "disorderly walkers" and advised them on how to correct their conduct. Often, the overseers were able to informally resolve the situation. If the informal approach failed or was not appropriate because of the seriousness of the transgression, the preparative meeting turned the case over to the monthly meeting.[14]

The monthly meeting made a formal investigation of the case and usually appointed a committee to try to persuade the delinquent Friend to mend his ways. If he still refused to uphold the Society's "testimonies" and satisfy its ethical requirements, the monthly meeting could "disown" him, which did not imply damnation. Disownment was a means to state publicly that some aspect of the person's behavior was incompatible with the Society's rules, that the person was unwilling to do what the Society required in order to repair the breach, and that, therefore, he or she was no longer a member of the Society.[15] Disowned but contrite Friends, willing to repent in public and reform their behavior, could petition the Society for readmission—and penitent disowned persons were readmitted.[16]

The monthly meeting actually comprised two meetings: a men's meeting and a women's meeting. The women's meeting handled discipline among women Friends and served as a forum in which women could express their concerns. The women's meeting was autonomous in many regards, particularly in the matter of disciplining women, but often depended on the men's meeting for funds. The parallel structure of men's and women's meetings continued upward through the hierarchy of Quaker meetings: quarterly and yearly.[17]

The monthly meetings in a given geographic area reported to a quarterly meeting, which served as an appellate body to which individuals or meetings could turn in cases of difficulty that could not be resolved on the local—monthly—level. In 1755 the quarterly meetings took on added importance when the PYM required its subordinate monthly meetings to read aloud—and answer in writing—a standard list of queries every three months, designed to assess the meeting's spiritual health and sectarian rigor. The PYM had adopted the practice in 1743, when it devised its own list of questions, patterned on original British queries. The requirement that the queries be answered quarterly—in writing—was one of the first measures taken by the reformers. Each monthly meeting answered the queries with detailed written responses, which were then summarized by the quarterly meeting, with the summary being forwarded to the yearly meeting.[18] The quarterly meetings of a larger geographic region, such as the states of Pennsylvania and New Jersey, reported to a yearly meeting, in this case, the PYM.

Any of these meetings, except for the weekly worship meetings, could appoint standing committees to manage on-going business between sittings of the meeting. For example, on October 2, 1795, the PYM appointed the twenty-nine-member Indian Committee to oversee Indian affairs during the interval between sittings of the yearly meeting. The official name of this committee described its function: "The Committee Appointed . . . for Promoting the improvement and gradual civilization of the Indian natives."[19]

But the RSF was much more than structure and organization. Its unique form of worship, its testimonies, and its discipline all distinguished it from other Christian denominations and sects.

Most congregations of Friends met at least twice a week for worship, every First Day, or Sunday, and once during the week. Some congregations in metropolitan Philadelphia offered a third meeting during the week. Worship meetings were held in simple, unadorned meeting houses. There was no music, no hymn singing, no recitation of standardized prayers, and no formal reading of scriptural passages. The congregation sat quietly in attentive silence, patiently waiting for the Holy Spirit to move one of its members to speak. In theory, anyone could speak who felt moved by the Spirit to offer a spontaneous prayer or to communicate some particular exhortation, insight, or concern. In practice, most speaking during worship meetings was done by recognized ministers. A particular congregation might, at any given time, have one, several, or no ministers. During a worship meeting, a minister might feel called upon by the Spirit to deliver what amounted to an extemporaneous sermon, explaining a biblical text and applying it to matters of belief and behavior. The worship meeting concluded with a round of handshaking, as a sign of fellowship.[20]

The Society eschewed a specially trained, ordained, paid, full-time clergy. Friends viewed this as a hireling ministry. They believed that religious truth would be discovered by all men and women who hearkened to the light of the Spirit shining within their own hearts and allowed the seed of Christ's kingdom to grow within and claim their souls.[21] They practiced literally the "priesthood of all believers." But, some individuals, when speaking during worship, consistently delivered messages that met with general approbation. Such individuals, both men and women, became recognized as ministers, persons especially gifted at communicating the revelations of the Holy Spirit.[22]

Ministers were formally recognized by the monthly meeting, which also appointed a group of elders to cultivate the ministry. The elders served as spiritual advisors for the ministers, encouraging them in the development of their special gift, guiding their study of scripture, and counseling them in the ways of humility. The elders had to discern, and help ministers discern for themselves, whether a message, which was supposed to come from the Spirit, came from the Spirit or from the minister. No compensation was paid to any of the ministers, elders, trustees, overseers, clerks, or any of the other officers within the hierarchical structure of Quaker meetings. Traveling ministers and missionaries, however, were reimbursed for their traveling expenses. The Quaker church, thus, was a lay church, or, perhaps more accurately, a church in which the laity had been abolished in favor of a universal priesthood.[23]

By 1783 after roughly 130 years of Quakerism, Friends had developed several important testimonies. A testimony consisted of the body of divine revelation concerning a fundamental religious or spiritual truth that Friends had collectively and cumulatively experienced in their meetings for worship, in the preachments of their ministers, and in the writings of their enlightened men and women; and it was also the witness borne to the revealed truth by Friends in all aspects of their lives—marriage, family, work, private and public business, education, and philanthropy. At times, bearing witness to the truth required sacrifice and exposed Friends to suffering.

The quintessential Quaker testimony—the "inner light"—was a metaphor for that measure of the divine principle that Christ placed in every soul.[24] That measure present in every man existed as but a seed, which "draws, inclines, and invites to God," but could sprout into life only if man cooperated with the grace of Christ. Friends believed that human nature was totally corrupt, and that man, through his own powers, could not even begin to find his way to salvation. God, however, gave to each man and woman, Jew and Gentile, Christian and "heathen," a spark of His own life which, "if not resisted" but "received and closed within the heart," led to sanctification and salvation.[25]

The Quakers bore witness to the inner light not only in their meetings for worship, in their theory and practice of a lay ministry, and in their publications, but also in their attitude toward non-Quakers. One did not have to become a Quaker in order to be saved.[26] Christians of all stripes, from Puritans to Catholics, could find salvation if they heeded the inner light. Jews, Muslims, and heathens were also visited by the inner light, and, if they "resisted it not" but responded to it positively, they too could be saved—even if the gospel was never proclaimed to them. Friends did not believe that all men were saved automatically. It was possible to resist the inner light, to bruise the seed, and to find deserved damnation—as did many men, Christians as well as heathens.[27]

Inextricably linked to the inner light was the Quaker testimony regarding "immediate revelation." Friends did not believe that divine revelation had ended at the close of the Apostolic era. True, Scripture already revealed all that was necessary for salvation, but the Spirit could reveal anew "the good old gospel and doctrines."[28] The Spirit, moreover, could communicate to individuals God's will concerning their own specific lives. As George Fox, first publisher of the Quaker vision, reported of his own experience, "[T]hen I heard a voice which said, 'There is one, even Christ Jesus, that can speak to *thy* condition.'"[29]

Friends believed that "the inward immediate manifestation and revelation of God's Spirit" could shine "into the heart, enlightening and opening the understanding." This on-going process of revelation was necessary because scripture alone could *not* be "esteemed the principle ground of all truth and knowledge, nor yet the adequate primary rule of faith and manners." Scripture was "a secondary rule, subordinate to the Spirit."[30] Scripture also did not address all the circumstances encountered in the present: "[T]here be many truths, which as they are applicable to particulars and individuals, and most needful to be known by them, are in nowise to be found in the Scripture." And, "[T]here are numberless things, with regard to their circumstances, which particular Christians may be concerned in, for which there can be no particular rule had in the Scriptures."[31]

THE QUAKER PEACE TESTIMONY

Friends are probably best-known for their peace testimony, which led to their withdrawal from Pennsylvania's government during the French and Indian War and from politics altogether during the American Revolution. Believing that war and all violence were contrary to the teaching of Jesus Christ, Friends refused to render military service. Over the course of the French and Indian War and the American Revolution, increasing numbers of Friends refused to pay taxes levied specifically for financing war.

George Fox had based his pacifist principles on "immediate revelation" provided by the workings of the Holy Spirit. Later, Friends such as William Penn appealed to the more secular argument that, in the end, war was nothing but a cruel and savage barbarity, destructive to the humanity of all participants, including the victors. By the close of the seventeenth century, Friends began citing texts from the New Testament to demonstrate the incompatibility of war with the teachings of Jesus.[32]

During the first half of the eighteenth century, Quakers generally dropped the secular and humanitarian argument; they came to base their pacifism almost exclusively on the New Testament texts. At the same time, Friends became less concerned about the evil of war itself, concentrating instead on the elimination of any Quaker complicity in war.[33] In other words, rather than emphasizing their objection to war itself, Quakers focused their objections on any attempts by the state to make Friends bear arms or otherwise participate in military activities.

For three-quarters of a century, the children of Onas had been shielded from the ethical challenge of war by their elected representatives, who until 1756 composed the overwhelming majority in the Pennsylvania Assembly, so conscientious Friends did not have to contemplate even the prospect of being called upon for military service. Indeed, from its founding in 1682 until 1755, Pennsylvania had no need for a militia.[34] It faced no foreign threat from the French or Spanish. William Penn's enlightened policies toward American Indians had helped to create a set of conditions in which the colony was altogether spared from Indian wars. A real military threat to Pennsylvania arose only with the French incursions into the Allegheny River Valley in 1753–54 and with the accumulated and rising resentment of Indians defrauded of their lands by the sons of William Penn and the executive branch of the Proprietary government.

For seventy-five years the only care that Pennsylvania Friends had to exercise for their peace testimony was to ensure that their legislators did not enact conscription laws, direct the undertaking of any military operations, or expend moneys for military purposes.[35] The legislators could, however, appropriate funds "for the King's use," provided that the king made an official demand or request for such funds. The king could then expend the moneys to equip his armies and pay his troops.

The legislators could even levy taxes to pay for the king's war. In 1711 during Queen Anne's War, which did not involve Pennsylvania, the Quaker assembly levied a tax to raise funds for the queen's use, which was to prosecute the war against France and Spain.[36] Good Quakers were expected to pay the tax, based on their duty to the king. Although it significantly tempered their peace testimony, the Quakers justified this deference to their earthly sovereign based on Christ's words in the Gospel of Matthew. "Render therefore unto Caesar the things which are Caesar's, and unto God the things that are God's."[37]

Quakers Protest War Taxes and Requisitions

The Quaker legislators, still in control of the assembly at the start of the French and Indian War, could have hewed to the traditional practice of levying taxes and appropriating funds for the king's use, and then left the actual spending for military purposes to the king, or in this case, to the king's agent—the governor. The Quaker legislators, however, violated the traditional ethic by appropriating funds and appointing a committee to expend those funds for military purposes.[38] The appropriation was ethical, at least according to traditional norms, but the spending committee was not. Now, the legislators were not just rendering to Caesar, they were acting as Caesar.

For more than a decade, the Pennsylvania Assembly had been locked in a power struggle with the governor and the Proprietary family. The political bickering between the assembly and Thomas Penn had been particularly bitter and nasty. The authority to disburse moneys was an important and jealously guarded prerogative of the assembly, and the assemblymen were not willing to concede it to the governor, who was essentially Penn's lieutenant. If they relinquished this authority in wartime, especially to a man like Penn, they might not get it back when the war was over. In this case, jealousy trumped scruple and blinded the legislators to their traditional ethic, or caused them to simply shut their eyes to it. But the reformers within the Society saw the ethical breach very clearly.[39]

In November 1755 a group of twenty prominent Friends addressed the assembly to protest the violation of the peace testimony. The protesters warned the legislators that their unethical behavior could ultimately endanger Quaker religious liberties. They threatened to disobey the law and refuse to pay the tax that had been levied to finance the war. This was a significant step in the development of the Quaker peace testimony, although the majority of Friends did not, at that time, follow the step taken by the twenty protesters. But some did.[40]

The assembly was unmoved by the protesters. In April 1756 the war-spending committee asked the governor to declare war on the Delaware Indians and to set bounties for Delaware scalps with bounties to be paid from funds made available by the assembly. The Quakers on this committee were therefore disowned by the end of the month. The governor declared war and offered the scalp bounties. Despairing over the conduct of the war-spending committee and the governor, six Friends resigned from the thirty-six–seat assembly. Quakers remained in the majority, however.[41]

These resignations marked the beginning of a Quaker exodus from all branches of government. Some officeholders left voluntarily, torn between the demands of office and the dictates of conscience. Others went unwillingly, ousted at the polls or dismissed from the executive and judicial branches by an ascendant anti-Quaker faction. The exodus was gradual, taking place over a period of two decades.[42]

The Quaker exodus from the assembly was a little faster and, almost certainly, less voluntary than from the other branches. In the October 1756 election the Quakers failed for the first time to win a majority in the assembly, though they did retain one third of the seats. Under increasing pressure from religious activists, four of the Quakers victorious at the polls resigned their seats even before the new legislative session began.[43]

Defeat at the polls came after three-quarters of a century of Quaker governance. As early as 1700 the Quakers had become a minority group within Pennsylvania's population. By 1756 after massive immigration of German Lutheran and Reformed groups, and Scots-Irish Presbyterians, the Quakers accounted for no more than one-fifth of all Pennsylvanians. Yet for more than half a century, the non-Quaker majority had continued to vote for Quaker legislators.[44]

A combination of factors operated to change that voting pattern in the autumn of 1756. In press, pamphlet, and parliament, anti-Quaker partisans reviled Quaker pacifism, accusing the Quaker-dominated assembly of leaving the beleaguered frontier defenseless against Indian attacks. This accusation was ironic in view of the fact that Quaker legislators had actually voted huge sums for defense, levied a war tax, and gone out of their way to trample their own traditional peace ethic.[45] Nevertheless, anti-Quaker politicians claimed that Friends' hands were stained with the blood of frontier settlers.[46]

In addition, fewer Friends were willing to run for office because they could not reconcile the demands of office with their religious beliefs.[47] This reduced the pool of attractive and viable Quaker candidates. Some Quaker voters boycotted the polls, disgusted and revolted at what the outgoing assembly and the governor had done in offering scalp bounties.[48] But, in the main, the election defeat was caused by public reaction to the Quaker peace testimony. When war finally came to Pennsylvania, that testimony cost Quaker politicians their offices, even though many of them had done their best to skirt and subvert it.

A small minority of Friends joined in the 1756–57 war-tax protest. Those who refused to pay the tax suffered the penalties imposed by the government: distraint of property and, in a few cases, imprisonment. When a Friend refused to pay the tax, the tax collector enlisted the constable, who seized some of the protester's property, usually household goods, livestock, or tools used in a craft or trade. The constable auctioned the distrained goods, and from the proceeds, paid the tax and fine to the collector, kept his own costs, and returned any surplus to the protester. If the protester resisted any part of the distraint procedure, he was subjected to double fines.[49]

Conscientious Quaker protesters, however, did not resist the distraint procedure. Willingness to suffer the legal consequences of civil disobedience went right to the heart of the Quaker concept of "testimony." To try to evade any of the legal consequences would only cheapen the testimony. A Friend could render worthy testimony and bear true witness to Quaker convictions only by submitting to the legal authorities and suffering the consequences of his protest.[50]

The 1756–57 war-tax protest produced some divisions within the PYM. Within Philadelphia, Bucks, and Chester Counties, where most Quakers lived, the tax collector and the constable, as well as the judges and the county commissioners, were likely to be Quakers.[51] These officeholders could claim, with tradition and orthodoxy to back them up, that their legal prosecution of tax protesters was entirely ethical. The PYM beheld the unseemly spectacle of Friends prosecuting Friends.

The Society did not require its members to protest the war tax in 1756–57. The traditional, orthodox position was that Friends should pay the tax. But, significantly, the Society did not require the protesters to pay. The Yearly Meeting, sitting at Philadelphia in September 1756 and September 1757, decided that the time was not yet ripe for changing the traditional peace testimony, but it deliberately refrained from disciplining the protesters on account of their nonpayment of the tax.[52]

Though the reformers made limited progress on the war-tax issue, they did steer the Society toward reaffirmations of its peace testimony in two other respects. In 1756 and 1757 Pennsylvania's governor proclaimed days of fasting and prayer related to the war, during which citizens were not supposed to work and were expected to close their places of business. Quakers believed it grossly improper for the state to compel any particular religious practice or observance. Quakers, moreover, balked especially at being required to pray on behalf of a war effort. Some Friends in Philadelphia did hold a religious meeting, apparently innocently, ignorant of the Quaker scruple on this matter. The PYM required them to acknowledge their mistake. It also printed and distributed 2,000 instructional pamphlets to Friends to prevent ignorance from leading to ethical breaches in the future.[53]

In 1758 when Gen. John Forbes was organizing his expedition against Fort Duquesne, a law passed during the preceding year came into play and challenged the Quaker peace testimony. The act authorized constables to requisition wagons and horses from civilians for use in transporting military supplies. Owners of requisitioned wagons and horses had no recourse but to lease them to the government. If they refused, they were fined, and if they refused to pay the fine, their property was distrained.

Many Friends, assured by Quaker constables and magistrates that no ethical violation was involved, complied with the requisitions and received payment. The leasing of wagons and horses under these circumstances, however, was a violation of the Quaker peace ethic. The proper course was to refuse to lease the wagons and horses, refuse to pay the fine, and to suffer distraint of one's property. The Yearly Meeting, sitting in September 1758, reiterated this fact and directed monthly meetings to counsel violators and win their promise not to repeat the error. In addition, it ordered Quaker magistrates to resign from any public office in which they could not avoid prosecuting other Friends or non-Quakers who resisted requisitions for reasons of conscience. If a Quaker magistrate persisted in enforcing requisitions, fines, and distraint, he was to be barred from all Quaker meetings, except those for worship. He would not be disowned, but he would be excluded from any voice or role in the Society's policy, a disciplinary practice sometimes referred to as "partial disownment."[54]

Implementation of the Yearly Meeting's directives and orders regarding the "wagon affair" was less than vigorous. The spirit of reform that reigned in the Yearly Meeting did not exactly permeate monthly meetings, which opted to rely more on persuasion than on coercion. From 1758 through 1764, thirty-two Friends were formally disciplined for leasing wagons and horses to the military. They were required to publicly disavow the error and promise not to repeat it. Many more cases, however, were handled informally. A committee privately visited known offenders, to counsel and reprimand them as needed, and to exact their promise not to lease wagons or horses to the military again. Reformers labored continually to correct recidivists.[55]

The Paxton Boys

The Quaker peace testimony, reform, and discipline were all dealt a serious blow by the murderous rampage of the Paxton Boys from 1763 to 1764. The primary goal of the Friendly Association, founded in 1756, was to restore and preserve peace with the Indians, and to do so entirely through nonviolent, pacific measures. The Association wanted to show that the Indian raids could be stopped without resorting to military measures and to promote justice in the provincial government's land transactions with the Indians. The Association also raised money for ransoming frontier settlers who had been taken captive by the Indians. Part of neither the government nor the PYM, the Friendly Association injected itself into the negotiation and treaty process. The government did not like this interloping, but the Indians did.[56]

The cause of Indian hostility was the relentless dispossession and displacement of tribe after tribe through inequitable and fraudulent land dealings perpetrated by the governor and Proprietors. According to the Association, the Indian war had been caused by Proprietary greed and abuse, and did not represent a failure of Quaker pacifism. By playing a prominent role in the restoration and preservation of peace through purely pacific measures, the Friendly Association hoped to vindicate Quaker pacifism and show that Proprietary malfeasance had caused the war. Although the Friendly Association enjoyed some notable and well-publicized successes in its early years, it had virtually ceased to function by 1763.[57] Its reputation, however, lived on.

Pontiac's Uprising in 1763, during which frontier forts and settlements were destroyed, tended to discredit both the Friendly Association and Quaker pacifism, at least in the mind of the general public.[58] Quaker critics and political adversaries were quick to denounce the Friendly Association and Friends in general for the sympathetic approach they had taken toward the "horrid and perfidious" Indians. Rabid Indian haters also circulated and exaggerated reports, some of which needed little exaggeration, of frontier depredations committed by the hostile Indians. These malefactors deliberately fanned the flames of racial animosity and incited mobs to violence against all Indians, even those who had taken no part in the uprising. In Northhampton County, a group of 140 peaceful Indians, frightened by death threats, fled to the protection of Friends in Philadelphia.

In December 1763 a band of fifty armed men rode from Paxton Township, near present-day Harrisburg, Pennsylvania, to Lancaster, where they murdered twenty peaceful Conestoga Indians, who had nothing to do with Pontiac's Uprising but were convenient targets for indiscriminate rage. In February 1764 the Paxton Boys, now numbering 250 armed riders, headed toward Philadelphia with the announced intentions of killing the Indian refugees there and teaching the Quakers a lesson. Their approach to the city so alarmed the inhabitants that hundreds of men mustered into infantry and artillery regiments—including 200 young Friends. The Paxton Boys backed off, preferring more vulnerable targets. But the rush to arms by so many Friends impugned Quaker pacifism.

In the wake of this incident, anti-Quaker pamphlets appeared in unprecedented numbers. Detractors accused Friends of being pacifists only so long as their own lives and property were not at risk. The "wealthy" Quakers had allegedly remained content in their pacifism, while the Indians "slaughtered" hapless frontier families, most of whom were poor, Scots-Irish, and Presbyterian. When the Quakers found themselves threatened, however, they had tossed aside their pacifist principles in an instant.

The real damage to the Quaker peace testimony came in the Society's failure to rigorously apply its own disciplinary procedure to the men who had taken up arms during the Paxton-Boys incident. Disciplinary proceedings were initiated, and a special committee worked with the violators for more than a year. The committee then allowed some men to repent more or less privately, in the presence of the committee. These men were not required—as they should have been—to condemn their actions in front of their monthly meeting and in written documents that could be posted for the public to see. The committee continued to work with the others, who did not repent at all, for an additional two years. In the end, only six violators publicly renounced their error, and the unrepentant delinquents were not disowned, leaving Friends open to the charge of hypocrisy.[59]

Quakers and the American Revolution

The American Revolution became the vehicle by which Friends redeemed their peace testimony, heightened their ethical scruples against war, and advanced the reformation within their own Society. The cost to the Society was high; Friends left or were disowned, and those who remained were despised by many of their fellow Pennsylvanians. Radical patriots used their wartime control of the Pennsylvania state government to persecute pacifists. Friends suffered fines, penalties, distraint of property, imprisonment, and in a few cases exile from the state of Pennsylvania, as well as violence and vandalism at the hands of revolutionary mobs. This ordeal winnowed out the "sunshine Quakers," those who were unwilling to suffer for the sake of Quaker testimony.

At the beginning of the Revolution Quaker ethics obligated Friends to remain loyal to the Crown.[60] The obligation of loyalty to the civil authority was based on Paul's words in his letter to the Romans: "Let every soul be subject to the higher powers. For there is no power but of God: the powers that be are ordained of God."[61] In 1775 and 1776 the king and the parliament were, technically, still in power, and the upstart revolutionaries were mere insurrectionists.[62] Ethical considerations aside, there is no doubt that many prominent Quakers were Tories in their political sentiments, though not active participants in the political and military struggle. During the years leading up to the Revolution, some of the PYM's pronouncements revealed a decidedly Tory bias, with which all Friends might not have agreed, but for which all were blamed.[63]

In May 1775 following the fighting at Lexington and Concord, the Pennsylvania Assembly levied an estate tax to support mobilization. Within the Society, traditionalists as well as reformers objected to the tax. The reformers' highly developed scruples regarding the peace ethic caused them to object. They knew that war destroyed persons and property, and they refused to be a party to it in any way. Traditionalists objected to paying a tax that supported what was, in their view, an illegal uprising. "That would not be rendering to Caesar but overthrowing him."[64] Refusal to pay war taxes remained a controversial testimony among Friends and was never added to the Society's discipline. The Yearly Meeting commended the refusal to pay, but the decision was left to the dictates of individual conscience. Hundreds of Friends voluntarily refused to pay war taxes during the Revolution, and willingly suffered the consequences.[65]

In November 1775 the assembly required all able-bodied men between the ages of sixteen and fifty to join militia units. Nonassociators would be fined. Quaker ethics constrained Friends from paying fines imposed for refusing to render military service. They believed that the state had no right to require military service of anyone who conscientiously objected. To pay the fine would be to tacitly acknowledge that the state had such a right. The only course for the objector was to stand peacefully aside when the sheriff came to seize his property and offer no resistance to the civil authority. Similarly, when imprisonment was added to the penalties for resisting military service in 1777, it would have been improper for a Friend to flee. Rather he was expected to surrender peacefully to the authorities who came to arrest him.[66]

During the summer of 1776 the Continental Congress declared the independence of the United States, and the crisis escalated from insurrection to revolution. Pennsylvania got a new constitution that summer, and a radical regime took the reins of state power. In September the PYM resolved that any of its members holding public office of any kind must resign or be disowned. Friends should also no longer vote in elections. The Quaker withdrawal from politics was at last complete.[67]

The new state government revised the militia act, changing the age range to eighteen to fifty-three and raising the fines for not mustering. The only method provided for exemption was the hiring of a substitute. This, of course, was out of the question for a conscientious Friend—objecting to war himself, he could hardly pay someone else to go fight in his place. Over the course of the war, the fines for not mustering skyrocketed because of the tremendous depreciation in the value of the Continental currency. The fines had to be increased enormously, lest they become nominal in real terms.[68]

In 1776 the revolutionary state regime prescribed oaths of allegiance for voters and public officeholders. These oaths presented no problems for conscientious Friends because the PYM had directed its members not to vote or hold office. In 1777, however, the radical assembly prescribed an oath of allegiance by which all citizens had to swear or affirm. Friends could not swear an oath of any kind; they were prohibited from doing so by one of their most ancient and revered testimonies.[69] Additionally, they could utter an affirmation only to the "powers that be."

To Friends the issue came down to fundamental honesty. Friends believed they must always be truthful and honest. Taking an oath or affirmation implied that one was not ethically obligated to speak truthfully and act honestly at all times.[70] Friends took Christ's words in the Gospel of Matthew very seriously: "Swear not at all; neither by heaven, for it is God's throne: Nor by the earth; for it is his footstool. . . . Neither shalt thou swear by thy head. . . . But let your communication be, Yea, yea; Nay, nay: for whatsoever is more than these cometh of evil."[71]

Quaker ethics compelled conscientious Friends to be nonjurors. The legal penalties on nonjurors were harshly punitive and constituted a significant disenfranchisement. Nonjurors could not sue to collect debts. They could not buy, sell, or transfer land or other real estate. In 1778 fines and imprisonment were added to the penalties for a nonjuror's first refusal to swear or affirm allegiance. Upon second refusal the nonjuror forfeited his estate and became subject to exile from the state. Certain non-jurors, including schoolteachers and tutors, were barred from the practice of their professions. This effectively prevented Quakers from operating their schools. Regardless, throughout the Revolution, the Society routinely disowned erring Friends who swore or affirmed oaths of allegiance.[72]

As was the case with fines for refusal to muster into the militia or hire a substitute, Quaker ethics prevented Friends from paying any of the fines associated with refusal to swear or affirm allegiance. Again, their property was distrained. Quite often, magistrates distrained more than the law required, and kept the surplus. But even if magistrates had made an effort to return such surpluses, Friends were ethically obligated not to accept them. The PYM kept records of the value of all property distrained from its members. The valuations were not subjective; at the very least the property, when auctioned, had to fetch the value of the fines and penalties. The sheriff or constable would otherwise have seized additional property. Altogether, members of the PYM lost about £40,000 of distrained property and goods. This included the property lost to requisition by American armies. The Continental Congress offered compensation for such requisitioned property, but Friends were ethically obligated to refuse it.[73]

Imprisonment of Friends was not common, but some prominent Quakers were exiled to Virginia for a few years. Two elderly and infirm exiles died there; another went into decline while exiled and died after returning home.[74]

Throughout the war Friends frequently suffered violence and vandalism at the hands of Revolutionary mobs. Yearly, the state government declared a day of fasting in April and a day of thanksgiving in December. On these days, all businesses were to close. Most people also illuminated the windows in their homes, as a sign of observance. They did this whether they wanted to or not because roaming mobs insisted upon it. Ethical Friends could not observe such state- or mob-mandated practices. They neither closed their shops nor illumined their windows. As a result mobs vandalized Quaker businesses and hurled rocks through the darkened windows of Quaker homes. The worst riot, however, occurred when Philadelphia celebrated the surrender of General Cornwallis and his army at Yorktown in October 1781. Many Quaker houses were destroyed by the rioting mob.[75]

Relief for the harassed and beleaguered Quakers finally came with the elections of 1782, in which Friends could not, ethically or legally, vote or otherwise participate. Pennsylvania voters ousted the radicals from both the assembly and the Supreme Executive Council, and replaced them with moderates. Most of the prosecution and all of the persecution of Quakers stopped.[76]

FRIENDS AND TEMPERANCE

Prior to the reformation, temperance had long been a highly recommended virtue among Friends. The Society tended to focus on the most obvious results of alcohol abuse, public drunkenness and disorderly conduct, instead of on the abuse itself. The Society routinely disciplined drunkards. But, amid widespread heavy drinking in the general society and culture, Quaker discipline alone was not effective as counseling or treatment. Habitual drunkards were rarely rehabilitated; they usually ended up being disowned. The Society began its temperance effort by trying to prevent Friends from becoming drunkards. It cautioned and disciplined Friends who served liquor and became inebriated at weddings and funerals. The incidence of drunkenness among Friends continued to rise, however, reaching "scandalous" proportions by the middle of the eighteenth century. Reformers started promoting abstinence and prohibition as the surest measures for preventing Quaker drunkenness.[77]

In 1762 the Society began discouraging Friends from keeping taverns. Monthly meetings admonished, but generally did not discipline, their tavern-keeping members. In certain exceptional cases, such as one in which a habitual drunkard obtained a liquor license, tavern keepers were disciplined and even disowned.[78] The rising concern among Friends about drunkenness paralleled the rise of the whiskey industry in Pennsylvania. During the 1770s many distilleries sprang up and whiskey began to supplant rum as the hard liquor of choice among Americans. Disruptions in the rum trade, which occurred during the prelude to revolution and during the war with Britain, only hastened the ascendance of whiskey.

In 1777 the PYM made it a requirement of discipline that Friends cease and desist from all aspects of the liquor business, from producing to retailing. The Society not only forbade Friends to enter the alcohol trade, but it required those already engaged in it to find another livelihood. As a matter of discipline, the Society also forbade Friends to drink any whiskey at all. It even proscribed the selling of grain to anyone who would use it to produce whiskey.[79]

FRIENDS AND ABOLITION

At the midmark of the eighteenth century, many Pennsylvanians, including wealthy Friends, owned slaves. Some Friends were even importers of slaves into Pennsylvania. Prior to midcentury and the reformation, a few abolitionist Friends were actually disciplined and disowned for having condemned slaveholders. During the 1740s, however, some Friends began quietly to manumit their own slaves. Once the reformation started, antislavery sentiment within the Society grew into something more than individual dissent. It developed into a new testimony.[80]

In 1755 the PYM prohibited its members from importing slaves into Pennsylvania and from buying slaves who had already been imported. The PYM directed its monthly meetings to admonish any of their members who purchased a slave. In 1758 reformers pushed the PYM a bit further and obtained an order that any Friend who purchased or sold a slave was to be barred from all Quaker meetings except those for worship. He would not be disowned, but his exclusion from meetings for business and discipline would prevent him from hindering the pace of reform.[81] That same year the Society followed an identical course with Quaker magistrates who refused to resign their public offices and persisted in prosecuting pacifist protesters.

Enforcement of the antislavery directives was somewhat uneven at first. But, gradually, during the 1760s, some monthly meetings began to disown members who bought or sold slaves—instead of just barring them from business and disciplinary meetings. When these disowned Friends appealed to the Quarterly and Yearly Meetings for reinstatement, they found their petitions rejected. Slave purchasers who repented and wanted to remain in the Society were required to emancipate the slave(s) they had purchased.[82]

The Society viewed selling a slave as an even more pernicious evil than buying one. It insisted that Friends who still held slaves from purchases made prior to the 1755 directive treat those slaves humanely and educate them. When a Friend sold one of his slaves, the Society lost its ability to promote the slave's welfare. As for Quakers who wanted to end their personal status as slaveholders, the Society allowed only one course. They must manumit—not sell—their slaves. In some cases, a Friend who sold a slave was required to buy the slave back and immediately free him or her.[83]

By 1770 the antislavery demands being imposed by monthly meetings, such as manumission, far exceeded the requirements of the discipline. Abolitionist sentiment had outrun the disciplinary code, which was, therefore, revised in 1774. Quakers who bought, sold, or transferred slaves were to be immediately disowned. Friends who still owned slaves were called before the Yearly Meeting to explain if infirmity, minor age, or lack of education and skills made their particular slaves unready for emancipation. The PYM reiterated its insistence that slaveholders educate their slaves, instruct them in religion, and manumit them as soon they were prepared for liberty. The PYM further required Quaker slaveholders to treat African-American slaves exactly as the law required masters to treat "white" indentured servants, which meant not only humane treatment and care, but a fixed limit on the length of servitude. Slaveowners who did not take these steps, or otherwise failed to show progress toward the emancipation of their slaves, were barred from meetings for business and discipline.[84]

In 1776 the PYM resolved to disown all slaveholders who would not commit to freeing their slaves. For slaveholders who wanted to remain in the Society, the only option was manumission, under circumstances that provided for the needs of aged, infirm, or minor freed persons. By the end of the American Revolution, the children of Onas had effectively purged themselves of the abomination known as slavery, although a small number of extraordinary cases dragged on until the turn of the century.[85] They had become "the first community of people in Western history to corporately espouse and practice the abolition of slavery."[86] Having done so, they were uniquely positioned and qualified to turn their attention toward the larger communities of state and nation, and hold up their new testimony as an example.

RISE OF QUAKER BENEVOLENCE

Philanthropy evolved significantly during the reformation. By the end of the 1700s Quaker philanthropy had become nonsectarian, extending to oppressed people who were neither Quaker nor Christian. But it was nonsectarian in another, more distinctive way. What made late-eighteenth-century Quaker philanthropy unique for its time was the fact that, while extending their charity and charitable services to non-Quakers and non-Christians, Friends refrained entirely from proselytizing. Their benevolence was not in any way contingent upon the recipients' acceptance, or even progress toward acceptance, of Quakerism or Christianity.

The children of Onas believed that philanthropy toward groups like the American Indians and African-American slaves and freemen was justified wholly on the basis of humanitarian concerns.[87] This situation differed considerably, however, from that which had pertained just half a century earlier. In 1750 Quaker charity did not extend much beyond the Quaker religious fellowship. Friends extended charity to other Friends strictly out of a religious sense of obligation for the physical and spiritual well-being of less fortunate members.[88] During the second half of the 1700s, this view was transformed in the crucibles of reformation, war, and revolution.

The monthly meeting had always supervised the mutual aid that its members provided to one another.[89] At the beginning of the reformation, the monthly meeting could be analyzed as a religious association, or fellowship, that performed two basic functions for its members: mutual aid and mutual surveillance.[90] Mutual surveillance involved each Friend's responsibility to caution or reprove any brother whom he noticed to be faltering, either morally or ethically. Surveillance also touched the workings of Quaker discipline, informally within the preparative meeting and formally within the monthly meeting.

Mutual aid activities of the monthly meeting included relief for needy Friends, placement of orphans in suitable homes, placement of older children in apprenticeships, and operation of schools, which made available a rudimentary education to the children of even poor Friends. The monthly meeting took care of its own in many other specific ways. The meeting provided financial assistance to the families of members imprisoned for civil disobedience committed in the name of a Quaker testimony.[91] Assistance was also provided to members who suffered financial distress or economic hardship caused by distraints imposed for the same reason.[92]

The meeting supplied its poor members with food, clothing, and shelter, or the cash with which to purchase these necessities. It made loans to help financially struggling members set up in a trade or open a shop. As early as 1704 Philadelphia Quakers operated an almshouse to shelter poor Friends. By 1746 they had constructed a complex, consisting of eight tenement or apartment buildings, to house poor and elderly Friends. Philadelphia Friends, of course, could tap resources far beyond those available to country meetings, whose relief projects did not match those of city Friends in scope or magnitude.[93]

The meeting was very generous to Friends who had lost their homes to fire or Indian raid. It was always solicitous of the children of Friends, including children of disowned Friends. But the monthly meeting withheld aid from adults who had been disowned. Members who were under disciplinary "dealings," however, were still eligible because they might yet repent and submit to the discipline, and not be disowned. The threatened withdrawal of the meeting's social safety net, implicit in disciplinary action, was thus a powerful incentive for recalcitrant Friends to submit.[94]

At mid-eighteenth century, Friends tended to look upon the duty to render mutual aid as an obligation owed by the monthly meeting primarily to its own members.[95] The meeting's mutual aid was precisely that, aid reserved for members by members. By 1750 monthly meetings were refusing to accept new members on certificate from other meetings if the migrants appeared to be indigent, unless the meeting that issued the certificate of removal agreed to bear the cost of providing relief.[96]

Extraordinary circumstances, however, had always forced the children of Onas to look beyond their own monthly meeting when it came to extending charity.[97] Compared with the Philadelphia Monthly Meeting, the membership of some country meetings was quite small. When fire claimed the home of a member family, the burned-out dwelling could not be replaced without assistance from the surrounding monthly meetings. In the construction of a new meetinghouse, a monthly meeting could count on contributions even from distant meetings, including those within the jurisdiction of other quarterly and yearly meetings.[98]

During the French and Indian War, the plight of frontier families riveted the attention of all Pennsylvanians, including Friends. The children of Onas were compelled to lift their gaze beyond the boundaries of their monthly meetings by reports of Indian raids, in which families were driven or burned out of their homes, often with several members being killed, wounded, or captured.

During 1755 and 1756 the Society sent help to the frontier people in the form of money, clothing, and an offer to place refugee children in foster homes. The Friendly Association also assisted frontier settlers by negotiating an end to the Indian attacks and arranging the release of prisoners. It also tried to regain the Indians' friendship for the province by giving them presents and addressing the cause of Indian alienation. It pressured the provincial government to treat the Indians fairly and launched an independent investigation of the Indians' charges that the Proprietors had cheated them in numerous land transactions, including the infamous Walking Purchase of 1737.[99]

The Friendly Association even assisted Teedyuscung, chief of the Delawares on the upper Susquehanna River, in his efforts to establish a permanent reservation in the Wyoming Valley. The Association advanced money and supplied craftsmen for construction of a Delaware village, where the Indians could live under the tutelage of the Quakers and other pacifist sects, such as the Mennonites and the Moravians, and learn the ways of "civilized" life. Only a few houses were built, however, before raids by hostile Indians aborted the project.[100]

The Indian crisis certainly presented opportunities for institutional charity toward the Indians. Moreover, such benevolence could be readily justified on the very practical and laudable basis of promoting peace and opening the door to material progress for the Indians. In addition to its role in constructing the Delaware village, the Friendly Association got involved in an effort to reform the Indian trade, focusing mainly on fair prices for trade goods and prohibition of liquor. This effort, however, was sabotaged by independent traders.[101] The PYM, in contrast, did not involve itself in any of these projects. Although composed of wealthy and prominent Friends, the Friendly Association was not a part of the PYM, nor even officially connected with it. It was a "private society to do good."[102]

Though a "private" society, the Friendly Association was still very involved in politics and public affairs, which is probably why the PYM decided against officially sponsoring it.[103] Reformers in the PYM feared that the Association's political machinations, aimed at embarrassing the Proprietary government, would reflect negatively on the Society. Even when the objectives of philanthropy were less obviously political, the PYM left its members to act individually or collectively through private societies, if those objectives extended beyond the Quaker religious fellowship.[104]

In 1755, for example, Pennsylvania was required to accept a quota of Acadian exiles. These were French-speaking Nova Scotians who had been deported for refusing to swear an oath of allegiance to the British king. The provincial government was supposed to resettle the exiles by dispersing them throughout the more populated counties. The idea was to separate the exiles from one another, scatter them among the king's subjects, and thereby obliterate their group identity. Friends provided funds that were used to keep the Acadians together in Philadelphia, while English Quakers lobbied the British government to reverse its policy of expulsion and dispersal. Individual Friends acting collectively provided the funds, but the PYM itself was not involved. Similarly, several Friends, acting collectively but not as part of the PYM, answered the call of a Moravian bishop to supply relief for a mixed group of refugees, both white and Indian, who, displaced by the French and Indian War, had collected at Bethlehem, Pennsylvania.[105]

It was the struggle against slaveholding within their own ranks—together with the political and legal persecution they themselves suffered—that finally enabled the children of Onas to see the need for philanthropy practiced corporately toward outsiders, with whom they shared nothing in common except oppression at the hands of society in general. The persecution they endured during the war gave them some insight into and sympathy for the plight of African-American slaves, (as well as American Indians).[106] Reform-minded members realized that the Society's corporate responsibility to slaves extended beyond merely requiring its members to manumit them. A major wrong remained to be righted, even after an ex-slave had been liberated. While enslaved, the African American had been unjustly deprived of his natural right to liberty and of his God-given opportunity to grow and develop as a free person. Legal emancipation was only the first of several steps necessary to even begin to repair the damage done by generations of enslavement.

The Society recognized the need to prepare slaves and ex-slaves for earning a living as free men. We have already seen how it required its slaveholding members to undertake this task. But the PYM was not content to leave the task in the hands of slaveholders. To look after the spiritual welfare of African Americans, the PYM conducted religious meetings for them. These segregated meetings were not aimed at making African Americans into Quakers. They were intended to provide an opportunity for worship and to promote certain virtues commonly identified as Christian that actually enjoyed a much more universal esteem: nonviolence, lawfulness, honest work, earning a living for one's family, educating one's children.[107]

The PYM also looked after the temporal needs of former slaves and their children. It helped them in the areas of housing, employment, and vocational training. In 1770 the Philadelphia Monthly Meeting founded a special school that was open to the children of all free African Americans. Soon it was open to the children of slaves as well. Over the next few years, as rural monthly meetings addressed the same issue, limited resources forced some of them to restrict their educational assistance to providing school tuition only for the children of ex-slaves who, at one time, had been owned by Quakers.[108]

Slaves and ex-slaves were not the only non-Quakers to receive humanitarian aid from the Society. From the beginning of the Revolution, the PYM directed its relief efforts to Friends and non-Quakers alike. It distributed cash assistance to persons of all denominations throughout New England and the southern states, in addition to the mid-Atlantic region. Even English and Irish Quakers sent relief supplies across the Atlantic to help distressed non-Quaker Americans, as well as American Friends.[109]

By the end of the American Revolution, therefore, an important new precedent had been set among Friends. The Society, acting corporately through its own institutions, had extended practical benevolence to non-Quakers and non-Christians, never pressuring the recipients to convert to Quakerism or even to Christianity. This precedent would soon redound to the benefit of American Indians—the Allegany Senecas in particular.

After the wartime tumult, the PYM gradually turned its attention once again to the situation of the American Indians.[110] This renewed interest was abetted by the continual procession of Indian chiefs who arrived in Philadelphia when that city was the seat of the federal government from 1790 to 1800. The chiefs came to confer with Congress and the president, but they usually met too with the children of Onas, as did Cornplanter during his 1790–91 visit.[111] At the request of the Indians and with the consent of the federal government, delegations of Friends attended several treaty negotiations during the early 1790s, where they acted as observers, witnesses, and, on occasion, as advisors to the Indians.[112]

During the negotiations at Canandaigua in 1794, the delegation of Friends became particularly interested in the situation of the Six Nations of New York. The war for the Old Northwest Territory, however, delayed corporate action by the Society on behalf of the Iroquois. After peace was formally established by the Treaty of Greenville in 1795, the PYM established its Indian Committee, the PYMIC. The PYMIC's 1796 circular letter to the Six Nations of New York resulted in the previously described mission to the Oneidas. The PYM subsequently transferred its Oneida concern to the New York Yearly Meeting and shifted its own efforts to the Allegany Senecas in 1798–99.[113]

QUAKER MILIEU

From 1755 onward the children of Onas had turned increasingly toward their Society's sectarian discipline to perfect their old testimonies on pacifism and temperance and to develop new ones on abolition and humanitarian benevolence. The stern discipline, together with the political oppression during the Revolutionary War, had culled the lukewarm and indifferent from Quaker ranks. The Society's discipline, however, extended far beyond the upholding of old testimonies and the uplifting of new ones. It meshed with a Friend's personal story, pervading all the interstices of his daily life.

Monthly meetings exercised constant supervision over their members through overseers. The close scrutiny of the meeting was interrupted—but only briefly—

when a Friend moved far enough to have to transfer to a different monthly meeting. Before moving, the Friend had to apply to his old monthly meeting for a "certificate of removal." The meeting tasked a few members with making an inquiry to ensure there was no obstruction to his moving away. Obstructions included familial responsibilities, legal complications, debts and creditors, or a jilted fiancée. If satisfied, the meeting would issue and date a certificate, which the migrant was required to present to his new meeting, upon arrival in his new location.[114] The certificate of removal attested to his status as a member in good standing. If his standing was something less than good, it was so noted on his certificate.

The new meeting would then "receive him on certificate." If the relocating Friend delayed in presenting himself to his new meeting, he would be closely questioned as to the cause of the delay. An inordinate and unreasonable delay could result in disownment. With very few exceptions, the Society required that Friends live continuously under the supervision of a monthly meeting.[115]

Simmons's father, Henry Sr., knew these requirements very well. While still a bachelor, he transferred from Wrightstown Monthly Meeting, or MM, to Middletown MM in 1757.[116] Both meetings were in Bucks County, Pennsylvania. The reasons for moving were most likely related to employment and, perhaps, to his search for a suitable wife. Four years later, on June 23, 1761, he married Mary Paxson, also of Middletown MM.[117] Henry Sr. and Mary continued to reside in Bucks County, remained members of Middletown MM, and started a family. That his move from Wrightstown to Middletown and his marriage were duly noted without comment in the Quaker records indicates that Henry Sr. and Mary were both Friends in good standing, who observed all the requirements of the Quaker marriage discipline.

Quaker Marriage

The Quaker marriage discipline was exhaustive and rigorous. A Friend could marry only another Friend. After the reformation, marrying a non-Quaker was a sure way to be disowned. The reformers' chief objection to mixed marriages was that such unions could not be relied upon to provide a proper Quaker upbringing and religious education for the children. Even if the non-Quaker spouse agreed to have the children receive Quaker religious instruction and be raised as Quakers, the children would still see the confusing example of one parent who was not convinced of Quaker beliefs and did not observe Quaker practices.[118]

A young man intent on marrying a young woman had to secure not only her agreement, but also the approval of her parents and of his own, even though he and she had both attained majority. Before he could even begin to court a girl, he had to declare his intentions and ask her father's permission.[119]

Once a couple decided to marry, they had to do so "within the meeting." They could not go to a justice of the peace or to a hireling clergyman of some other denomination. That would be "marrying outside of meeting" or "marriage out of unity," a disownable offense. The only way to marry a non-Quaker was to do so outside of meeting. But even exclusively Quaker couples sometimes married outside of meeting, often because the young woman was pregnant, and a marriage ceremony of any kind—even if not Quaker—would square things with the law, though not with the Society. Fornication was a disownable offense, even for a couple who subsequently married. The surest way for a couple to get disowned was to marry "within the meeting," and then deliver a child six or seven months later. Theirs was a double offense: fornication and the "sullying" of Quaker marriage. They should have confessed their fornication and publicly repented *before* marriage. The only offense more likely to result in disownment was adultery.[120]

The Society took the position that mixed marriages and marriages between Friends outside of meeting were legitimate and valid, but not holy. If the parents of a young Friend, who married outside of meeting, had failed to oppose the marriage, they were disciplined and could be disowned. If Friends even attended a wedding in which an erring Friend married outside of meeting, they were disciplined.[121]

The Society insisted on supervising every aspect of the marriage process, which included a meticulous assessment of both parties, each of whom had just been vetted by the other's parents. The procedure started when the betrothed couple appeared before the monthly meeting and announced their intention to wed. Both sets of parents gave their permission, either in person or in writing. If a potential marriage partner did not belong to the meeting in which the wedding was to be performed, he or she was required to produce a "certificate of clearness for marriage" from his or her own meeting. This was usually the man because the woman preferred to be married in her own meeting, where her family could more conveniently play a major role in the preparations.[122]

Provided that the parental permissions and, if needed, the certificate of clearness were all in order, the monthly meeting appointed two overseers or elders to investigate the couple's backgrounds further. The investigators tried to uncover any actual or potential impediments to an impeccable Quaker marriage: prior marriage; previous engagements or promises from which one of the parties had failed to obtain an honorable release; false or misleading representations by either party regarding the size of estates, dowries, or incomes; unresolved disciplinary issues with the Society; lack of matrimonial qualifications, such as insufficient income or resources to support a family or financial complications such as debt; or any hint of fornication. At a second appearance before the monthly meeting, the affianced pair restated their intentions and the investigators reported their findings. The meeting then gave its approval for the wedding to proceed. It also appointed two overseers to advise the parents regarding the nuptial celebrations, lest the festivities become too extravagant and the merriment too undignified.[123]

The wedding ceremony was essentially a meeting for worship in which the bride and groom stood and said their vows to each other. At the conclusion of these simple rites, husband and wife signed the marriage certificate. Guests signed as witnesses. Following the ceremony, the couple entertained their guests with a meal or a feast, the sumptuousness of which depended on the financial circumstances and social station of the couple and their families.[124]

The Society's solicitude—indeed anxiety—over the formation of sound, durable, and dependable marriages stemmed from its desire to ensure that the children of each Quaker union would be raised in a thoroughgoing Quaker household, receive from both their parents good examples as well as religious instruction, and grow up to be solid Friends. For the Society, this was a matter of self-preservation. Its discipline, which became increasingly ascetic and sectarian as the reformation progressed, not only culled and reduced the Quaker ranks, it also discouraged conversions. The reformers understood and accepted these losses in membership and placed their trust in the marriage discipline to create robust and religious Quaker marriages that would regenerate the Society.[125]

Quaker Family and School

The Society required all Friends, including Henry Simmons Sr. and Mary Paxson, to adhere to this strict regimen for making a marriage. The couple's wedding day, however, did not mark the end of the Society's intrusive supervision. Several times during the course of the reformation between 1755 and 1777, the PYM initiated lengthy top-to-bottom inspections of all its constituent meetings, to ensure that business and discipline were being executed in good order. The yearly meeting appointed a committee to inspect its quarterly meetings; the quarterly meeting, in turn, appointed a committee to inspect its monthly meetings; and the monthly meeting designated a few "weighty" Friends to visit and "inspect" each of its member families. Weighty Friends were solid, widely respected Friends with unimpeachable reputations, known for their undeviating personal adherence to the Quaker code; they were often active reformers.

By appointment, the visitors called upon the family at its home. The entire family, including any servants or apprentices, had assembled beforehand. The visitors and the family sat in silence for a while, marking the seriousness of the occasion, recollecting themselves, and waiting upon the Lord's Spirit. The visitors then made their observations. The possession of such luxuries as ostentatious furniture, ornate decorations, fancy clothing, silver teasets or goblets, or embossed china was inconsistent with Quaker views on simplicity, plainness, and humility. If the family's attendance at meetings for worship had been irregular, the visitors were sure to remark on that. They also noted the children's comportment. The visitors offered advice and counsel, and exhorted the family to persevere in the quest for holiness. Then the family served some refreshments, enjoying a more relaxed and informal atmosphere before the visitors departed.

In the years preceding the marriage of Henry Sr. and Mary Simmons in 1761, Bucks Quarterly Meeting had been somewhat lax in implementing the family visitation program. Monthly meetings everywhere had difficulty finding sufficient weighty Friends who had the time and inclination to perform what must have been a thankless task. In Bucks quarter prior to 1760, furthermore, some meetings apparently resisted the imposition of family visitations. But, the inspection programs initiated by the PYM in 1762 and 1777 very likely included the Simmons family of Middletown MM.[126]

Born on September 15, 1768, Henry Simmons Jr., hereafter referred to simply as Henry Simmons, was the youngest of the five children born to Henry Sr. and Mary. Less than ten months after Henry was born, his mother died, at age thirty-one.[127] Henry Sr. remarried in 1771 and with his new wife, Sarah Dun, had eight more children.[128] Henry Sr.'s second wedding was performed in Abington MM, the meeting to which Sarah Dun's family belonged. Presumably he did not have to get his own parents' permission to marry again, but he had to get permission from Sarah's parents, and he had to produce for Abington MM a certificate of clearness for marriage issued by Middletown MM.[129]

If Henry Simmons did receive some formal schooling as a child, it is possible that his instructors were neither well-qualified nor very competent. Older than his eight step-siblings, he might also have been required to work or help at home. At times, there might have been no schoolmaster available to conduct classes. That Simmons served as schoolteacher, first at Oneida from 1796 to 1797 and then at Cornplanter's village from 1798 to 1799, would seem to indicate that he had attended school himself, at least for some period of time; but his exposure was probably limited to the bare rudiments of education.

In their journals and letters, Halliday Jackson, John Pierce, and Joshua Sharpless all express themselves more clearly and narrate more fluently than does Simmons. Their sentences are better constructed, their paragraphs better organized, and their narratives better structured than are Simmons's. His inferiority in writing is evident in the original version of the Simmons 1799 Journal that appears in the appendix. Jackson was so adept at composition that he kept one of his journals in pseudobiblical prose. Simmons's comparative deficiency might have resulted from a personal disinclination to reading and writing, as well as from a restricted and uninspired education.

The lack of educational resources within the rural monthly meeting to which Simmons belonged meant that operation of the local school was probably sporadic; that the school had to be funded almost entirely through tuition payments; that even when funds were available, a schoolmaster often was not available; and that when a schoolmaster could be retained, he frequently was not very capable. A lack of financial resources would also have made it difficult for the Simmons family, with its eleven surviving children,[130] to pay tuition, either for school attendance or for a private tutor.[131]

The Quaker schools in Philadelphia, in contrast, enjoyed the financial support of a large subscription base and plentiful endowments. So well funded were the Quaker city schools that Friends opened them to the children of all denominations. Because the schools were open to all, they were often called public schools; but they were not financed with public funds or supervised by the local government. The Society of Friends provided the funds and governed the schools through a quasi-independent board of "overseers of the public schools." In general, city schools were able to attract better qualified teachers than country schools, and were conducted on a much more regular basis.[132]

Operating funds for the city schools were derived primarily from voluntary subscriptions, pledged on a yearly basis by all Friends regardless of whether they had school-age children. The resulting lower tuition fees relieved the parents of school-age children, especially poor parents, of a considerable financial burden. Subscriptions were supplemented by income derived from endowments and by rates, the tuition charged on a sliding scale according to the parents' ability to pay. By 1775 the Quaker schools in Philadelphia had amassed a substantial endowment fund, which came from bequests of all sizes, made by Friends from a variety of financial strata.

Country meetings, with many fewer subscribers and much smaller endowments, had to rely heavily on tuition fees in order to operate their schools. This placed a considerable financial burden on the parents of school-age children. Families with numerous children sometimes hired a single tutor to teach all their offspring, rather than pay multiple tuition fees. The tutors available in the country were, generally, no better qualified than were the schoolteachers. This practice also diverted funds from the school, increasing the tuition burden on the parents of those children who did attend. Some poor rural children simply received instruction from their parents and older siblings. Country Friends tolerated this situation because their expectations regarding their children's educational achievement were not ambitious.

The minutes of the Middletown MM contain only sporadic references to a school, which was permitted to use the meetinghouse as a facility. The school did not come under the control of the meeting until after 1750, the year in which the PYM recommended that each monthly meeting assume financial responsibility for the Friends' school(s) within its verge, or territory, and exercise direct supervision over the school operation, administration, and curriculum. The Philadelphia MM and the board of overseers had been doing this for decades, and the larger monthly meetings, when prompted by the PYM, followed suit, although they substituted standing committees in place of the quasi-independent board.

Country meetings initially balked at the PYM's recommendation as impractical, arguing that their membership was too sparse and scattered. The PYM, however, continued to urge Friends to designate legacies of cash and land in their wills, for their own meeting's educational endowment. The Middletown endowment received its first legacy in 1755. By 1785 Middletown's endowment, along with those of other country meetings, had grown to the point that country schools were finally implementing the reforms first recommended by the PYM in 1750 and reiterated in 1778.

The reforms required that meetings hire only religious Friends to fill the position of schoolmaster. Before country meetings assumed control over Friends' schools, organizers accepted non-Quakers and Friends who were less than enthusiastic about their own religion. The reforms stipulated that poor children and orphans should be allowed free attendance at school. To end the days when the schoolmaster had to conduct classes in his dwelling, the meeting should provide the schoolmaster with living quarters separate from the school building. To attract married men to the position of schoolmaster, the meeting was to provide both a salary and a house large enough for raising a family. A large house would also enable the schoolmaster to accept boarding students under decent conditions.

These reforms came to Middletown when Henry Simmons was already seventeen years old, looking for work, not elementary school. Simmons's educational handicap did not impede his selection as the schoolteacher at Oneida and at Cornplanter's village. Basic reading, writing, and arithmetic were deemed a sufficient curriculum for Indian as well as rural Quaker children.

Even after the educational reforms, leading Quaker educators still thought it was most important for a prospective schoolmaster to be a solid and religious Friend. In terms of religious fervor, steadfastness of faith, and reliability of character, Henry Simmons ranked high. Simmons might have undertaken the undesirable job out of a strong sense of religious duty.

Discipline in the Society of Friends

Aside from a notation about his birth, the Quaker records ignore Henry Simmons until 1796, when he was twenty-eight years old and volunteered to be of service in helping the Indians. At that time he had not yet married—and would not until 1800, after he had returned permanently from the missions. Nor had he run afoul of the ubiquitous Quaker discipline, which permeated the various aspects of a Friend's life: marriage, religion, education, business, and public affairs.

In addition to the major offenses—drunkenness, fornication, adultery, and military activity—there were many other offenses which Simmons had to avoid. Some are not surprising: profanity, quarreling, gambling, swearing oaths, conducting business unethically, dispensing liquor, loose conduct, failing to attend worship meetings regularly, and violating "Gospel Order."[133] Loose conduct was a catch-all for comporting one's self in a vain or undignified manner, wearing extravagant clothes, and keeping bad company. A good Quaker was also expected to avoid places, persons, and activities that could result in the temptation to sin: pubs, disreputable women, and card games, for example. Loose conduct also involved infractions like "strong speech without slander, anger without assault or threats without violence, flirtations without fornication, and liaisons without adultery."[134] If a Friend's behavior was not above reproach, he was subject to a charge of loose conduct.

Failure to regularly attend worship meetings rarely resulted, by itself, in disciplinary action or disownment. Usually this offense operated as an aggravating factor when the meeting considered a delinquent Friend's other, more serious offenses.

"Gospel Order" was the Quaker term for arbitration of disputes by the monthly meeting. Arbitrated disputes ranged from ownership or boundaries of land, to wills, wages, and business contracts. The arbitrators were a committee appointed by the monthly meeting, to which the disputing parties also named representatives. Once the arbitration committee rendered a decision, both parties were bound by it. If one party failed to comply, the meeting disowned him and granted the other party permission to pursue the matter in the public courts. The monthly meeting, acting as amicus curiae, informed the court of the arbitrators' decision. The Society imposed Gospel Order because it did not want Friends suing each other in court. Such public legal wrangling between Friends damaged the Society's reputation, belying the profession of true Christian friendship among the Society's members.[135]

Using the law against a Friend, defaulting on a debt or loan, and entertainment were offenses in the Quaker discipline. Using the law against a Friend consisted of taking a fellow Friend to court without first submitting to the Quaker arbitration process known as Gospel Order, and without first obtaining permission from the monthly meeting to sue in court. Friends could sue non-Quakers without recourse to Gospel Order. Non-Quakers did not recognize the Society's authority and were not bound by its discipline. The Society, therefore, had no powers of arbitration in disputes between Friends and non-Quakers.

If a non-Quaker sued a Friend in court, the Friend found himself in trouble with his meeting, if it turned out that he was guilty of wrongdoing. The Society strictly enforced its discipline requiring the practice of ethics in business. Forbidden were the cheating of business partners or customers by shorting them on weights or measures, the defrauding of anyone while investing in land and real estate, and the tricking or hoodwinking of any party into a contract of any sort. The Society forbade Friends to otherwise cozen, bamboozle, or swindle while engaged in commercial or financial affairs of any kind. Considering that even a non-Quaker could alert the monthly meeting to unethical business practices by one of its members, very few Quaker businessmen ever attempted anything shady or underhanded. Quaker businessmen were renowned for their honesty, which was a factor that contributed to their enormous mercantile success.[136]

The problem with a Friend defaulting on a debt or loan was, in part, the disrepute it brought upon the Society. But it also indicated that, potentially, the defaulter was lacking in prudence, judgment, and self-discipline. When a Friend defaulted or declared bankruptcy, the meeting tried to determine to what extent, if any, the failure had resulted from negligence, greedy miscalculation, or profligacy. Guilt on any of these points could lead to disownment. But if the Friend's pecuniary calamity was due to forces beyond his control, the meeting offered him a loan to help him back toward solvency. He was always required to satisfy his creditors eventually, and to stay out of financial straits in the future.[137]

Entertainment included activities like dancing, singing, acting in or watching plays, racing on foot or horseback, watching a race, reading novels, fox-hunting and other "hunting for sport," and playing at cards, dice, billiards, ninepins, shuffleboard, or "any other kind of game whatsoever, now invented or hereafter to be invented." Entertainment distracted one from proper and sober pursuits in religion, charity, and business. It not only wasted time and energy, but excited the baser passions of human nature, which detracted from a Friend's true calling to personal holiness and moral rectitude. Dancing could lead to lust; singing and acting, to vanity and pride; racing, to conceit and wagering; novel reading, to romantic and fanciful daydreaming; sport hunting, to needless cruelty; gaming, to avarice and dishonesty. Useful and instructive pastimes, however, were permissible and encouraged as needed recreation. Acceptable hobbies included gardening; horticulture, and the cultivation of medicinal herbs; studying botany, geography, and geometry; and reading history.[138]

This then was the ascetic religious discipline, which formed the young Henry Simmons from childhood through early adulthood. Perhaps this background helps explain his outbursts against the raucous singing and dancing of the Allegany Senecas, his charges of idolatry and vanity in connection with their worship practices, and his frequent harping about their drinking, extravagant clothing, and personal adornments. Considering that the Quakers did not even indulge in hymn singing during their meetings for worship, it is a bit easier to understand Simmons's outrage when he observed Seneca worshipers loudly beating drums, shaking rattles, singing, and dancing. His experience among the Oneidas, who had already been extensively Christianized by the Rev. Samuel Kirkland, did not prepare him for what he saw at Cornplanter's village.

FRIENDS AND THE INDIANS

In 1796 when Henry Simmons informed Middletown MM that he was interested in helping the Indians, the meeting evaluated him and concluded that he was suitable for mission work. Middletown issued a certificate of approval on his behalf to the PYMIC, which was looking for volunteers to go among the Indians. The certificate began, "Our Friend Henry Simmons, Jr., having for some time had a concern on his mind to go and reside for a while with the Indians, in order to instruct them and assist them in farming, which he laid before our last monthly meeting. . . ." The certificate recommended Simmons to the PYMIC "as a sober young man in good repute amongst us, and a diligent attender of our religious meetings."[139]

Simmons presented his certificate to the PYMIC on May 20, 1796.[140] A subcommittee interviewed him, considered his credentials, and accepted him.[141] In June Simmons and two other missionaries, in company with a delegation of PYMIC members, traveled to Oneida. After the delegation held a series of conferences with the Indians and reached an agreement governing the mission, it departed, and the three missionaries stayed to build and operate the Oneida mission, which eventually consisted of a model, or demonstration, farm and a school. Simmons served as schoolteacher during the winter of 1796–97. In May he visited the Onondagas and Cayugas, to explore the possibility of expanding the Quaker missionary effort. Those nations, however, declined the offer.[142] In October Simmons returned home to spend the winter with his family.

The following March Simmons and two other young Friends, Halliday Jackson and Joel Swayne, appeared before the PYMIC and volunteered to answer its call for "suitable Friends who may feel their mind drawn to go into this country . . . of the Seneca nation of Indians . . . for the purpose of instructing them." The PYMIC had issued this call in October 1797, the same month that Simmons had returned home from Oneida. Jackson and Swayne presented certificates from their monthly meetings in New Garden and London Grove, respectively, and passed muster with the PYMIC's personnel subcommittee. Simmons was already cleared for service based on his work at Oneida and his 1796 certificate from Middletown. In May 1798 the three missionaries set out for the Seneca country and Cornplanter's village, accompanied by elders John Pierce and Joshua Sharpless.[143]

The Quakers were not at all concerned that Indians become Quakers, nor even immediately concerned that they become Christians. Friends believed that the Indians must first become civilized, before they could become Christian in anything but name. Many Friends probably assumed that, in general, the temperament and disposition of most Indians was ill-suited to Quakerism. Indians Christianized by other denominations loved hymn singing and ritual, although some denominations stinted on the latter. French Catholic missionaries had exerted great appeal before they were quarantined to Canada. But even the Presbyterians and Congregationalists seemed extravagant compared with the Quakers. Friends seem to have been right; late-eighteenth-century Indians evinced no more than passing interest in Quakerism.

During the 1790s when Friends were traveling to Indian treaties and establishing the missions at Oneida and Allegany, they recorded few occasions of Indians attending a meeting for worship. When two or three Quakers away from home on a diplomatic mission in Indian country met for worship, the meeting was frequently silent, or mostly so. If the Spirit did not move one of them to speak, the companions simply sat in meditative silence. Indians who sat in on one of these meetings usually got up and left after a few minutes.

Following initial exposure to the Quaker religion, Indians almost always lost interest. The gulf between Quakers and Indians in method of worship was revealed by an incident that took place at Canandaigua, New York, during the treaty negotiations there in 1794. James Emlen, an official Quaker observer, described a worship service held jointly by Friends and Indians.

> In the afternoon we had a meeting with the Indians at their camp. . . . A scene was here acted, the like of which I do not recollect to have heard of in a Friends' meeting before, which was the singing of a hymn. . . . Having been taught to sing psalms in their own language by Kirkland, a missionary who resides among them, the poor Indians requested of Friends liberty to proceed in their usual way. Being desirous of not unnecessarily thwarting their inclinations, we condescended accordingly. The Indian language being one of the softest in the world, their singing exceeded anything of the kind that I remember to have heard. The voices of the squaws were truly melodious. To a mind which could drop its [spiritual] exercise and listen with satisfaction to the harmony of sound, it would have been truly delightful. But being most easy [comfortable] to endeavor to center to the true place of waiting, I must acknowledge that that part of our meeting in which they were engaged in singing was to me the most exercising.[144]

Good Quaker that he was, Emlen wanted to meditate in quiet and listen for the voice of the Spirit. For him, the beautiful singing was nothing but a distraction. Emlen's sentiments show that Friends would never consent to hymn singing, except in the most extraordinary circumstances. If Indians wanted to sing hymns on a regular basis, they would have to do so somewhere besides a Quaker meeting for worship.

In any case, Friends saw "civilization" as an essential prerequisite for Christianity. As the Indians learned the ways of civilization, it was important for them to be exposed to good Christian behavior. The Quaker missionaries would be role models, as they instructed and guided the Indians. As the Indians learned to read, they would gain independent access to the Scriptures. In time, the Holy Spirit would turn their hearts toward Christ, but the Indians had to be given time to come to Christ in their own way, following the lead of the inner light. Their souls, meanwhile, were not doomed to certain damnation. Indians could find salvation, even in their unconverted "heathen" state. The children of Onas had only to concentrate on teaching the ways of civilization. Quaker good example, the Holy Spirit, and the Indians' inner light would take care of the rest.[145]

The individual Quakers involved in the Allegany mission definitely believed that the Holy Spirit operated in the hearts of unconverted Indians. In 1798 when Quaker elder Joshua Sharpless was at Allegany helping set up the mission, Cornplanter asked him if the Bible said anything about the Indians.

> We informed him the Bible mentioned all nations, kindreds, tongues, and people, and that included the Indians. We would have been glad to have told him that, though the Indians could not read the Bible, yet they were not wholly deprived of the benefits of the coming of Christ . . . a manifestation of his Spirit or measure of his grace was placed in each of their hearts, and would if minded or given way to, reprove for all wicked words and wicked actions and also produce peace for well doing. But this was too refined and delicate a subject for our interpreter to handle.[146]

Halliday Jackson too expressed his belief in the power of the Spirit to guide the Indians toward Christ. The occasion of this expression was a visit in 1820 to the Senecas living at Cattaraugus, New York, where a man named Chief Warrior was headman.

> At the close of this interview . . . Friends present communicated some sentiments on the subject of religion and the nature of true worship to the Great Spirit—stating that it might be performed while engaged in their fields, on the road, or while sitting with their families by their firesides. This they appeared fully to comprehend; and the chief warrior replied, "it was his religion, and the only one with which he was acquainted."
>
> This short though sincere confession of faith from a native Indian was a corroborating evidence that they were not destitute of the divine principle operating in the heart of man, which teaches him what constitutes the true worship of God, and requires not the aid of men or books to accomplish it, but is performed according to Christ's testimony "in spirit and in truth," arising from the sincere homage of a devout heart.[147]

During the same visit, the issue of religious factionalism came up. Under the influence of non-Quaker missionaries, some of the Cattaraugus Senecas had begun to observe the Sabbath, while others—nativists—refused to do so. The nativists asked the visiting Quakers for advice. Friends told them not to allow the community to become divided over the issue.

> Brothers . . . although it is our practice to meet together to worship . . . yet we do not wish to force upon you any of our performances in religion. . . . They were again recommended to attend strictly to the one unerring guide, the voice of the Good Spirit in their own hearts, which was sufficient to direct them in the right path, without the teachings of any man; and that as they were obedient to this principle, it would gradually enlighten their understandings, and by degrees they would come to see more light.[148]

As for Quaker motivation in extending humanitarian benevolence to American Indians and African Americans, historians have cobbled together various theories. Sydney V. James, in his study of eighteenth-century Quaker benevolence, *A People Among Peoples,* published in 1963, argued that during the Revolution, the Society's pacifism became identified with Toryism and garnered Friends much disrepute and ill will among their fellow Americans. Philanthropy offered the Quakers a way to refurbish their image and "win a place for themselves in American society." Its disinterested benevolence would demonstrate the Society's value to the nation at large.[149] According to James, the Quakers were very attuned to the public relations benefits of philanthropy. "Friends expected the good will of the public in return for benevolence,"[150] and "they often expected charitable acts to put their virtues and views before the public, at least as a secondary objective."[151]

On the other hand, Jack D. Marietta, in his 1984 book, *The Reformation of American Quakerism,* argues that late-eighteenth-century Friends were not trying to win the hearts of other Americans. Rather, they went deeper into sectarianism, and withdrew from the mainstream to the periphery of American society and culture. Standing on the fringes of the national community, the Quakers, like a corporate Jeremiah, appealed to the minds and consciences of their fellow citizens. Like Jeremiah they pointed to the two great evils of their day: the enslavement of African Americans and the gradual dispossession and extirpation of American Indians.

The period examined in Marietta's study, 1748 to 1783, ended before Quaker missionary work among the Indians began. He focuses on the Quaker abolition testimony, pointing out that Friends had purged the practice of slavery from their own ranks, before calling on their fellow citizens to do the same. He also points out that its strong abolitionist stand was ill-calculated to win the Society admirers in the United States of the 1790s, when slaveholding was widespread, even in the North, and when Christian doctrine was regularly employed to accommodate—if not justify—slavery. The practice of slavery was enshrined in the Constitution of the new nation, because even those Americans who personally opposed it were willing to compromise and tolerate it.[152]

The Society stood apart from the rest of the nation because it was the first entity, corporately as a whole, to eradicate the practice internally and to call for its abolition everywhere. This made the Society even more reviled in some quarters than had its pacifism during the war. Quaker benevolence toward American Indians during the 1790s was not well-suited for ingratiating Friends with their fellow Americans. Almost all of the Indians had fought on the British side during the Revolutionary War and the United States had finally managed to win the war for the Old Northwest Territory only in 1794. Many Americans had been killed by Indians; and to many Americans, "the only good Indian was a dead Indian." By seeking justice for the Indians, Friends courted the resentment of federal and state officials bent on turning Indian land into public land, and then into revenue. Friends also earned the enmity of land speculators and developers, such as Joseph Ellicott of the Holland Land Company, and the hostility of European-American settlers who wanted the Indians cleared from the landscape so they could take possession.

Whatever the Quaker "secondary objectives" in terms of propaganda might have been, Friends were motivated primarily by a deep sense of the injustice American Indians had suffered—as Sydney James himself points out. John Woolman, a leading reformer, expressed this feeling that the Indians had been terribly wronged.

> Having for many years felt love in my heart towards the natives of this land who dwell far back in the wilderness, whose ancestors were formerly owners and possessors of the land where we dwell, and who for a small consideration assigned their inheritance to us . . . I fell in company with some . . . natives [from] Wyalusing [who were visiting Philadelphia].[153]

James Emlen expressed the same sentiment at Canandaigua, when considering ways in which Friends might be able to help the Indians.

> It ought to excite a deep consideration whether any substantial good can be done for the help and benefit of this greatly injured people, to whom we in gratitude are so deeply indebted.[154]

This sense of injustice included an appreciation of how much the Indians had lost in lives and land since the European advent. This, in turn, led to a sense of moral indebtedness and obligation to the American Indians, both for their lands and for their suffering. To a great extent, this sense of obligation motivated the philanthropy shown by the Quakers toward American Indians.[155]

Regardless of Friends' motivation, there was, from the perspective of the Allegany Senecas, a single concern. What would "civilization" at the hands of the children of Onas mean for Seneca society, religion, and culture?

CHAPTER FOUR

Iroquois Games

G ames can tell us about the people who play them, but sometimes it is necessary to know about a people before we can appreciate their games. Iroquois games reveal a people who valued both individual prowess and group solidarity. They had no use for standardized rules and regulations governing the playing of games, but would perform intricate game-preparation rituals to the most exacting specifications. The Iroquois loved the excitement of wagering, but had developed channels for controlled, communal betting. Religious beliefs permeated every facet of life, including play. The messages of many religious faiths are that God is pleased with our righteousness, our suffering, our labor, or our sacrifice—the Iroquois proclaimed that the Good Spirit delights in watching our play.

The Iroquois bowl game, lacrosse, and snow snake were played for amusement and entertainment, but also for religious reasons or as medicine to cure the sick, to prevent illness, and to bring favorable weather. To better understand the medicinal purposes of these games, we will examine aspects of Iroquois social structure and spiritual belief.

LINEAGE, CLAN, AND MOIETY

The basic social, economic, and political unit of the Senecas and of all the Iroquois was the extended family group known as a lineage. The extended families of the Iroquois were matrilineal, successive generations were traced through the female line, rather than the male. As a simplified example, assume that two sisters are both grandmothers and that their own mother is deceased. In this case the lineage consists of them, their sons and daughters, and the children of their daughters, but not the children of their sons. Their grandchildren fathered by their sons belong to the lineages of their sons' wives.[1]

Working up the hierarchy of social, economic, and political structures, the next unit after the lineage was the clan. The clan was a group of exogamous lineages that never intermarried but were united in a fictive kin relationship, such as that of the Bear or the Hawk totem, the animal that symbolized the clan.

The clan system originated during Early Woodland times, 1200 B.C. to 200 A.D., as a means of precluding incest. A few extended families, or lineages, would band together to form a community in which there would be no intramarriage. Partners for marriage-eligible individuals had to be found in other communities. In the cultural milieu of aboriginal northeastern North America, the only basis for community was kinship. If the community could not be based on real kinship ties between its con-stituent lineages, then a fictive kinship had to be invented to hold it together. Clans-men related to each other as if they were really kinsmen, but there was no tradition that all members of the clan were descended from a common human or animal an-cestor. Clan membership was ascribed at birth and members associated under the symbol of the totemic animal after which their clan was named. In keeping with the Iroquois matrilineal organization of kinship ties, children were members of their mother's clan.[2]

The significance of clans gradually evolved beyond the realm of incest taboos. During Middle Woodland times, 200 A.D. to 1000, communities became more com-plex as segments of several clans settled together in the same village. This made find-ing a suitable mate for marriage-eligible individuals much more convenient. It was no longer absolutely necessary to go to another village to find a potential spouse. More importantly, members of the same clan living in different villages readily extended hospitality to each other in the form of food and shelter. Visitors and travelers could thus be sure of finding a welcome in villages other than their own—among their clansmen. This broadened the linkage between villages beyond that provided by indi-vidual intermarriages.[3]

Within a given village, the lineages of the same clan cooperated with each other as a unit in a variety of activities such as clearing fields, cultivating, planting, har-vesting, hunting, fishing, and making war. The Seneca population was divided into eight clans. The clans were associated in two groupings called moieties. In the moiety of the land were the Bear, Beaver, Turtle, and Wolf clans. In the moiety of the air were the Hawk, Heron, Snipe, and Deer clans. The Deer was associated with totemic birds because when it ran, it seemed to fly. For ceremonial and religious functions, the clans present in a Seneca village were associated into balanced moieties. By the end of the 1700s, no village contained lineages belonging to all eight clans. For ex-ample, the two moieties in a village might consist of the Wolf and Bear clans on the one hand and of the Deer and Heron clans on the other.[4]

Each moiety had reciprocal obligations to the other, especially in matters related to funerals and condolence. This clan system, with its pattern of reciprocal obliga-tions within and between clans and moieties, figured prominently in the ceremonial life of the village. Usually, the two moieties sat on opposite sides of the ceremonial fire, passing calumet pipes of tobacco back and forth and taking turns at different parts of the rituals used to celebrate various festivals.[5] And in any intravillage bowl games or lacrosse games, one moiety usually played the other.

BOWL GAME
The bowl game was sacred, in part, because it symbolized the struggle between the Good Twin and the Evil Twin during the days of creation. There were secular ver-sions of the game, however, that were played within nonsacred contexts for fun and

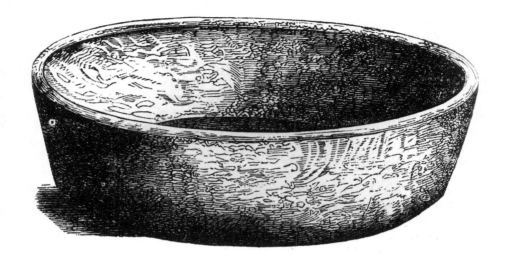

Wooden bowl and peach stones used to play the sacred bowl game (originally published by Morgan in 1851). The bowl was about a foot in diameter at its base; its sides were four to six inches high.

DARLINGTON LIBRARY, UNIVERSITY OF PITTSBURGH.

entertainment.[6] The sacred version of the game was always played between the two moieties of the village. The sacred bowl game was an ancient feature of Iroquois culture, with documented references dating from the 1600s. Numerous European-American observers wrote eyewitness descriptions of the game.[7]

The bowl game was named for the large, flat-bottomed, wooden bowl with which it was played. Also used were six peach or plum stones, each ground down into a flattened oval, scorched black on one side, and left its natural light color on the other. The stones were placed in the bowl, the bottom of which was then thumped on the floor or on a blanket laid on the ground, causing the stones to bounce upward. They were caught again in the bowl as they fell downward. The bowl was about a foot in diameter at its base so that when the stones fell back into the bowl, they did not collect in a pile on top of each other—as they would in a curved bottom. The sides of the bowl were four to six inches high and angled outward, so that the mouth was wider than the base.

Each throw was scored according to the color combination presented by the stones after the bowl had been thumped—all black or all white yielding the highest score. A throw resulting in fewer than five stones showing the same color produced no score. The color that predominated—white or black—was immaterial. Beans were used as counters; typically there were 102 beans, which were awarded on the basis of the score thrown. Initially the beans came out of a common pile, but once that was exhausted, beans were awarded from the opposite moiety's accumulated winnings. When one moiety accumulated all the beans, it won and the game was over.

Two players sat opposite each other, with the bowl between them and the members of their respective moieties ranged behind them. As soon as a player took the bowl to throw the stones, members of the opposite moiety started hurling imprecations against the player's luck, making faces, and gesturing wildly. At the same time, members of the player's own moiety began yelling countercurses, displaying similar antics, and trying to drive bad luck back to the opposition. Both sides kept this up until the stones settled from the throw. A player continued thumping the bowl until he or she threw a scoreless combination, at which point the bowl passed to the opposing moiety. The player who threw a scoreless combination was replaced by another person from his or her moiety before their next turn. In this way, many, if not all, members of a moiety had a chance to try their luck with the bowl and stones during the course of the game.

Both sexes played the bowl game, and sometimes the men and women played against each other, instead of moiety versus moiety. During the Midwinter Rites, for example, Onondaga women played against the men to foretell the result of the new year's harvest. If the men won, long ears of corn could be expected; if the women won, short ears were likely. This curious belief was based on the fact that generally men were taller, that is, longer than women. The bowl game was often played as a means of foretelling or divination.[8]

The bowl game shared certain aspects with lacrosse. Both games were frequently played against neighboring villages, with heavy wagering on the outcome.

Ritual preparations often preceded both, ranging from tobacco sacrifices to fasting and sexual abstinence. Both sometimes went on for days. Additionally, each game was often played as a healing ritual to help cure a sick person.

LACROSSE

This athletic ball game was the Iroquois' favorite sport. But it was much more than a "sport" in our modern European-American sense of the word. American Indian lacrosse had a profound spiritual and religious dimension difficult for European Americans to appreciate.

The emotional responses of European Americans who witnessed the game and reported on it in the 1700s and early 1800s run the gamut from astonishment and amazement, through excitement and enthusiasm, to admiration and awe. Samuel Woodruff, who witnessed a lacrosse game played between the Seneca and Mohawk nations in 1797, wrote in his notes: "The match was played with great spirit, and the display of agility and muscular strength was surprising. . . . Every nerve was strung. . . . The scene was full of excitement and animation . . . and . . . afforded . . . a greater degree of satisfaction than any game or pastime . . . ever beheld."[9] Writing almost a hundred years later, William Beauchamp said, "It is one of the most picturesque and exciting of ball games, the contestants racing, dodging, throwing, struggling, digging up the ball in the liveliest manner possible."[10]

American Indians loved to play the game on a grand scale. Forty, sixty, sometimes a hundred or more "warriors" took to the playing field, which was often four or five times longer than a modern football field, with the goals as far apart as a quarter of a mile. There were no sidelines; field width was limited only by the size of the clearing and contours of the surrounding terrain. One game in 1797 at the Grand River Reservation in southeastern Ontario, between the Mohawk and Seneca nations, was played on a 100-acre field. Each side had a reserve of 600 players and fielded 60 of them at a time, for a total of 120 players continuously on the field.[11]

Naked except for breechcloth, body decorated with red warpaint, each player was armed with a 5-foot-long lacrosse stick.[12] The stick was sharply curved at the business end, with a web of rawhide, or untanned deer hide, netting stretched inside the curve. The web was taut enough that the ball could be effectively thrown, but not so taut as to preclude carrying the ball on the web in a very shallow depression—more like a saucer than a cup or pocket. The ball was of buckskin, stuffed with hair, grass, or sand, and sewn around the circumference.[13] The ball was round and about 2.5 inches in diameter.[14]

The game alternated between general melee and running battle. When a ball grounded, a tumultuous melee erupted as players on both sides scuffled for the ball. Touching the ball with hand or foot was forbidden, so it all came down to stick work.[15] The webbing of the lacrosse stick was used to bat the ball. Batting a grounded ball was the main method of getting it into a position where a teammate could take control of it. It was permissible to strike an opponent's stick at any time, and although it was considered very bad form for a player to deliberately strike an opponent with his stick, virtually any other form of unarmed combat was allowed.

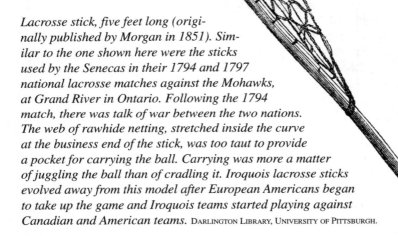

Lacrosse stick, five feet long (origi-
nally published by Morgan in 1851). Sim-
ilar to the one shown here were the sticks
used by the Senecas in their 1794 and 1797
national lacrosse matches against the Mohawks,
at Grand River in Ontario. Following the 1794
match, there was talk of war between the two nations.
The web of rawhide netting, stretched inside the curve
at the business end of the stick, was too taut to provide
a pocket for carrying the ball. Carrying was more a matter
of juggling the ball than of cradling it. Iroquois lacrosse sticks
evolved away from this model after European Americans began
to take up the game and Iroquois teams started playing against
Canadian and American teams. DARLINGTON LIBRARY, UNIVERSITY OF PITTSBURGH.

Melees were attended with confusion. Most players—and spectators—could not
see the ball because of the teeming throng that surrounded its suspected location, with
the result that sometimes multiple melees erupted simultaneously. Because grabbing,
tripping, and tackling were all permitted, the individuals assigned to cover each other
often got into tussles. Opposing teams had equal numbers of players and, before the
game started, each player was paired against a personal adversary who matched him,
at least roughly, in strength, fleetness of foot, and skill. Paired adversaries played opposite each other throughout the game. Hand-to-hand confrontations, in which two
personal adversaries dropped their sticks and settled their differences with fisticuffs or
by wrestling, were ignored by the rest of the players, as the general melee rolled
along the field, leaving in its wake scattered pairs of brawling players.[16]

With dozens of players jostling, with dozens of sticks clattering against each
other, and with the ball ricocheting like a pinball, a melee could go on for several
minutes before the ball emerged.[17] Eventually, a player would be able to balance
the ball on his webbing and get sufficiently clear of the melee to raise his stick off

the ground. At this point, he either ran with the ball or threw it toward the target goal. In either case, the running battle was on.

To run with the ball, a player had to hold his lacrosse stick horizontally and keep the ball from rolling off the web. "Cradling" the ball was actually more a matter of juggling it on the nearly flat web. The player had to run at full tilt, darting and dodging as opponents tried to cut off his dash toward the goal. His teammates ran interference for him, but if he sensed that an opponent was about to close, he would throw the ball—in the general direction of the goal—in hopes that a teammate would be able to advance it. If he was close enough, he would try to throw the ball through the goal, thereby scoring a point.

Typically, the goal posts were thirty to fifty feet apart and ten to fifteen feet high. A player preferred to score by running through the goal, carrying the ball. This was considered an admirable feat because the goal was defended by players from the other team specifically assigned to guard the goal. The team thought of the goal to be scored upon as *their* goal. According to this notion of a "home goal," members of the opposing team who played a guard position were trying to block "your" team from bringing the ball home.[18]

As played by the Iroquois two hundred years ago, the aerial portion of the game did not consist of passing the ball to be caught by a teammate in the webbing of his stick. The netting simply was not loose or deep enough to catch the ball. Rather, the ball was lobbed down field in a high arch to keep it above the waving sticks of opponents closing in on the thrower, in hopes that a teammate would knock it out of the air and scoop it up or recover it after it had grounded. The risk was that a player from the opposing team would do so instead. A player threw the ball by swinging underhand, or, preferably, by turning his back toward his goal and swinging backwards over his head.[19]

During these running battles "for the ball, when it is up—where hundreds are running together and leaping, actually over each other's heads, and darting between their adversary's legs, tripping and throwing, and foiling each other in every possible manner, and every voice raised to the highest key, in shrill yelps and barks—there are rapid successions of feats, and of incidents, that astonish and amuse far beyond the conception of anyone who has not had the singular good luck to witness them."[20]

American Indians did not establish a standardized set of rules and regulations to govern lacrosse for a very good reason. The absence of standardization left the game infinitely scaleable—it could be adjusted to fit the circumstances between any two parties who wanted to play each other. Two nations could play a game, or two villages, or two moieties in the same village. Each game—down to the smallest sandlot or pickup game—was preceded by negotiations during which all the variables were agreed upon for that particular game: the number of players on each team, including the number to be fielded and the number to be allowed in each team's reserve, the distance between goals, the size and the shape of the playing field, the number of points required to win, and who would keep score.[21]

Although American Indian lacrosse was widely scaleable, the games fit into distinct classes: exhibition, intervillage, and intravillage games. The major portion of all lacrosse played by Indians was played in intravillage contests, usually between members of opposing moieties. These were informal affairs, arranged spontaneously, except when being played as part of a training regimen preparatory to an intervillage or exhibition match. Virtually every Indian boy in the Eastern woodlands grew up playing lacrosse with the other boys in his village.[22] Later, when he became a young man and well into his adulthood, the informal, pickup lacrosse game remained his favorite pastime. Prior to one of these informal pickup games, the players themselves worked out and agreed upon the details governing play.

Intervillage games were usually between neighboring villages of the same nation, and between just two villages. But sometimes a group of villages would combine to oppose another group—all within the same nation—creating a sort of intranational game. Intervillage games were preceded by formal negotiations between the headmen of the respective villages regarding the details of play. Wagering was a prominent feature of intervillage games.

Exhibition games were played between two different nations and on the grandest of scales. Wagering on these games was heavy. Revered elders from both nations were selected to jointly keep score. They were empowered to adjust the point value for goals scored, provided that the scorekeepers from both sides agreed to do so. If the score started to become lopsided, the leading team might have to run the ball through their goal twice before another score was added to their tally. This was done deliberately to prolong the game—sometimes for as long as three or four days.[23]

Preparations, Wagers, and Feasts

Activities always associated with Iroquois lacrosse were ritual preparations, widespread wagering, and dancing and feasting. Ritual preparations were performed by the village shaman and the players. Players made wagers with opposing players. Similarly, members of one village or nation made wagers with members of the opposing team's village or nation—always for their own team to win. Feasts and religious dances were held in conjunction with lacrosse games. In the case of the Iroquois, it seems that these usually followed the game.

Preparation of players for a game was not limited to physical exercise and practice sessions. It included acts of ritual cleansing and purification such as fasting, purging, and bathing.[24] Iroquois players took a decoction of the bark of spotted alder and red willow—as an emetic. Players tied charms into their hair and onto their lacrosse sticks.[25] And prior to the game, they applied body paint—usually red, the color of war and victory.[26]

Favorite charms for wearing in the hair were feathers from birds of prey, such as eagles, ospreys, and goshawks.[27] The belief was that these charms would impart the attributes of the bird to their wearer through a process that some have dubbed "sympathetic magic."[28] The keen eyesight that allows the soaring hawk to spot a rabbit in a field far below or the gliding osprey to see a fish beneath the surface of the water was transferred to the player, enabling him to spot and track the ball flying through the air, lying in the grass on the field, and ricocheting inside a thicket of shins and lacrosse sticks. The speed of an eagle diving from aloft enabled the player to run quickly and reach the ball before an opponent. The goshawk's maneuverability enabled the player to dodge opponents and to dart swiftly after the ball as it continually changed direction.

Charms, such as a piece of bat wing, might be affixed to the stick.[29] In a widely occurring American Indian legend about the origins of lacrosse, a story is told about a lacrosse game between the quadrupeds and the birds. In all the versions of this tale, the central question is how to classify the bat—that is, on which team should it play? In most versions neither side wants the bat at first. But eventually, one team or the other, quadruped or bird, depending on the version, accepts the bat. The bat then plays a pivotal role in winning the game for the team with which it found acceptance. By attaching a piece of bat wing to his lacrosse stick, an American Indian player invoked the spirit of the bat to assist him and his team during the game.[30]

The services of a shaman or medicine man were employed, probably invariably. He brewed the decoctions used for purging. It was often the shaman who called for the game to be played, sometimes as a prescription to help an ailing patient, who did not himself play, and sometimes as a means of bringing favorable weather, such as rain during a dry spell. Indeed, the village shaman often filled the role of team owner, coach, and promoter. He decided when a game would be played, which neighboring village would be challenged, what strategies his players would use, and what charms they should wear and attach to their sticks. He also performed rituals over the players and their gear to give them strength, endurance, and resilience.[31]

In later times—by the end of the 1800s—individual players hired shamans to "exert their supernatural powers in their own behalf and for their side, and when a noted wizard openly espoused the cause of one of the parties the players of the other side felt to a certain extent disheartened."[32]

A discussion of traditional American Indian lacrosse is not complete unless it touches on the wagering universally associated with the game.[33] From earliest contact times, European observers noted that wagering was an integral part of Indian lacrosse.

Father Jean de Brebeuf, a Jesuit missionary writing in 1636 about the Hurons, noted that villages not only played lacrosse against each other but also bet against each other.[34] Nicolas Perrot, a French trader writing sometime around the year 1700 about observations he had made during the preceding three and a half decades, reported: "Men, women, boys, and girls are received into the parties which are formed; and they bet . . . for larger or smaller amounts, each according to his means."[35] Samuel Woodruff, eyewitness to a 1797 Seneca-versus-Mohawk game, reported that significant stakes were wagered in conjunction with that game and an earlier match in 1794. Lewis Henry Morgan, writing in 1851 about observations he had made during the preceding decade, observed: "Betting upon the result [of games in general, and of lacrosse in particular] was common among the Iroquois." This practice remained unchanged as late as the end of the 1800s, when J. N. B. Hewitt wrote: "Like all other public games of the Iroquois, the ball-game [lacrosse] was to the spectators a favorite opportunity for betting."[36]

Indians did not give odds or handicaps nor did they bet on point spreads; theirs was strictly winner-take-all wagering.[37] Until the latter half of the 1800s, cash was not wagered. The stakes were usually goods and, sometimes, services. The stakes at the Seneca-versus-Mohawk games during the 1790s were all goods: rifles, hatchets, swords, belts, knives, blankets, beads, brooches, etc.[38]

Aside from presenting an opportunity for individuals to obtain valuable articles by winning personal bets, wagering performed other important functions for American Indian lacrosse. It raised the stakes in the game, heightening the anticipation and excitement surrounding the game for all the stakeholders, including the players. Each player wagered individually with his personal adversary on the opposing team. Wagering between nonplayers from opposing villages was less structured. People looked for someone they knew from the other village and made a bet with him or her, or they simply found someone who had an article of equal value to wager. High stakes increased the significance of the game for everyone and provided strong motivation for the players to perform their best.

As a mechanism for spectator involvement, wagering made nonplayers active participants in the contest by giving them a personal stake in the outcome of the game. Virtually everyone in the village placed a bet. Indeed they were encouraged to do so by their spiritual leader, the shaman, or medicine man. Morgan wrote, disapprovingly, that "this practice was never reprobated by their religious teachers, but, on the contrary, rather encouraged."[39] The act of betting was more important than any monetary value attached to the stakes.

Wagers made on lacrosse games were expressions of community support, solidarity, and pride as much as they were attempts by individuals to win bets.[40] The notion of betting on the team from the opposing village was totally alien to the culture of American Indian lacrosse, as were the notions of odds, handicaps, or point spreads. Indians would probably have disapproved of such foreign practices as greedy. What seems to have been important to Indians was that all of the individual wagers made by the villagers, both players and nonplayers, combined to form a "collective bet," placed by the village as a whole. The collective bet represented not only the commitment of the village to its team, but also of each individual to the village. As a visible expression of the community commitment represented by the collective bet, the stakes wagered by both villages were all kept in the same place, out in the open, guarded by elders from both villages.[41] Displayed for all to see, the stakes bore witness to the strength and solidarity of each community.

Accounts of lacrosse among Southeastern tribes, such as the Cherokees, are replete with detailed descriptions of feasts and religious dances associated with the game.[42] The literature describing Iroquois lacrosse, however, is comparatively sketchy about associated feasts and dances. And in contrast to the Southeastern pattern in which the dancing occurred during the night prior to the game, the Iroquois seem to have held their dancing and feasting in the evening, after the game.

Harriet Converse, writing in 1908 about her observations—gleaned over two decades—on Seneca myths and legends, stated that when famine or epidemic threatened the people, the shaman would order a game of lacrosse to be played. At the end of the game, all the players engaged in religious dances and ceremonies. Hewitt, describing Iroquois lacrosse, wrote in 1892 that the game "is usually followed by a dance at night, accompanied by a feast." Frank Speck, writing in 1949 about the Cayuga Thunder Rite, noted that a ritual lacrosse game between the old men and the young was followed by the War Dance and a feast—on corn mush. And Morgan reported that the War Dance was usually performed in the evening.[43]

Lacrosse for Good Health and Weather

Lacrosse was sometimes played to effect beneficial changes in health and weather. The practice of playing lacrosse for these purposes predates the advent of Europeans and is deeply rooted in ancient Iroquois religious beliefs and spirituality. Brebeuf wrote of the Hurons in 1636:

> Of three kinds of games especially in use among these peoples—namely, the games of crosse, dish, and straw, the first two are, they say, most healing. . . . There is a poor sick man, fevered of body and almost dying, and a . . . sorcerer [shaman, medicine man] will order for him, as a cooling remedy, a game of crosse. Or the sick man himself, sometimes, will have dreamed that he must die unless the whole country shall play crosse for his health; and no matter how little his credit, you will see then in a beautiful field, village contending against village.[44]

The "game of dish" referred to here is the bowl game. The straw game was played with straws or sticks of uniform length and thickness, about eleven inches long and "not so thick as the cord [used] for a salmon-net."[45] More than a hundred straws or sticks—but always an odd number—were placed in a jumbled pile. Players inserted a small pick, or pointed bone, into the pile and used it to draw off some of the straws. Any odd number of straws so obtained always beat any even number. The highest odd number beat all other odd numbers.[46]

In 1815 the Onondaga played a game of lacrosse to help Handsome Lake, who lay on his deathbed. Some historians have reported that the reason for this game was an attempt to lift Handsome Lake's spirit by amusing and honoring him. But Thomas Vennum, author of *American Indian Lacrosse,* believes that "it represented a desperate effort to save his life." I agree with Vennum, although the game was certainly intended to honor and entertain the Prophet as well. Handsome Lake himself had recognized the spiritual significance of lacrosse.[47]

In May of 1637 the Hurons of present-day Thunder Bay, Ontario, played a lacrosse game to help ensure good weather for germination of the corn crop, the seeds for which had just been planted. As late as the 1940s the Cayugas were still performing a rite in spring and summer when rain was needed which honored the Seven Thunders, and which included a ritual lacrosse game. The Thunders benefited mankind by causing the wind and rain to cleanse the earth and by keeping certain monsters and serpents imprisoned beneath the earth where they could not harm people. In the ritual lacrosse game, which was the principal part of the Thunder Rite, the number seven was featured to honor the Seven Thunders. Seven old men played seven young men, the goals were seven paces wide, and seven points were needed to win the game.[48]

Spiritual Underpinnings of Lacrosse

How could playing a game of lacrosse be related to curing or preventing illness or influencing the weather? The connection between lacrosse and the weather is fairly easy to establish, because the Seven Thunders controlled the winds and rains. The Iroquois believed that the sound of thunder was produced by the sticks of the seven Thunder Spirits striking their lacrosse ball as they played the game inside the thunderheads. Streaks of lightning traced the path of their lacrosse ball through the sky as they batted it across the heavens.[49] It was only natural to propitiate and entreat the Seven Thunders for favorable weather by playing their favorite game.

The starting point for tracing the relationship between lacrosse and healing is the cult of dreams. Iroquoians believed that illness could be caused by an unsatisfied wish of the soul. The soul might disclose in a dream its wish for a lacrosse game to be played in the dreamer's honor. Typically, a person would dream that he sponsored a lacrosse game by providing presents for the players—tobacco, for example—and food for the postgame feast. A sick person could sponsor the game as a preventive or a curative measure, depending on whether the disclosure occurred before or after the onset of illness. In either case, the person would consult a shaman about the dream. If the soul never disclosed its wish in a dream, causing the person to become ill, the services of a shaman were essential in descrying that the soul secretly wished for a lacrosse game.

Part of the relationship between lacrosse and healing lay in the fact that both healthy and sick persons believed that dreams of lacrosse expressed their soul's wish for a game.[50] And the frequency of such dreams tended to validate a shaman's diagnosis that an illness unaccompanied by dreaming was caused by the soul's secret wish for a lacrosse game, or that a game must be played to prevent an epidemic.[51] Cultural conditioning and predisposition probably caused people to dream often about lacrosse games.

Lacrosse was sacred, a gift from the Creator. The Good Twin gave the game to the Indians so that they could entertain and amuse him by playing it. This explains why players were required to undergo ritual purification before a game. By playing lacrosse Indians pleased the Creator and disposed him toward curing or preventing illness, and sending clement weather. The game of lacrosse and its associated activities also exhibited one of the most powerful forces in Iroquois spirituality—alliance.

To the Iroquois, alliance was the ideal relationship—not dominance or competition. The Iroquois sought to build alliances at all levels of human interaction—between individuals, extended families, clans, and nations—not just because of the obvious benefits, but also because such alliances were believed to be the source of great spiritual power that was needed to hold at bay a whole host of misfortunes: crop failure, defeat in battle, accidental death, or the malevolent spell of a hostile witch to mention a few.[52]

When the Good Twin created fauna, flora, and people, he did so by growing them all out of the earth, infusing that earth with supernatural power drawn from prototypical spirit beings who dwelled in the sky, under the ground, and beneath the waters. Everything, and every person, that the Good Twin created retained a link with its prototypical spirit being—a conduit through which power from the spirit world could flow.[53] When persons united in alliance, the total reservoir of spiritual power that could be tapped increased in proportion to the number of persons involved and the quality of their alliance. The Iroquois recognized degrees in the quality of alliance. The relationship holding people together might be superficial and easily broken, symbolized by a flimsy "everyday rope." Or, the relationship might be deep and unbreakable, symbolized by a "bright chain of friendship."[54]

Lacrosse was the preeminent peacetime exercise in alliance, next in degree only to actual war against a common enemy. Although war did represent the failure of alliance, within the Iroquois League and its related political Confederacy, it also functioned to strengthen the internal alliances—until the Confederacy finally split during the American Revolution. Known as "little brother of war," lacrosse called for extensive training and preparation, and for bravery, skill, and strength in execution. Like warfare, lacrosse called for the whole team, backed by the entire village or nation, to pull together.

Lacrosse could be played against a friendly village and did not result in loss of life—normally. It did, however, produce many injuries—some of them serious and permanently disabling. The Iroquois, like all American Indians, did not have any protective gear to wear until the second half of the 1800s. Although the stakes in war greatly outweighed those in a game of lacrosse, the practice of universal wagering on the outcome of a game increased the significance of the game for all and motivated the players to perform at near warlike levels.

The formation of a village lacrosse team was an alliance among a small, select group. This small alliance was extended to include the rest of the village through the mechanism of wagering. The collective bet placed by the playing and nonplaying members of the village symbolized a spiritual alliance of friendship.

The alliances forged in preparing for a lacrosse game went beyond the team and village members. A lacrosse match represented a duel between the shamans of the opposing villages, and was not just an athletic contest between the two teams. It was the shaman's responsibility to enlist every spirit ally possible to assist his team. He did this by performing certain rituals and by having his players employ certain charms or fetishes, such as feathers or bits of bat wing. In the case of the Iroquois, little else is known about the shaman's rituals or the charms and potions he prescribed for players.

The details of shamanism performed for Southeastern Woodlands tribes such as the Cherokee and the Creek Indians are much better documented. We can look at some of these details, but only with the understanding that they might or might not be similar to the details of shamanism surrounding Iroquois lacrosse. The information in the following two paragraphs on Southeastern lacrosse shamanism is drawn from Thomas Vennum's book, *American Indian Lacrosse.*[55]

The shaman supervised the manufacturing of his team's lacrosse ball, providing specific instructions on how to obtain and assemble the components. In the case of the Cherokees, the skin used for the ball cover had to come from a squirrel killed without being shot. The Cherokee version of the legend about the lacrosse game between the birds and quadrupeds included a flying squirrel, in addition to a bat. The shaman required the man who made the ball to undergo ritual purification before dressing the squirrel skin to form the ball. Sometimes the shaman directed that certain charms or fetishes be incorporated into the stuffing that went inside the ball. The Creeks included inchworms in the stuffing for their lacrosse balls, because they believed that inchworms were invisible to birds. By sympathetic magic, the worms would make it difficult for members of the opposing team to spot the ball.

The night prior to a game, the shaman "doctored" his team's lacrosse ball, together with the players' sticks. "Doctoring" consisted of the recitation or chanting of a magic formula by the shaman while the players applied potions, which the shaman had prepared, to their lacrosse gear. In the case of the Cherokees, the shaman lined up his players along a riverbank and instructed them to dip their lacrosse sticks into the water. Because rivers and streams were sacred to the Cherokees, immersion of the sticks therein increased their potency in attracting the ball. In the case of the Creeks, the shaman supervised his players as they applied a potion to the netting of their lacrosse sticks to attract the ball into the net. Potions were also poured on the lacrosse ball to make it fall out of an opponent's net.

The common theme in all shamanistic practices revolving around lacrosse was the solicitation, invocation, and enlistment of spirit allies: the prototypical bird of prey, bat, squirrel—even the inchworm. These practices all rested on the widespread American Indian belief that everything encountered in the world—human, animal, vegetable, mineral—was not only linked to the spirit world but also possessed some kind of personhood.[56] Each person, including nonhuman "persons," had unique characteristics: speed, maneuverability, visual acuity, stealth.

It was the shaman's function to tap into the special powers possessed by nonhuman persons and to forge alliances with spirit forces for his team and village. He had the same task in war and used similar shamanistic practices to accomplish it. In some cases, belief in the power of these spirit forces was so great that they were seen as determining the outcome of a game or battle irrespective of the relative skill and stamina of the opposing players or warriors, who were merely instruments of the contending spirit forces marshaled by rival shamans.[57]

Thus, it was the tremendous spiritual power summoned by the alliances forged around lacrosse that culturally predisposed people to dream about the game and shamans to prescribe it as a preventive and cure for illness. Short of war itself, there was nothing like its "little brother" for exercising the spiritual power of alliance.

Little Brother of War

Some history writers, most notably Thomas Vennum, author of *American Indian Lacrosse,* have emphasized the similarity between the rituals and symbolism related to lacrosse and those related to warfare. Vennum sees the affinity between American Indian lacrosse and warfare as "a native North American example of ancient and universal relationships between game and battle. It was not by accident that on the prize table at Olympia, seat of the original, Greek, Olympic games, the statue of Agon, the god of the games, stood immediately next to that of Ares, the god of war."[58]

There are distinct ways in which he says that lacrosse served as a surrogate for war. The game provided an outlet for generalized aggressive impulses.[59] Lacrosse served as a safety valve to vent aggressive feelings and behaviors that might otherwise have been directed as violence at members of the village or of nearby, friendly villages.

Lacrosse provided a comparatively harmless outlet for hostility that was directed at a specific target within the village or nation, "funneling group aggression into peaceable rivalry."[60] Many fights in lacrosse games could be "attributed to grudges, either personal or at a group level, such as family or clan."[61] Lacrosse again served as a safety valve, this time to preserve domestic tranquility within the village and the nation.

Lacrosse also provided an alternative or substitute for actual combat in resolving disputes between American Indian nations. Vennum asserts that "long before Europeans arrived in North America, tribes settled territorial disputes with lacrosse games"[62]; however, there is no documentary evidence for events predating the arrival of Europeans.

Vennum cites only three examples of lacrosse as a direct substitute for warfare as a means of settling a dispute between two nations, and they all pertain to Southeastern tribes. In one instance, according to Cherokee oral tradition, "[T]he Cherokee won a huge tract of land in present-day Georgia by beating the Creeks in a ball game."[63] According to another report, "[I]n the early 1790s an argument between the Creeks and the Choctaws over rights to a large beaver pond in what is now Noxubee County, Mississippi, was supposed to be settled by a lacrosse game, although the outcome was contested and bloody fighting erupted . . . five hundred were dead by the next day."[64] A similar outcome occurred in this contest; "Another Creek-Choctaw game over territory between the Tombigbee and Black Warrior Rivers likewise ended in a battle."[65]

In two of the cases cited by Vennum, lacrosse failed as an alternative to actual fighting. And those are the cases for which documentary evidence exists. Only in the episode based on an oral tradition does lacrosse appear to have been successfully substituted for war in resolving a territorial dispute.

BOWL GAME REVISITED AND SNOW SNAKE

The spiritual underpinnings of lacrosse also applied to the bowl game, which was considered sacred because its outcome was directly determined by the battle between the spirit forces summoned on behalf of each village—or, in the case of an intravillage game, on behalf of each moiety. This explains why the bowl game was played to cure the sick or prevent illness. The bowl game—like lacrosse—was an exercise in alliance building—within and between each village or moiety and the spirit beings enlisted on its side.

Alliance building for the bowl game assumed many of the forms associated with lacrosse. Village or moiety wagered against its counterpart, and various rituals, such as tobacco sacrifices, fasting, and sexual abstinence, were employed to invoke the assistance of spirit persons. Medicine men practiced "bowl-game shamanism" on

Snow snake and snow snake head (originally published by Morgan in 1851). At mid-nineteenth century, Seneca snow snakes were 7 feet long, 1 inch wide, and ¹/₄ inch thick—like a very long, narrow cross-country ski. Snow snakes used by the Allegany Senecas at the turn of the nineteenth century were probably quite similar. DARLINGTON LIBRARY, UNIVERSITY OF PITTSBURGH.

behalf of their village or client moiety, much like they did in the case of lacrosse. The shaman, or a patient prompted by a dream, called for the game as a curative or preventive measure. Shamans also supervised the ritual preparations and used all their occult powers to influence the outcome of the game.

Unlike lacrosse, however, the bowl game allowed no room—or certainly very little room—for human skill or talent. Some bowl game players were recognized as luckier than most, but their good fortune was attributed to the fact that they were able to summon more powerful spiritual allies. The outcome of each throw in the bowl game was solely the result of the contending supernatural alliances forged by the two sides. In this sense, the bowl game was purely spiritual—and sacred. In the early 1800s Handsome Lake added the bowl game, already an ancient religious and curative ritual, to the Midwinter Festival.[66]

The game of snow snake was—and remains—a Seneca favorite. Wooden snakes were launched onto frozen waterways or crusted snow to see how far they would slide. The snake was essentially a long, narrow ski, typically five to seven feet in length, a quarter inch thick, and tapering in width from an inch at the head to a half inch at the tail. "The head was round, turned up slightly, and pointed with lead to increase momentum."[67] To launch his snake, a player made a running leap and thrust the snake forward. After a sihort trajectory, the snake landed on the icy surface and slid onward, traveling a total distance of up to 440 yards. Snow snake was played by teams, with half a dozen or so men on each side. After all the players threw their snakes, the score was tallied. One point was awarded for each snake that had outrun all the snakes of the opposing team.

CHAPTER FIVE

Great Eaters
with Big Bellies

In his entry for March 26, Simmons reported that a contingent from Cornplanter's village had gone to the Buffalo Creek Reservation to collect the Allegany Seneca share of a tribal annuity cash payment. Members of the Seneca nation resident in the United States then received, as a group, cash payments anywhere between $3,000 and $6,000 in annual interest from a $100,000 trust set up as compensation for the sale of the Seneca lands in New York State at the Treaty of Big Tree in 1797. The Senecas had decided to divide and distribute the national annuity cash payment among the reservation communities—Buffalo Creek, Tonawanda, Cattaraugus, and Allegany—in proportion to population. The total population of the Seneca nation living in the states of New York and Pennsylvania was about 1750 persons,[1] of which 362—or about one-fifth—lived along the Allegheny River in Pennsylvania and New York under Cornplanter's supervision.[2] Cornplanter and the Allegany Senecas thus were entitled to about 20 percent of the national annuity payment, amounting roughly to between $600 and $1,200 per year—depending on interest rates. Cornplanter also received a personal annuity of $250 per year that he used to support his own family and to assist members of the Allegany community.

Members of the Six Nations resident in the United States also received, as a group, a yearly stipend of $4,500 from the United States, as promised at the Treaty of Canandaigua in 1794. The stipend was not delivered in cash, however, but in goods and services: clothing, blankets, domestic animals, tools, and payments to craftsmen, such as smiths and millers, who provided services for the Indians. The Senecas had also decided to divide and distribute their portion of these goods and services among their communities on the basis of population.

When the contingent returned from Buffalo Creek with the annuity money, Simmons wrote:

> Cornplanter sent nine of his men to Buffalo to receive their annuity money. They returned in fourteen days with $1,560. They also brought back some goods, which they receive yearly from the British as a favour for the Senecas' adherence to the British side during the war between the British and Americans. . . . A few days after the men returned, the money and goods were divided.

In September 1796, a full year before the Senecas sold their lands at the Treaty of Big Tree, Red Jacket voiced a premonition that the Senecas were about to lose their lands: "We are much disturbed in our dreams about the great Eater with a big Belly endeavoring to devour our lands. We are afraid of him, believe him to be a conjurer, and that he will be too cunning and hard for us, therefore request Congress will not license or suffer him to purchase our lands."[3] Robert Morris, the subject of Red Jacket's disturbing dream, did possess a voracious appetite for land. Morris, who had won renown as the "financier of the American Revolution" but had for some time been speculating wildly in frontier land schemes, held the preemption rights to 4 million acres of Seneca territory. And, within a year of Red Jacket's premonition, Morris together with the Holland Land Company (HLC) did indeed dispossess the Senecas of 3.8 million acres.

Red Jacket's unflattering but accurate description of the corpulent Morris served as an apt metaphor for many European-American individuals and institutions who hungered for Indian land. No matter how much land the Indians relinquished, European Americans always wanted more. Red Jacket reportedly told the following story—or variations of it—on several occasions. An Indian was sitting alone on a large log. A white man walked up and asked for a place to sit down, just a single seat—for himself. There was plenty of room on the log, so the Indian slid over, making a space for him to sit down. Soon another white man came along with an identical request, and then another, and another. Still others came, and all asked only for a single seat, just for themselves. And each time, the Indian slid along the log just far enough to allow one more seat; until he was eventually pushed off the log.[4]

The alienation of the Seneca people from their own lands was a complex process that climaxed, but did not end, at the Treaty of Big Tree in September 1797. In the years and decades following that treaty, European Americans continued to gnaw at the 200,000 acres the Senecas had held onto at Big Tree. All subsequent Seneca land cessions, however, pale in comparison to the scope of the 3.8 million acres sold at Big Tree.

The road to Big Tree stretched back to the 1500s and the eastern shores of North America when American Indians and Europeans first came into contact. We will trace the road to Big Tree, however, from Fort Stanwix, located near present-day Rome, New York, where in 1768 the Six Nations signed a treaty with the British Crown that was supposed to firmly establish a fixed boundary between native and colonial territories.

FIRST TREATY OF FORT STANWIX, 1768

The idea of an official boundary between colonial and native territories was not new; it had inspired the Proclamation of 1763, which established such a boundary along the crest of the Appalachian Mountain chain. The British ministers in London who drew the Proclamation Line intended, in part, that it reassure the Indians who had participated in Pontiac's Uprising that the Crown would protect their lands from further encroachment by the colonists. Transacted seven years before the outbreak of the American Revolution, the first Treaty of Fort Stanwix was an attempt by the

British and the Six Nations to preserve the principle of a fixed boundary between colonist and Indian. Adjustment was necessary because, although the crest of the Appalachian Mountain chain had provided the British ministers with a conveniently defined boundary, that boundary did not entirely conform to political and demographic realities on the ground—even when it was first drawn.[5]

The 1763 line, for example, ran to the west of the still-occupied Oneida and Tuscarora homelands, placing them on the wrong side and exposing them to white encroachment. Conversely, the line ran to the east of white settlements—some of which were twenty years old—in the New and Greenbriar River Valleys, in present-day southwestern Virginia and southern West Virginia.[6] Located on the western slopes of the Appalachians, these settlements were not abandoned after 1763. They remained as a dagger pointed at the heart of a vast, unoccupied territory in present-day Kentucky and Tennessee. This area had become depopulated of Indian inhabitants during many generations of warfare between Northern and Southern tribes. Used only as a hunting ground by the Shawnees and the Cherokees, this virtually empty no-man's-land beckoned to land-hungry colonists, its vulnerability enticing them to step through the door left open at New River.[7]

To make matters worse, the line had been seriously breached within a few years of its being drawn. By the end of 1766 hundreds of illegal squatters had crossed the mountain barrier, following two military roads through the wilderness—Braddock's Road from Virginia and Forbes's Road from Pennsylvania. British troops from the garrison at Fort Pitt repeatedly evicted the squatters, who repeatedly returned.[8] The existence of Fort Pitt—terminus of Braddock's and Forbes's Roads—was ironically the single most important factor in facilitating this breach of the 1763 line. Nothing short of shifting the boundary westward to or beyond Fort Pitt could even begin to restore the integrity of the line.

By 1768 the original imperfections—plus the more recent breaches—in the Proclamation Line cried out for correction. To leave them unattended any longer was to invite the outbreak of a new Indian war.[9] Early in 1768 the British ministry authorized its two Indian superintendents in North America to negotiate adjustments to the boundary line. Sir William Johnson, superintendent for the Northern Department, was to negotiate adjustments where the line ran through New York, Pennsylvania, and Virginia. John Stuart, Johnson's Southern counterpart, was to negotiate adjustments where the line ran through the Carolinas and Georgia.[10] The Indians of New England had long since been subjugated and dispossessed of their national lands.

In April of 1768 Johnson sent invitations to the chiefs and sachems of the Six Nations to attend a formal treaty, to be held that autumn on the deserted grounds of Fort Stanwix. Johnson also invited the Delawares and the Shawnees, but only as observers. Negotiations got underway in late October and the treaty was signed on November 5, 1768.[11]

At this first Treaty of Fort Stanwix, the British and the Six Nations agreed on a continuous boundary line between Indian and colonial territory that ran southwest from a point near Fort Stanwix in present-day central New York State to present-day Kentucky. To the north, the boundary was moved eastward, placing the Oneida and

Sir William Johnson (1715–74),
Britain's superintendent of Indian
affairs for the Northern Department.
Portrait by John Wollaston, Jr., 1750.
ALBANY INSTITUTE OF HISTORY AND ART.

Tuscarora homelands back on the Indian side of the line. To the south, the boundary was moved westward—all the way to the mouth of the present-day Tennessee River, at that time called the Cherokee River. This was at least 300 miles farther west than would have been necessary to accommodate the settlements in the New and Greenbriar River Valleys. The Six Nations did not just accept this outlandish adjustment, they had proposed it to Johnson in the first place—in 1765.[12]

The Six Nations wanted the boundary to shift more and more to the west as it ran south from Fort Stanwix. They believed that this would protect their New York homelands and their lands in Pennsylvania by channeling white migration southwestward into Kentucky.[13]

The Six Nations also wanted to punish the Shawnees and the Delawares for failing to obey Iroquois orders to cease and desist from hostilities against British troops and colonial settlers during the French and Indian War and again during Pontiac's Uprising. By selling the lands in West Virginia and Kentucky, the Six Nations "proved"—by a perverse kind of logic—that the lands were theirs to cede, and, thereby, demonstrated their authority over the Delawares and the Shawnees.[14] Because their claims in Kentucky were likely to entangle them in a war with expansionist Virginia, the Six Nations were happy to jettison the troublesome claims and shift to their British allies all the responsibility for keeping peace and order in Kentucky.[15]

At the 1768 treaty Johnson accepted the three-year-old Iroquois offer, even though in so doing he ignored instructions from his superiors in London.[16] The British ministry wanted to limit the westward shift in the boundary to no farther than the mouth of the Kanawha River, at present-day Point Pleasant, West Virginia, about a hundred miles to the west of the 1763 Proclamation Line.[17] There it would join with the boundary being negotiated by Stuart to form a continuous line running from central New York to southern Georgia.

Johnson wanted to open the lands in present-day West Virginia and Kentucky to settlement. He believed that some Indian land somewhere would have to be opened to the designs of land companies and would-be settlers—just to take the pressure off the rest of the line.[18] Moreover, he had close ties to the land companies that had formed to lobby for westward adjustment of the line and to petition the Crown for charters to Western lands.[19] Some historians have suggested that Johnson violated

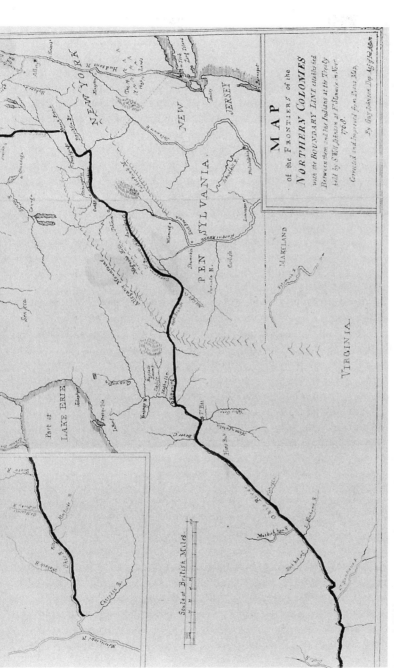

Map of 1768 Treaty Line (from The Papers of Sir William Johnson, vol. 6, between pp. 450 and 451). In addition to restoring the Oneida and Tuscarora homelands to the Indian side of the boundary, the line drawn in 1768 ran along the Ohio River far to the southwest, all the way to the mouth of the Cherokee (present-day Tennessee) River. This opened the lands in present-day West Virginia and Kentucky to settlement and had the temporary effect of channeling the tide of European-American westward migration to the south, bypassing the Iroquois homelands and the Ohio country. NEW YORK STATE LIBRARY.

his orders and accepted the Iroquois cession of Kentucky specifically to satisfy the needs of certain Virginia land speculators.[20]

In agreeing to the 1768 boundary adjustment, the Six Nations relinquished their claims to northeastern and southwestern Pennsylvania, present-day West Virginia, and Kentucky. Although significant, the cession of southwestern Pennsylvania and West Virginia was more a recognition of the *status quo* than the surrender of securely held territory. British strongholds at Fort Loyalhanna, present-day Ligonier, and Fort Pitt, present-day Pittsburgh, represented too much of a military inroad by European Americans for the Iroquois to exercise control over that region. The bastion at Fort Pitt, which commanded the forks of the Ohio River and had withstood a six-week-long siege during Pontiac's Uprising, stood athwart the lines of communication to West Virginia, effectively removing that territory from Iroquois influence. Besides, the valleys of the Monongahela River and its tributaries in southwestern Pennsylvania and West Virginia were already infested by hordes of illegal squatters, and British troops had proved singularly ineffective at keeping them out.[21]

As for the cession of northeastern Pennsylvania, the Six Nations had already sold that land to the Susquehanna Company—a Connecticut land company—in 1754.[22] So, in this case, the Iroquois did not give up anything they had not already given up before. Connecticut settlers had begun moving into the Wyoming Valley of present-day northeastern Pennsylvania in 1762. In ceding the same land to Pennsylvania in 1768, the Iroquois set the stage for conflicting colonial claims.

The Penn family had prevailed upon Johnson to obtain for them a cession of land between the upper Delaware River and the west branch of the Susquehanna River, including the Wyoming Valley. This would establish a counter claim to Connecticut's. In return for Johnson's assistance, Thomas Penn used his influence in London to help the superintendent secure a patent of his own to an 80,000-acre tract north of the Mohawk River in New York.[23]

In 1769 armed conflict broke out in northeastern Pennsylvania between people from that colony, called Pennamites, and settlers from Connecticut, called Yankees. Combat continued sporadically for three years and then erupted again in 1775, continuing until halted by the American Revolution. While the settlers were busy fighting one another, pressure from that quarter on the Iroquois frontier was greatly reduced. The final installment in this series of miniature civil wars—known as the Yankee-Pennamite Wars—came too late (1783–84) to help the Six Nations with their tactical situation.[24]

As far as the lands in Kentucky were concerned, the Six Nations had never exercised anything like true hegemony over those distant territories, having never done more than periodically traverse them with war parties on their way to raid the Iroquois' traditional Southern Indian enemies, such as the Cherokees and the Catawbas. The Six Nations' claim to Kentucky was highly dubious, especially in the opinion of other American Indians.[25]

In exchange for degraded and doubtful claims to distant territories, the Six Nations received for the cessions south of the Ohio River more than 10,000 British pounds in cash and goods from the Crown, and for the cessions in Pennsylvania 10,000 Spanish dollars from the Penns.[26]

The land claims retained by the Six Nations at the first Treaty of Fort Stanwix were as significant as the claims they relinquished. The Six Nations retained their claim to parts of Pennsylvania. They even retained some rather tenuous claims to lands in present-day Ohio. The Iroquois based their claims to all these territories on the right of conquest.

The Iroquois claimed the territory in northwestern and north-central Pennsylvania based on their extirpation of the Erie Indians in 1656 and their subjugation—supposedly by military conquest—of the Susquehannock Indians in 1675. Their claim to northwestern Pennsylvania overlapped somewhat with their claim to the Ohio Country, which included the watersheds of western Pennsylvania, present-day northern West Virginia, and present-day Ohio.[27] The Iroquois based their claims in the Ohio Country on a series of military expeditions against other Indians during the second half of the 1600s. Although these expeditions ranged as far west as the Mississippi River, an alliance of French and Indians had, by the end of the 1600s, driven the Iroquois from all territory west of present-day Cleveland, Ohio.[28]

During the 1720s the Six Nations allowed displaced tribes such as the Delawares and the Shawnees to settle in western Pennsylvania and Ohio. During the 1740s another refugee tribe, the Wyandots, a remnant of the Huron nation that the Iroquois had decimated and scattered in 1649,[29] relocated to the area around present-day Sandusky, Ohio.[30] After 1740 significant numbers of New York Iroquois began migrating to the Ohio Country.[31] The Iroquois who settled in Ohio drifted out of close association with the Six Nations of New York and gradually took on a new identity, becoming known as the Mingos.[32]

Although the non-Iroquois tribes in western Pennsylvania ostensibly deferred to the Six Nations in all matters of policy, the Indians living in Ohio, including the Mingos, exhibited considerable independence and asserted their own rights to the lands on which they lived and hunted. By the 1760s the Ohio Indians had come to look on the Six Nations of New York less as arbiters of policy and more as intermediaries in dealings with British imperial and American colonial powers.[33]

The territorial integrity of Iroquois homelands was significantly improved by the first Treaty of Fort Stanwix. Prior to that treaty, the extent of Iroquois homelands had been diminished somewhat, but the losses had been limited to the Mohawk River Valley, where the Mohawk nation had been hemmed into two "castles," Canajoharie and Tiononderoga, neither of which included much land.[34]

Mohawk confinement within these close quarters had not been the result of military defeat, but rather of the incremental encroachment that inevitably occurred as the settlements of friendly European-American pioneers crept ever closer. By 1768 European Americans had been nibbling at the homelands of the Mohawks—easternmost of the Six Nations—for more than a century. The Mohawks still retained some territory north of the Mohawk River Valley, along Kayaderosseras Creek in present-day Saratoga County, New York, where they could hunt. Even this last reserve, however, was the target of Albany land speculators who had been trying for over half a century to gain recognition for a fraudulent title to a vast tract of several hundred thousand acres, which encompassed the Kayaderosseras hunting grounds.[35] The treaty specifically guaranteed to the Mohawks the security of the little land they still possessed east of the new boundary line.

The tribes living on or hunting in the ceded lands in southwestern Pennsylvania and West Virginia, such as the Delawares and the Shawnees, viewed the 1768 treaty as a sellout. They received no share of the payments; the Six Nations kept it all. The Ohio Shawnees were particularly incensed because Kentucky was their favorite hunting ground.[36]

Despite their considerable diplomatic and political successes at first Stanwix, the Six Nations still labored under a deteriorating strategic situation. British—not Iroquois—power lay behind the Iroquois achievements. For their own reasons, the British propped up the Six Nations in several ways: economically through preferential trade arrangements and generous gifts, politically by making the Iroquois their closest Indian ally, diplomatically by treating the Iroquois as the first-ranking Indian nation and dealing through them with other nations, and legally by protecting Iroquois homelands from colonial encroachment. If the British had remained in control, the subsequent history of the Iroquois would doubtless have been different. As it was, the American Revolution was about to split the Six Nations apart and knock all British props from under the New York Iroquois.

IROQUOIS AND THE AMERICAN REVOLUTION

The American Revolution was just as much a seminal event in Iroquois history as in American. For the Iroquois, it marked the dissolution of their ancient political confederacy and the death of national independence. To Americans, at least to white Americans, the Revolution bequeathed a legacy of self-determination and the promise of prosperity. To the Iroquois, it brought civil war and destitution. The war and its aftermath completely shattered the political confederacy known as the Six Nations. Just as patriots fought loyalists, so did pro-American Oneidas fight pro-British Mohawks. As a result of the war, thousands of Iroquois emigrated from New York to Canada, where they set upon a political course separate from that of their brethren who remained in the United States. Those who remained behind in New York were reduced to the status of "dependent" nations, dispossessed of all—or all but a fraction—of their ancestral lands, and confined to reservations. They were among the first American Indians to endure the process of being forced to recognize the political sovereignty of the United States and to accept the reservation system.

During the years 1775 and 1776, as rebellious Americans on one side and British troops and loyalist partisans on the other squared off against each other and got down to the deadly serious business of war, both sides courted the Six Nations, who had adopted a neutral stance.[37]

From the first, the British sought to enlist the Six Nations and other Indians.[38] They had immediate need of the Indians as auxiliary forces, especially in light of the American invasion of Canada during the autumn and winter of 1775. The British had fewer than 800 regular troops available to defend Canada against an American army of more than 2,000 men.[39] And, indeed, the British did find Canadian Indians who could be persuaded to take up arms in the king's cause—especially among the predominantly Mohawk residents of Caughnawaga.[40]

British Indian superintendent Guy Johnson[41] also recruited a few hundred Iroquois warriors in New York and led them into Canada. But these loyalist—or Tory—warriors, both those from Canada and those from New York, fought only in Canada and only to repel the American invasion.[42] Throughout 1775 and 1776, the number of Indians fighting—even in Canada—was not large, never amounting to more than a few hundred warriors.[43] Not until the middle of 1777 did the British have any real success in swaying the Six Nations away from their neutral stance.

Iroquois reluctance to get involved in the war stemmed from their perception of their own best interests. They inclined naturally toward the British side because British authority had so often interposed itself between them and the land-grabbing colonists. The Mohawks—already hemmed in closely on all sides by colonists—had good reason to hope for a British victory and continued royal protection against white encroachment.[44] Most of the other Iroquois nations appreciated this royal protection too, especially as it had manifested itself in the Proclamation Line of 1763 and the Treaty Line of 1768.

But even the Mohawks calculated that it made more sense to let the British do the fighting. Besides, there was always the outside chance—British assertions to the contrary—that the Americans might win. By staying out of the war the Indians had little to lose. By entering the war on the British side, they had little to gain, other than American enmity, and much to lose—if the Americans won.[45]

The Oneidas and the Tuscaroras stood as exceptions to the general Iroquois inclination toward the British. These two nations had come under the strong influence of Samuel Kirkland, a Presbyterian missionary, who eventually prevailed upon them to take up arms on the American side.[46] But initially the Oneidas and the Tuscaroras were just as determined as the rest of the Six Nations to remain neutral.[47] In 1775 the Oneidas put their position this way: "We are unwilling to join on either side . . . for we love you both—old England and new. Should the great King of England apply to us for our aid—we shall deny him—and should the Colonies apply—we shall refuse."[48]

In general, non-Iroquois Indian nations followed the neutral example set by the Six Nations and adopted a wait-and-see attitude. But, if the Six Nations decided to enter the war, most other Indian nations would be right behind them—particularly the "Western" tribes: the Shawnees, the Delawares, the Wyandots, and the Mingos of the Ohio Country.[49]

With neutralist sentiment running so strong in 1775, one might wonder how it came to pass that by the middle of 1777 most of the Six Nations had taken up arms either on the side of the British, in the case of the Senecas, the Cayugas, the Onondagas, and the Mohawks or on the side of the Americans, in the case of the Oneidas and the Tuscaroras. One might also wonder how it came to pass that Senecas and Mohawks were killing and being killed by Oneidas and Tuscaroras. There were a number of reasons for this tragic turn of events.

The strategic location of the Iroquois homelands athwart major routes between the Hudson River Valley and Lake Ontario and Upper Canada ensured that sooner or later a European-American army would march through Iroquoia. When that finally happened, each of the opposing European-American foes would demand that the Iroquois join its side and treat any neutrals as enemies, forcing the Iroquois to choose.[50]

The Americans, in contrast with the British, initially urged neutrality upon the Six Nations. American leaders such as Philip Schuyler seemed to sense that if the Iroquois entered the war, most of them would take the British side.[51] The Americans also seemed to understand that if the Six Nations joined the fight, the floodgates would be thrown open to widespread participation in the war by many Indian nations—and mostly on the British side.[52] But these realizations did not keep the Americans from making a series of mistakes that steadily alienated most of the Iroquois.

For example, at a treaty conference at Albany, New York, in August 1775, the Iroquois pledged to remain neutral and in return the Americans promised to respect Iroquois neutrality and not to make any demands for support. Yet, the Americans turned around and seized Oswego, a small port and trading post on the southeastern shore of Lake Ontario and definitely within Iroquois country.[53] In January 1776 American general Philip Schuyler marched 3,000 New York militiamen into Iroquois country to intimidate loyalists and disarm a well-known Tory leader—John Johnson, son of the deceased Indian superintendent Sir William Johnson. In May Schuyler sent 300 men back into Iroquois country to capture Johnson, who nevertheless escaped to Canada.[54]

The Iroquois viewed both of these incursions as violations of the Albany neutrality agreement, which became so tattered by August that another round of treaty negotiations was held—this time at the German Flats, along the Mohawk River near present-day Herkimer, New York. The Iroquois again pledged neutrality and the Americans again promised to respect it.[55] Yet, within a month the Americans had occupied old, moldering Fort Stanwix—abandoned by the British a decade earlier and, once again, definitely in Iroquois country. The Americans began to rebuild the fort and the only thing that quieted Iroquois outrage was the opening there of a trading post.[56] The war had already badly disrupted trade and the Iroquois would have greeted any new trading venue with relief. The problem was that the Americans provided too few goods to trade.[57]

The most serious American mistake was not supplying the Iroquois with the trade goods and gifts upon which, under the British regime, the Iroquois had come to depend. Iroquois loyalty ran in the direction of trading partners. If the Americans would not or could not meet the Iroquois need for trade and presents, the Iroquois would turn to the more cooperative British. The Americans did practice some gift giving,[58] but they were not willing or able to match the munificence of the British.[59]

British diplomacy, therefore, seized upon these American failures. British negotiators such as Maj. John Butler continually plied the Iroquois with gifts, rum, and dogged solicitations to "take up the hatchet" on behalf of the king.[60] Butler was not an exceptionally shrewd or subtle negotiator; but he was crafty and not above resorting to trickery. What he lacked in finesse, he made up for in persistence—and in his lavishly generous gift giving.[61]

Joseph Brant—a Mohawk chief—served as a veritable agent provocateur in the British interest. He spent the entire year from July 1776 through July 1777 traveling through Iroquoia, jawboning any receptive warrior. If the untrustworthy Americans won, he argued, the Iroquois would lose their lands, whereas the British could be trusted to protect the Iroquois landholding. The Iroquois had an ancient covenant with the king, to whom they owed their allegiance. Brant had tremendous influence among the Mohawks. In the spring of 1777 he began recruiting and organizing Indian auxiliary units that would be ready to assist British forces under Gen. Barry St. Leger when they assaulted Fort Stanwix and then thrust down the Mohawk River Valley to Albany, to effect a juncture with Gen. John Burgoyne's army, which was to strike from Canada via the Lake Champlain route.[62]

St. Leger's expedition against Fort Stanwix and the Mohawk River Valley was the fateful march of a European-American army through Iroquoia that finally forced the Six Nations to choose sides. Once the St. Leger and Burgoyne campaigns were in motion, Iroquois entry into the war was inevitable. The only question was which side to take.

The influence of Presbyterian missionary Samuel Kirkland over the Oneidas and the Tuscaroras exacerbated the factionalism that would soon rive the Six Nations with fratricidal strife. Kirkland was virtually an American agent: He collected intelligence; he passed information from Congress and committees of safety to the Oneidas and the Tuscaroras; and he advised Congress and General Schuyler on how best to court the two tribes.[63]

The warriors and war chiefs finally slipped the institutional reins that had traditionally restrained their ability to take to the war path.[64] The institutional constraints consisted of the prestige and influence of the league sachems and other civil chiefs, and of the clan mothers and lineage matrons. The fifty league sachems were the highest-ranking civil chieftains and constituted the grand council of the Iroquois League. The main purpose of the league was to keep peace among the Six Nations, but it also played a role in maintaining peace in general with external entities, such as non-Iroquois Indian nations and European-American states. The lower-ranking civil chiefs acted in like fashion when war tensions were high. The matrons, one at the head of each lineage, and the clan mothers, one at the head of each clan, also usually urged peace in times of crisis.

Joseph Brant (1742–1807), pro-British Mohawk chief. Portrait by Charles Willson Peale, 1797. INDEPENDENCE NATIONAL HISTORICAL PARK, PHILADELPHIA.

In earlier times if these peace advocates determined that war was ill-advised, they had been able to sway the young men away from the war path. A war chief would find it very difficult to organize a war party in the face of determined opposition from the "institutional" peace advocates. But over the course of the seventeenth and eighteenth centuries, the prestige and influence of the peace advocates had been steadily eclipsed by the rising power and authority of war chiefs.

The Iroquois had always turned to outstanding warriors in emergencies when an external enemy posed a clear and present danger to the nation and when peace was not a current option. But, in the past, as soon as the fighting had ended, the influence of the war chiefs waned. The problem was that for almost two centuries—ever since the advent of Europeans on the St. Lawrence and Hudson Rivers—the Iroquois had been caught up in an ever-intensifying storm of violence and warfare: over a dozen trade wars with other Indian nations, four major imperial contests between Britain and France,[65] interminable border warfare with European-American frontiersmen, and now a war of rebellion by European Americans against Europeans, which was also a civil war between American loyalists and American patriots. The increased incidence of warfare allowed war chiefs to consolidate their influence.[66] The voices of the peace advocates were gradually drowned out by those of war hawks, such as Joseph Brant.[67]

An Onondaga spokesman described the situation this way: "Times are altered with us Indians. Formerly the warriors were governed by the wisdom of their uncles the Sachems but now they take their own way and dispose of themselves without consulting the Sachems."[68]

In January 1777 an event occurred that represented the final act in the long process by which civil authorities lost control over the warriors and war chiefs. An outbreak of illness at Onondaga, where the council fire of the Iroquois League had burned from time immemorial, resulted in the deaths of several league sachems. The league council fire was extinguished until the sachems could be replaced. The voices in the middle that spoke for peace and neutrality were silenced at a critical moment. Meanwhile, the war hawks on both sides continued to agitate and to recruit followers.[69]

During July large elements of the pro-British nations formally "took up the hatchet" against the Americans—thanks largely to Maj. John Butler and to Joseph Brant.[70] Almost immediately, pro-British and pro-American factions found themselves fighting each other in the bloody battle of Oriskany. An Iroquois civil war had begun.[71] The Six Nations were now divided; the ancient League of the Iroquois was torn asunder.

Gen. James Clinton (1732–1812). New York State Library.

The Iroquois—the pro-British nations in particular—eschewed participation in pitched battles, preferring instead to conduct lightning raids deep into enemy territory. They unleashed a remarkably effective campaign of economic disruption and psychological intimidation that devastated not just the New York and Pennsylvania frontiers, but also agricultural hinterland regions throughout present-day central New York State and northeastern Pennsylvania. Their hit-and-run tactics allowed the Iroquois to desolate a wide area by burning houses, barns, and crops; by slaughtering livestock; by destroying the economic infrastructure such as sawmills, gristmills, and blacksmith forges; and by turning the European-American farming population into a mass of refugees who either sought safety in the closest fort or fled east. The Iroquois and Tory raiders effectively paralyzed the local militias, kept them "forted up," ambushed them whenever they sallied forth, and prevented them from mobilizing to help in campaigns farther to the east.

Indeed it was precisely the effectiveness of Iroquois guerrilla warfare during 1777 and 1778 that prompted the American commander in chief, Gen. George Washington, to make an attack on the Iroquois homelands the main element of his military campaign for 1779. The Iroquois strategy had seriously hurt the American war effort.[72] Historian Barbara Graymont summed up the significance of Indian-Tory depredation of the American frontier this way: "[T]he economy was being seriously disrupted. . . . Burned barns and ruined crops meant less food for both the populace and the Continental army. New York had frequently been unable to meet its quota for provisions on this account. . . . Governor [George] Clinton warned that soon New York's western frontier would be the Hudson River."[73]

Washington's plan called for a three-pronged attack on the homelands of the hostile Iroquois nations that would inflict on them the same kind of punishment they had been visiting upon the Americans. Before Washington's plan was put into motion, however, a gratuitous and, in fact, counterproductive stroke was aimed at some neutralist Onondaga villages. In April 1779 a force of 500 men under Col. Gose Van Schaick razed three Onondaga villages during a brief sortie, which drove the formerly neutralist Onondagas firmly and finally into the British camp.[74]

The first stage of Washington's 1779 plan got under way in mid-August, when Gen. James Clinton (brother of the New York governor, George Clinton) and 1,600 men floated down the Susquehanna River from Otsego Lake in New York State, burning three Tuscarora towns along the way. The Indians themselves fired two other villages, rather than allow the Americans the satisfaction of doing it.[75] The main effect of the Clinton expedition was felt when it linked up with Gen. John Sullivan's army at Tioga, present-day Athens, Pennsylvania. Sullivan had initiated the second stage of Washington's plan by moving up the Susquehanna River from Wyoming, present-day Wilkes-Barre, Pennsylvania, and destroying the Indian village of Chemung, located on the lower Chemung River, near Tioga. The combined Clinton-Sullivan force, under Sullivan's command, amounted to 5,000 officers and men.

Sullivan had been slow in getting his campaign off to a start. He had not even entered the Iroquois country until the end of August. The Iroquois had not been idle. Sullivan's delay had given them five months of good fighting weather in which to terrorize the frontiers of New York and Pennsylvania. Ironically, when Sullivan's blow finally fell, the Iroquois were not prepared to mount an effective resistance. No longer believing that Sullivan would strike, the Iroquois were scattered in dozens of war parties across hundreds of miles. Only 500 Iroquois warriors and 250 Tory rangers could be gathered to meet the vastly superior American force at the Battle of Newtown, on the Chemung River, near present-day Elmira, New York, in late August 1779. Sullivan's army overwhelmed the Iroquois and then went on to ravage the Iroquois homelands in the Western Finger Lakes district and the Genesee River Valley.

Sullivan's troops marched into Iroquois country from the southeast and destroyed "all of the surviving Indian towns on the Susquehanna River and its tributaries, all the main Cayuga settlements, and most of the Seneca towns."[76] The Americans imitated Iroquois tactics of burning every structure and all caches of food and of destroying field crops and livestock. They inflicted few casualties, however, because Iroquois villagers simply fled before the army's slow advance. The Iroquois retreated west of the Genesee River to regroup. But the Americans turned around at the Genesee in mid-September and retraced their steps, destroying whatever they had missed on their outbound march.

Just as Sullivan's army was leaving Eastern Iroquoia, the third prong of Washington's plan, a force of 600 men under Col. Daniel Brodhead, moved into Western Iroquoia from Pittsburgh. Brodhead's expedition razed Iroquois towns and crops on the upper Allegheny River in present-day northwest Pennsylvania and southwest New York state, including Jenuchshadago—future site of Cornplanter's village.[77]

Gen. John Sullivan (1740–95). Painting attributed to Richard Morell Staigg, 1876. INDEPENDENCE NATIONAL HISTORICAL PARK, PHILADELPHIA.

During the winter of 1779 to 1780 the Iroquois warriors and their families reassembled under the protection of the British fort at Niagara. There they had access to arms and ammunition and to a strained supply of other provisions, including food and clothing.

From a military perspective, the American campaign of 1779 was not very successful. It failed to knock the Iroquois out of the war and had the effect of attaching them even more firmly to the British, upon whom they became almost completely dependent for supplies. The Clinton, Sullivan, and Brodhead invasions did not even relieve the pressure on the frontiers and exposed districts of New York and Pennsylvania. While their women and children sheltered at Niagara throughout 1780, Iroquois warriors returned to the frontiers and hinterlands of New York and Pennsylvania, where they wreaked havoc.[78] The Iroquois maintained the intensity of their offensive in 1781.[79] And they would have continued the battle in 1782, if their British allies had not restrained them and urged them to conduct only defensive operations.[80] British general Charles Cornwallis had surrendered his army at Yorktown in October of 1781, effectively ending the British military effort to suppress the American rebellion. Cornwallis's defeat brought about the collapse of the wartime ministry in London. In the spring of 1782 a new ministry opened peace talks in Paris with the Americans and with the French, who had entered the war on America's side in 1778. These talks produced the Treaty of Paris, signed September 9, 1783, by which Britain formally recognized the independence of the United States. The American negotiators won an astounding concession from Britain—the United States would extend westward all the way to the Mississippi River. As historian Randolph Downes put it, "The United States was presented with victory in the shape of new boundaries that included the very lands that the Indians had just successfully defended.[81]

During the treaty negotiations, British peace commissioners completely ignored the status of the Iroquois and all the other Indian as allies of the British. Not only did the British recognize the political sovereignty of the United States south of the Great Lakes and the St. Lawrence River and westward all the way to the Mississippi River, but they left the Iroquois and other Indians to fend for themselves in dealing with the Americans to arrange a cease fire, negotiate a peace treaty, and settle the status of Iroquois lands within the boundaries of the new United States.[82]

In the autumn of 1784 Iroquois leaders came to Fort Stanwix to arrange a formal cessation of hostilities with the United States. The Iroquois delegation consisted of war chiefs and warriors who had come to participate in the customary rites by which warriors on both sides mutually "removed the hatchet from the head" of their former enemy and "buried it forever." They were also prepared to arrange for the release and repatriation of war captives. The American "peace commissioners" came with a very different agenda; they wanted to establish in principle and precedent that the United States had subjugated the Iroquois; and they intended to demand land cessions to prove it.

SECOND TREATY OF FORT STANWIX, 1784

By comparison with the results of the 1768 Treaty of Fort Stanwix, those of the second Treaty of Fort Stanwix represented a precipitate drop in Iroquois fortunes. By this treaty, "negotiated" and signed in October of 1784, the United States and the Six Nations of New York made peace following the American Revolution. For the Iroquois it was a punitive treaty.

The United States forced the Six Nations of New York not only to recognize its political sovereignty but also to renounce their Ohio claims and cede approximately one million acres of Seneca homelands—all without any compensation. The Seneca territory annexed by the United States consisted of the southwest angle of the present-day state of New York, along the southeastern shore of Lake Erie, west of present-day

Buffalo, and of a narrow strip along the east bank of the Niagara River, between Lakes Erie and Ontario.[83] The United States also annexed a thirty-six square-mile tract surrounding the site of Fort Oswego, near present-day Oswego, New York.[84] Furthermore, the United States, by asserting and exercising a "right of conquest," grievously undermined Iroquois "rights to the soil" in those territories in which it "allowed" the Iroquois to remain—on "sufferance." In separate negotiations, also conducted at Fort Stanwix in 1784, the Commonwealth of Pennsylvania pressured the Six Nations into selling all of their remaining lands in northwestern and north-central Pennsylvania, permanently erasing the Iroquois' southern buffer zone.

The United States asserted that the Iroquois and the Ohio Indians were a vanquished people, that in fighting against the United States the Indians had forfeited their rights to the soil, and that the United States could simply take land from the Indians as war reparations without paying for it.[85] At second Stanwix the United States made these assertions stick by unilaterally voiding Iroquois claims to Ohio and taking Seneca homelands without paying for either.

This drop in Iroquois fortunes was not the result of an American victory over the Iroquois on the battlefield. Nor was it really even due to the fact that the Iroquois had fought on the losing side. It was, rather, the result of British failure to look out for the interests of the Crown's Indian allies during peace negotiations with the Americans and of British refusal to participate in or support renewed hostilities in defense of Indian rights. It was, finally, the result of American covetousness of Indian land and vindictiveness over the ravages suffered by the American frontiers and hinterlands at the hands of Iroquois warriors.

Several historians have pointed out that the Iroquois emerged from the Revolutionary War unbroken militarily.[86] Although this is true, it is also irrelevant. Without a guarantee of British support—political, diplomatic, and matériel—the Iroquois could not possibly continue military operations against the United States after the British themselves had withdrawn from the war. The British refused to give the Iroquois such a guarantee. If British matériel assistance and active engagement in the war had not been sufficient to stop the American invasions of 1779, how would matériel support alone be sufficient in the future?[87]

Although the United States had not actually defeated the Iroquois militarily, it certainly had the potential to do so. During the Revolution, the paramount military objective for the United States had been to secure its independence from Great Britain—not to crush the Iroquois. If the United States had deployed its superior resources against the Iroquois, they would have been forced to capitulate or flee their homelands.

The real question is whether the United States, which at that time was still constituted under the feeble Articles of Confederation, could have mustered the political will and discipline to marshal its resources and effectively prosecute an expensive war against the Iroquois, if the Six Nations had refused to sign at second Stanwix. As it turned out, the Six Nations did sign and never militarily contested the terms of second Stanwix.[88] The confederated United States did not need to fight the Iroquois, so we cannot know whether or not it would have found the resolve to do so, had the Iroquois used force to resist.

The federated United States, under the Constitution of 1788, did wage and win a protracted Indian war.[89] In the war for the Old Northwest Territory (from 1790 to 1794), the United States, despite initial military reverses, persisted until success on the battlefield enabled it to pry from the Indians the land cession it wanted at that time. In that case, both the subdued Western Confederates and the lands secured were at a much farther remove from the centers of American power than were the Iroquois people and their homelands.

Given that the strategic balance vis-à-vis the Iroquois was tilted overwhelmingly in favor of the United States at the conclusion of the Revolution, it is not really so surprising that the Iroquois got a raw deal at second Stanwix—despite their status as being militarily unvanquished. Immediately following the treaty and for years afterward, Iroquois leaders—such as Cornplanter—who were parties to second Stanwix, endured bitter criticism from some of their own people.

American demands at second Stanwix were driven by the need for land, which stemmed not just from the yearning of would-be settlers for space, but from the desperate fiscal condition of the new United States government. The national government was in debt to foreign and domestic creditors who had financed the Revolutionary War, and it owed back pay to the former Continental troops and officers who had fought to win American independence. But it had nothing with which to pay either its lenders or its soldiers, except badly depreciated currency.

The Continental currency literally was not worth the paper it was printed on. Some soldiers had been paid, in full or in part, with the worthless Continental script. To placate these soldiers, the government issued them "certificates of depreciation," which could be redeemed for land at a future—unspecified—date. The government thus promised those soldiers that they would receive compensation someday in the form of land.[90]

Individual state governments were in much the same fiscal condition as the confederation government, although their specie-based currencies were generally in better shape. The individual state currencies consisted of, or were backed by, gold or silver coins issued by European nations such as Spain and Britain. The Continental script had been based on nothing but its alleged purchasing power. Land—public land—was to be the salvation of the cash-strapped central and state governments.[91]

Cessions of land were to be extracted as war reparations from those nations and tribes that had sided with the British. Only if absolutely necessary would the Indians be paid anything at all for their lands—and then they would be given no more than a "trifling." The national government could then immediately sell this "public" land to speculators for cash with which to meet its obligations to bankers at home and abroad. The speculators would be, as they had been in colonial times, large land companies that acquired vast tracts—sometimes consisting of millions of acres—at heavily discounted prices. Over time, the land companies sold small parcels to individual settlers; or they sold large subdivisions to other, smaller land companies, who in turn parceled the land to settlers. Always, the land companies strove to make a profit per acre.[92]

The government could also donate lands to the war veterans, who were then free to use the lands themselves or to turn around and sell them, which they usually did—to land speculators. Public lands set aside for remunerating veterans became known as donation lands. Holders of depreciation certificates could redeem them for public lands, which they usually sold to the speculators, who paid in specie—gold or silver coinage. Public lands set aside for redeeming depreciation certificates became known as depreciation lands.[93]

Obviously the land speculators were the principal underwriters for the whole scheme of transforming public lands into government funds and discharged obligations. They were the market makers, creating both the primary market for public lands sold directly by the government and the secondary market for donation and depreciation lands sold by veterans and currency exchangers. The speculators were, arguably, the primary beneficiaries of the transactions in public land, and, as market makers, they wielded enormous influence. Because the land companies snatched up vast territories sight unseen, however, they sometimes found themselves stuck with poor land that was almost impossible to sell. The costs of development—building roads and bridges, constructing store houses, transporting goods and sometimes settlers—also gobbled up profits. Some land companies consequently actually lost money.[94]

To help convert Indian land into "public" land, the United States advanced a theory-of-conquest argument. When the king ceded the territories south of the Great Lakes and east of the Mississippi River, more than just the political sovereignty was transferred to the United States. This was because, in "conquering" the king, the United States had "conquered" the king's Indian allies who inhabited the Trans-Appalachian West.[95] If the Indians of western New York, western Pennsylvania, and present-day Ohio had stood neutral during the conflict with Great Britain, then, when political sovereignty passed to the United States, they would have retained their "rights to the soil"—their ownership of the land. But, because most of the Indians had taken up arms against the United States, they had forfeited their rights to the soil.[96] When the king ceded the Trans-Appalachian West, all of that vast territory thus became public lands of the United States, except for those formerly Indian lands that fell within the recognized boundaries of existing states, such as New York and Pennsylvania, which became public lands of those individual states.

Under the rubric of the conquest theory, the United States expropriated land not only from the Iroquois at second Stanwix in 1784, but from the Delawares and the Wyandots of Ohio at the Treaty of Fort McIntosh, near present-day Beaver, Pennsylvania, in 1785 and from the Shawnees at the Treaty at the Mouth of the Great Miami River, near present-day Cincinnati, Ohio, in 1786. As they had at second Stanwix, negotiators from Pennsylvania followed the United States' commissioners to the treaty grounds at Fort McIntosh. This time the Pennsylvanians prevailed upon the Delawares and the Wyandots to quit their claims to all lands within the boundaries of Pennsylvania. Prior to the Revolution, many tribesmen of these two nations had lived in present-day western Pennsylvania—and a few still did. For their quitclaim, the Delawares and the Wyandots received a quantity of goods amounting to $2,000.[97]

In the case of the McIntosh and Great Miami Treaties, the American strategy of annexing land while imposing peace collapsed into the bloody and protracted war for the Old Northwest Territory. In the case of second Stanwix, the United States succeeded at imposing peace because the Six Nations of New York were well within striking distance of American forces. The fact that 5 million acres of Seneca home-land had not been annexed at second Stanwix also meant that the Senecas still had something significant to lose by taking up arms against the United States. Without Seneca participation, the Six Nations could not be effective militarily.

Several circumstances that arose during the war of the Revolution and its imme-diate aftermath placed the Iroquois in a precarious position and portended an unfa-vorable outcome at second Stanwix. Beyond British neglect of Iroquois interests during peace negotiations with the United States, British unwillingness to do any-thing on behalf of the Indians that might involve the Crown in another war, and American designs on Indian land, were several other circumstances that hinted at a looming diplomatic debacle for the Six Nations.

The end of the war found the Mohawk nation, mostly under the leadership of Joseph Brant, making arrangements for relocation en masse to Canada. The one thing the British were willing to do to counter or offset Iroquois territorial losses in-curred as a result of the failed war against the American rebels was to set aside land in Canada for the use of its displaced Indian allies. Most of the Mohawks settled on the Grand River Reservation in southeastern Ontario, established in October 1784—the same month during which second Stanwix was "negotiated" and signed. In 1783 a small band of Mohawks under the leadership of John Deseronto had settled on the Bay of Quinte, along the north shore of Lake Ontario.[98] The Mohawks at Grand River were joined by groups from the other Iroquois nations—including a small number of Senecas—and by groups from some non-Iroquois nations. Their interests and policies began to diverge from those of the Iroquois who remained in the United States. Iroquois leadership became increasingly fragmented.

Aside from the wartime split between the pro-British and the pro-American na-tions, a rift had opened within the pro-British camp in 1777 between the hawkish Brant and the more neutralist Seneca leaders such as Cornplanter and Old Smoke. The Seneca leadership generally wanted to stay out of the war—though many of the Seneca warriors, persuaded by British gifts and rum, may have been itching to take up the hatchet against the Americans. Brant called the Senecas cowards and it be-came impossible for Cornplanter and Old Smoke to restrain their warriors. After the decision to go to war had been made, Cornplanter and the other Seneca leaders and warriors fought with great skill and bravery.[99]

The rift between Mohawk and Seneca leaders grew wider after the war, as Brant pursued his policies of relying on the British and emigrating to Canada, which al-lowed him to take a more hard-line position on the subject of Iroquois claims to the Ohio country than the Seneca leaders remaining in the United States could afford.

Another crucial circumstance, arising directly from the Sullivan-Clinton-Brod-head expeditions of 1779, was the Seneca, Cayuga, and Onondaga memories of the fact that none of the Western tribes who were so truculent about holding the "Indian-white" boundary line at the Ohio River had been able to help the Iroquois defend their New York homelands against the American invaders. Nor had the British sent more than about 250 Tory rangers to help. No regular British troops had been deployed in defense of Iroquois homelands—even when the British had been at war with the United States. Seneca and other Iroquois leaders remaining within the boundaries of the new United States probably sensed that in any conflict with the Americans, they would be on their own.

Treaty councils were traditionally attended by large numbers of Indians—not just by the chiefs but by hundreds of warriors and women, who came not only to enjoy the continual round of feasting and drinking, but to be able to caucus with their representatives during the negotiations and to prevent the European-American side from trying to overawe or intimidate the Indian negotiators. The interests of factions who were not well represented on the treaty grounds might not receive much consideration during the negotiations.

Second Stanwix was attended by very few delegates from the Western tribes, Wyandots, Delawares, and Shawnees, who refused to participate in any council held farther east than Niagara.[100] Their reasoning seems to have been that locations east of Niagara were too far removed from their geographic power base in the Ohio Country—and from British succor. Perhaps the Western delegates, who congregated at Niagara in early September, could have been prevailed upon to go to Fort Stanwix—if the United States commissioners had arrived sooner than the beginning of October, by which time most of the Westerners, weary of waiting, had gone home for the fall hunt.[101]

Sickness among the displaced Iroquois still bivouacked in the environs of Fort Niagara further reduced the number of Indians who were able to travel to Fort Stanwix and attend the treaty. More than 2,000 Indians had attended first Stanwix in 1768; no more than a few hundred attended second Stanwix.[102] The puny gathering of Indians present on the council grounds as negotiations with the United States began was another circumstance that augured ill for the Iroquois.

The Iroquois had been deliberately deceived by the British about the terms of the November 1782 Preliminary Articles of Peace and were still confused about the impact of the September 1783 Treaty of Paris on the status of Indian lands in British and American eyes. They knew that the king had quit the war and recognized American independence, but they did not realize how completely the British had betrayed Indian interests.[103] Even after British officers in Canada had failed in their effort to conceal the terms of the Preliminary Articles, they continued to assure the Iroquois that the king had ceded only his political sovereignty and not their lands, and to insist that Indian possession of the land was not in doubt.[104] Despite these assurances, the Iroquois voiced continuing suspicions about how they had fared in the British-American settlement. The British reassured them that the Americans would not be so presumptuous as to try to take Indian lands under the pretense of having conquered them.[105]

The Iroquois headmen who came to Fort Stanwix intended only to make peace in the sense of laying down arms. They did not intend, nor were they empowered, to sell land—let alone to cede it. Nor did they intend to recognize the political sovereignty of the United States. Yet, by the conclusion of the treaty, they had accepted dependent-nation status, surrendered some Seneca homelands, and yielded Ohio—all without any compensation except a vague promise on the part of the United States to "order goods to be delivered to the said Six Nations for their use and comfort."[106]

The Six Nations came to Fort Stanwix divided, weak, and uncertain of what the British and Americans had already agreed upon. The tactics to which the Americans subjected them during the council were a masterpiece of intimidation and coercion. When taken together with the overall Iroquois strategic situation and the attendant political and diplomatic circumstances, these tactics explain how the war chiefs were brought to sign on October 22.

The American peace commissioners arrived with an armed detachment of 300 troops at their disposal, a number sufficient to overawe the Indian assemblage and seize hostages.[107] From the beginning to the end of the meeting, the domineering commissioners disdained the Indians. No less a personage than the Marquis de Lafayette rebuked the Indians for their perfidy in opposing the American patriots— champions of liberty and defenders of humanity.[108]

Hearing the 1783 Treaty of Paris read aloud shocked the demoralized Indians. For many of the Indians present, it was the first time they had heard the actual terms of the treaty. The commissioners told the stunned Indians that they were mistaken in supposing themselves to be "a free and independent nation" that could make peace on its own terms. "You are a subdued people; you have been overcome in a war which you entered into with us." The American terms were a take-it-or-leave-it proposition and the commissioners warned the Iroquois that the United States would never offer such "moderate" terms again. They cautioned that, by right of conquest, the United States could simply take all the land of its "vanquished" Iroquois enemies and force them to retire "beyond the Lakes." In a spirit of magnanimity and mercy, however, the United States would—for the time being—refrain from doing so, and, instead, would annex only a comparatively small tract—just a million acres.[109]

The commissioners refused to provide the Indians with a written copy of the American demands. The Iroquois had long ago learned the importance of getting European-American promises and proposals in writing. Even if they themselves could not read, the Indians would find someone who could translate and read for them: an educated Indian, a literate person of mixed blood, a captive adoptee, a trader, or a missionary. The commissioners brushed aside the Iroquois request for a written copy: Certain Indians who knew English and could read might intentionally misrepresent the specifics of the American proposals so as to incite the Indians against the treaty. With this specious argument the commissioners managed to insult Indian veracity and integrity—and to place the Iroquois councilors at a serious disadvantage.[110]

As a pretext for rejecting the Indian proposal, the commissioners invited the Iroquois to propose a boundary line, anticipating the Iroquois desire for a reaffirmation of the 1768 treaty line. The commissioners pounced on the "obstinate" Indians, denounced them for their lack of contrition about the war, and proceeded to dictate the terms of Iroquois capitulation.[111]

Taking some of the Iroquois chiefs hostage was actually an article of the treaty. The troops were to hold the hostages until the Iroquois delivered up all the prisoners and captives they had taken during the war—despite the fact that some captives wanted to remain with the Indians.[112]

Viewed against the backdrop of their fragile strategic position and the perilous political and diplomatic circumstances which the Iroquois faced, it is not surprising that the war chiefs acceded to the unpalatable terms of second Stanwix. As Mohawk chief Aaron Hill reported to the British deputy superintendent at Niagara, asking him not to think too harshly of the chiefs for whatever they might be forced to do at Fort Stanwix: "[T]hey were obliged to comply with whatever the commissioners dictated—that in short they were as prisoners."[113]

The chiefs knew—or believed—that a coerced treaty would never stand. The war chiefs traditionally had not the power to cede or sell Six Nations land. Perhaps they were counting on the grand council of the Six Nations to reject the treaty, thinking that such rejection would render the treaty null and void. If so they were relying on the institutional authority of the very council whose powers they had been steadily usurping. It does seem that in signing, the war chiefs were merely agreeing to lay the treaty before the grand council for ratification. The treaty did stand, despite rejection by the grand council.

The Iroquois war chiefs came to second Stanwix intending only to make peace with the state of New York and, if the American commissioners ever showed up, to arrange a formal cessation of hostilities with the United States. They were also willing to explore a definitive and permanent treaty with the national government. Joseph Brant had explained this in August 1784: "We the war chiefs who go at present are not empowered to conclude a final peace with the United States, but are sent by the Six Nations and the several Western Nations in alliance with them to settle some points necessary to be arranged previous to a more general meeting, which is intended to be held to establish an everlasting peace and friendship between all the [Indian] nations and the United States."[114] The "more general meeting" would no doubt have included some league sachems who would be empowered to make some reasonable land cession as indemnification to the United States. As it was, not a single league sachem signed at second Stanwix.[115]

The sequel to the treaty between the United States and the Six Nations at second Stanwix did further injury to Iroquois interests. That sequel was a separate round of negotiations and a separate treaty between the Commonwealth of Pennsylvania and the Six Nations, by which Pennsylvania extinguished Iroquois claims to the northwestern and north-central portions of that state. For their quitclaim, the Six Nations received a quantity of goods amounting to about $5,000.[116]

The Pennsylvanians timed their negotiation for the day after the American treaty, while the Iroquois were still reeling from the national commissioners' extortionist tactics. In this case, it seems quite possible that the threat posed under the right of conquest theory, as it had just been enunciated and applied by the United States, might have contributed to Iroquois willingness to sell their Pennsylvania lands. If they did not accept Pennsylvania's offer, the state might simply expropriate the land without paying them anything. The chiefs evidently felt that the most they could do was press for more compensation than Pennsylvania was offering. The state did agree to pay $1,000 more—in goods—beyond its original offer of $4,000.[117] Whatever their motivation, the Iroquois sold the last of their Pennsylvania lands at second Stanwix. There were no more Indian national or tribal lands in the entire state; the Cornplanter grant was not made until 1789—and that was a grant of private property to a single individual and his heirs, not to a tribe or nation.

If Pennsylvania's separate treaty was the sequel at second Stanwix, then New York's had been the prelude. In September 1784 the state of New York had held its own treaty at Fort Stanwix with the Six Nations. But that had been before the United States commissioners arrived with their troops; the Iroquois war chiefs had successfully resisted all efforts to extract a land cession. New York, however, would not be frustrated for long—and could not afford to be. In 1783, that state—eager to discharge some of its obligations—had "donated" most of the Cayuga and Onondaga homelands to its veterans before even treating with the Indians, arranging a purchase, or reaching any other kind of agreement. In 1785 the state extracted a cession from the Oneidas and the Tuscaroras of the present-day counties of Chenango, Broome, and Tioga. These nations, ironically, had been American allies during the war. Next were the Onondagas, who ceded most of their land to the state in 1788, followed by the Cayugas in 1790.[118]

By 1784 the claims of the New York Iroquois on Ohio were already in tatters. The Ohio Indians had for decades been asserting their own rights to the soil on which they lived and hunted. The Six Nations had not been able to rein them in during the French and Indian War and Pontiac's Uprising, when the Ohio Indians ignored Iroquois orders to cease and desist from hostilities against British troops and colonial settlers. As if first Stanwix, at which the Six Nations sold the Kentucky hunting grounds out from under the Shawnees, had not itself sufficiently highlighted the divergence of interests between the New York Iroquois and the Ohio Indians, Lord Dunmore's War accentuated those differences even more in 1774.[119] The Six Nations refused to help the Shawnees fight the Virginians in defense of Kentucky and worked to diplomatically isolate the Shawnees from the other Ohio Indians.[120]

In the perception of those New York Iroquois who criticized the war chiefs for having given away too much at second Stanwix, something real was lost in relinquishing the claims of the Six Nations on Ohio: Iroquois preeminence among Indian nations; Iroquois status as power brokers between European Americans and other Indians; and Iroquois standing as the indispensable Indian nation in diplomacy and treaty making. By 1784, however, the station occupied by the Six Nations of New York within the ranks of Indian nations was already much less than exalted. Relinquishment of the New York Iroquois' Ohio claims was simply a recognition and reflection of the fact that the balance of power in the affairs of Ohio had shifted long ago to the inhabitants of Ohio. Once the United States had cleared the Iroquois claims, it could directly attack those of the Wyandots, the Delawares, and the Shawnees, which it did during the negotiations at Fort McIntosh and at the mouth of the Great Miami. The New York Iroquois could afford to relinquish their claims on Ohio, whereas the Ohio Indians could not afford to relinquish theirs. They lived in Ohio and would continue fighting until 1794 to keep their lands.

As bad as the uncompensated cessions of homeland territories made by the Senecas at second Stanwix seemed in 1784, most of that land turned out to be retrievable. Red Jacket and other Seneca chiefs, including Cornplanter, won most of it back in 1794 at the Treaty of Canandaigua, except for the Erie Triangle.[121] The acreage in the southwestern angle of New York restored to the Senecas at Canandaigua was four times greater than that permanently yielded to Pennsylvania in the Erie Triangle. The southern two-thirds of the four-mile-wide strip along the Niagara River was also returned to the Senecas—at Red Jacket's insistence.[122]

Even the potent threat posed by the right-of-conquest theory to the remaining Iroquois homelands was dropped by the United States within a decade of second Stanwix. The long and costly war waged by the Ohio Indians played no small role in convincing the United States that the theory was of limited use, and that its time had come and gone. This development, ironically, redounded more to the benefit of the New York Iroquois—the Senecas in particular—at the Treaty of Canandaigua in 1794 than it did to the Indians of Ohio at the Treaty of Greenville in 1795.

It is easy to overlook what the New York Iroquois did not lose at second Stanwix. The Oneidas, the Tuscaroras, and the Cayugas were all left in possession of substantial tracts of territory, though not for long, and the Senecas still held claim to some 5 million acres in western New York State.[123] The conquest theory posed some threat to these lands for a few years, and it might have contributed to the pressure on the Onondagas and the Cayugas to sell some of their homelands, which they began to do in 1788. But, in view of the fact that the Oneidas and the Tuscaroras, who had been American allies during the war, ceded—under duress—large tracts of their homelands to the state of New York in 1785, it seems that factors other than the conquest theory were responsible for creating the pressures that caused New York Indians to sell their lands.

As for the Mohawks, virtually all of their homelands were gone forever, although this was not a result of second Stanwix. The Mohawks, rather, had been forced to retire from their lands during the fighting in the Revolution—first to the environs of the British fort Niagara and then into Canada. Once New Yorkers began seizing abandoned Mohawk land as war reparations, it became impossible for any treaty to reverse the process and restore to the Mohawks even a fraction of their former homelands.

FROM THE CONQUEST TREATIES TO
FORT HARMAR TO CANANDAIGUA

As much as the Americans craved Indian lands, they also needed peace with the Indian inhabitants of western New York, western Pennsylvania, and present-day Ohio. The "public" lands in that region, which the government hoped to sell, would attract few settlers until the Indians had been pacified, either by negotiating peace with the Indians or by imposing it upon them. In the conquest treaties, the United States attempted both to annex Indian land and to impose peace.[124]

This strategy worked best at second Stanwix partly because the Six Nations of New York were well within the striking distance of massive American armies—as the Sullivan-Clinton-Brodhead forays had shown—and partly because the United States annexed no more than about one sixth of the Seneca homelands. The Senecas were left with about 5 million acres, which they stood to lose by fighting the Americans. Without participation of the Seneca nation—the most populous of the Six Nations, the other Iroquois nations residing within the United States could not hope to resist the United States militarily. During the grand council of the Six Nations of New York held at Buffalo Creek in 1786, the Six Nations repudiated second Stanwix and denied that the war chiefs had been empowered to make any land cessions. But neither the Seneca nation nor any of the other Six Nations of New York resisted second Stanwix militarily, and so the terms of the treaty stood—for ten years.[125]

The McIntosh and Great Miami "conquest treaties" did not hold up nearly so well as second Stanwix. In these cases, the United States attempted to annex a huge amount of territory, extending from the Ohio River westward to the Great Miami River and including much of present-day Ohio. The Delawares and the Wyandots were "given" a reservation in northern Ohio between the Cuyahoga and Maumee Rivers.[126] The Shawnees were "given" a reservation consisting of the northwest corner of Ohio and part of northern Indiana.[127] The main reason that the McIntosh and Great Miami treaties fell apart was that the United States was attempting to extort territory from Indian nations who were beyond the reach of all but the most strenuous efforts that the American military could manage from 1784 to 1794.

The Delaware and Wyandot nations repudiated the Treaty of Fort McIntosh, claiming that the Indian signatories were not recognized representatives of those two nations, but merely a handful of chiefs, most of whom had been drunk, and who had acted on no authority but their own. The Shawnee nation, by 1786 a union of two tribes and the remnants of three others,[128] repudiated the Treaty at the Mouth of the Great Miami because the Shawnee chiefs who signed it represented only a minor portion of the nation.[129] The Shawnees, the Delawares, and the Wyandots did more than repudiate and protest these conquest treaties—they waged war against the United States. From 1786 until 1794 these nations, joined by other tribes of present-day Ohio, Indiana, and Michigan, fought to defend the Ohio River as the boundary between the United States and "Indian country." Until 1794 and General Wayne's victory at Fallen Timbers, the Western Confederates had the best of the fighting.

Although the Iroquois struggle to reverse the concessions wrung from the war chiefs at second Stanwix was diplomatic in nature, the threat of armed resistance—usually implicit but occasionally explicit—underscored Iroquois diplomacy. This threat remained a potent consideration in the calculations of the national government as long as the Western Confederates remained a viable military coalition, which they did until 1794. The national government under the Articles of Confederation and later the federal government under the Constitution were concerned that the Six Nations—the Senecas in particular—might join the Western Confederates on the warpath. This gave the Six Nations some leverage, which was augmented by the federal government's repeated requests that the New York Iroquois act as intermediaries in trying to arrange a peaceful settlement with the Confederates. Between 1789 and 1793 Cornplanter and other Seneca leaders held numerous councils with the Western Confederates, and made several trips to the Maumee and Sandusky Rivers in present-day northwestern Ohio, in order to mediate the dispute between the Ohio Indians and the United States. But by signing second Stanwix and refusing to take up arms against the United States the Senecas and the rest of the New York Iroquois had forfeited the last of their influence with the Ohio Indians, many of whom, such as the Shawnees and the Miamis, remained intransigent until the battle of Fallen Timbers in 1794.[130]

The conquest theory began to unravel almost as soon as the busy "peace commissioners" of the United States had finished "negotiating" the trio of treaties that invoked it. All three treaties, second Stanwix, McIntosh, and Great Miami, were repudiated by their Indian signatories. The ascendancy of the Federalists with the Constitution of 1788 brought a group of men into the federal government who saw nothing but disadvantages in connection with the conquest theory, and who favored an alternative approach to Indian affairs. Three individuals in particular set the new policy: George Washington, who took office as president in 1789; Henry Knox, secretary of war; and Timothy Pickering, commissioner of Indian affairs under Knox.[131]

The views of these three men on Indian affairs did not coincide precisely, but the bases of their policies were similar. Indian wars represented an unnecessary waste of money and blood—including the blood of women and children on both sides. An "enlightened' policy, which would entail abandonment of the conquest theory and recognition of Indian rights to the soil in those territories they still possessed, would redound to the credit of the United States in the eyes of the world. The United States would have to pay for Indian lands; but purchasing land as it was needed would be cheaper than fighting to conquer it and then trying to defend and secure it. Additionally, the Indians could take up "civilized" ways through agricultural, technical, and educational assistance programs provided by the government, charities, and churches.[132]

A darker side to this policy acknowledged that as land peacefully purchased from the Indians filled up with European-American settlers, nearby lands would become less suitable for Indian habitation. As the game decreased, the Indians would be unable to earn a living from hunting and from trading pelts and hides. In debt to European-American merchants and traders, they would become willing to sell more of their lands for cash and/or goods. The Indians would gradually retire westward, and the process would repeat itself. The only alternative was for the Indians to adopt

Henry Knox (1750–1806), secretary of war from 1785 to 1794. CLEMENTS LIBRARY, UNIVERSITY OF MICHIGAN.

the ways of "civilization" and start living like white people, in which case they would no longer need such vast tracts in which to roam and hunt, and so would become more willing to sell their land. In either case, more land would become available to European Americans.[133]

George Washington expressed himself on this subject as early as 1783, when he was still commander in chief of United States military forces:

> [P]olicy and economy point very strongly to the expediency of being on good terms with the Indians, and the propriety of purchasing their lands in preference to attempting to drive them by force of arms out of their country which, as we have already experienced, is like driving the wild beasts of the forest, which will return as soon as the pursuit is at an end. . . . [T]he gradual extension of our settlements will as certainly cause the savage, as the wolf, to retire; both being animals of prey, though they differ in shape. In a word there is nothing to be obtained by an Indian war, but the soil they live on, and this can be had by purchase at less expense.[134]

By 1787 Secretary of War Henry Knox was ready to negotiate a new, general treaty that would include the Six Nations and the Ohio Indians. The United States was prepared to drop the conquest theory and pay for Indian lands. However—and this was the sticking point with the Western Indians—the United States was not willing to forego expansion north and west of the Ohio River, which was precisely the boundary for which many of the Western Confederates were prepared to fight and die. The Ohio Delawares and Wyandots were willing to compromise with the United States and move the "Indian-white" boundary westward as far as the Muskingum River in eastern Ohio. However, the inept diplomacy of Arthur St. Clair, governor of the Northwest Territory, failed to exploit this willingness to compromise. In addition, the militant Shawnee and Miami core of the Western Confederacy was adamant about maintaining the Ohio River boundary.[135]

The result was that the Shawnees and the Miamis totally boycotted the negotiation when it was finally held in December 1788 and January 1789 at Fort Harmar, near present-day Marietta, Ohio. The transactions at Fort Harmar basically confirmed the cessions that had been made at the treaties of Fort McIntosh in 1785 and Fort Stanwix in 1784 by the Wyandots and "other Western Nations" and by the Six Nations, respectively. St. Clair—sole commissioner for the United States—reverted to the same arrogant and imperious language that his predecessors had used at second Stanwix and McIntosh. Almost the only representatives of the "Six Nations" present were Senecas, including Cornplanter. The legitimacy of the Delaware and Wyandot representatives was dubious.[136]

The United States transacted two treaties at Fort Harmar on January 9, 1789: one with the Wyandots and other Western Nations, and one with the Six Nations, principally the Senecas. The treaty with the Senecas confirmed the Indian land cessions made at second Stanwix but provided compensation: a quantity of goods amounting to $3,000, which were delivered at the treaty grounds.[137]

Commissioners from Pennsylvania again followed the United States to an Indian treaty ground. This time the Pennsylvanians were after the Erie Triangle, which lay within territories that had been claimed by New York and Massachusetts,[138] until those two states ceded their western land claims to the United States in 1781 and 1785, respectively.[139] After Pennsylvania's western boundary had been surveyed northward from the terminus of the Mason-Dixon line all the way to Lake Erie in 1786, and after its northern boundary, 42 degrees north latitude, had finally been surveyed westward all the way to Lake Erie in 1787, it was found that the state had only about five miles of frontage on the lake and no harbor. Desiring more frontage and a harbor on Lake Erie, Pennsylvania arranged to purchase the triangle from the United States. On June 6, 1788, the United States Congress, still operating under the Articles of Confederation, ceded the Erie Triangle to Pennsylvania in consideration for payment at the rate of $0.75 per acre. Although the boundaries of the triangle were clearly defined, the acreage enclosed could not be determined until a survey was completed, which did not occur until 1790, when it was found to contain 202,187 acres, for which Pennsylvania paid the United States $151,640.25 in 1792. At that point the new federal government, operating under the Constitution, issued a land patent to Pennsylvania and the transaction was finally consummated. The confederation Congress, however, had already transferred the right of jurisdiction to Pennsylvania on September 4, 1788.[140] With the triangle, Pennsylvania gained over 200,000 acres, the excellent Presque Isle harbor, the site of the present-day city of Erie, and 30 miles of frontage on Lake Erie.[141]

By late 1788, when the United States was preparing for what it hoped would be a general Indian treaty at Fort Harmar, Pennsylvania decided to avail itself of the opportunity to quiet the Indian claim to the triangle—even though the triangle was part of the cession the Six Nations had already made to the United States in 1784 and were about to confirm at Fort Harmar. In quitting their claim to the triangle in favor of Pennsylvania, the Six Nations, chiefly the Senecas, were not relinquishing anything they had not already relinquished before. They were, in fact, obtaining compensation from Pennsylvania for land just paid for by the United States. Pennsylvania was willing to do this to ensure the legality of its title to the triangle.[142]

The treaty of Fort Harmar failed to bring peace to the Ohio Country, so the United States set about trying to forcibly subdue the Ohio Indians—only to suffer two major military debacles. The Western Confederates dealt the United States a devastating blow in October 1790 at the battle of Kekionga, near present-day Fort Wayne, Indiana. There, warriors from several Indian nations, including the Shawnees and the Miamis, thoroughly routed an American force under the command of Gen. Josiah Harmar, which consisted of 300 U.S. Army regulars and 1,200 militiamen from the state of Pennsylvania and from the Kentucky District of Virginia (Kentucky did not become a state until 1791). A year later, General St. Clair, now commander of the U.S. Army as well as governor of the Northwest Territory, personally led an expedition to retrieve the situation. In early November 1791, St. Clair's army suffered an even greater catastrophe on the Wabash River near present-day Fort Recovery, Ohio, than Harmar's had experienced at Kekionga.[143] Numerous smaller battles and minor skirmishes brought little credit to American arms.[144]

The Harmar and St. Clair defeats so diminished American prestige that the United States found it counterproductive to negotiate directly with the Western Confederates and relied instead on intermediaries such as Joseph Brant, Red Jacket, and Cornplanter. As Secretary of War Henry Knox put it, "The pride of victory is too strong at present for them to receive the offers of peace on reasonable terms." A "strong coercive force" would be required to bring the militant tribes to terms.[145] Throughout 1792 the United States concentrated on recruiting and training that force. President Washington appointed Maj. Gen. Anthony Wayne as commander of the army with instructions to rebuild it and prepare it for a decisive military campaign against the Western Confederates. By the spring of 1793 Wayne had assembled and trained a new army; but before he was authorized to use it, the United States—its hand strengthened somewhat by Wayne's new army—attempted direct negotiations with the Western Confederates one more time.[146]

The Washington administration dispatched a team of negotiators, including Timothy Pickering, to offer the Confederates some concessions. The United States was willing to abrogate its Fort McIntosh and Fort Harmar treaties and restore to Indian title all lands north of the Ohio River that had not already been sold. In lieu of that, the United States would pay $50,000 plus an annuity of $10,000 as compensation for the Indian cessions at Fort McIntosh and Fort Harmar. By 1793, however, too much land had been sold north of the Ohio and west of the Muskingum for the Confederates to accept the *status quo*.[147] As for the alternative offer, the Confederates replied that "no consideration whatever can induce us to sell the lands on which we get sustenance for our women and children."

They went on to suggest that the moneys appropriated for compensating the Indians and funding their annuity, plus the vast sums that would be spent on armies to drive them from their lands, be applied, instead, to indemnifying those Americans already settled north of the Ohio River, so as to compensate them for withdrawing from their settlements and "improvements" to the south side of the river. The Confederates reiterated their resolute determination that the Ohio River should be the boundary between them and the United States. If the Americans would not agree to that, there was nothing to talk about. The Confederates' uncompromising stance was partly based on covert British instigation.[148]

General Wayne was given the go-ahead for his expedition in the autumn of 1793. Logistical problems, a vulnerable supply line, and harassment by Indian raiders de-

Josiah Harmar (1753–1813). CLEMENTS LIBRARY, UNIVERSITY OF MICHIGAN.

layed until the summer of 1794 his penetration to the "breadbasket" of the Confederacy, at the confluence of the Auglaize
and Maumee Rivers near present-day
Fort Defiance in northwestern Ohio. The
towns and crop fields in that locale were
called Grand Glaize, or simply the
Glaize.[149] By August Wayne's army was
burning the Glaize, much the same as the
armies of Sullivan, Clinton, and Brodhead had done in the Iroquois country in
1779. This, and Wayne's subsequent approach to the British fort at the foot of
the Maumee Rapids, called in those days
the Miami Rapids, precipitated the battle
of Fallen Timbers on August 20. The
British had just erected the fort in April,
partly as a defensive outpost for their
larger fortification at Detroit, and partly
as a facility from which to aid and abet
the Western Confederates in their struggle with the United States.[150]

*Arthur St. Clair (1736–1818), governor
of the Northwest Territory and major
general in command of the U.S. Army.
From an engraving of a pencil drawing
done from life by John Trumbull.*
CLEMENTS LIBRARY, UNIVERSITY OF MICHIGAN.

The U.S. Army routed the Western
Confederates, who fled the battlefield and sought refuge at Fort Miami—only to find
the gates barred against them. Defeated by the Americans and betrayed by the
British, the Confederacy ceased to function as an effective military coalition. They
signed a treaty at Greenville, Ohio, on August 3, 1795, by which they permanently
relinquished all of present-day Ohio, except for a reservation in the northwest corner
of the state. As compensation, the Confederates received a quantity of goods
amounting to $20,000 and an annuity of $9,500. The United States did not, however,
abjure its sovereignty nor its preemption right to purchase any land that the Indians
might decide to sell in the future.[151]

Although the Western Confederates waged war in defense of their rights, the
Senecas followed a policy of peace and cooperation to secure theirs. Cornplanter in
particular became strongly identified with American interests.

In early 1789, at the treaty of Fort Harmar, he had been instrumental in helping
Pennsylvania quiet Indian claims to the Erie Triangle. To express its gratitude for his
assistance in obtaining the Indian quitclaims, the state awarded him a private grant
of 1,500 acres. The grant was originally to be located within the Erie Triangle; but,
at Cornplanter's request, it was changed to three tracts along the Allegheny River,
which were all surveyed between July 2 and July 12, 1795. The tracts contained a
total of very nearly 1,700 acres: 780 acres surrounding Jenuchshadago and on two
nearby islands in the river, referred to as "the grant"; 614 acres around the site of
Goshgoshing, present-day West Hickory, Pennsylvania, referred to as "Richland";

and 303 acres at the site of present-day Oil City, Pennsylvania, referred to as "the gift." Cornplanter sold Richland to Gen. John Wilkins, Jr., in 1795, and the gift in 1818 to two partners, whose failure to perfect the title caused considerable confusion over the years.[152]

Cornplanter's aid to the garrison at Fort Franklin and the exposed settlers in French Creek Valley at Cussawaga, present-day Meadville, Pennsylvania, was symptomatic of his increasing alignment with the United States. His warriors scouted the region north and west of the fort, on the lookout for Western Confederate war parties infiltrating from Ohio. They warned the settlers to "fort up" or evacuate when hostile Indians approached. In 1791 when Cussawaga was under threat of imminent attack by the Western Confederates, a group of Allegany Seneca warriors escorted the settlers to the safety of Fort Franklin, and Cornplanter and his warriors were ready to fight in defense of the fort.[153]

The fort at Franklin was as important to Cornplanter and the Allegany Senecas as it was to the settlers in the region and to the state and national governments. It was built not just to protect the frontier and the settlers, but also to demonstrate the United States' commitment to its relationship with the Allegany Senecas. Constructed in 1787 near the confluence of French Creek and the Allegheny River, the fort provided, through its army commander, a direct link to the secretary of war and the president of the United States. In addition, Cornplanter's people could carry on some of their trade at Franklin, reducing their need to travel all the way to Pittsburgh; and when they did have to go to Pittsburgh, Fort Franklin provided a convenient intermediate stop and safe haven.

The fort also served to deter the most pugnacious members of the Western Confederacy, who, angry at Seneca neutrality in general and at Cornplanter's decidedly pro-American tilt in particular, had threatened to obliterate Fort Franklin and "shake Cornplanter by the head and sweep this [Allegheny] river from end to end."[154] Tension in the region was so high that the Munsees living on the Allegheny River in the vicinity of Goshgoshing and the Missisaugas living on the Lake Erie shoreline at present-day Conneaut, Ohio, fearing they might be caught in the cross fire, fled to Cattaraugus and Buffalo Creek, respectively.[155] The need for a common defense underpinned the alliance between Allegany Senecas and European Americans.[156]

Gen. Anthony Wayne (1745–96). From an engraving of a portrait painted by John Trumbull. CLEMENTS LIBRARY, UNIVERSITY OF MICHIGAN.

Cornplanter's monthslong visit to Philadelphia was clearly indicative of his policy of peace and cooperation with the United States. In Philadelphia he sought redress of Seneca grievances through conciliation and compromise; he sought compensation for offenses against his people that, left uncompensated, could have led to more violence and to war; and he sought technical and educational assistance for his people.

His diplomatic missions to the Western Confederates—performed at great personal risk—on behalf of the United States provided further evidence of how far Cornplanter was willing to go to accommodate American interests. In a 1790 conference the Western Confederates presented Cornplanter with the scalp of a Virginian and told him that if he did not join the fighting, they would treat him "the same as the Big Knife [the Virginian]."[157]

Cornplanter was not the only Seneca leader seeking an accommodation with the United States in the early 1790s. Red Jacket emerged as an important spokesman for peace and compromise. Red Jacket first came to American attention in November 1790 at an emergency conference held at Tioga Point, near present-day Athens, Pennsylvania, with Timothy Pickering—U.S. postmaster and Indian commissioner.

The conference was called following the murder of two Seneca hunters who had come peaceably to trade at the Pine Creek settlement in north-central Pennsylvania, near present-day Jersey Shore. As news of the murders spread, people living along the frontier feared that enraged Senecas would retaliate with indiscriminate border raids. The state and federal governments feared that the Senecas might take up arms on the side of the Western Confederates. The lieutenant of militia for Northumberland County was so concerned about further alienating the Senecas that he declined to send troops to Pine Creek as requested by the inhabitants of that settlement, who wanted troops to guarantee their safety. The Northumberland lieutenant also declined to jeopardize the safety of important state commissioners who were at that very time exploring the state's western water ways.[158]

To help "quiet the minds of the Senecas," the state government issued a reward of $200 apiece for each of the four accused killers. The Supreme Executive Council of Pennsylvania wrote to the chiefs of the Seneca nation lamenting the murders and informing the chiefs that the state was offering an $800 reward for the apprehension of the accused. The chiefs replied that the chain of friendship was rusty and the governor of Pennsylvania himself should come to brighten it personally. The governor, however, was preempted by President Washington, who, upon hearing of the Pine Creek murders, dispatched Timothy Pickering to denounce the murders, to reaffirm the friendship of the United States toward the Seneca people, and to "make pecuniary satisfaction."[159]

The Tioga Point conference provided Pickering—still new at his part-time job as Indian commissioner—with useful training and experience. He learned the customs, protocols, and language of Iroquois diplomacy. His teachers were Red Jacket and Farmer's Brother—Cornplanter was in Philadelphia meeting with state and federal officials. Pickering gained additional experience at Newtown Point, New York, in 1791 when he and Red Jacket kept the Senecas out of the war in the Old Northwest.

By the summer of 1794 Cornplanter was reevaluating his own policy. His efforts on behalf of the United States and his willingness to cooperate with the Americans had brought him charges of treason from his own people, as well as less and less in the way of a payoff from the United States and Pennsylvania. By late summer of 1794 Cornplanter was on the brink of abandoning his peace and cooperation policy toward the United States and throwing in his lot with the Western Confederates. News of their defeat at Fallen Timbers, including reports of how the British had slammed the gates on them at Fort Miami, arrived just in time to prevent him from leading his Allegany men onto the war path.

With the end of the war in Ohio, the Senecas were ready to work out an accommodation with the United States; and the Americans were finally prepared to treat with the Senecas on the basis of Indian rights to the soil—instead of on the basis of American conquest. The stage was set for a new treaty of peace and friendship between the United States and the Six Nations of New York.

The treaty negotiations were held at Canandaigua, New York, during October and November of 1794; Cornplanter and Red Jacket were the chief negotiators on the Indian side; Timothy Pickering was sole commissioner for the United States; some 1,600 Indians—mostly Senecas—attended. Ostensibly a transaction between the United States and the entire Six Nations, the treaty focused on Seneca affairs, although Indian rights to the soil were also recognized on lands that the Oneidas, the Onondagas, and the Cayugas had reserved for themselves in their separate treaties with the state of New York.[160] The Tuscaroras[161] relied on the Oneidas to represent their interests, and there was a separate treaty a month later—held at Oneida—between these two nations and the United States.[162]

Four Quaker observers also attended the treaty negotiations: William Savery, James Emlen, David Bacon, and John Parrish. They had been invited both by the president of the United States and by the chiefs of the Six Nations. The Friends were particularly concerned that Iroquois complaints about previous treaties at least be addressed, if not satisfied. The Friends provided little direct advice to the Indians, but they did verify for the Indians that the two copies of the treaty documents, retained respectively by the Six Nations and the United States, were true and identical. Although the Quaker observers registered no objections to the treaty, they did not sign it as witnesses because there were plenty of other witnesses present and, as they put

Timothy Pickering (1745–1829), secretary of state (1795–1800). Engraving by T. B. Welch after a portrait by Gilbert Stuart. MASSACHUSETTS HISTORICAL SOCIETY.

it, "we wish not to be held up to public view . . . we do not interfere with govern-ment."[163]

The preamble stated the treaty's purpose: to remove from the minds of the Six Nations all causes of complaint and to establish friendship. [164]

In Article 1 it was declared that peace and friendship between the United States and the Six Nations "shall be perpetual."

The Americans, in Article 2, acknowledged the rights to the soil of the Oneidas, the Onondagas, and the Cayugas on those lands which they had reserved to themselves in their respective treaties with the state of New York, but stipulated that, if the Indians should ever decide to sell any of their reservation land, only the "people of the United States" could purchase. Regarding these reservation lands, Article 2 stated that "the United States will never claim the same, nor disturb them [the Six Nations] . . . in the free use and enjoyment thereof." By the time of this treaty, the three nations had already sold most of their lands to the state of New York. The treaty did nothing to restore any of those lands, but it did provide some protection for the remaining reservations.

The boundaries of the Seneca nation were defined in Article 3, which extended the Article 2 guarantee to cover Seneca lands. The United States reserved the pre-emption right to purchase if the Indians decided to sell any of their land. Most of the negotiating on the treaty grounds concerned the boundaries of the Seneca lands.

Pickering came to the council fire prepared to return to the Senecas the bulk of the lands annexed by the United States at second Stanwix. Specifically, he was will-ing to restore the land in the southwestern angle of New York State, eastward of the Erie Triangle and westward of the Buffalo Creek meridian.[165] He was not prepared to restore the Erie Triangle. Nor was he prepared to restore the four-mile wide Nia-gara strip, because the United States wanted to build a wagon road from the southern terminus of the Niagara portage to Buffalo Creek. Additionally, he wanted to secure the right-of-way for the United States to extend the intended wagon road from Buf-falo Creek to Canandaigua.

Cornplanter came to the treaty grounds wanting the Erie Triangle returned to the Senecas. Red Jacket came wanting the southern two-thirds of the Niagara strip re-turned to the Senecas, to preserve the Niagara River fisheries and keep white influ-ences at a distance from Buffalo Creek. In return he had to agree to a right-of-way for the wagon road as far as the mouth of Buffalo Creek.

A reciprocal quitclaim between the United States and the Six Nations, in Article 4, specified that the Six Nations would never claim any other lands within the boundaries of the United States, outside the boundaries of what had just been delin-eated as the lands belonging to the Oneidas, the Onondagas, the Cayugas, and the Senecas. Nor would the Six Nations ever disturb the people of the United States in the free use and enjoyment thereof.

The provisions for the wagon road and right-of-way, plus additional rights of free passage on waterways and harbors were contained in Article 5.

According to Article 6, the United States was required to compensate the Six Na-tions with a quantity of goods amounting to $10,000 and with a $3,000-increase in their annuity, from $1,500 yearly to $4,500 yearly. The annuity was to be expended "in purchasing clothing, domestic animals, implements of husbandry, and other utensils . . . and in compensating useful artificers [blacksmiths, millwrights, carpenters, etc.], who shall reside with or near them, and be employed for their benefit."

Article 7 required both the Six Nations and the United States to prevent acts of private revenge or retaliation between their respective peoples. American citizens injured by members of the Six Nations were to file their complaint with the federal superintendent for the Six Nations, who would take up the matter with the chiefs of the Six Nations. Members of the Six Nations injured by Americans were also to lodge their complaint with the federal superintendent, who would take up the matter with the president. These procedures were necessary because the Indians were not citizens of the United States.

The treaty of Canandaigua marked one of the rare high points in Seneca affairs with European-American governments during the late-eighteenth century. The Senecas recovered over a million acres of their ancestral homelands, leaving them in possession of 4 million acres in western New York State, west of the Genesee River.[166] They received compensation, in the form of a onetime payment and an annuity, for Iroquois land claims that had been unilaterally disallowed or disregarded by the United States under the conquest theory. The United States also recognized Seneca rights to the soil, which meant that the Senecas owned their land and did not have to sell any of it—unless they wanted to.

Congress exercised its prerogatives under the Constitution of 1788 by passing a series of so-called nonintercourse acts, which prohibited the sale of any Indian lands to anyone, including state governments and preemption-rights holders, "unless the same [sale] shall be duly executed at some public treaty, held under the authority of the United States."[167] This meant, in practice, that a federal commissioner, appointed by the president, had to oversee and approve any land transactions, which then had to be submitted to the president and the Senate for final ratification.

In 1797 at the Treaty of Big Tree, despite the protections afforded under the treaty of Canandaigua and the federal nonintercourse acts, the Seneca nation was maneuvered into selling all but 200,000 acres of the land it had held at the close of Canandaigua in 1794.

TREATY OF BIG TREE, 1797

The Treaty of Big Tree was transacted under the regime established by the Treaty of Canandaigua and the federal nonintercourse acts.[168] However, an important prologue to Big Tree had transpired in 1788—before the federal Constitution had gone into effect and before Canandaigua or any of the nonintercourse acts. In the Phelps and Gorham purchase of 1788, the Senecas sold 2 million acres of their lands in New York, east of the Genesee River.

Oliver Phelps and Nathaniel Gorham were land speculators and developers from Massachusetts. From that state, they purchased the preemption rights to 6 million acres of Seneca land in New York State.

Following the American Revolution, both states asserted claims to the land in present-day western New York. Massachusetts based its claim on its colonial charter.

New York based its claim on a 1701 treaty with the Iroquois. After repeated failures by Congress—at that time still operating under the Articles of Confederation—to mediate the dispute, bilateral negotiations held on the "neutral ground" of Hartford, Connecticut, finally produced a compromise in December 1785. By the Treaty of Hartford the territory that had been in dispute was recognized as being within the political boundaries of the state of New York. However, the exclusive right to purchase land from the Indians was reserved to the state of Massachusetts.[169]

The extent of the territory over which Massachusetts held the preemption rights was established by the "preemption line." The preemption line was a longitudinal line that ran from Sodus Bay on the south shore of Lake Ontario, southward through Seneca Lake, to the eighty-second milestone on the northern boundary of Pennsylvania.[170] East of the preemption line, New York held both political sovereignty and the preemption rights. West of the preemption line, Massachusetts would have the preemption rights, but New York would have the political authority and civil jurisdiction.[171] If Massachusetts exercised its preemption rights, the land purchased by Massachusetts within the boundaries of New York did not become part of Massachusetts.

Massachusetts—desperate for cash—had no intention of purchasing land from the Senecas. In 1787 Massachusetts sold its preemption rights on all 6 million acres in western New York to Phelps and Gorham for a million dollars, payable in three installments. Phelps moved quickly to acquire the Indian title to as much of the 6 million acres as he could. In July 1788 he exercised his preemption right on some 2 million acres located west of the preemption line and east of the Genesee River, which he purchased from the Senecas. During the negotiations, which were held at Buffalo Creek, near present-day Buffalo, New York, Phelps was assisted by the Reverend Samuel Kirkland—the missionary who had helped sway the Oneidas and the Tuscaroras to the American side during the Revolution.[172]

Within a year of the purchase a dispute arose between Phelps and the Senecas as to what terms had actually been agreed upon at Buffalo. The Senecas claimed that the agreed-upon purchase price was $10,000 cash, of which only $2,500 had been paid at Buffalo, plus an annuity of $1,000 per year. Phelps claimed that the price was $5,000 plus an annuity of $500.[173] During his 1790 Philadelphia visit Cornplanter laid the dispute before President Washington, who told the chief that he found no evidence of wrongdoing on the part of Phelps. The boundaries of the Seneca lands, as they would be drawn at Canandaigua in 1794, provided a de facto confirmation of the Phelps and Gorham purchase.

Phelps and Gorham, however, were not without troubles of their own. They had scraped together enough money only for the initial installment on their $1 million payment to the state of Massachusetts. They failed to make their second installment payment. The state of Massachusetts, in consideration of the first installment which the pair had paid and which amounted to one-third of the total price, recognized their preemption rights to the 2 million acres east of the Genesee, which Phelps had purchased from the Senecas in July of 1788 at Buffalo. Preemption rights on the 4 million acres west of the Genesee River, however, reverted to the state of Massachusetts.[174]

At this point another land speculator—Robert Morris of Philadelphia—moved into the picture. Renowned "financier of the American Revolution," Morris had for some time been speculating in frontier lands. In 1791 he paid Massachusetts $1.3 million for preemption rights on the 4 million acres west of the Genesee that had reverted from Phelps and Gorham, virtually eliminating Massachusetts from the picture in western New York State. Eager to turn a profit, Morris concluded a series of deals in 1792 and 1793 with six Dutch banking houses, which had pooled their resources and eventually incorporated their American land interests into the Holland Land Company (HLC).[175]

The arrangements between Morris and the HLC covered a total of 3.3 million acres west of the Genesee River in New York State. The HLC would buy the lands from Morris, provided that he furnished a clear title in which all Indian claims to the soil were absolutely extinguished. Numerous difficulties, including the war for the Old Northwest, delayed Morris four years in complying with this critical provision.[176]

Morris was concerned that any pressure to sell that he might exert on the Senecas would only drive them into the arms of the Western Confederates. As long as the British retained possession of the lakeside forts, especially Niagara and Detroit, there was fear that the Senecas, if pushed too far on land sales, might put up armed resistance—financed and supplied by the British. Even after Wayne's victory over the Western Confederates and Jay's treaty by which the British finally agreed to evacuate the lakeside forts, Morris could not move on the Seneca lands because his finances were in disarray. He had to borrow money from the Dutch just to stay out of debtor's prison; then he had to borrow more with which to conduct an expensive treaty.[177]

It was not until 1796 that Morris was prepared to request that the president appoint a federal commissioner to oversee a proposed treaty with the Senecas to be held for the purpose of purchasing some of their lands.

In September 1796 Red Jacket had raised his objection to a treaty conference, requesting that "Congress will not license or suffer him [Morris] to purchase our lands." Red Jacket's remarks had been addressed to Cap. James Bruff, U.S. Army commandant of Fort Niagara, which had only recently been yielded by the British. Captain Bruff informed President Washington that Red Jacket and other Seneca chiefs opposed the sale of any land. This information caused Washington to put off naming a treaty commissioner until March 1797,[178] because naming one was tantamount to granting permission for the holding of a land-sale treaty.[179]

Robert Morris's son Thomas had settled in Canandaigua, New York, in 1791, the same year in which his father had obtained the preemption rights from Massachusetts. There Thomas became friends with the U.S. superintendent for the Six Nations, Israel Chapin, and with his son Israel Chapin, Jr., who succeeded his father to that same post. Thomas Morris had advised his father to postpone any attempt to purchase Seneca land until the war with the Western Confederates had been concluded and the friction with the British over the lakeside forts had been resolved. To Thomas Morris fell the task of persuading the Senecas to sell.[180]

In February 1797 Thomas Morris arranged for Joseph Brant and Cornplanter to visit his father in Philadelphia. Robert Morris was heartened by Cornplanter's view "that it will promote the happiness of his nation to sell at least a part of their lands and place the purchase money in the public [national or tribal] funds so as to derive an annual income therefrom." It was only after Cornplanter made this statement that Washington appointed a federal treaty commissioner.

As for other Seneca leaders like Red Jacket and Farmer's Brother, although Robert Morris did not entertain them in Philadelphia, he did direct his son to visit them. In the spring of 1797, Thomas Morris toured the Seneca country, talking up the notion of a sale. In a meeting held during May with some sixty warriors and chiefs in a tavern near Buffalo Creek, Thomas Morris persuaded Red Jacket to drop his objection to holding a conference on the subject of a potential sale.[181]

At last the Senecas had agreed to hold a treaty and a federal commissioner had been appointed. Big Tree on the Genesee River, at present-day Geneseo, New York, was the agreed-upon place and mid-August of 1797 was the agreed-upon time. By July wagon loads of supplies and presents for the Indians were en route. Nearly $5,000 of provisions, including beef, flour, whiskey, and tobacco, were shipped to the treaty grounds to feed and entertain the Indian attendees. Also transported were over $15,000 of presents: blankets, cloth, leggings, shirts, kettles, knives, gunpowder, and lead shot. The Dutch were willing to advance the money needed to extinguish the Indian title. Robert Morris was finally going to get the chance to exercise his preemption rights—acquired back in 1791—and consummate his deals with the HLC.[182]

Robert Morris could not attend, however, because he was trapped in his own house in Philadelphia, virtually under house arrest, hiding from summonses issued in law suits filed by his numerous and angry creditors. To set foot outside his door during the summer of 1797 would have immediately landed him in jail.[183] So he gave his son Thomas full power of attorney to act for him at Big Tree and instructions to deceive the Indians as to the true reason for his father's absence. Thomas was to convey his father's apologies: "I grow old, am corpulent, and not very well, and am fearful of traveling so far during the hot weather in the month of August."[184] If the Senecas had known that Robert Morris was foundering financially, they would never have treated with him or his son. [185]

Big Tree was no exception to the general rule that treaties rarely started on time. In this case, the Americans were late because a replacement treaty commissioner had to be named at the last minute. The original appointee, offered a seat on the New Jersey Supreme Court, left the federal government in the lurch for a commissioner. Jeremiah Wadsworth of Connecticut was the last-minute replacement. By August 30 Wadsworth and Thomas Morris plus several representatives of the HLC, including William Bayard, a New York banker handling the Dutch interests, and Joseph Ellicott, the company's recently appointed chief of survey, were all on hand, together with more than 1,200 Indians—almost exclusively Senecas.[186]

The arrangement that came out of the discussions at Big Tree seemed aboveboard and was quite simple. The Senecas agreed to sell to Robert Morris all but 200,000 of the 4 million acres they held. In return Morris would pay $100,000 into a trust fund, with the president of the United States as trustee, which was to be set up for the Seneca nation as soon as the Senate ratified the treaty. The money was to be invested in Bank of the United States stock, and the interest accrued yearly was to be paid to the Seneca nation as an annuity.[187]

Under the table, the arrangements at Big Tree were more complicated. To induce the chiefs and headmen into consenting to the terms he offered, Thomas Morris—acting in his father's name—made several "private settlements" with individual Seneca leaders, which today would be called bribes. In return for their cooperation, or for at least dropping their opposition to his terms, Morris gave onetime "cash grants" of $600 to Red Jacket, $300 to Cornplanter, and $1,000 to several other sachems to be divided among them. He promised, additionally, personal lifetime annuities of $250 to Cornplanter, $100 to Red Jacket, $100 to Farmer's Brother, $100 to Young King, and similar sums to a few others.

Thomas Morris initiated the rocky discussions. He "warned" the Seneca negotiators that their nation might not always be guided by leaders as wise as they. The day might come when feckless chiefs would "waste the property given to you by the Great Spirit." They therefore had best sell their lands while they could get the most favorable terms that had ever been, or ever would be, offered to Indians. He offered $100,000 for all their lands, excluding some reservations of reasonable extent. Should they seek to reserve an excessive amount of land, he would reduce the purchase price in proportion to what they reserved. He claimed that the income derived from investing the $100,000 would forever liberate them from hunger and want. They could retain their hunting rights on any lands they agreed to sell to his father, but as long as his father held the preemption rights to purchase their lands, they could not make a bargain with anyone else. "My father alone can buy your lands, and if after making you the greatest offer that ever yet has been made to Indians for land, you reject it, he will never again treat with you on the same favorable terms."[188] The Senecas took a few days to think over what Thomas Morris had said, and for a while it looked as if they might accept his offer.

A novel feature of the proceedings at Big Tree, a brainchild of Joseph Ellicott, chief of survey for the HLC, was to withhold the whiskey that had been stockpiled in great quantities at the treaty grounds until all the essential business had been transacted. This differed from the customary practice of dispensing whiskey rations throughout the proceedings, from the time the Indians began arriving at the treaty grounds until they left. Ellicott's idea was to parade the whiskey before the Indians with the promise that the liquor would flow in abundance once the business was done.[189]

"But some son of a woman had got a barrel of whiskey and privately sold by retail to the Indians, several of whom got drunk, and amongst them Red Jacket, so they were obliged to stop the treaty for him to sober again."[190] Several of the Indian delegates engaged in a three-day drinking spree, which was halted only when Farmer's Brother managed to stave in the unauthorized whiskey casks.[191]

Red Jacket's overindulgence did not dispose him toward cooperation. When the treaty discussions resumed, he declared his opposition to the sale. The Indians refused to sell more than a small tract of thirty-six square miles on the Pennsylvania border. After several days without headway, banker Bayard, in concert with commissioner Wadsworth, who announced he was ill and anxious to leave for home, urged Thomas Morris to adopt a harsher tone. Laying aside his keen instincts for dealing with the Indians, Morris took the advice of the banker and commissioner and fell into a trap sprung by Red Jacket. Morris told the Senecas that, if the tiny border tract was the best they could do for him, he might as well adjourn the conference at once. Red Jacket leaped to his feet and railed against Morris.[192]

> We have now reached the point to which I wanted to bring you. You told us when we first met, that we were free, either to sell or retain our lands; and that our refusal to sell would not disturb the friendship that has existed between us. I now tell you that we will not part with them. Here is my hand; I now cover up this council fire.[193]

Red Jacket's fiery words ignited Seneca emotions; pandemonium erupted as the Indians hooted at Thomas Morris and company—some of whom feared they were about to be tomahawked. Bayard, with ailing commissioner Wadsworth in tow, told Thomas Morris that if he could find a way to resuscitate the collapsed talks, they would interfere no more and allow Morris an entirely free hand.[194]

Soon thereafter, Farmer's Brother came calling on Morris, who used the occasion to point out that Red Jacket had violated Iroquois diplomatic protocol when he had covered the council fire. Traditionally, only the person who had called and sponsored a council could close it. Thomas Morris had lit the council fire and only he could cover the fire. Farmer's Brother concurred, promised to call Red Jacket's breach of etiquette to the attention of the other chiefs, and pledged to use his influence to revive the talks.[195]

The next morning, Morris appealed directly to the women in general and to the clan mothers and lineage matrons in particular. In a special meeting of the women and some of the warriors—but no sachems or civil chiefs—he explained that, in rejecting his offer, the sachems had not considered the needs of the women. The annuity money from the sale of their lands would secure them and their children from hunger and want forever, and it would afford them many conveniences—even luxuries. Morris declared that the obstinacy of the sachems was no reason for the women and children to suffer. He accordingly directed that the trove of presents, normally not bestowed until the successful conclusion of a treaty, be distributed immediately. "Clothes, beads, brooches, yard goods, kettles, and fancy articles of many types were eagerly seized and gleefully carried away as tokens of the great heart of Big Bear [Seneca name for the corpulent Robert Morris]."[196]

That same afternoon, Morris and the commissioner met with the warriors and war chiefs, including Cornplanter. Farmer's Brother announced that the council fire was indeed still burning. He added, "It is an ancient custom that when a difference arises among us [the sachems and civil chiefs] that it should be referred to the warriors as being the greatest number. We the sachems have therefore referred this business to the warriors and head women and hope they will give an answer that will be satisfactory to all parties." Even before Red Jacket had covered the council fire,

Cornplanter had already publicly declared that the warriors disagreed with the sachems and civil chiefs, and favored a sale. After Thomas Morris's munificence toward them that morning, so did the women.

Formal negotiations resumed, but this time Cornplanter sat on the Seneca side of the council fire, speaking for the warriors and women. In short order, Morris had his deal—everything except for the tracts that the Seneca communities reserved for themselves to live on. The 200,000 acres on which the Senecas retained their rights to the soil were unevenly divided into ten reservations, the largest of which were Buffalo Creek, Tonawanda, Cattaraugus, and Allegany. Precise boundaries for these reservations were not drawn at Big Tree; only the acreage and general location of each reservation were determined.[197]

Then came the last-minute snag, in the form of the sachem Young King, twenty-five years of age and a descendant of Old Smoke. Young King wielded considerable influence, derived from his ancestry and his position as a sachem. He exercised his influence rarely, so that when he did use it, it had maximum effect. Late in the proceedings at Big Tree he announced his opposition to the sale. Morris thought it unreasonable that one man should be able to subvert the will of the entire nation, but Farmer's Brother and the other chiefs told Morris they could not defy Young King. Then, suddenly and mysteriously, Young King stood aside and let the transaction go through. Perhaps it was because Morris bribed him; or, perhaps he had just wanted to get himself on record as protesting the alienation of the Senecas from such a huge chunk of their ancestral lands.[198]

The night before the treaty documents were to be signed, Red Jacket stole surreptitiously to Thomas Morris's lodgings to disclose that he would not sign the papers in public during the next day's ceremony. But Red Jacket wanted Morris to leave a blank space near the top of the list of signatures where he could sign later. Lest we judge Red Jacket as nothing but duplicitous, it should be recalled that he was an orator and at Big Tree he was speaking for the sachems and civil chiefs, many of whom opposed the sale—at least until Thomas Morris's "private settlements" persuaded them to drop their objections. Perhaps he thought it would damage his credibility to suddenly assent to the sale after his vehement opposition. On this basis, he could have signed clandestinely at the bottom, the last of the signatories. But that would never do for Red Jacket; his name had to be near the top. Morris obliged him and reserved a vacant space for Red Jacket's signature, where it was subsequently inserted in private.[199]

Red Jacket's maneuvering at Big Tree was not restricted to the document signing. Earlier in the proceedings, when he first voiced public opposition to the sale, he had already secretly confided to Thomas Morris that his speeches against the treaty did not reflect his own views, but those of the sachems. He added that if Morris would but persevere, he would achieve his purpose.[200]

Behind-the-scenes maneuvering at Big Tree was not limited to Red Jacket. In May, about the time Red Jacket was in the tavern at Buffalo dropping his objection to the holding of a treaty, Cornplanter had called a secret meeting of the warriors and war chiefs. The purpose of the meeting was to organize opposition to the sachems, whom Cornplanter expected to block any sale. He wanted to use the warriors to counter or at least check the sachems by having the warriors demand, if necessary, that the land be divided so they could sell their share.[201]

On the European-American side of things Thomas Morris promised a "gratification" of $4,000 to be divided among the three interpreters at the treaty, who were known to have considerable influence with the Indians. Agents of the HLC went even further. They made conditional promises of $1,000 to each of the three interpreters, and of $2,000 to Israel Chapin, Jr., federal superintendent of the Six Nations. The condition, upon which these "extraordinary gratifications" depended, was that the Senecas be convinced to reserve no more than 200,000 acres, which is exactly what happened.[202]

Chapin ended up receiving a total of $5,000. He rendered a service of incalculable value to the Morrises and the HLC. In late August, while everyone was waiting for the federal commissioner to arrive, the Indians became restless. Chapin chose this moment to distribute the gifts presented yearly by the U.S. government. This not only kept the Indians on the council ground until the treaty started, but also restored their good humor.[203]

The selection of Jeremiah Wadsworth as the last-minute replacement commissioner was probably no accident either. Wadsworth was one of the largest land speculators in the Genesee Valley. His cousin William Wadsworth, in charge of parceling off Jeremiah's Genesee holdings, lived in Big Tree, and the American negotiators stayed at his house throughout the treaty. As federal treaty commissioner, Wadsworth was responsible for ensuring that the Indians were genuinely willing to sell and that they were treated fairly and honorably. The conflict of interest here was astounding—at least by present-day standards.[204]

Late in March 1799, when Henry Simmons witnessed the return of the Cornplanter contingent from Buffalo Creek with $1,560 in annuity and other moneys, plus a few goods from the British, he was seeing the outcome of three centuries of struggle against "the great eaters with big Bellies." That was all the compensation that had come to the Allegany Senecas from their once vast land holdings in western New York. It worked out to a paltry $4.30 per person per year.

CHAPTER SIX

The Seasonal Round

The seasonal round, which on occasion caused the village to be virtually deserted, explains the conspicuous absence of any entries in the Simmons Journal from the beginning of March until the middle of May, except for a single entry dated March 26. Every year, at various times during March, April, and the first half of May, the village broke up, as entire families moved to scattered camps throughout the surrounding countryside to exploit seasonally available natural resources. During these periods, some of which lasted for weeks, nothing much went on in the village itself. This situation left Simmons with little to report during the late winter and early spring of 1799.

The seasonal movement, in which children were fully included, explains the endemic truancy that plagued missionary schoolmasters until the era of Indian boarding schools. Even when the families were living in the village, the seasonal round brought many activities that taught the children how to make a subsistence living. No child was to be deprived of these activities, which the Senecas viewed as important and also fun. The Senecas wanted their children to learn thankfulness to the Creator for all his blessings and allowed the children to witness all of the religious ceremonies, some of which lasted as long as a week.

The annual cycle of Iroquois life proceeded in two synchronous orbits: one economic, the other religious. The schedule of seasonal subsistence activities was intertwined with a busy calendar of religious observances. Everyone participated in the pleasant and fulfilling yearly round of sustenance and celebration.

CELEBRATION

The religious calendar began with the Midwinter Rites in late January or early February.[1] This was the most important and the longest of all religious feasts and marked the beginning of the Iroquois new year. At the close of the 1700s Midwinter celebrations lasted for more than a week. Thanks-to-the-Maple came in early March when the sap began to rise in maple trees, which the Iroquois tapped for making sugar. May brought the Corn Planting Ceremonial, held at a convenient time during the planting season. In mid-June, usually soon after the Planting Ceremonial, came the Strawberry Festival, a first-fruits celebration that coincided with the ripening of wild strawberries. The second-most important religious celebration, the Green Corn Festival, occurred in late August when the first ears of corn were ripe and ready for eating. At the close of the 1700s Green Corn lasted for four days.[2] Following the harvest and after the corn was dried and stored, the Harvest Feast was held, usually in November. Except for Midwinter and Green Corn, all religious holidays were one-day affairs.

The Midwinter Rites revolved around themes of thanksgiving, hope, and renewal. A preliminary rite of communal confession was held first. Unlike Roman Catholics, who in the sacrament of penance confess their sins privately to a priest to obtain absolution from God, the Iroquois confessed their misdeeds publicly to obtain forgiveness from each other. Halliday Jackson described the Iroquois confessional rite as practiced at the close of the eighteenth century.

> After they are generally collected, both men and women, with the children, an examination takes place, whether any uneasiness or dissatisfaction exists among them, and whether any have committed offenses or evil acts. Of these it is often the case that the offender makes confession, the design of which is that all wrong things may be done away and reconciliation take place, where any differences have occurred, and a promise on the part of the aggressor to try to do better for the future; which done, the council then assembled forgive them.[3]

Jackson reported the confessional rite as part of the main sequence of rites performed at Midwinter. Morgan, writing at mid-nineteenth century, reported that it took place a few days before the opening of the main ceremonies, as a preliminary or preparatory rite. He noted that every religious holiday was preceded by a rite of communal confession, but that the one prior to Midwinter was more thorough and lasted up to three days, longer than any other confessional rite.[4]

Morgan also reported a commencement rite performed by two costumed individuals, known during the twentieth century as the Big Heads, who served as heralds of the Rites. Dream guessing was a prominent part of Midwinter, and the Big Heads' brains were puffed full of dreams waiting to be interpreted, hence their name. Their costumes, which combined symbols from the hunt and from horticulture, consisted of bearskin robes secured about the body with ropes of braided corn husks. Each Big Head carried a four-foot-long wooden pestle, normally used for pounding corn, but decorated on this occasion with diagonal stripes of red dye. They went through the village together, stopping at each house to visit. Upon entering a house, they struck their corn pounders against the floor to command attention. They announced that the Midwinter Rites were beginning and instructed the inhabitants to prepare their wooden shovels for the upcoming "ashes-stirring" rite and to hold nothing back when reporting their dreams during the guessing ritual. Anyone who held back would find his brain "stuck to the ceremony" and suffer all manner of psychological distress.[5]

Although not mentioned by Jackson, the Big Heads were mentioned by Jerediah Horsford, who observed the Midwinter Rites at Squawky Hill on the Genesee River in 1816. In that case, however, the Big Heads were not heralds, but singers who made their rounds in the evening. Horsford recorded his observations in a diary, which was used by Lockwood L. Doty in his 1876 publication, *A History of Livingston County,*

New York. Doty supplemented Horsford's description with information from George W. Patterson, who attended the Squawky Hill Midwinter Rites in 1819.[6]

The ashes-stirring ceremony, performed only at Midwinter, symbolized the renewal promised by the start of a new year and the much-anticipated spring season. According to Morgan, two men dressed as warriors, "plumed and painted," went through the village in the same way as the Big Heads. Instead of corn pounders, however, the warriors carries wooden shovels. Upon entering a house, they greeted the occupants and moved to the fireplace. One of them stirred the ashes and scooped up a shovelful, which he sprinkled on the hearth while reciting a prayer: "I thank the Great Spirit that he has spared your lives again to witness this New Year's celebration." He repeated the process with another shovelful of ashes, this time praying: "I thank the Great Spirit that he has spared my life, again to be an actor in this ceremony. And now I do this to please the Great Spirit." The two warriors then joined in a thanksgiving song, after which they moved on to the next house. After the warriors had visited a house, neighbors came and repeated the ashes-stirring ceremony.[7]

Although not mentioned by Jackson, this ceremony was described in two other Midwinter accounts dating from the first quarter of the nineteenth century: Jerediah Horsford's and Mary Jemison's. Jemison, born at sea during her parents' immigration to Pennsylvania from Ireland, was captured by a Shawnee war party in 1758, when she was about fifteen years old.[8] Almost immediately the Shawnees gave her to the Senecas, among whom she chose to remain for the rest of her ninety-year life, despite many opportunities to return to European-American society.[9] She had two Indian husbands and eight children, and spent most of her life in the Genesee Valley. In 1823 James Seaver interviewed her over a period of several days and obtained her life story, which he published the following year. He included several appendices, one of which dealt with Seneca religious observances. Although the reliability of some of the information in that appendix is questionable, Seaver did cite Jemison as his source of information on Midwinter.[10] Jemison, eighty years old in 1823, seems to have described the Rites as practiced by the Genesee Senecas around the turn of the nineteenth century.[11]

Elisabeth Tooker has speculated that, at some time in the ancient past, the ashes-stirring ceremony had been a new-fire rite, in which all the old fires were extinguished and new ones kindled.[12] Indeed, Mary Jemison confirms that the ceremony, as practiced by the Genesee Senecas, was a new-fire rite. Each warrior "carries a paddle, with which he takes up ashes and scatters them about the house in every direction."

> In the course of the ceremonies, all the fire is extinguished in every hut throughout the tribe, and new fire, struck from the flint on each hearth, is kindled, after having removed the whole of the ashes, old coals, etc.[13]

Horsford did not mention the kindling of new fires, merely the stirring—or scattering—of ashes.

> Five Indians appeared with long wooden shovels, and began to scatter fire and ashes until the council house became filled with dust and smoke. This ceremony was repeated at each house several times during the day.[14]

Several days of the Midwinter Rites were given over to three special activities: the performances of small dance companies, the antics of beggar or "thieving" companies, and dream guessing.

According to Morgan, at mid-nineteenth century, each dance company adopted a unique dance and went from house to house performing it. These dance companies are also reported in all written accounts of Seneca Midwinter Rites, dating from the first quarter of the nineteenth century.[15] Some of these so-called dance companies—perhaps all of them—were composed of medicine society members, who performed abbreviated versions of their curing rituals at the homes of people who belonged to or had dreamed of their society, or who were currently sick and needed a cure. The Iroquois had a plethora of medicine societies: the Society of Faces, members of which wore grotesque wooden masks called false faces, the Eagle Society, the Little Water Society, which drew upon the spiritual power of dwarfs who dwelt in the woods, the Buffalo Society, the Otter Society, and so on. Halliday Jackson observed the False Faces making their circuit through the village. The men were:

> dressed in the most frightful manner imaginable, being covered with bear skins, and a bag of ashes tied round their middle, behind them, with a hole to suffer the ashes to fly about as they move. Their faces are covered with a large painted mask, having a high mane on the crown, made of long coarse hair standing almost erect, and with large eyes encircled with a flame colored ring. The mouth is open and shows their own teeth with which they grin in a terrific manner, and their hands are blackened so as to leave marks on every person they lay them on. They carry the shell of a mud tortoise [snapping turtle],[16] which has been dried for the purpose, with a stick thrust through it, which stretches the neck and a large head to their full extent, and inside the shell are a quantity of pebbles, with which they make a wonderful rattle. These men go from house to house and rub this shell on the side up and down the door posts.[17]

The Iroquois believed that a shaman had clairvoyant powers and could look into the soul of a sick person and see the cause of the illness. Often, the prescription for a cure was the performance of the healing ritual of a particular medicine society. The society specified by the shaman would send some of its members, dressed in their distinctive regalia, to conduct their unique healing ritual. If the sick person survived the illness, he or she was thenceforth a member of the society and could be called upon to participate in healing rituals for others. Another avenue to membership in a medicine society was to have a dream about its spirit guardian, costume, or dance.

For a medicine-society cure to last, a "booster" ritual had to be repeated annually as a sign of thanksgiving to and remembrance of the spirit forces that had effected the cure. Hence, the medicine-society rituals at Midwinter, which were performed privately in the homes of people who needed their annual booster ritual, or who were currently ill and in need of a ritual. Some medicine-society rituals were secret and could be performed only by individuals who attributed their own personal cure to the ritual.

The small dance companies—or medicine-society members—were followed around the village by a company of teenage boys, disguised in rags and face paint, who begged for tobacco and food, which were to be used, respectively, as incense in upcoming ceremonies and as provisions for a forthcoming communal feast. In return for these gifts, the beggars entertained their benefactors with a dance or with some silly antics, such as barking like dogs. If the householder refused to give, the beggars were at liberty to purloin anything they could make off with.[18]

In the dream-guessing rite, or as the Iroquois called it "turning the brain upside down," people ran madly from house to house, acting out their dreams in charades, demanding that their dreams be guessed and satisfied. They were not allowed to tell their dreams directly; others had to guess their meaning, based on the dreamer's pantomime. Once guessed, the dream had to be satisfied, at least symbolically. Dreamers could hardly loose. Observers who guessed wrong were supposed to give a compensatory gift to the dreamer. When the dream was correctly guessed, people vied with each other to fulfill it and satisfy the dreamer's wish.

At the turn of the nineteenth century, the Senecas devoted a minimum of five days to the performance of the Midwinter activities described thus far.[19] The Rites continued for another four or five days, however, with additional ceremonies, including the sacrifice of the white dog, the performance of sacred dances, the rite of personal chant, and the playing of the sacred bowl game At mid-nineteenth century, in the Sand Hill Longhouse on the Tonawanda Reservation, the entire course of the Midwinter Rites was passed in seven days.[20]

Little is known about Thanks-to-the-Maple. It was held in late February or early March when the sap started to rise. Each family went to its private maple grove and burned tobacco offerings at the foot of a large maple tree. The smoke carried the prayers of thanks to the spirit of the maple tree and to the Creator.

> O partake of this incense, you the forests! We implore you to continue as before, the flowing waters of the maple. It is the will of the Creator that a certain tree should flow such water. Now may no accidents occur to children roaming in the forests. . . . We give thanks, oh God, to you who dwell in heaven. We have done our duty, you have seen us do it.[21]

There were social dances in the evening.[22]

Sometime during May, the Corn Planting Ceremonial was held. Religious officials known as Faithkeepers went to each house in the village and collected seeds for corn, beans, squash, and other vegetables. These were taken to the council house, where they were soaked in water. Prayers of thanksgiving were offered to the Good Spirit and to all the lesser spirits for their past beneficence and future bounty. The Thunders, seven spirits who dwelt in the dark, rain-making thunderheads, were entreated to send water for the crops, and the sun was asked to spare the crops from its harshest rays.[23] The Good Spirit was addressed as follows:

> Great Spirit . . . we thank thee for this return of the planting season. Give to us a good season, that our crops may be plentiful. . . . Preserve us from all pestilential diseases. Give strength to us all that we may not fall.[24]

June brought the Strawberry Festival, which was celebrated when the "berry moon" was five days old. The villagers assembled, and the Faithkeepers once again thanked the pantheon of spirits for preserving the people and letting them live to see another festival. They also thanked the Good Spirit for providing all the wild and cultivated fruits, of which the strawberry is the first to ripen. They beseeched the spirit forces to bring all the berries: strawberries, raspberries, blackberries, elderberries, blueberries, and huckleberries; and all the orchards: apple, cherry, peach, pear, and plum, to fruition.[25]

Late August saw the Green Corn Festival, and the Harvest Feast was usually held in November, after the harvest had been gathered. The theme was one of thanksgiving to the Creator for a bountiful harvest. A hearty feast was the central feature of this festival.

SUSTENANCE

The first seasonal subsistence activity of each new year was the collecting of maple sap and the making of maple sugar. Each extended family had its own designated grove of sugar maples and adjacent "sugar camp."[26] In March the entire family moved to its camp, tapped the trees in its maple grove, collected the sap, and rendered it into sugar by boiling. Because each family did this, the village was virtually deserted for a month or more. The sugar season could extend well into April.[27] Rebecca Gilbert and her cousin Benjamin Gilbert, Jr., white captives who had been adopted into the family of a Seneca chief at Buffalo Creek, reported[28] that in the spring of 1782, "the whole Family moved about six Miles . . . where they staid [sic] about two Months to gather their annual Store of Maple Sugar, of which they made a considerable Quantity."[29]

The maple sugar season among the Allegany Senecas was described by Halliday Jackson as follows:

> The Third month is generally their season for making sugar, when whole families retire into the woods contiguously to a grove of sugar maple, the sap of which they extract by making an incision into the trunk near the ground. They convey the sap by means of a small tube into troughs set for the purpose. This is collected and taken to the camp, where it is boiled in large kettles till reduced to sugar. And when cleanliness is observed in the operation, they will make this valuable article of an excellent flavor and quality. . . . At this season the Indians remain several weeks in the woods. The men assist the women with the labor of making sugar, besides attending to their hunting to procure supplies of meat. They also trap those amphibious and other animals which furnish furs, and especially the beaver, the meat of which they esteem a luxury."[30]

If the sugar season ran late, lasting into the middle of April, the men and boys also started fishing the streams near their sugar camps. Fish were an important food source at this time of year and were consumed as fast as they were caught. Fishing in the creeks and brooks that flowed through the hills down to the Allegheny River was done mostly by spearing, although some nets were dragged where practical.[31] Trout were the prize.

After the sugar making was done, the people returned to the village, where they remained from two to four weeks—until pigeon time. During their stay the spring fishing season was resumed, now in the streams near the village, and this time the women and girls joined in. Once again, even though the people were back in the village, all hands, including the children, were fully engaged.

The passenger pigeon hunt occurred sometime in late April or early May. During the late 1790s prodigious numbers of passenger pigeons were still present in northwestern Pennsylvania and southwestern New York. They moved in flocks so dense that they blotted out the sky when alighting in the treetops of a forest. In contrast to sugar time, which lasted for a month or more, pigeon time lasted only a week or two. The hunt was timed to occur just before that year's hatchlings were ready to fledge, because the prize of the hunt was not adult pigeons but young squabs still unable to fly. Timing the hunt to just anticipate fledging ensured that the squabs taken would be at their fattest. To this end, hunting for adult pigeons was banned throughout the nesting season.[32] The parents were left unmolested to brood, feed, and fatten the squabs.

While still in their sugar camps, the Senecas watched the skies for the huge flocks of passenger pigeons migrating to their breeding grounds. The gregarious pigeons nested in large rookeries, for which they preferred beech groves where there was a large store of beechnuts on the ground. The enormous flocks, however, overflowed the beech trees and many birds nested in low trees and shrubs. There were numerous nesting grounds in northwestern Pennsylvania and southwestern New York, only a few of which were used in any given year, and there was no way to predict from year to year which nesting grounds would be used. When the pigeons flew over, usually in late March, the Senecas sent scouts to follow them to the nesting grounds and monitor the development of the squabs. From the time of nesting until the onset of fledging required four to five weeks.[33] After the young hatched, the adult pigeons were engaged full-time in feeding them.[34]

Horatio Jones, another captive-adoptee of the Senecas, described the scene as he witnessed it in the early 1780s.

> The pigeons, in numbers too great to estimate, had made their temporary homes in a thick forest. Each tree and branch bore nests on every available spot. The birds had exhausted every species of nesting material in the vicinity, including the small twigs of the trees, and the ground was as bare as though swept with a broom. The eggs were hatching and thousands of squabs filled the nests. Every morning the parent birds rose from the roosts, the noise of their wings sounding like the continuous rolls of distant thunder, as flock after flock soared away to obtain food. A little before noon they began to return to feed their young; then arose a deafening chorus of shrill cries as the awkward younglings stood up in the nests with wide open mouths. . . . Soon after noon the old birds departed again to return about sunset, when they came in such dense flocks as to darken the woods. All night long the sound of breaking branches caused by overloading the roosts, and the whirring and fluttering of falling birds trying to regain their foothold, disturbed the usual silence of the forest."[35]

The scouts periodically sampled the developing squabs and estimated the time until fledging. They sent word to the village when they thought it was time for the people to move to the pigeon grounds. They included some sample squabs for experienced connoisseurs to evaluate and confirm their assessment. The village was again empty. Depending upon the vagaries of weather, maple sap flow, and pigeon behavior, the village might be reoccupied for as little as two weeks following the end of the sugar season. This time all families converged on the nesting grounds, setting up individual family camps around the margins of the rookery. When it was finally determined that the squabs were on the verge of fledging, the hunt began.[36]

Col. Thomas Proctor of the U.S. Army, while on a diplomatic mission to the Seneca in 1791, observed pigeon time among the Allegany Senecas—in early May:

> Red Jacket and Captain O'Beel [Cornplanter][37] came to see me, when the former acquainted me with the reason why no council would be held this day, to wit: That it was their pigeon time, in which the Great Spirit had blessed them with an abundance; and that such was his goodness to the Indians that He never failed sending them season after season, and although it might seem a small matter to me, the Indians will never loose sight of those blessings. This is, therefore, the reason why our men, women, and children are gone from their towns, but on tomorrow our headmen will return and your business shall again be taken up. 'Tis a matter worthy of observation, that at some convenient distance from every one of the Indian settlements, the pigeons hatch their young in this season of the year, and the trees which they commonly light on, are low and of the bushy kind. The pigeons are found in such great abundance, that more than a hundred nests, a pair of pigeons in each, are common to be found in a single tree. So that I have seen in one house, belonging to one family, several large baskets full of dead squabs. These they commonly take when they are just prepared to leave their nests, and as fat as it is possible for them to be made.[38]

Colonel Proctor neglected to mention just exactly how the squabs were taken. From his description it seems that some could be easily taken from low bushy trees. But many would remain out of reach in the more substantial trees such as beeches. The Seneca method for getting these squabs was to cut down the trees. The men felled a tree and everyone rushed in to capture the squabs. The adult birds escaped by flying away. The squabs were taken by hand and killed by knocking them on the head with a club or by wringing their necks. While the men set to work bringing down another tree, the women and children gathered and gutted the dead squabs. Later the feathers were plucked and most of the fat squabs were cured for future use by a combination of drying and smoking.[39]

Horatio Jones described the process: "The Indians cut down the roosting-trees to secure the birds, and each day thousands of squabs were killed. Fires were made in front of the cabins and bunches of the dressed birds were suspended on poles sustained by crotched sticks, to dry in the heat and smoke. When properly cured they were packed in bags or baskets for transportation to the home towns. It was a festival season . . . and even the meanest dog in camp had his fill of pigeon meat."[40] Benjamin Gilbert, Jr., reported a similar method for curing the birds, "which they dried in the Sun and with Smoke, and filled several Bags, which they had taken with them for this Purpose."[41]

Pigeon time was very festive and no one wanted to miss pigeon camp. The people feasted sumptuously every day on fresh squab, which they considered a delicacy.[42] This tasty treat was especially welcome at this time of year when the stores of corn laid up the previous autumn were beginning to run low.

The people returned to their village sometime during early May, in time for the Corn Planting Ceremony and its related seasonal subsistence activity. The planting was done by the women and the girls. The men and the boys continued to fish and hunt. When the Quakers first arrived at Cornplanter's village on May 17, 1798, they found that the women were already hard at work planting. The women were so busy that they could not attend the first general council between the Indians and the Quakers, which was held the next day. By the twenty-eighth, however, when the second general council was held, the senior women were able to attend.[43]

Halliday Jackson, betraying some of his cultural prejudices while at the same time displaying remarkable insight, described the women's work in the fields:

> The females, who are subject (as amongst other uncivilized Nations) to almost every kind of domestic drudgery, are industrious in the culture of Indian corn, beans, squashes, melons, potatoes and many other vegetables. And, although each family have their separate pieces of ground to cultivate with the hoe and hold the fruits of their industry as distinct property, yet they frequently join in large companies to assist each other, on which occasions they are remarkably loquacious and lively, as also expert in using the hoe, each patiently assisting her neighbor till her own turn comes in rotation. Thus they enjoy a kind of convivial intercourse which greatly tends to ameliorate the weight of the labor assigned them, and in many instances, no doubt, afford them a satisfaction equal to, if not surpassing that enjoyed by many of the white females in their most social entertainments.[44]

The next big event in the round of seasons was strawberry time, which peaked in the first part of June and included the Strawberry Festival. After the long winter months when the only fruit and vegetables available had been dried, the appeal of fresh strawberries is easy to understand. But the Senecas' craving for strawberries went much deeper than that. The earliest of the wild strawberries were believed to have potent medicinal properties and were much sought after. A tonic was made from the juice. It was also thought that the road to the afterworld was lined with wild strawberries for the deceased to eat during their journey. When a person recovered from a near-fatal illness, she or he would remark, "I almost ate strawberries."[45]

The people were living in their village at strawberry time. "Toward the beginning of June, small groups of women, with children, and sometimes with menfolk, made picnic parties into the hills, picking wild strawberries and carrying them home in baskets of woven splints, to make into a syrupy tonic beverage and to dry and preserve for later seasons."[46]

There was a summer hunting season, in July and August, during which many small hunting parties left the village on expeditions that lasted from several days to several weeks. Hunting parties continually rotated into and out of the village. Prior to the harvest, which began in late August, the men often took their wives and children with them, especially on the longer expeditions, when a hunting camp was set up for the families.[47] Summer hunts were not very productive and probably did not provide much more than enough to meet daily needs.

Halliday Jackson described the procedure:

In their hunting excursions they generally take their wives and families with them, and remain several weeks in the woods, sometimes twenty, forty, or even one hundred miles from their villages, and generally up or down a river or some large stream of water, where they can go in canoes. Their household furniture being mostly portable, they carry as much with them as answers their purpose during their hunting tour. On getting to the place they have chosen for a hunting ground, they erect a temporary shed, generally so situated as to command an extensive view of the river or smaller streams where they may have a favorable opportunity of seeing the deer or other wild animals pass and repass. And thus it frequently happened that they had an opportunity of shooting them from the door of their cabin.[48]

Large fish drives were held during the summer hunting season. These were communal activities in which everyone who happened to be in the village participated. The fish drives were held on the Allegheny River in certain eddies that contained just the right height of water when the river was low, as it usually was in July and August.

Some of the men built a large, V-shaped stone weir across the downstream end of the eddy, across the upper end of the riffle that invariably lay immediately below the eddy. The weir was oriented with the converging sides of the V running downstream. The two sides did not actually meet; the bottom of the weir opened into a pen or corral of wooden posts. The posts were driven vertically into the riverbed, right next to each other, forming a stockade. The weir thus served as a giant funnel to channel fish into the stockade as they were driven downstream.

To drive the fish, people working on the shore constructed a huge brush seine long enough to span the width of the river. The seine consisted of a floating wooden boom from which was suspended a brush net. The boom was made of hickory or ash poles, three to four inches in diameter, cut by the same team that supplied the posts for the stockade. The poles were overlapped at the ends and lashed together with strips of inner hickory.

While the men were working on the weir, the stockade, and the boom, the women and children were cutting brush to use for the net. They cut any kind of bush or shrub that grew along the river bank, except for willow, which was not stiff enough. They interwove the branches to form sections of stiff netting about four feet in height. As sections of netting were completed, they were attached to the boom. When everything was completed, a brush-net seine long enough to stretch across the river lay along the shoreline, parallel to the river, just above the upstream end of the eddy.

Everyone took up their positions for the actual fish drive. Some of the women and children massed inside the stockade, armed with spears and clubs. Others, similarly armed, lined both shores of the eddy. A line of men stationed at intervals along the boom floated the seine by swinging its upstream end out into the river and pivoting until it was stretched across the river at the upstream end of the eddy. The net hung down into the water, suspended from the floating boom. The boom handlers faced downstream, the boom just in front of them. Another line of men armed with spears took up positions just behind the boom handlers.

As the drive began, the boom handlers started moving in unison downstream through the eddy toward the weir, keeping the seine perpendicular to the shores. The fish were gradually driven before the seine. Any that managed to swim under the net were speared by the line of men following behind the boom handlers. Any that swam in close to either shoreline were speared or clubbed by the women and children stationed there. Most fish, however, fled downstream, swimming into the wide-open jaws of the weir, which funneled them into the stockade, where they were clubbed or speared by the waiting women and children. The seine eventually reached and closed with the mouth of the weir and all hands joined in slaughtering the fish.

Great numbers of fish were taken this way, some of which were consumed shortly thereafter, but most of the catch was smoked and dried. Once driven, it is unlikely that a given eddy could be profitably driven again for some time, until it became restocked with fish, which probably required a period of high water that allowed fish from other parts of the river to move in. This consideration together with the fact that there were a limited number of suitable eddies probably limited the number of fish drives to a half dozen or so per summer. Fish taken included bass, perch, pike, and suckers.[49]

By late August all the hunting parties had returned to the village, in time for the Green Corn Festival and the harvest. Gathering, preserving, and storing the harvest occupied September and October. Again, all hands participated, including the men and boys.

> The winter was on its way now, and the surplus of vegetable stuffs had to be put away for later use. Corn and other vegetables were taken in from the fields; some corn was husked and hung up in braids to dry, and the rest was shelled and buried in baskets in bark-lined pits or stored on the ear in elevated cribs. Tobacco was hung for curing, beans were dried. In this work both men and women participated, for any failure to make the maximum use of what the earth had yielded might mean hardship or even starvation later.[50]
>
> When the harvest was in and before the people moved out for the fall hunt, they devoted one day more to the Harvest Festival, thanking the Creator and His spirit forces for permitting them to reap a full harvest, and testifying to the happiness of the corn now that it had again been returned safely into storage to rest for the winter.[51]

The fall and winter hunting season was long, lasting from November past the middle of January. Once again, whole families packed up and moved to winter hunting camps, leaving the village almost empty.[52] Unlike the summer hunting season, the winter season was generally very productive, supporting not only day-to-day needs but, also, the accumulation of a store of meat for the winter. Halliday Jackson described the winter routine:

> The man sets out in the morning taking his course along some stream of water, making, as he travels on, a kind of way, marked by once in a while breaking down a bush. And in this way traverses the country for many miles in the course of the day, exploring the haunts of the deer or elk, as these animals resort to certain places called "deer licks" [salt springs or seeps], with which the country abounds, where the water issuing from them is somewhat impregnated with salt.

When the hunter kills a deer or other animal, he takes off the skin which he generally carries [away] with him. Dividing the carcass in quarters, he hangs it up in a tree and then makes his way [back] to the path along the water course, breaking down the bushes from the deer, till he reaches the stream, where he scrapes with his feet in the leaves or snow [to mark the point at which the trail to the deer kill branches off from the watercourse path]. In case of snow falling, which would cover his marks on the ground, he cuts down a bush and, sharpening a stick, he sets it in a position pointing in a direct line to the deer he has killed. This furnishes a mark for his wife to find the deer he has killed, whose business it is to carry it home to the camp. He then pursues his hunting again and, if he kills several deer in the course of the day, he marks the way from each in the same manner to the main path by the water. In the evening he returns to his cabin, tired with his day's work, where his wife furnishes him a supper of such as she has to prepare.

He then relates the success he has had through the day, regales himself with fumes of tobacco, and retires to rest on a deerskin in his Native dignity as aboriginal lord of the soil. If too late in the evening when he returns, his wife goes off next morning, directed by his marks, to find the deer he has killed. She brings it home on her back, one at a time, often from a great distance. In winter time, when they have great success in hunting, they leave much of the flesh in the woods, which is devoured by wolves or other animals of prey.

They sometimes watch the deer licks in the night season, where those animals more frequently resort than they do in the daytime, and sometimes in great numbers. The huntsman takes his station in the evening at a proper distance, and kindles a small fire, which he is careful to conceal, until he hears some deer in the lick, and then having some torches, or dry wood, presently makes the light shine round about, by which he can discover his prey, and the poor animals will stand gazing at the light, while he discharges his gun at them. In this manner, he frequently kills several deer in a night.

As the snow falls deep in the winter, in their country frequently from one to three feet, it renders traveling difficult. The Indians therefore have recourse to snowshoes, on which they can travel with much facility, and sometimes catch the deer by running them down, without either dog or gun. These snowshoes are made of a tough piece of wood curved before, and somewhat of an oval form, making a span of about two feet long, and perhaps one foot wide in the middle. Two straight braces cross this again at proper distances to support the foot, and the intermediate spaces are laced with great neatness, with thongs of deer or elk skin. They vary in size according to the person wearing them.

On these the huntsman wanders over mountains, hill and dale, in pursuit of the wild animals of the wood. Should he get benighted at too great a distance to reach his cabin, and providing he has killed any deer, he strikes up a fire in the woods and roasts a ham or shoulder of venison on a sharp stick stuck in the ground before it. He begins to eat as soon as one part is done, while more of the venison cooks, and so on, until he is satisfied or the whole is consumed. It is said that some of the hunters when very hungry will eat a ham of venison without much difficulty.[53]

By late January all of the people had left their hunting camps and returned to the village in time for the Midwinter Rites, the beginning of a new year, and the start of a new round of seasonal subsistence activities.

Breaking the children out of this seasonal round so that they could stay in school required a basic alteration in cultural patterns—not because of the children's contributions to these activities, which were probably marginal, but because this was the traditional way Seneca children were taught subsistence skills. Besides, having the children participate was fun, for both the children and the adults.

The benefits of formal schooling for the children were to most of the Seneca people at this time largely intangible. It was extremely difficult for parents to see any real benefit in requiring their children to attend school regularly. If they happened to be in the village and the weather inclement, they might send their children to school.

CHAPTER SEVEN

A Victory in the Struggle for Sobriety

A month or more after the annuity contingent returned from Buffalo Creek, Handsome Lake's band of drunken hunters returned from Pittsburgh, where they had traded their winter's accumulation of pelts for a large quantity of whiskey. Widespread bingeing ensued for a week or more. The injuries and deaths resulting from the tumult left Simmons aghast and alarmed at the immediate threat to Indian well-being posed by alcohol abuse.

The alcohol-induced turmoil of May 1799 was not an isolated incident, as is made clear by Halliday Jackson, writing of the Allegany Senecas at the time of the Quakers' first arrival.[1]

> These Indians in general—their young people excepted—were unhappily the victims of great intemperance, when they could obtain strong liquors. . . . This article of strong drink was sometimes carried among them by white traders, who also furnished them with abundance of silver trinkets, beads, and like ornaments adapted to their taste. The Indians themselves were also in the practice of trading to the frontier settlements of white people, and exchanging their skins and furs . . . for liquor, which they often brought home to their villages and sold out by retail. This kept many of them continually in a state of intoxication while they could obtain the liquor, and many scenes of human wretchedness were the fatal consequences thus produced. Their aged women in particular were conspicuous sufferers of this evil, and were often seen lying beside the path, overcome by it.[2]

As Simmons put it, "Their deplorable condition by reason of that destructive article of strong drink greatly augmented our concern and exercise for the promotion of their present and future happiness. So much so that we were desirous of having them collected in council." It is not clear whether Simmons consulted with Halliday Jackson and Joel Swayne before asking Cornplanter for permission to address a general assembly of the community, but he made certain the other Friends were in attendance. "And a day being agreed upon for that purpose, I informed my companions thereof."[3]

According to Jackson, the temperance council was held on May 15. Simmons added, "All three of us attended. I was—I think I may say—divinely favored to communicate some pertinent and judicious counsel to them on various subjects, to the furtherance of civilization and their future well-being." According to Jackson,

Cornplanter and the other headmen met with the Quakers later that same day, after the general council. The Allegany Seneca leadership assured the Quakers that they would make every effort to "put away the accursed thing [liquor] from among them."[4] It seems, however, that the leadership required several more days to forge a consensus among the general populace to ban alcohol from the village. Only then did Cornplanter summon Simmons to yet another council, by which time Jackson and Swayne had already departed, returning to their farm. Cornplanter informed Simmons that the community had resolved to ban alcohol from the village, and that two sober warriors had been appointed to enforce the ban.

> The Indians spent several days deliberating the issues we had raised. Then, a large number of them assembled in council and made reply on each subject that we had spoken to them upon. By this time, my companions had returned to Genesinguhta and I was the only one still present. . . .
>
> They had made inquiry and conversed with each other about us, and said they could not find any fault with us, but found we were just and upright in all our ways and proceedings among them, etc. And that the fault and bad conduct lay on their own side. They wished us to be easy in our minds, for they would take our advice and try to learn to do better. They had concluded with a resolution not to suffer any more whiskey to be brought among them to be sold. Then, they had chosen two young men as petty chiefs, to have some oversight of their people in the promotion of good among them. They intended to take up work, and do as we said, and would assist their wives and women on the labor of the field, etc.
>
> After a pause, I arose on my feet and told them I had paid great attention to their words, and thought I should remember them a great while. I felt my heart truly thankful to the Great Spirit for their new resolve. And I felt newly encouraged to persevere in every branch of good instruction to them that I was capable of. Also, I had an earnest hope of seeing their own words verified, which would more and more encourage us who were working among them. I told them that if they lived up to their words, it would also encourage our Friends at home, to whom we wrote frequently letting them know what progress is being made among our Indian brethren, etc. Cornplanter then covered the council fire. Thus it ended.

THE LONG FIGHT TO STAY DRY

Simmons certainly acted as a catalyst in the Allegany Senecas' decision to ban alcohol from the village. But neither that decision, nor the concern over personal and social problems associated with excessive alcohol consumption, originated with Simmons or the other Friends. Cornplanter had appealed to President Washington in 1791 that the Indian trade be regulated as a means of reducing the importation of alcohol into Indian country. And the sober Cornplanter was not unique, neither as an individual nor as a headman. Many Indians did not drink, and many headmen made similar appeals.[5] The historical record is replete with urgent pleas by American Indian headmen that officers of the Crown, colonial or state officials, and federal agents act forcefully to prohibit traders from hauling liquor into Indian villages and to compel them to bring, instead, goods that the Indians really needed, such as blankets, clothes, kettles, tools, and hunting supplies.[6]

At a 1727 council held in Philadelphia between the governor of Pennsylvania and a delegation of Iroquois—mostly Cayuga—chiefs, authorized to speak for the whole of the Five Nations, the Indians complained that "there come many sorts of traders among them . . . and though they [the traders] get their [the Indians'] skins [pelts, hides], they give them very little in pay. . . . Those traders bring but little of these [powder and shot], but instead . . . they bring rum, which they sell very dear." The Cayuga chiefs went on to request that no rum be shipped up the Susquehanna River above Paxtang, at present-day Harrisburg, Pennsylvania, nor any transported over the mountains to the remote Allegheny River.[7]

In 1753 when missionary Timothy Woodbridge went among the Iroquois at Oquaga, a mixed town of Oneidas and Tuscaroras on the Susquehanna River, near present-day Windsor, New York, he told the Indians that their use of liquor would impede the success of the gospel among them. One of the headmen had Woodbridge take down a letter to Sir William Johnson, the Crown's superintendent of Indian affairs for the Northern Department. The headman implored Johnson to staunch the flood of distilled spirits, "My brother, my dear brother, pity us; your bateaux is often here at our place and brings us rum; and that has undone us. . . . I would have you tell the great men at Albany, Schenectady, and Schoharie not to bring us any more rum. I would have you bring us powder, lead, and clothing. . . . This is the third time that I have sent and told you that I would have no more rum brought here." Addressing himself to Woodbridge, the headman went on, "I would have you tell him [Johnson] to bring no more rum to my place. He has sent a great deal of it here, and we die many of us only by strong drink."[8]

At the Albany Congress in 1754, where the Six Nations met with representatives of New York, Pennsylvania, and several other colonies, the Mohawks, speaking on behalf of all the Iroquois, said, "There is an affair about which our hearts tremble and our minds are deeply concerned; this is the selling of rum in our castles [villages]. It destroys many both of our old and young people. We request of all the governments here present, that it may be forbidden to carry any of it amongst the Six Nations." The Cayugas declared in their own name that they would not allow any rum to be brought up their river; those who tried to bring any would suffer consequences. Speaking for themselves, the Mohawks said, "We the Mohawks of both castles have also one request to make, which is that the people who are settled round about us may not be suffered to sell our people rum. It keeps them all poor, makes them idle and wicked, and if they have any money or goods they lay it all out in rum. It destroys virtue and the progress of religion amongst us."[9]

In 1758 during a conference at Fort Johnson, the superintendent's baronial estate on the Mohawk River, near present-day Amsterdam, New York, the Oneida and Tuscarora chiefs addressed their remarks to Sir William, "[W]e, not only in the name of ourselves but also in that of the Onondagas and Cayugas, apply to you for having a stop put to the selling of any strong liquors to our people . . . it not only disturbs us in our meetings and consultations, where the drunken people come in quarreling and very often have weapons in their hands, but it likewise carries off many of our people, both old and young. Wherefore we earnestly beseech you to have no more liquor brought among us to be sold. All we desire to be sold is dry goods as usual for necessary clothes and ammunition to hunt with."[10]

In 1770 the sachems of Oquaga, perhaps including the one who had corresponded through missionary Woodbridge in 1753, sent a letter to Johnson, expressing their displeasure at the continuation of the rum trade.

> It always gave us great pleasure when our brethren (the whites) came to see us, and when we heard of canoes of goods coming down the river. Brother, we lately saw a canoe coming down the river, which at first sight much comforted our hearts; but when we came to look into it, we saw nothing but a heap of kegs and barrels filled with rum, which at once made us tremble. There are some among us so disordered by reason of rum that we are unable to keep them in any regulation. You know that of a long time, we very much dislike the appearance of rum in this town. Rum is [a] troublesome thing, 'tis master of us, and in every respect bad.[11]

Similar entreaties emanated from the chiefs of many nations besides the Iroquois.[12] In all these appeals, American Indian leaders sought to restrict the supply of liquor as a way to reduce problem drinking in their villages. British and colonial authorities, while not unsympathetic to the plight of the Indians, felt that their responsibilities in the matter were limited and that it was mainly the Indians' problem to solve. European-American authorities were content to place on the books laws that prohibited transportation of alcohol into Indian country, and to issue proclamations that proscribed trafficking in rum with the Indians. During the first six decades of the 1700s, the governors of Pennsylvania issued eight proclamations prohibiting or regulating the Indian rum trade, most of which banned the transportation of alcohol into Indian country.[13] The governors did little else.

No resources were allocated to enforce the ban on Indian rum trade; few offenders were prosecuted or punished; and fines and penalties were generally too light to deter traders from such a lucrative business—virtually all rum sold to Indians was watered-down, one part water to two parts rum.[14] Even if European-American authorities had wanted to enforce the ban, they would have been unable, because they did not have the resources to control or regulate the activities of traders who ventured into the remote and far-flung Indian country.[15] As one Pennsylvania governor put it, "the woods are so thick and dark we cannot see what is done in them."[16]

In fact, colonial authorities had a hard enough time working out a policy on liquor sales to Indians in the colonial settlements, where they, nominally, exercised control. Within the space of twenty years, the Pennsylvania colonial government seesawed from a blanket ban on the sale of alcohol to Indians, to the total deregulation of such sales, and back to some minimal government regulation of the Indian rum trade. In 1682 the colony passed its first law "against the selling or exchanging of rum, brandy, or other strong liquors to Indians."[17] This ban did not last long, however, partly because the Indians wanted to be able to buy alcohol when they visited colonial settlements. In 1684 Indians in the hinterland of Philadelphia agreed to sub-

mit to punishment under English law for infractions committed in the colony's settlements, provided that law against selling them rum be abolished. The Pennsylvania
legislature repealed the law that year.[18]

But complete deregulation was not the answer either. In 1701 Pennsylvania began
to regulate the Indian rum trade by forbidding sales to all Indians except chiefs, and by
limiting those authorized sales to "such quantities as the governor and council shall see
fit." The chiefs could then dispose of the liquor however they chose. The chiefs probably liked this arrangement because the entire Indian liquor supply had to pass through
their hands, which enhanced their own positions and status within their respective
communities. The Conestoga chief Oretyagh certainly like Pennsylvania's new policy.
While bidding farewell in 1701 to William Penn, who was taking his last leave of the
colony, the chief expressed his great satisfaction at the new law.[19]

However well Pennsylvania's policy did or did not work within its own settlements, traders routinely ignored the prohibition against trafficking in rum in Indian
country, where the law was toothless. The fact that traders transported considerable
quantities of alcohol into Indian country during colonial times is well established.
Sir William Johnson estimated that in 1764 alone, traders sold some 50,000 gallons
of rum to Indians in the "northern department," which consisted of present-day Ohio
and the central and western parts of present-day New York and Pennsylvania.[20] The
volume shipped in the "southern department" was perhaps twice as high. In 1767,
while thanking Superintendent Johnson for his role in facilitating the settlement of
Tuscarora emigrants from Carolina among the Oneidas, Chief Aucus al Kanigut recalled what it had been like for his people before they moved. "We return you many
thanks in bringing our people from Carolina, where they lived but wretchedly, being
surrounded by white people, and up to their lips in rum so that they could not turn
their heads anyway but it ran into their mouths."[21] In 1770 colonial traders purveyed
over a million gallons of rum to the Eastern Woodlands Indians.[22]

The Indian conferences of two Pennsylvania colonial governors, Charles Gookin
and Patrick Gordon, illustrate how badly the colony's policy to regulate the Indian
rum trade failed, how the flow of rum into Indian country continued unchecked, and
how European-American authorities tried to throw the problem back into the Indians'
lap. In 1715 when Sassoonan, chief of the Delawares living on the Susquehanna
River, complained that "they were much abused by the quantities of rum brought
amongst them" and requested that the governor put a stop to the practice, Governor
Gookin reminded the Indian delegation of the "very strict laws made against it." He
pointed out that "it was impossible for us to know who came thither into the woods
amongst them without their information." He countered the Indian complaint, claiming that it was "in their power . . . to prevent it if they would stave all the rum [kegs or
other vessels] that came amongst them." He then authorized and directed them to do
so "without fail as often as any [rum] came [among them]." Sassoonan requested and
received a written copy of the governor's order.[23]

In 1727 the Cayuga chiefs received much the same response when they complained about Pennsylvania traders who came into their villages with little more than
rum for sale. Governor Gordon told them that "we have made . . . laws to prohibit it

and made it lawful for an Indian to stave all the rum that is brought to them . . . they [the traders] carry it privately out of town, without the governor's knowledge. . . . We desire them [the Indians] not to seize any for that is not lawful, but that they would break the casks and destroy it. . . . The Indians may stave any rum they find in the woods, but . . . they must not drink or carry any away." Like Sassoonan, the Cayuga chiefs requested "a writing to show that the governor allowed them to stave any rum they met with in the woods, which was promised with this limitation, that they should not meddle with any rum they found in any houses whatsoever, and that they should not on any account seize any to drink or carry it away. And with this caution, a writing [written copy] was ordered."[24]

In granting the Indians permission to stave in any rum casks that invaded Indian country, Governors Gookin and Gordon were only reiterating a license that had been issued originally by none other than William Penn—or so the Indians believed. The Conestoga chief Tawenna reminded Gordon of this in 1729, "William Penn told them that he would not suffer any large quantity of that liquor to be brought among them, and that they might stave the casks and spill it, if they found any in the woods."[25] Temperate Indians did avail themselves of this remedy from time to time. In 1738 some chiefs of the Shawnees living in the lower Allegheny watershed wrote to Proprietor Thomas Penn that they had collected all the rum in their towns, staved in the casks, and spilled the liquor in the street. Furthermore, they had "appointed four men to stave all the rum or strong liquor that is brought to the towns hereafter."[26]

The license to smash rum kegs in Indian country had not done much to curtail the liquor trade. Indian individuals highly regarded their own personal freedoms and liberties, and respected those of others. Indian societies had no coercive agencies like the police and courts, either to prevent disorderly drinking or to compel the smashing of rum casks. Aside from murder, bodily harm, and theft, which were punished by the victim's kin, all other forms of human intercourse and behavior were pretty much unfettered. Community leaders, such as sachems, war chiefs, and matrons, wanted to intervene to curb the alcohol trade and abusive drinking; but they had no traditionally sanctioned mandate to do so—and no coercive powers.[27] Public opinion and family disapproval carried some weight, but not enough to deter those who would purchase alcohol and then consume it or resell it for a profit. In short, while the Indians were at liberty within Indian country to stave in liquor kegs, there was nothing to prevent individuals from seizing the traders' alcohol, drinking some, and carrying the rest away for later consumption or resale to other Indians.

The chiefs of the Scioto Shawnees told Alexander McKee as much in 1771. McKee, an agent of Sir William Johnson, transmitted the Shawnee complaints to the superintendent in a letter. "Our chief complaint was that your traders brought too great quantities of rum amongst us, which has been the cause of the death of many of our dearest friends and relations, as well as the reason of our foolish young men abusing your traders; though they [the traders] themselves are to blame for all the mischief it produces. It gives us great uneasiness and we expected you would have done something to put a stop to it before this. As to our parts, the measure that we intended to take was to stave all that was brought amongst us. But we fear this would not answer the end we expected, for we find in the execution mischief must undoubtedly happen and probably draw on what we are endeavoring to avoid. Brethren, you have laws and government amongst you. It is you that make the liquor, and to you we must look to stop it."[28]

This was not the first time the Shawnee chiefs had, with the greatest sense of urgency, raised the subject with Johnson. "It has been a subject we have spoke to you long upon, without your seeming to listen to us. We desire to hear from you as soon as possible, as the time draws near for the traders to be coming out; and if no method can be fallen upon to prevent their bringing rum into the country, the consequence must be dreadful."[29]

Johnson typified the attitude prevalent among European-American officials that no one was forcing the Indians to buy rum. Officials quickly pointed to Indian ambivalence about controlling the rum supply and to the Indians' divided counsel on what to do about the rum problem. For example, Pennsylvania governor Gordon rebuked the Oneida chiefs in 1727, telling them that the Indians did not stave in the rum casks, because they were "too fond of it themselves . . . [and] will not destroy it."[30] In 1729 when the Conestoga chiefs Tawenna and Civility took their complaints to Philadelphia, Gordon told them that "you complained much of your suffering by rum. Many laws you know have been made against it, but your people make all these laws of no effect; they will have it [alcohol]. . . .We can make no laws against your drinking it; you must make these yourselves."[31]

In 1758 Johnson expressed impatience and frustration when the Oneida and Tuscarora chiefs asked him to prevent the shipment of any strong liquor into their countries or those of the Onondagas and the Cayugas. "Your request in conjunction with the Onondagas that there should be a stop put to the sale of rum to the aforesaid nations, I must say appears to me very whimsical, as you well know what a noise was made about stopping it before." Two years previously the Six Nations had prevailed upon Johnson and the New York colonial governor and legislature to ban the importation of alcohol into Iroquoia. Within a year rising discontent among some of the thirsty Iroquois had forced the chiefs to go back to the colonial officials and ask that the ban be repealed. Indeed, as Johnson now taunted the chiefs, "[S]everal sachems now present told me unless it was allowed to be sold again, they were in danger of their lives." The ban had been repealed. "Now to desire the same law to be re-passed must certainly appear to everybody extremely odd," chided Johnson.[32]

The dilemma in which the Iroquois chiefs found themselves in the second half of the 1750s, and over which Johnson teased them, was nothing new. It fact it reprised almost exactly the embarrassing experience of Teganissorens, an Onondaga orator of the late seventeenth and early eighteenth centuries. In 1716 at the urging of Teganissorens, the provincial legislature of New York had imposed a blanket ban on the sale of alcohol to Indians throughout the colony, including trade emporiums such as Albany. Within a few months, Teganissorens came under intense pressure from young warriors, who found the dry spell intolerable. To extricate himself from an impossible situation, Teganissorens charged the New York authorities with having acted unilaterally in imposing the ban, demanded that the liquor trade be reopened without restriction, and threatened, if his demands were not met, to send his people to the French in Canada to trade. From that moment, prohibition was useless.[33]

Indian temperance initiatives were hindered by ambivalence[34] and divided counsel.[35] As early as 1728 sachems of the Six Nations drew a distinction between, on the one hand, European-American traders carrying rum to Indian villages, which they found to be objectionable, and, on the other hand, Indians traveling to European-American settlements and trading posts to buy and consume liquor, which they accepted.[36]

At the Albany Congress in 1754 the Six Nations protested the rising tide of liquor washing over Indian country, but were somewhat equivocal when insisting that the rum trade be shut down. "We are in great fears about this rum, it may cause murder on both sides. We don't want it to be forbid to be sold us in Albany, but that none may be brought to our castles."[37]

Scaroyady, the Iroquois superintendent of the Ohio Shawnees, had made a similar request of the governor of Pennsylvania the preceding year. "Your traders now bring scarce anything but rum and flour; they bring little powder and lead or other valuable goods. The rum ruins us. We beg you would prevent its coming in such quantities by regulating the traders. . . . We desire it may be forbidden, and none sold in the Indian country; but if the Indians will have any, they may go among the inhabitants [European-American settlers] and deal with them for it."[38]

The Delaware chief Sassoonan had been even more equivocal during a 1731 conference with Pennsylvania governor Gordon in Philadelphia. He too objected to the flood of alcohol pouring into Indian country. He conceded that the "Indians have made frequent complaints of rum being brought amongst them in great quantities, and that they themselves have too great a liking for it." But, he noted that lately "very large quantities are carried everywhere amongst them; that many horse loads of it pass by his door; and it all comes from Philadelphia." He could not "understand why such quantities should be sent up."[39]

The governor and his counselors then asked Sassoonan if he wanted a prohibition of all liquor shipments to Indian country. The chief responded, initially, that all shipments by European Americans—but not by Indians—should stop; he cited an Iroquois precedent for this. "There was lately a great council of the Five Nations and Mohawks where . . . it was agreed that the white people should not be suffered to bring any rum amongst them, and that if an Indian wanted any he should go to the white people and bring it himself." He explained why Indians, but not European Americans, could be allowed to continue bringing rum into their country. "There is not so much danger to be apprehended from the quantities that the Indians themselves may bring in this manner, as from the great quantities that are brought amongst them by the white people." He concluded, saying "no rum should be suffered to be carried amongst them by the English, but that if any Indians want it, they should come to Philadelphia for it."[40]

The following day, Sassoonan amended his statement to allow European Americans to haul some rum into Indian country. "The Indians do not desire that rum should be entirely stopped and that none at all should be brought to them; they would have some, but not much, and desire that none be brought but by sober good men, who will take a dram with them to refresh them and not . . . to hurt them." He specified that four men might be allowed to carry rum to "Allegheny" and that some rum be "lodged" at Tulpehocken, west of present-day Reading, Pennsylvania, and at Paxtang.[41]

And after the Albany Congress, Indians evinced ambivalence about completely stopping the traffic in ardent spirits. In 1759 the Beaver King, a chief of the Delawares living in the Ohio country, asked George Croghan, a key trader from Pennsylvania, to unstop the proverbial rum keg. British authorities, desperate to avoid further alienating the Indian chiefs over the pernicious rum trade, had bunged up the rum keg pretty tightly during much of the French and Indian War.[42] "At last the Beaver spoke in behalf of the Indians, that as they [the Indians] had stopped the bung in our rum kegs . . . they were now for having the kegs kept open for their people . . . that they might have it to buy . . . for they loved it."[43]

Even Pontiac, a great American-Indian champion, solicited rum from Croghan for the Indians present, upon completing negotiations at Detroit in 1765 to restore Indian-British relations to normal following the uprising of 1763–64. "You stopped up the rum barrel when we came here, 'till the business of the meeting was over,'" but since the business was "now finished we request that you may open the barrel that your children may drink and be merry."[44]

During the American Revolution, the Mohican Indians of Stockbridge, Massachusetts, fought on the rebel side. In 1775 while participating in the siege of British-held Boston, the Stockbridge elders petitioned the Massachusetts Assembly to regulate—but not stop—their liquor supply and to hold their combat pay in trust, lest they themselves be tempted to spend it all on liquor.[45]

The flood tide of spirituous liquors was not only the product of division within the Indian community, but the cause as well, as wives complained about their husbands' drinking, and as elders chastised their young men for getting drunk. As a Seneca sachem put it to New York governor William Burnet in 1726, "We desire that no rum may be sent up, for it produces all evil and contention between man and wife, between young Indians and the sachems."[46]

Dissension within the Indian ranks is reflected in the remarks Governor Gordon directed to a delegation of Indians from the Allegheny region in 1730. "The old men, whose advice you should take have complained, of the abuse and great injury you receive by it [the rum trade]. They complain that for drink you give away all the fruits of your labors, and are left naked and poor as if you had never hunted at all."[47] The intergenerational conflict was even more obvious when young men, preferring to drink, rejected the temperance initiatives of their own elders. In the late 1760s some young warriors refused to join their sachems and other civil chiefs in signing a petition to abolish the liquor trade in western Pennsylvania.[48] Sachems and chiefs frankly and openly acknowledged that their expostulation against the intemperate use of alcohol often fell on deaf ears. The Huron (Wyandot) chief who spoke at Pittsburgh in 1773 said, "You are all sensible that the complaints of all nations this way [west of the Allegheny and Ohio Rivers] have been frequent against spirituous liquors being carried amongst them. This, brethren, is the source of many evils and cause of a great deal of our unhappiness; by it our young men [are] not only reduced to the necessity of stealing to recover what they lose by drunkenness, but [are] deprived of their reason and rendered incapable of listening to or taking the advice of their wise people."[49]

Nothing exemplified the discord within Indian society more than the rum traders who were themselves Indians. As early as 1727 the Cayuga chiefs complained to Governor Gordon that "there come many sorts of traders among them, both Indian and English, who all cheat them . . . these traders bring little . . . but . . . rum."[50] To this Gordon helpfully replied that the method of all traders was "to buy as cheap and sell as dear as they can." Therefore, "every man must make the best bargain he can; the Indians cheat the Indians and the English cheat the English; and every man must be on his guard."[51]

The role of Indians in the liquor trade was mostly limited to dealing at the very end of the distribution network. Indian rum traders served a market consisting of Indian drinkers who lived at an inconvenient distance from white establishments that stocked a steady supply of liquor, or who wanted alcohol but not the trouble and danger sometimes associated with visiting a European-American settlement. In this way, liquor—like pathogens—far outran the limits of European-American penetration into the "wilderness," carried by Indians to Indians.

In 1730 a group of Iroquois purchased a large quantity of rum in Albany and transported it to a village of Delawares on the Allegheny River, which at that time was still quite remote from any continuously stocked source of liquor. To buy the Iroquois rum, Delaware drinkers sold their accumulation of furs and hides to local European-American traders, who had run out of rum. Some Delaware drinkers even robbed the traders to obtain more goods to exchange for Iroquois liquor.[52]

Evidence that Indians from many nations participated as dealers in the liquor trade is found in the actions of the Shawnee temperance reformers who lived in the lower Allegheny watershed in 1738. These were the Shawnees who spilled into the streets all the liquor in their villages, banned the importation of any more liquor, and appointed four enforcers to stave in any rogue rum kegs. In addition, they not only sent a petition to the government of Pennsylvania that liquor shipments be stopped, but they also sent wampum strings to the Iroquois, to the Delawares and the Shawnees living on the Susquehanna River, and to the French in Canada. The strings warned the recipients that if members of their respective nations brought any liquor to the Allegheny Shawnees, it would be spilled onto the ground—implying that in the past traders from these nations had carried liquor to the Allegheny.[53]

In 1758 Peter Bard, the provincial commissary officer at Pennsylvania's frontier Fort Augusta, located at the Shamokin forks of the Susquehanna River, near present-day Sunbury, Pennsylvania, reported that Teedyuscung, a chief of the Delawares on the Susquehanna, had purchased kegs of rum from local settlers, which he was transporting up the river to sell at Tioga, near present-day Athens, Pennsylvania.[54] James Kenny, storekeeper of Pennsylvania's provincial trading post at Pittsburgh from

1761 to 1763, reported that the Beaver King and his son were in the business of purchasing liquor from scofflaw traders and sutlers in Pittsburgh and transporting it to Indian towns in present-day eastern Ohio for resale.[55]

David Zeisberger, a Moravian missionary resident at the Indian refugee town of Goshgoshing on the Allegheny River, above present-day Tionesta, Pennsylvania, reported that a party of Senecas arrived in September 1768, bearing rum. Zeisberger and a local Munsee[56] headman named Allemewi prevailed upon the Senecas not to sell any rum in Goshgoshing.[57] Earlier, during the first part of August, Allemewi had directed that a string of wampum be carried down the Allegheny all the way to Pittsburgh, announcing "to all the Indians, that they are to bring no rum hither."[58] But rum made its way to Goshgoshing by traveling downstream as well as up. As Zeisberger put it, "Every spring and fall Goshgoshing was the rum market for the Senecas. . . . They secured the rum in Niagara and brought it thither for sale."[59]

In their 1770 letter to Sir William Johnson, the sachems of Oquaga complained bitterly about Indians who had become traders. "One thing more in an especial manner we very much dislike . . . Indians coming and trading among us. When we had white traders, goods seemed [to] be something reasonable and right; but Indians devour us, they extort from us everything we get with great pain and labor in the woods. . . . Therefore we desire, if any Indians apply for liberty [to trade], that you would forbid them. We expect you will answer us, that thereby we may be strengthened to oppose Indian traders."[60]

Indian women were extensively involved in the Indian side of the liquor trade. This may have started when women were sent to fetch liquor from European-American settlements and trading posts.[61] But by 1766, New Comer, a chief of the Delawares on the Muskingum River, was complaining to visiting Presbyterian missionary Charles Beatty that "there is another thing that we do not like and complain of very much." Some European-American traders did "at times hire some of our squaws to go to bed with them," and paid the women in rum. "This thing is very bad, the squaws again selling the rum to our people to make them drunk. We beseech you to advise our brothers against this thing and do what you can to have it stopped."[62]

During 1779 and 1780 missionary Zeisberger, writing up his notes on Indian history, life, manners, and customs, recorded the following observation: "Many engage in rum traffic, especially women, who fetch it from the white people and sell it at a considerable profit to the Indians, often taking from the latter everything they have, sometimes even their rifles upon which they depend for subsistence."[63]

The liquor trade continued throughout colonial times and beyond because of the complicity between Indian drinkers and European-American traders.[64] The latter were motivated by the promise of easy profits and the belief, shared by European-American authorities, that liquor was not only the essential lubricant for all intercultural exchanges, commercial and otherwise, but the indispensable commodity in the fur trade. The profit margin on liquor was unsurpassed, owing in no small part to the nearly universal practice of watering it before selling it to Indians.[65] Although profits on other trade goods averaged around 100 percent, the return on liquor ran as high as 400 percent.[66]

From early contact times, European-American officials offered liquor to Indian representatives at the start of treaty negotiations and conferences, as a sign of hospitality and friendship. They included liquor in the presents they gave Indians at the end of councils, the Indians giving pelts and hides in return. Reciprocal gift-giving symbolized and affirmed alliances—both military and commercial.[67] To curry goodwill, European-American traders customarily provided Indians with a few free drams before beginning to bargain. Most traders viewed liquor as a prerequisite for doing business in Indian country, both as a complimentary beverage and as a trading commodity.[68]

Many traders and government officials saw liquor, which the Indians consumed but generally did not produce, as the key to sustaining and expanding the fur trade.[69] The importance of liquor in this regard lay precisely in its nature as a consumable for which demand was both continuous and high. In contrast, demand for durable goods—like kettles, hoes, hatchets, and guns—fell off as Indians acquired as many of these items as they could reasonably use. Demand for wampum and vanity items, such as mirrors, combs, and body ornaments, was higher because, though durable, these goods were much desired. Even the demand for cloth, blankets, and clothing could be saturated. Demand for other consumable goods—such as ammunition, body paint, tobacco, and flour—was fairly constant; but the demand for liquor was even more reliable. Traders also saw liquor as essential for attracting distant Indians to British-American trading posts.[70]

A group of Albany merchants explained to the British Lords of Trade in a 1764 petition aimed at forestalling a ban on the liquor trade: "When the Indians have nothing farther to provide for than bare necessaries, a very small quantity of furs in trade will abundantly supply that defect. Whereas, when the vent of liquors is allowed amongst them, it spurs them on to an unwearied application in hunting in order to supply the trading places with furs and skins in exchange for liquors."[71] Later that same year, Sir William Johnson echoed the Albany merchants, when he wrote to his London superiors that, absent the liquor trade, "the Indians can purchase their clothing with half the quantity of skins, which will make them indolent, and lessen the fur trade."[72]

COSTS AND CAUSES OF EIGHTEENTH-CENTURY INDIAN DRINKING

The commercial and mercantile incentives for European Americans to continue the liquor trade are fairly clear.[73] Not so clear are the reasons that some Indians chose to drink and to keep on drinking, especially after the social costs became apparent to many in the Indian communities.

The social costs of Indian drinking were indeed high.[74] Too often, violence followed in the wake of binge drinking,[75] almost all of it Indian-on-Indian.[76] Drunken brawling resulted in deaths and injuries.[77] Deliberate murders were sometimes associated with drinking, in part because of a widespread sentiment among Indians that perpetrators were not responsible for acts of aggression committed while under the influence.[78] Some murderers apparently took the precaution of getting drunk before committing their foul deed.[79]

The rampant disorder caused by orgies of drinking disrupted the normal course of village and family life. Local councils were interrupted by drunks; or, councils could not be held at all because too many villagers were drunk, hiding, or sleeping it off.[80] The onset of group drinking prompted women to hide all the weapons in town, lest they be used to do harm. In some villages where the liquor supply was abundant, families were forced to move into the surrounding woods, to be free of continual disturbance and danger.[81] Drinking also disrupted family life; some families suffered domestic violence at the hands of their own drunken members.[82]

Drunkenness also led to many accidental deaths and injuries, ranging from hypothermia and frostbite, to drowning, perishing in a structure fire, falling from a height, or stumbling into a bonfire.[83] Health problems brought on by repeated drinking binges contributed to the overall population decline among Eastern Woodlands Indians, especially when acting in concert with pathogenborne diseases and the malnutrition common among war refugees.[84]

Drinking drove some Indians into poverty and debt. To pay for the liquor imbibed during chronic and episodic drunken sprees, drinking Indians used pelts and hides, which were virtually the only Indian commodities that European Americans valued. This left them with fewer furs and skins to use in purchasing necessities, like hunting supplies, tools, blankets, and clothes. Traders did extend credit, and some Indians went into debt to furnish themselves with essentials, having first expended their peltries on liquor.[85]

Given that the view we have of eighteenth-century Indian drinking comes to us almost exclusively through the eyes of eighteenth-century European-American observers, it is difficult to reconstruct the reasons that Indians of that time chose to drink the way they did. Most European Americans viewed Indian drinking through several layers of prejudice: the assumed superiority of white culture to Indian culture; the assumed moral superiority of "Christian" colonists to heathen Indians; the fear that drunken Indians were always violent and dangerous; and racism. The documentary record however, is extensive enough that, by peering through the layers of prejudice inherent in that record, the reasons for eighteenth-century Indian drinking can be partially and tentatively reconstructed.[86]

The drinking patterns and habits of Eastern Woodlands Indians throughout the 1700s can be summarized as follows. Indians drank communally, sometimes for ritual purposes in hospitality and mourning ceremonies, and sometimes with the deliberate intention of achieving a state of total intoxication.[87] This last intention was never more evident than when a group of Indians would find itself with insufficient liquor for all to get drunk. Oftentimes, in such cases, some members of the group were selected to drink all the alcohol, while everyone else totally abstained. Only as many were appointed to be "designated drinkers" as could be made completely drunk by the available liquor supply.[88]

The desire to be completely inebriated derived from the belief held by some Indians that in an inebriated state they gained access to spiritual forces that were sometimes dangerous, but always powerful.[89] For these Indian drinkers, inebriation imparted a sense of enhanced personal powers.[90] To them, the spatial and temporal disorientation induced by alcohol was revealing, challenging, and even self-affirming. Young men especially, full of bravado, sought to experience and survive the wild and uncontrollable sensations of total intoxication.[91]

Although such use of alcohol might be related to some sort of psychological or even spiritual quest, it was not necessarily related to vision or dream quests. The Indians themselves seem not to have connected drinking and dreaming (except in reverse, when false dreaming was practiced on European Americans to extort the obligatory dram or two).[92] The medical literature, furthermore, suggests that alcohol-related hallucinations occur only in chronic and heavy drinkers and only when they stop drinking—as a withdrawal symptom. Thus, "it is perhaps unwise to presume that Indians drank to induce visions."[93]

Many Indians could not drink chronically, even if they had wanted to, because their liquor supply was too sporadic. Indians living in close proximity to European-American settlements were an exception to this and could drink chronically, provided they could afford to purchase liquor in the quantities needed to sustain chronic drinking. But despite the best efforts of European-American traders and the internal Indian trading network, Eastern Woodlands Indians, on average, consumed only a fraction of the distilled spirits that their European-American counterparts did.[94] One estimate of colonial drinking habits put the average weekly consumption of hard liquor, mostly rum and whiskey, at three pints per week, or almost seven one-ounce shots per day.[95] Heavy drinking among Indians was more episodic than chronic. The problem was not the total quantity of alcohol consumed by Indians on an annual, per-capita basis; it was that when they did obtain alcohol, many imbibed to the point of stupefaction.

Many of the uses to which Indians put alcohol were not necessarily socially disruptive.[96] They incorporated the imbibing of alcohol into existing religious and social rituals. Believing that drinking together strengthened bonds of friendship and alliance, Indians included the sharing of liquor in hospitality rituals. They even adopted the custom of toasting and drinking to one's health.[97] Additionally, there is some evidence that they integrated alcohol into marriage festivities and into dances—both ceremonial and social.[98]

The religious, even sacred, connotations of the inebriated state are most obvious in the role that drinking came to play in funeral rites and mourning rituals.[99] Drunkenness was thought to facilitate contact with the spirit world and to help survivors mourn a loved one's passage into that world. In October 1768 Moravian missionary David Zeisberger traveled from Goshgoshing on the Allegheny River to visit the Seneca town of Geneseo, the Genesee castle, later called Big Tree, located on the Genesee River in western New York State. While there he witnessed a memorial vigil in which his hostess and some other women became drunk—as a requisite part of the vigil. "Our hostess with other women became very drunk and disturbed us the whole night." The women "excused themselves, asking us not to remember it against them, because they were obliged to drink for the dead." They were actually "obliged" to get drunk for the dead, and that is why "they were not able to offer us any of their liquor," which was a cause for thankfulness on Zeisberger's part.[100] The women needed all of their available liquor to achieve total intoxication.

Grief and insecurity may also have been significant factors in eighteenth-century Indian drinking. During the 1600s and 1700s, the Eastern Woodlands Indians were engulfed by a demographic catastrophe of staggering proportions. From time of contact through the end of the European colonial period, the American Indian population east of the Mississippi declined by 90 percent.[101] Epidemics of such pathogenborne diseases as smallpox, influenza, and measles caused most of the decline. War and the malnutrition that followed in the wake of wartime dislocations exacerbated the decline. Virtually every Indian suffered numerous painful personal losses in parents, siblings, spouses, children, kin, and countrymen.

Added to grief was the insecurity that came with repeated forced migrations. The Eastern Woodlands Indians were pushed out of their original homes and ever westward, as nation after nation was transformed into bands of refugees. Some Indian groups were displaced as often as once per generation, others were forced or felt compelled to move two and even three times in the same generation.

If some Indians, wearied with sorrow and fear, searched for escape, temporary respite, or even solace in drunkenness, they would not be the first nor the last people to do so.[102] And they certainly had sufficient cause.

TEMPERANCE ASSESSED

The available evidence suggests that the Allegany Senecas, under the leadership of Handsome Lake and under the continuing influence of long-time temperance advocates like Cornplanter and the Quakers, achieved and maintained a high level of sobriety during the thirteen years between the prophet's first vision and the outbreak of war in 1812. The evidence further suggests that the temperance movement associated with Handsome Lake spread to other Seneca communities and to other Iroquois nations.

The evidence is all anecdotal, of course, and most of it comes from the Quakers. But, on this subject, anecdotal evidence is the only kind available; if documentary evidence exists, it has either not surfaced or not been identified yet. As for healthy skepticism about the objectivity of Quaker authors, who might be suspected of slanting their reports on Indian temperance in such a way as to validate the effectiveness of their mission, it should be noted that when sobriety did slip during the War of 1812, the Quakers reported it.

In September 1799 after Henry Simmons had announced his intention of returning to the east, Cornplanter expressed his disappointment to some visiting Quaker elders. "He regretted the loss of the Friend who was about to leave them, and said he [Simmons] had been useful to him in keeping whiskey and other strong liquor out of their town; that they now drank much less than formerly." Cornplanter also conveyed some apprehension about waging the temperance campaign without Simmons. "He feared that when the Friend went away, he should not be able to prevent its [alcohol's] use so well as he had lately done."[103]

Simmons, however, was not indispensable to the temperance movement, which began to spread to the Cattaraugus Reservation in late 1799. The Senecas there resolved "to quit drinking whiskey, and not to allow traders to sell it" on the reservation.[104] By the early summer of 1800 the chiefs at Cattaraugus were able to report that the temperance message was being received favorably—even by their young people. "We are now determined to follow your advice as far as we are able, and to spill all the whiskey traders bring among us for sale. You must not think we are offended at you for trying to make us sensible of our weaknesses; for even our young men and young women rejoice to hear it, and are in hopes that their hands will grow stronger, that they may be able to overcome their weaknesses."[105]

Progress continued at Allegany too, where, according to Halliday Jackson, the Senecas continued "to be strong in their resolutions against the use of spirituous liquors, over which they had by this time [June 1800] gained a great conquest."[106] By 1801, temperance was the firmly established rule at Allegany. "The Indians now became very sober, generally refraining from the use of strong liquor, both at home and when abroad among the white people." Jackson noted that one of the Allegany Senecas had remarked to the Friends, "No more bark cabins, but good houses; no more get drunk here, now, this two year."[107]

The chiefs at Allegany, led by Cornplanter, reinforced the community's temperance standard by excoriating any backsliders. "Whiskey was not knowingly suffered to be brought into the settlement; and if any were found out to have been intoxicated, when they were out in the white settlements, they were sharply reproved by the chiefs on their return, which had nearly the same effect among Indians, as committing a man to the workhouse among white people."[108] The example set by the Allegany Senecas influenced other Seneca communities. A Quaker visitor to Allegany observed in 1802 that sobriety was "in some degree spreading to other settlements of the Seneca nation."[109]

By 1803 the temperance movement, inspired by continual exhortations from Handsome Lake, was flourishing far beyond Allegany and Cattaraugus. At a general council of the Seneca nation held that year at Cornplanter's village, a chief from the Tonawanda Reservation announced that the Senecas there had renounced strong drink.[110] According to a report published the following year in the *Massachusetts Missionary Magazine,* the Onondagas had "for two years greatly reformed in their intemperate drinking. . . . The impression he [Handsome Lake] made was so powerful, that different tribes held several councils on the subject, and finally agreed to leave off the intemperate use of strong liquors."[111]

The dramatic impact of the temperance movement on the Onondaga nation is described in a collection of reminiscences about the early days of European-American settlement in the locale of Syracuse, New York. This collection, called *Onondaga Reminiscences,* includes the recollections of a trader named Webster, who ran a trading post at the mouth of Onondaga Creek, around the turn of the nineteenth century. Webster stocked a plentiful supply of whiskey, and was actually quite generous with it. Sometime after Handsome Lake's 1799 visions, probably in 1800 or 1801, Webster was called upon briefly by "eighteen of the principal chiefs and warriors of the

Onondagas," who told him "they had just set out to attend a great council of the Six Nations, to be held at Buffalo." As was his custom, Webster produced a bottle, which "was plied with a right good will to the lips of all." As the Indians departed, Webster, long a favorite trader with the Onondagas, received extravagant demonstrations of friendship and mutual attachment.[112]

Later, on their way home from the Buffalo council, the Onondaga delegates stopped at Webster's store. As usual, the trader placed a bottle of liquor before them. To Webster's "utter astonishment . . . every man of them refused to touch it." At first, the trader took this as a sign of hostility and resentment, though he could not imagine the cause. He even feared, for a moment, that the Indians might be going to take his life. But, his anxiety was short-lived. "The chiefs explained that they had met at Buffalo a prophet of the Seneca nation, who had assured them . . . that without total abstinence from the use of ardent spirits, they and their race would shortly become extinct." Having "implicit confidence" in the prophet's warning, the principal Onondaga chiefs and warriors had "entered upon a resolution never again to taste the baneful article," and "they hoped to be able to prevail upon their nation to adopt the same salutary resolution."[113]

The *Onondaga Reminiscences* continues: "Many at this early day adopted the temperance principles, it is said at least three fourths of all the nation; and of all those who pledged themselves to the cause, not an instance was known of alienation or neglect; but to a man, they religiously adhered to their solemn pledge. . . . At this period, it [the Onondaga nation] was considered one of the most temperate communities in the land; only a very few of the nation indulging in the intoxicating cup, and these were treated with contempt by their more sober companions."[114]

Evidence from the year 1806 shows that the temperance movement continued strong at Allegany and Cattaraugus, and that Handsome Lake continued to carry his abstinence message to other communities. Regarding Allegany, Halliday Jackson reported "They continued strongly opposed to the use of spirituous liquors, and seldom held a council without some animadversions on their baneful effects—and nothing excited more wonder among the surrounding white people, than to find them entirely refuse liquor when offered to them. The Indians said that, when the white people urged them to drink whiskey, they would ask for bread or provisions in its stead."[115] The Pittsburgh trader John Wrenshall confirmed that Allegany Senecas, when offered alcohol, would decline and ask for sugar water instead.[116]

Jackson added: "Their continued resolutions against the use of spirituous liquors affords an encouraging prospect. . . . Several old men, whom I well knew had formerly been very much addicted to drinking and generally got intoxicated when they could obtain liquor, are now become sober and industrious, and there are very few instances of intoxication."[117] Jackson also reported that, during the summer of that year, "a company of Indians from Allegany with Connediu [Handsome Lake] (whom they call their prophet) at their head, paid a visit to several villages of their brethren, near the Genesee River, in order to dissuade them from the use of strong drink, and to encourage them in habits of industry."[118]

John Phillips, part of a delegation of Friends from the Indian Committee of the PYM, which visited the Seneca country in September 1806, recorded in his journal that the Quakers congratulated the Allegany Senecas on their sobriety. "Brothers, we have often heard of your strong resolutions against drinking whiskey . . . and it has made our hearts glad to find that you have kept these resolutions. . . . Quitting the use of it has been a great blessing to you."[119] Phillips also recorded the reply made by Blacksnake, nephew of Cornplanter. Blacksnake said that it had been seven years since the Great Spirit had first spoken to Handsome Lake, warning the Indians not to drink whiskey, and that for seven years the Indians had "declined the use of it." Furthermore, they "were determined never to let it rise again."[120]

The delegation of Friends also visited Cattaraugus in 1806. The foremost headman of the Senecas there, whose name was Chief Warrior, told the delegation that the Cattaraugus chiefs closely monitored the sobriety of their people and held regular temperance meetings. "They had taken up strong resolutions against the use of whiskey," and each of their chiefs "kept a daily watch over the rest of the Indians to caution them against drinking whiskey. . . . They were sensible that strong drink had done them a great deal of mischief and kept them poor, but now they had got master of it. . . . Since they had taken up these good resolutions, they had daily conferences on these subjects, and were continually trying to encourage one another."[121] Impressed by this thorough-going sobriety program, Halliday Jackson declared that "A great reform had taken place among" the Cattaraugus Senecas.[122]

On their way home from the Seneca country, the Quaker delegation stopped overnight at Batavia, New York. There the Friends encountered a "number of Indians" who were "on their way to the great council at Buffalo Creek. . . . They all behaved very sober and civilly without drinking a drop of liquor. . . . We noted with satisfaction that, during our journey among all the Indians on the Allegheny River, or either of the villages at Cattaraugus [the Seneca village and the nearby Munsee village[123]], we have not seen one Indian the least intoxicated with liquor—which perhaps would be a singular circumstance to observe in traveling among the same number of white inhabitants."[124]

The temperance movement remained strong and the general level of sobriety remained high throughout the remainder of the first decade of the 1800s. In a written speech sent in November 1807 to the PYM Indian Committee, Handsome Lake and the chiefs at Allegany stated that their young men, usually the hardest drinking segment of the population, had generally abstained from whiskey and other hard liquor.[125] That same year, in fact, two young chiefs had so overmastered their thirst, that they purchased some whiskey and hid it, for the purpose of retailing it to European-American passers-by on the river, as the latter traveled down the Allegheny in boats, barges, and rafts. This practice, however, was "much disapproved by the Indians generally."[126]

The Allegany Senecas valued their sobriety and did not appreciate it when a sly trader debauched some of them in 1809. This enterprising fellow, who had brought a load of goods up the river in a canoe, sold the Indians some cider royal, never letting on that it was anything other than regular apple cider, which he also sold. When several of the Senecas, including a few chiefs, turned up drunk, some members of the community uttered threats against the trader, while others, alarmed that things might be about to get out of hand, quickly fetched the Friends from their farm. By the time the Quakers arrived, the shifty trader had already shoved off in his canoe, probably in fear for his life.

William Allinson, the Quaker visitor who related the episode in his journal, concluded his remarks on the temperance of the Allegany Senecas with this observation. "The Indians of this settlement generally abstain from the use of spirituous liquors so that it has become very rare to see one of them intoxicated."[127] Allinson also visited the Cattaraugus Senecas in 1809, and reported nearly universal abstinence among them. They had quit "the use of spirituous liquors every man, but there were yet three women who would sometimes become intoxicated; yet they [community leaders] did not intend to cease laboring with them until they became reformed."[128]

In 1809 upwards of 1,000 Iroquois Indians assembled at Buffalo Creek for a general council of the Six Nations. In the preceding century, such councils had been occasions of much drunkenness. Quaker Jacob Taylor, who attended the 1809 meeting, remarked, however, "I think I never saw so many Indians together before that conducted [themselves] with so much propriety—the number could not be well ascertained, but it was though there were about one thousand, and I don't remember one drunken Indian amongst them.[129]

Not surprisingly, the temperance movement associated with Handsome Lake was not 100-percent effective. Despite the movement's overall effectiveness and Handsome Lake's vigilance, there was backsliding, most of it due to Indian traders who kept liquor as part of their stock. Handsome Lake fulminated against these individuals; and although he drove the liquor traffic underground and reduced it to minor proportions, he was not able to completely suppress it.[130]

Also, the temperance movement did not spread to all Seneca communities in western New York. While the movement enjoyed remarkable effectiveness at Allegany, Cattaraugus, and Tonawanda, it had little, if any, effect at the huge Buffalo Creek Reservation, at Tuscarora, or at the tiny Seneca enclaves strung along the Genesee River. The problem seems to have been one of proximity to European-American population centers.[131] Buffalo Creek was close to New Amsterdam, later called Buffalo; Tuscarora was close to Niagara, a major military installation surrounded by "white" settlements; and the Genesee enclaves were just that, enclaves surrounded by European-American settlers. Even if temperate-minded Indians had been able to keep liquor out of these villages and off these reservations, intemperate Indians had but a short distance to travel before finding a place to get drunk.

The Oneida Reservation is a special case, when it comes to the Handsome Lake temperance movement. The Oneidas had long been Christianized, and the Reverend Samuel Kirkland was working among them during the first decade of the 1800s. On the question of temperance, it is difficult to separate his impact from that of Handsome Lake; but neither achieved the result he desired. By Kirkland's own admission, his Christianized followers were hardly models of sobriety; and he reported that temperance among the Oneida "pagans," as he called Handsome Lake's followers, was not as high as it was among Handsome Lake's Onondaga followers.[132]

With the outbreak of war between the United States and Great Britain in the summer of 1812, the temperance movement suffered a severe setback. Anxiety levels rose among the Senecas and other Iroquois of western New York. They felt pressured by the Americans, upon whom their annuities depended, to take up arms against the British and their Canadian allies. But some of those British allies were Mohawks and other Iroquois who had emigrated to Canada after the American Revolution. The New York Iroquois dreaded the notion of being placed in a position where they might be called upon to kill their Canadian brothers.[133] Yet they also feared that if they "stayed at home on their seats," their land would be overrun by the victor, whichever side that might be, intent on punishing them for their neutrality. Additionally, the close proximity of the New York Iroquois to Canada threatened to turn their lands and villages into battlefields.[134]

Tension and panic were not the only reasons that intemperance rose again as the war came on. During wartime European Americans had always used liquor to recruit and retain Indians to their side as allies, and the Americans during the War of 1812 were no different. Many of the New York Iroquois took up arms on the American side, despite Handsome Lake's strenuous objections. (He wanted them to remain neutral.) Once in the American army as auxiliaries, the Indians were issued regular rations of whiskey.

Of the Allegany Senecas, Halliday Jackson reported that by 1813, "their war excursions had a demoralizing effect, by exposing them again to the use of intoxicating liquors, which gained an ascendancy over some."[135] By 1814 the final year of the war, the injurious effects of intemperance were once again causing problems for the Allegany Senecas and the other New York Iroquois.[136] As Jackson put it, "Some of their people had, during the war, got into habits of intemperance—and this tended to retard their advancement in the modes of civilized life."[137]

CHAPTER EIGHT

Dances and
a Dead Feast

S everal days after Cornplanter had informed Simmons of the community's decision to ban alcohol from the village, the Indians "held a worship dance." The temperance council had taken place on May 15, and several more days had elapsed before Cornplanter informed Simmons of the ban. The worship dance, then, would have occurred during the second half of May. Based on this timing and on Simmons's description of the dance, he probably witnessed the feather dance, performed as part of the annual Corn Planting Ceremonial.

> Men, women, and children wearing their best apparel were dancing in a circle around their wooden image, or God. There seemed to be no designated dancers. Those, who had a mind to step into the ring, did so, facing toward the image. Two men were seated flat on the ground, face to face within the circle, engaged with musical instruments. Their instruments were gourd shell and water turtle, dried with the entrails out, and bullets, shot, or corn in the place thereof. They beat these on a deerskin lying on the ground, making a very great rattle.
>
> The men in the circle, always moving round at a slow pace, dance and shout greatly. The women dance chiefly by keeping their feet set close together and moving them sideways, first the toes and then the heels, as they move round with the men. The women, however, remain silent.
>
> After they had taken two heats at dance, their minister, who was a very lusty Indian, said it was enough, and thanked them. Shortly after that, he addressed them with a long speech by way of advice, after which they concluded the business by eating some food, which had been prepared the fore part of the same day.

Simmons's use of the words "wooden image" is a bit too suggestive of graven images and idolatry. The Allegany Senecas did not worship their wooden statue, which was but a representation of the Good Twin, also known as *Tarachiawagon,* the Good Spirit, whom the Iroquois viewed as the supreme being. The Iroquois also acknowledged many other spirits and spirit forces, whom they appreciated, supplicated, placated, and thanked. But all these were inferior to Tarachiawagon, whose statue stood in an open area, in front of and facing Cornplanter's house, which served as the village council house. Halliday Jackson described the statue as "a huge block of wood" formed "into the similitude of a man, and artfully painted."[1]

The use of a large, outdoor, wooden statue during religious celebrations was not unique to the Senecas at Cornplanter's village. Some of the Genesee Senecas living at Caneadea used a similar statue. Colonel Proctor stumbled across it during his fruitless diplomatic travels in 1791.

> Arrived this day [April 3] at an Indian village called Canaseder [Caneadea], situated on a high bluff of land, overlooking the Genesee river. . . . In this place was erected a wooden statue, . . . fashioned like a fierce looking sage. This form they worship by dancing before it on certain festive occasions or new moons, looking on it as through a veil or assistant, whereby they pay adoration to the Supreme Spirit, as knowing it hath a form, but not a substance.[2]

The wooden statue at Cornplanter's village met its demise in 1802, when, rotted at the ground, it fell over. Jackson described the chagrin caused by this development.

> This circumstance occasioned very considerable agitation among them, to know what manner to dispose of it, without giving offense to the Great Spirit. . . . Some were for taking it into the woods, and leaving plenty of provisions beside it. Others were for erecting another in its place, and some were for discarding such a representation entirely.
>
> A son of Cornplanter [Henry] . . . reasoned with them . . . and told them it had grown up in the woods like other trees of the forest; that they had cut it down and made it into the form of a man; but it was still nothing but a block of wood. . . . If they would give it up to him, he would dispose of it. To this they reluctantly consented, but only on the condition that he would take all the responsibility for any harm that befell the nation in consequence thereof.
>
> Accordingly, he tumbled it into the [Allegheny] river, and let it swim down. The Indians carefully viewed the process to see if any evil would befall him. Some time later, several of them, passing along the river, discovered it lodged on an island, about eleven miles below its former station. At this, they appeared struck with astonishment and considerable alarm; but they let it remain as they found it.[3]

SENECA DANCES: FEATHER, DRUM, AND WAR

What follows here is by no means a comprehensive description of Iroquois dance. Lewis Henry Morgan, regarded as the father of American anthropology, reported that the Iroquois had thirty-two distinct dances, of which twenty-one were still performed at mid-nineteenth century. Gertrude P. Kurath, a professional dancer who studied Iroquois ethnic music and dance at mid-twentieth century, listed almost forty different Iroquois dances. The feather, drum, war, and dead dances examined in this chapter are those that figure prominently in the Simmons 1799 Journal or in the contemporaneous journals of Quaker missionaries and other European Americans.[4]

The feather dance was a sacred and ceremonial act of worship, consecrated to the praise and adoration of the Good Spirit.[5] Featured, in this case, as part of the Corn Planting Ceremonial, the feather dance was performed during each of the major religious celebrations: Midwinter Rites, Thanks-to-the-Maple, Planting Ceremonial, Strawberry Festival, Green Corn Festival, and Harvest Feast.[6] The feather dance was open to all who were physically able to participate. The male version of the feather dance was quite strenuous and required a good deal of stamina; older men shuffled their way through with a few heel bumps. The female version was based on an altogether different dance step, which was, perhaps, a bit less taxing than the exertions of the men.[7]

The name of the dance came from the feathers in the ceremonial headdress worn by the men. Seneca headgear of the late-eighteenth century did *not* consist of the peacocklike feathered bonnets of the Plains Indians. Rather, it consisted of a buckskin skull cap, formed on a frame of wooden splints, and decorated on top with a bouquet of split feathers. The quill of a single eagle feather, much larger than the split feathers, was inserted into a tube, which allowed the feather to spin as its wearer danced, waving it through the air. The Seneca name for this ceremonial head-piece is *gustoweh.*[8]

Simmons's description of the feather dance is similar in essentials to that published by Morgan in 1851. Morgan's description was based on observations made, mostly on the Tonawanda Reservation, during the 1840s. By then, this dance—and the Corn Planting Ceremonial of which it was a part—had moved indoors. By Morgan's time, most formal religious rituals were held inside a dedicated building, specif-

Gustoweh, *or men's ceremonial headdress (originally published by Morgan in 1851). This example is typical of the mid-nineteenth century Senecas, and is probably quite similar to what Allegany Seneca men wore a half century earlier.* DARLINGTON LIBRARY, UNIVERSITY OF PITTSBURGH.

Nineteenth-century Seneca Gustoweh, *from the Grand River Reservation, Ontario, Canada. Made from eagle and pheasant feathers and wampum beads attached to a leather cap, this gustoweh includes a decorative silver band.* COURTESY, NATIONAL MUSEUM OF THE AMERICAN INDIAN, SMITHSONIAN INSTITUTION (06.0354). PHOTO BY DAVID HEALD.

ically reserved for ceremonial use, which came to be known as the longhouse. This designation referred to the long houses in which the Iroquois once dwelled and to the Iroquois League, which itself was represented symbolically as the Great Longhouse.

Morgan, a much more careful and thorough ethnographer than Simmons, made his observations on a different reservation, Tonawanda versus Allegany, and a half century later than Simmons. Variations in Seneca dance and ritual occurred locally, from village to village, and temporally, over the years and decades—although it seems that they varied less with time and more with locale. Aside from the outdoor location and the presence of the wooden statue, Simmons's 1799 description of the feather dance at Cornplanter's village is nevertheless consistent with Morgan's 1851 description of the dance at Tonawanda. There are some differences in detail, however.

In Morgan's description, dancing was initiated by a corps of male dancers, composed of fifteen to thirty men who were the most proficient performers. Simmons does not mention a core group of dancers, but in his description, every villager turned out in his or her finest regalia. In Morgan's description, only the members of the male dance corps dressed in ceremonial costume, which consisted of gustoweh, kilt, moccasins, and a belt worn around the waist and over one shoulder. Except for the shoulder strap, the men were naked from the waist up, though they also wore arm- and wristbands, made of various materials ranging from deerskin to velvet. The dancers also wore knee rattles or bells, which consisted of numerous deer hooves or tiny bells attached to kneebands. These rattled and jingled as the dancers moved. Although Simmons does not mention it, the men wore breechcloths, not kilts, at the end of the eighteenth century.[9]

Simmons and Halliday Jackson both witnessed another feather dance, performed in conjunction with the Green Corn Festival in late August. Their descriptions of the August feather dance add important details to Simmons's description of the May dance. As Simmons put it: "Many of the men were almost naked and painted greatly

round their bodies, arms, and about their heads, in different colors and in various figures. Most of the men and boys were painted, a little or a lot." Jackson wrote: "The men are all naked from the waist up, and their bodies painted a variety of hues." Morgan too described the men as "nude down to the waist . . . exposing their well formed chests, finely rounded arms, and their smooth, evenly colored skins, of a clear and brilliant copper color," but said not a word about them being painted.[10]

As the dance continued, the less proficient men joined in, then the older men, then the women and children. In this way, the dance was "cumulative." Simmons described the dancers as arranging themselves in a ring around the

Men's regalia typical of mid-nineteenth-century Senecas (originally published by Morgan in 1851). Shown are kilt, leggings, moccasins, feathered head-gear, and lightweight ceremonial war club. A half century earlier, among the Allegany Senecas, men's ceremonial costumes had consisted of nothing more than breechcloth, moccasins, body paint, and headgear. DARLINGTON LIBRARY, UNIVERSITY OF PITTSBURGH.

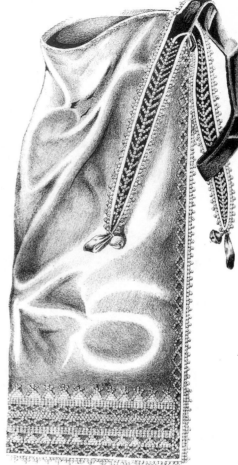

Male moccasin and legging (originally published by Morgan in 1851). The ornate embroidery with beadwork was typical of the Seneca men's ceremonial costume at mid-nineteenth century. Before the availability of commercially manufactured glass beads, porcupine quills were used for decorative embroidering. At the turn of the nineteenth century, Allegany Seneca men had preferred to dispense with leggings when dancing. Many midcentury Seneca men did the same. DARLINGTON LIBRARY, UNIVERSITY OF PITTSBURGH.

wooden statue, facing it. Presumably they moved sideways, revolving around the statue, as the entire ring rotated. Morgan described the dancers as arranging themselves in a single column, one following the other, in a long, counterclockwise spiral, with the male dance corps at the head of the line.[11]

The feather dance proceeded according to the musical accompaniment provided by the two male singers and their turtle-shell rattles, which set the rhythmic beat and

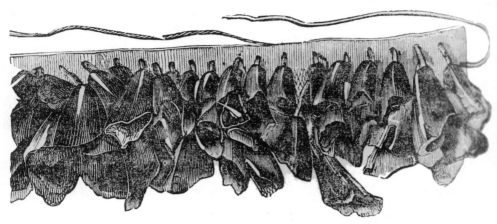

Knee rattle (originally published by Morgan in 1851). It was made of deer's hooves suspended individually from a leather strap, which was tied onto the leg, just above the knee. Men wore them while dancing, to set up a rhythmic rattling sound, perfectly synchronized with their dance step. Sometimes tiny bells were used instead of or in combination with the deer's hooves. Similar rattles were worn around the ankles. DARLINGTON LIBRARY, UNIVERSITY OF PITTSBURGH.

tempo for both the singing and the dancing. Morgan found the two singers seated astride a wooden bench in the center of the dance space, facing each other, pounding their turtle-shell rattles on the bench. In his description, they sang a series of songs that praised the Good Spirit, and lesser spirits too. The lyrics expressed sentiments of appreciation for past favors and supplication for continued protection. Each song lasted several minutes and was separated from the next by an interval of a minute or two. During these intervals, the singers continued to beat their rattles, but at a slow, restful pace. This gave singers and dancers a chance to catch their breath. Dancing ceased during these intervals; the dancers simply sauntered along to the slow beat of the rattles. The tempo increased as the next song began and the dancing resumed. Simmons mentioned "two heats at dance," which does not correspond closely to Morgan's series of songs. But the notion of "heats" or rounds is consistent with alternating periods of intense dancing and restful walking.[12]

In his description of the Green Corn feather dance, Simmons linked variations in song to variations in dance.

> Two men were seated on a deerskin just at the foot of the image. Each of them had a water turtle shell, with corn or shot within, which they beat on the deerskin so as to make music for the dancers. The men on the deerskin also made changeable noises by way of song. The dancers paid great attention to the sound of the music and the tone of the song, and as these changed, so did their dancing. They changed the twisting of their arms, heads, and bodies; they also varied their yelling and shouting. All of which would be very astonishing to those who had never beheld Indians.

At mid-twentieth century, only the male dance corps performed during the first song, according to anthropologist William N. Fenton and music-and-dance ethnologist Gertrude P. Kurath, who, collectively, made their observations at Allegany between 1933 and 1951. With each subsequent song, more and more of the men joined in the dance. By about the third or fourth song, the women and children began to join in too, their numbers increasing with each succeeding song. Perhaps it was a cumulative aspect similar to this in the 1799 feather dance that led Simmons to write: "There seemed to be no designated dancers. Those, who had a mind to step into the ring, did so."[13]

In both of his feather dance descriptions, Simmons mentions the shouts and yells of the male dancers, and the silence of the females. Jackson also mentions a "frightful halloo or scream" given by the dancers. Morgan is silent on this point. Fenton and Kurath, however, both describe antiphonal calls between the lead dancer and his followers, and, just before the start of a new song, between the lead singer and the people. Perhaps similar antiphonal calls passed between the dance leader and the dancers in 1799.[14]

As Morgan described it, the men's feather-dance step was based on very energetic, yet rhythmic and graceful, heel stomping. The foot was raised "two to eight inches" and then the heel was brought "with great force as frequently as the beat of the rattles." The tempo was frenetic—two or three beats per second. Dancers stomped one heel two or three times, before alternating to the other. The rapid stomping motions shook the knee rattles and bells, creating a rhythmic clatter and jingle, which complimented the turtle-shell rattles of the singers. The men maintained an erect posture throughout the dance, with none of the bending at the waist seen in other dances. Nor were there any contortions of body or face. All movement

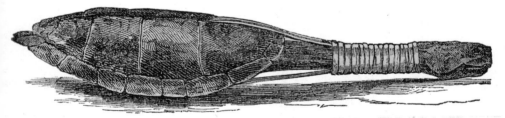

Turtle-shell rattle (originally published by Morgan in 1851). It was made from an eviscerated turtle, with a handful of dried chokecherry pits added to the interior. The head and neck were strengthened with wooden splints or rods to form a handle. Various species, including box turtles, were used to make rattles. The great turtle rattles, used in connection with the feather dance and false-face rituals, were made from snapping turtles (Chelydra serpentina) found in the Allegheny River. These animals grow carapaces of more than sixteen inches in length and can weigh over sixty pounds. Some snapping turtle rattles, therefore, were very large indeed.

and expression was graceful and dignified.[15] Fenton and Kurath described male feather dancers at mid-twentieth century, as raising their feet "as high as they are able" and doing "a powerful stamping two-step, with raising of the free knee."[16]

Descriptions of the women's feather-dance step remained virtually unchanged over the century and a half spanned by the historical and ethnographic sources used here. Simmons: "The women dance chiefly by keeping their feet set close together and moving them sideways, first the toes and then the heels." Morgan: "They moved sideways in this figure, simply raising themselves alternately upon each foot from heel to toe, and then bringing down the heel . . . at each beat of the rattle." Fenton: "The step of the women is a side-ward shifting of toe and heel, coming down on heel with the rattles, shoulders erect and swaying with the music." Kurath: The women face the center and glide to the right, "shoulder to shoulder with the women's feather dance step: a smooth swivel twist of parallel feet."[17]

Simmons said nothing about the women's costume in connection with the Planting Ceremonial feather dance. Later in his journal, however, he did say a few words about it, in connection with the Green Corn feather dance. He described "the women's manner of dress" as "superfluous to such a degree that some of their strouds and petticoats must have cost them twenty dollars. Their petticoats were overlaid with silk ribbons of diverse colors." He made the same charge of superfluity against the men's ceremonial attire.

Halliday Jackson too described the Seneca woman's apparel of about 1800. The skirt was "an open garment," secured at the waist by a belt, and reaching to midcalf.[18] From Jackson's somewhat opaque description, it is difficult to de-

Women's regalia typical of mid-nineteenth century Senecas (originally published by Morgan in 1851). Shown are overdress (or smock), skirt, leggings, moccasins, and blanket. A half century earlier among the Allegany Seneca women, hemlines had been at about midcalf, allowing more of the leggings to be visible. DARLINGTON LIBRARY, UNIVERSITY OF PITTSBURGH.

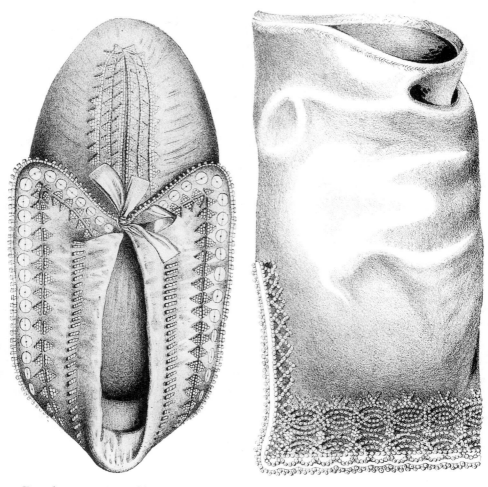

Female moccasin and legging (originally published by Morgan in 1851). These are typical of Seneca women's ceremonial costume at mid-nineteenth century, when leggings were gathered above the knee and extended to the ankle. A half century earlier, among the Allegany Senecas, women's leggings had been a bit shorter, gathered just below the knee and extending to the ankle. DARLINGTON LIBRARY, UNIVERSITY OF PITTSBURGH.

termine whether the skirts were simply a bolt of broadcloth wrapped around the waist and secured there, or whether they were made by actually sewing together the vertical edges of such a bolt. Twenty some years later, skirts were definitely sewn together.[19]

Jackson noted that the hem was "often covered with ribbons or embellished with silver brooches, with a considerable degree of skill and taste." The women also wore "a short frock or vest, which reached to the waist and flowed loosely about them." In addition, they wore leggings that extended from just below the knee, where they were gathered and fastened, down to the moccasin. A colorful blanket was "spread over the whole." Jackson added that various garments were "fancifully fringed and ornamented with needle work, set in with beads and porcupine quills, variegated and disposed with much skill and ingenuity."[20]

By Morgan's time, hemlines—at least those on ceremonial skirts—had fallen to the ankles. Women still wore leggings, however, which had risen and were gathered and fastened above the knee. The "short frock" had grown into an "overdress," which was a long-sleeved, pullover dress, gathered somewhat at the waist, and falling almost to the knees, like a smock. A blanket was still worn as a shawl.[21]

Clearly, Morgan was describing the ceremonial garb of his day, while Jackson seems to have given a more generalized description that touched on both the everyday clothing and the ceremonial costume of his day. Some of the differences in their descriptions might thus be due to differences between everyday and ceremonial clothes, as much as they are to changes in fashion over the decades.

The drum, or thanksgiving, dance was a sacred dance quite similar in external form to the feather dance. The theme of the songs, however, was given over to thanks-

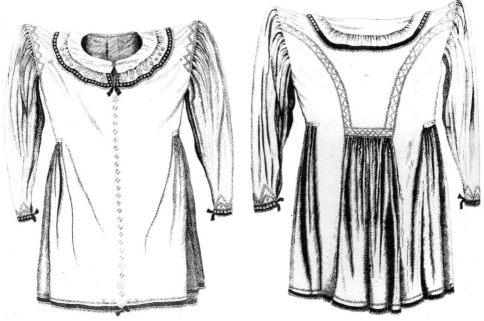

Women's overdress, front and back (originally published by Morgan in 1851). This garment was worn over the skirt, which in turn was worn over the leggings. A half century earlier, among the Allegany Senecas, women's smocks had been more like large shirts, with the tails untucked and falling only to the waist or the top of the hips. DARLINGTON LIBRARY, UNIVERSITY OF PITTSBURGH.

giving to the Good Spirit and all the lesser spirits that played a role in Seneca well-
being. During the walk-around between songs, people offered spontaneous prayers of
thanksgiving. When the drum dance was performed at Green Corn and Harvest Feast,
religious officiators recited set speeches or prayers during the intervals between the
singing and dancing and the walking. The alternate name for the thanksgiving dance
came from the water drum used to set the rhythm and tempo, which was a bit slower
than that of the feather dance. According to Morgan, the thanksgiving dance was performed at Midwinter Rites, Green Corn, and Harvest Feast.[22]

Morgan found the thanksgiving dance so similar to the feather dance that he did
not elaborate on the details of the dance itself.[23] He did note, however, that the thanksgiving prayers given between song-and-dance bouts were consolidated into a thanksgiving address to the Good Spirit, which was recited during the white-dog sacrifice of
Midwinter and Green Corn. (The white-dog sacrifice is no longer performed by prac-
titioners of the Longhouse Religion.) A much abridged version of the thanksgiving
address follows.[24]

> We return thanks to our mother, the earth, which sustains us . . . to the rivers and
> streams, which supply us with water . . . to all herbs, which furnish medicines for
> the cure of our diseases. We return thanks to the corn, and to her sisters, the beans
> and squashes, which give us life. We return thanks to the bushes and trees, which
> provide us with fruit . . . to the wind, which, moving the air, has banished diseases.
> We return thanks to the moon and stars, which have given to us their light when the
> sun was gone. We return thanks to our grandfather *Heno* [the thunder], that he has
> protected his grandchildren from witches and reptiles, and has given to us his rain.
> We return thanks to the sun, that he has looked upon the earth with a beneficent eye.
> Lastly, we return thanks to the Great Spirit, in whom is embodied all goodness, and
> who directs all things for the good of his children.[25]

Curiously, Morgan described the thanksgiving-dance singers as using turtle-
shell rattles, whereas twentieth-century observers reported the use of a water drum
and cow-horn rattles.[26] Jackson described the 1799 version of a drum as follows:
"[T]wo men, being seated near the feet of the image, make music by pounding on a
skin drawn over the mouth of a kettle, or some other vessel, the sound of which has
some resemblance to that of a drum."[27] He did not say whether the "vessel" contained water.

Mid-twentieth-century observers described the water drum as a wooden vessel,
open at the top, with a hide cover stretched over the opening. The drum's pitch is adjusted by varying the tightness with which the hide is stretched. The drum is partially filled with water, which is added through a bunghole on the side. The water is
needed to keep the hide drumhead wet. If it dries out, it will contract and collapse
the wooden stays of the drum. Thus, the drum must be inverted periodically during
use and continuously during storage.[28]

The war, or brag, dance of the late-eighteenth century was not described by Simmons or Jackson. Surveyor John Adlum, however, witnessed a war dance at Cornplanter's village in August 1794, and described it in his memoirs. Quaker elder James
Emlen witnessed a brag dance at Canandaigua in October 1794, and wrote a brief de-

scription of it in his journal. Morgan also wrote a detailed description of the war dance at mid-nineteenth century; Fenton and Kurath described it at mid-twentieth century.[29] The following description of the war, or brag, dance is a synopsis of these references, with emphasis on the earlier sources.

At one time, this dance had been performed upon the departure and return of war parties. It was not a sacred dance and came to be performed for a variety of reasons, not all of them war-related: adoption of a war captive, installation of a new sachem, and entertainment during treaty negotiations or during the visit of a noteworthy guest.[30] The dancing was performed only by a corps of male dancers, numbering from fifteen to thirty, and dressed in traditional Iroquois battle attire, which consisted of nothing more than breech clout, moccasins, and war paint. They also wore "clusters of small deer hoofs tied around their knees and ankles, to rattle as they danced."[31]

The dancers performed to the accompaniment of up to four singers, with one or two drums, "made of a kettle covered with parchment," and a couple of cow-horn or gourd rattles. War whoops preceded each song. The songs for this dance expressed emotions associated with war: undaunted courage, steadfast resoluteness, implacable fierceness, unyielding defiance, stoic fatalism. The spirit of these songs was captured in the following example, which had also been sung by war captives during torture rituals in the sixteenth and seventeenth centuries.

> I am brave and intrepid. I do not fear death, nor any kind of torture. Those who fear them are cowards. They are less than women. Life is nothing to those who have courage. May my enemies be confounded with despair and rage.[32]

This dance was structured in the familiar pattern of two- or three-minute periods of singing and dancing to a quick-time beat, alternating with one- or two-minute periods of walk-around to a half-time beat.[33] The dancing warriors, each armed with a tomahawk or a small war club, clustered within a circular dance space. The dancers, however, each gave a solo performance, as they faced in independent directions, and pantomimed the contorted movements and violent actions of close combat: aggres-

Wooden drum, one foot in height, with hide drumhead (originally published by Morgan in 1851). The wetted hide was stretched over the top of the hollow drum and held in place by a cloth-wrapped hoop. As the partially cured hide dried, it became very taut. The drumhead could be rewetted simply by inverting the drum, which contained several mouthfuls of water, blown into the interior through a bunghole, which was then plugged with a wooden stopper. DARLINGTON LIBRARY, UNIVERSITY OF PITTSBURGH.

sive lunging, defensive ducking, springing from a crouch in ambush, throwing a tomahawk, swinging a war club, parrying blows, stabbing with a knife, and scalping. The only ground plan for this dance was spontaneous chaos, and the basic step was a leaping jump-kick.[34]

A unique feature of the war dance were the brag speeches, given not by the dancers or singers, but by some of the onlookers, who sat or stood in a circle around the dance space. The would-be speaker, at his own whim and irrespective of the state of the dance, active or walk-around, stood, took up a tomahawk, strode to a wooden post, and struck it with all his might. This produced a loud crack or rap, which instantly halted the singing, drumming, rattling, and the dancing or walk-around. Performers and spectators all shifted their gaze and full attention to the speaker, who then delivered an animated address that lasted anywhere from a few seconds to a few minutes.

Some speeches boasted of war exploits or hunting feats. Others contained pleasantries and compliments, or barbs and criticisms, directed at someone present. In either case, such speeches rarely failed to elicit a response-in-kind from a subsequent speaker. Still other speeches were composed of witticisms, jests, or taunts—occasionally aimed at someone present. Speeches of this sort, delivered in the high, grand style of Iroquois oratory, were the source of much amusement. Spectators delighted in the repartee, greeting some speeches with cheers, other with jeers. The brag speeches turned an hour's dancing into a two to three hour session, good for a whole evening's entertainment. The war dance was usually performed in the evening or at night.

Adlum had an unforgettable experience at the August 1794 war dance, held at Cornplanter's village, under the night sky, by firelight. The Indians seated him next to the war post, where the hatchet blows struck uncomfortably close to his head. To make a lasting impression, the dancers occasionally surrounded the post and rained their tomahawks upon it. This situation seemed so dangerous that Adlum was deserted by his interpreter, Nicholas Rozencrantz, who scurried off into the darkness, after the fire had burned down a bit, before it could be restoked. Adlum, however, remained seated while the dances and speeches continued.

The older speakers prefaced their brags by addressing some remarks directly to Adlum. They told him they would not relate any war exploits done against the "whites" because "possibly I had lost some of my relations or friends, and they did not want to hurt my feelings. Then they would relate something that had been done against the Cherokees, or other southern Indians."[35] Adlum described the braggadocio typical of war-dance speakers.

> And if the braggart thought he had related a feat, that none present could exceed, he would throw on the ground a small piece of tobacco wrapped in a leaf or other substance, at the same time saying, 'if any of you can beat that,' (meaning the story) 'take it up and let us hear what you have to say.' It was always taken up, and sometimes a more extraordinary story told.[36]

Cornplanter finally rose and struck the war post. He stood in the bright light of the freshly stoked fire, holding a tomahawk in one hand and a pair of moccasins in the other. He glared at Adlum, who stood up and glared back, but later confided in his memoirs that he had held his breath and clenched his jaws to keep the color in his face.

Cornplanter then delivered a speech that was less of a brag and more of a threat. That whole summer, Cornplanter had been thinking about taking up the war hatchet in earnest. He was disillusioned with the United States, which still insisted on keeping all of the territorial concessions it had extracted from the Senecas in the 1784 Treaty of Fort Stanwix. His policy of peace and cooperation with the United States appeared to have brought nothing but new indignities and affronts to the Seneca nation. Some Senecas had been maligning him and his policies for a decade, and maliciously impugning his motives. The Western Confederates utterly detested him and occasionally threatened to kill him. Both Cornplanter and his policies seemed thoroughly discredited.

Cornplanter liked Adlum, but he did not like what the surveyor was doing—laying out tracts for European-American settlement and development north and west of the Allegheny River, all the way to Lake Erie. The Senecas were particularly sensitive about surveys in that portion of their homeland that had been annexed by the United States in 1784—the southwest tip of the present-day state of New York plus the Erie Triangle. Cornplanter might have been trying to send a message through Adlum to the federal and state authorities that Seneca forbearance was wearing thin in the face of repeated provocation. He also might have wanted to advertise to his own people his willingness to go to war; or perhaps he hoped that a fearsome display within the dramatic setting of the war dance would redound to his advantage in Seneca domestic politics. Whatever his motives, Cornplanter delivered one of the most intimidating brag speeches ever given at a war dance.

> You are the most dangerous man we know of as an enemy. You know every path and avenue in our country, and you have acquired an influence that no [enemy] ought to have. . . . You are now here and in our power, and it would be but common prudence for us to keep you here. But we have promised that, while you are with us, you and all your people [Adlum's survey teams] shall be safe. We will now be as good as our words . . . tomorrow you must depart from this place. . . . We are at peace now, but in a few days it will be otherwise.
>
> If the piece of country we have asked for is not returned to us, war will follow. And we will break up the frontier, from the Genesee River to Pittsburgh. Also, that part of the West Branch of Susquehanna, where two of our people were murdered, . . . will not escape our vengeance. That place [Pine Creek] I understand is not far from your home. . . . We suppose that when that settlement is invaded, you will turn out and act like a man. And as I have always seen you wear moccasins when you are with us or in our country (I suppose you can move in them more alertly than with shoes), I therefore present you with this pair . . . that you may be ready for us, and meet us, when we make a stroke on your settlements.[37]

Adlum reached out with one hand to take the moccasins, and with the other to take the tomahawk. Then he struck the war post and delivered a reply that showed the true spirit of the brag dance. He grieved greatly that they were "so determined for war and to rush on certain destruction." He would go home and "endeavor to be prepared for them. And . . . if they invaded the settlement I lived in, or anywhere within reach of me, I would take care that none of them should ever return to their towns to tell what became of them. Then they gave a great shout, which ended the bragging and dancing."[38]

A few months later Quaker elder James Emlen witnessed a war dance near Canandaigua, staged as entertainment during the weeks of waiting for all the Indians and the American representatives to assemble prior to the treaty talks between the Senecas and Timothy Pickering. General Wayne, by this time, had defeated the Western Confederates at Fallen Timbers, and both the Senecas and the Americans were ready to strike a deal. With the threat of war lifted, this dance was suffused with a spirit of mirth and merriment that contrasted sharply with the ominous atmosphere that had surrounded the one at Cornplanter's village. When writing the name of this dance in his journal, Emlen initially wrote the word "war," but then crossed it out, and continued with "brag dance."[39]

According to Emlen, "[A]ny of the spectators have a right, after presenting a bottle of rum, to . . . boast of what great feats . . . they had done . . . in their lives. This was done in rotation by the bystanders, both Indians and Whites." They took turns recounting all the heroic deeds of their lives: battles fought, scalps and prisoners taken. A doctor who happened to be present, delivered a bottle and made his own, novel brag. He declared "that he had been a man of peace all his days, that his profession was . . . to save men's lives, . . . that a child was capable of taking the life of a fellow creature, but that it required a man of judgment and skill to save it." The Indians found this boast so unique and original, that it "gained their universal applause."[40]

FEAST FOR THE DEAD

Simmons had this to say about the feast for the dead, which occurred sometime in late May or very early June, 1799:

> About a week after the worship dance, they had a great feast as a form of remembrance of their dead, which was according to their ancient custom. They have such strange ideas. They believe that they and their deceased ones will receive some benefit on account of their holding the feast. The present one was being held on account of the old chief's daughter, who had been dead upwards of four months. They prepared much food of different kinds and took it to a cabin near their burying ground where they ate it. They were, old and young, a very great number. Their custom is that each one must taste the other's dish.

Jackson's coverage of the dead feast ritual was also brief:

> They are also in the practice of collecting together and making feasts in remembrance of their dead, some months after the interment, under an apprehension that the deceased will receive some benefit thereby. And if an Indian . . . dreams a remarkable dream, respecting a deceased relative being hungry, or in need of sympathy or assistance in any way, the Indians of the deceased's particular tribe [clan] are informed of it, and a deputation is sent out to hunt. The game thus taken is prepared and cooked, and a feast and dance in a religious way is instituted, which continues for a day or more, whereby they apprehend the wants of the deceased are satisfied.[41]

Though Jackson wrote of a religious aspect to the dead feast and dance, this ritual ceremony was transacted directly between the living and the dead. Perhaps the most appropriate way to think of the dead feast is as a village reunion, attended by the dead as well as the living. The dead were summoned to the feast, where they joined in the dancing and shared in the food.

Although the immediate purpose of the feast was to feed the dead, something more than mere nourishment was carried away from the feast by the living and the dead. Both benefited from the renewal of kinship bonds and the fulfillment of reciprocal obligations that transcended death. The living fulfilled their obligation to remember and feed the dead, who, in turn, continued acting as chthonic powers in spiritual alliance with their living relatives. Thus, the dead would refrain from bothering the living by haunting their dreams or visiting illness upon them. In addition to nourishment, the ancestors received satisfaction in knowing they were not forgotten, which brought them peace.[42]

The Senecas conducted the dead feast within three separate contexts: as a night-long, communal memorial for all the ancestors of the village; as a private ritual for curing illness; and as a "booster" rite at Midwinter for those who had been cured through a dead feast. As a curing ritual, the dead feast was conducted in the house of the sick person, and lasted only about half as long as the communal version. The renewal ceremony at Midwinter was even briefer.[43]

From Simmons's description of the late-May (or early-June) community meal at Cornplanter's village in 1799, it is not clear whether the dead feast was held during the day or at night, nor whether the feast included anything beyond the meal—such as songs, dances, and processions. Jackson, however, did mention dance, which, presumably, would have been performed to the accompaniment of singing, and perhaps drumming. He also wrote that the dead feast "continues for a day or more," which suggests the possibility of a daytime celebration.

Simmons reported that the feast was held "on account of the old chief's daughter, who had been dead upwards of four months." Her death was still on everyone's mind, and, most likely, this was the first communal dead feast since she had died, all of which might explain why Simmons associated this feast with her in particular. But there is no reason to believe that the feast was not held for all the other village ancestors too.

Morgan, writing at mid-nineteenth century, described the ritual as a nightlong series of dances performed to a cappella singing (no drums or rattles); he also made brief mention of a community repast. At mid-twentieth century too, the communal memorial started before midnight and lasted until dawn.[44] The remainder of this description is based on Fenton and Kurath's description of the dead feast at mid-twentieth century.

In keeping with the matrilineal kinship ties of the Senecas, the duty of maintaining friendly connections with the ancestors fell mainly on the women. They organized the feast, presided over it, and performed the dances to the attendant music of the *ohgiwe* songs, the chants to the dead. The "chanters to the dead" consisted of a mixed group of male and female singers, who were accompanied by a drum.[45]

The feast began with a tobacco invocation, in which a man burned tobacco and invited the dead to come and participate. The tobacco served both as an offering and as incense. Then came the ohgiwe songs and dances. It is generally believed that the ohgiwe dances, unlike others, proceeded in the clockwise direction, as did the ritual distribution of food which followed the dances. Everyone partook of a communal meal. Next came a series of social dances, in which men and women both participated. Then presents were distributed to the organizers, cooks, helpers, singers, and ohgiwe dancers, in short, to everyone responsible for putting on the feast. Finally, just before dawn, a number of corn bread cakes were carried overhead in a procession formed by a single-file column of men and women. As the cakes were carried around, onlookers reached up and snatched them out of the upheld arms. This represented the spirits of the dead claiming their share of the food.[46]

Though as laconic as Simmons in describing the dead feast, Jackson did describe the related topic of Seneca mortuary practice of about 1800, in which the corpse was buried soon after death, in an underground grave, where the remains were left permanently. Jackson observed no contemporaneous practices involving prolonged exposure of the corpse above ground on scaffolds, until microbes and the elements left nothing but bones. Nor did he observe any familial ossuaries, village ossuaries, or mounds.[47]

> Their funeral rites are observed with great solemnity, and succeeded by deep mourning. Whatever might have been the ancient custom, as stated by some writers, with respect to a place of general deposit of the bones of their dead, I find no such tradition among them at the present day. A spot of ground contiguous to each village is occupied as a place of interment, and each grave has a separate covering of boards, or clefts of wood.
>
> The corpse, dressed in the best apparel, is put into a coffin made of boards, when they can be procured; otherwise bark is laid beneath and over it in the grave. Sometimes a new blanket and small kettle is enclosed with it, and frequently other articles, to which the deceased was attached while living.
>
> They believe in the resurrection of the spirit, and that, for some time after death, it is common for the . . . [spirit to return to the body]. Therefore, in order to afford the spirit easier access to its former tabernacle, a hole is cut in both the head of the coffin and the covering of the tomb, the ground not being considered any obstruction to its entrance or egress.[48]

At mid-nineteenth century, Morgan confirmed several of the features described by Jackson. The spirit of the deceased was still believed to linger in the vicinity of the body, hovering about it, sometimes reentering it. Some Senecas still bored holes in the coffin to facilitate the spirit's comings and goings.[49]

CHAPTER NINE

Witches and Wives

S immons recorded two disturbing events in Cornplanter's village on June 13, 1799, a week or two after the dead feast.

> By command of the old chief, three of his men took the life of a woman, with knives. They supposed that she was a witch or that she had poisoned others, and that she had threatened the day before to do the like again. This threat reached Cornplanter's ears. However worthy of death she might have been, I know not, but I took her to be a bad woman. The same day, I, with the assistance of an Indian, rescued a woman whose husband was beating her with his fist in a cruel manner, he being somewhat intoxicated.

WITCHES

The old woman was suspected of having used witchcraft to kill Cornplanter's daughter, whose memory was honored at the recent dead feast. The chief's daughter had suddenly become gravely ill in late May or early June 1798. Cornplanter had, at that time, been forced to cancel his plans to accompany Quaker elders John Pierce and Joshua Sharpless to Buffalo, saying "that one of his daughters had been taken very bad, and was now likely to die."[1] She finally died in late January or early February 1799.[2]

On June 13, 1799, Cornplanter, still mourning the loss of his daughter, received reports that the old woman had threatened to kill a child living in his household—probably one of his grandchildren. Cornplanter ordered three men—his own sons, according to Jackson—to kill the old woman. They did so that day, falling upon her as she worked in a field, and stabbing her to death. They buried her immediately, there where she had fallen, with no ceremony and no opportunity for public mourning.

News of the bloody deed flashed through the village, causing "no small stir." A general council, convened that same day to consider whether the killing had been justified, decided that the woman had indeed been "worthy of death."[3] To late-eighteenth-century Senecas and other Iroquois Indians, practicing witchcraft was equivalent to committing murder, and the victim's kin had the right and duty of retribution. In fact, it was not necessary to first hold a trial or obtain a confession before killing a witch, though such a formal procedure did often prevail. Accusers, such as Cornplanter and his family in this case, could take matters into their own hands, and an inquiry would be held after the fact, to determine whether their action had been warranted.[4]

Simmons, though he too "took her to be a bad woman," did not condone the killing, nor the fear of witchcraft that had occasioned it. Having had no foreknowledge of the slaying, nor any opportunity to prevent it, he chose to say nothing about it. This contrasts rather sharply with his forceful denunciations of drunkenness, diatribes against dancing, and comments on the Indian forms of worship. Perhaps perceiving witchcraft fear to be not only endemic, but intractable, he did not want to further alienate the nativists. The fact that Cornplanter had ordered the slaying may also have deterred him from speaking out.

The fear of witchcraft was widespread among the Senecas.[5] Illness, accidental injury, and death were often blamed on the malevolent power of a witch. Many people feared that some individuals had mastered the powers of witchcraft and used those powers against persons whom they viewed as enemies.

The pervasiveness of witch fear was recognized, acknowledged, and accommodated by Seneca beliefs pertaining to the false faces and *Tawiskaron,* the Evil Twin of creation days. The false faces, or in Seneca, simply "faces," *gagosa,* were wooden masks carved with grotesquely twisted facial features, such as deep-set eyes, staring or squinting from beneath an impossibly furrowed brow, a protuberant nose bent to one side, and a misshapen mouth with exaggerated and weirdly distorted lips. False faces were used throughout the year in private curing rituals; during Midwinter and Green Corn, when the medicine societies performed their maintenance rituals for previous cures; and during spring and fall in general village exorcism rites. The exorcism rites were conducted to expel disease; to prevent natural disasters ranging from windstorms to insect plagues; and to banish the powers of witchcraft.[6]

The faces derived their power to nullify witchcraft from the archetype of all false faces—the defeated and chastised Tawiskaron. At his birth, he had killed his own mother by bursting forth from her side, instead of leaving her womb by the normal route, as his elder brother Tarachiawagon had just done. The Good Twin proceeded to do the work of creation, while the Evil Twin followed him about, spoiling as much of his brother's creation as he could. The Good Twin was able to repair much of the damage done by the spoiler, but not all of it. So the Indians, created by the Good Twin, were left with good things, such as the sun and the moon, the three sisters, corn, beans, and squash, the rivers and their fish, the forests and their game animals. But they were also left with blights on their crops, disease, pestilence, winter, snakes, and witches.

When the creation was finished, the Good Twin made one final tour of inspection to see if anything was left undone, and whether he could undo any more of his brother's evil works. As he approached the western rim of the world, he found a giant, who claimed to be the author of creation. This Great World Rim Dweller, *Shagodyoweh,* was none other than the Evil Twin, in a different guise.[7] After arguing over whose handiwork the creation really represented, the two brothers decided to settle the dispute by means of a contest, the winner of which would hold undisputed claim to the title of Creator.

The test was to see who could move the mountains at the rocky rim of the world the farthest—one version of this story specifies the Rocky Mountains. The twins faced eastward, their backs to the mountains. Shagodyoweh shook his huge tortoise rattle, the ground trembled, and the mountains moved—a short distance. The twins turned around to see what Shagodyoweh had accomplished, and then faced eastward again. Next, the Good Twin commanded the mountains to move, and they did—right up to the brothers' backs. Shagodyoweh spun around to see what had happened. He smacked his face into the mountain, bashing his nose over to one side, and contorting his mouth in pain.

Humbled, Shagodyoweh acknowledged his brother as the Creator and reformed his own behavior. He could not repair the harm he had already done to creation, but he promised to become a benefactor to the Indians, if they would but remember him by wearing masks to represent his battered face, burning tobacco to honor him, and offering him an occasional bowl of cornmeal mush. In return, he would protect the Indians against the evils he had introduced into the world: pestilence, natural disasters, and witches. The false faces thus acquired their power to cure disease, restrain the destructive forces of nature, and counter the effects of witchcraft.[8]

By serving as a ritualized countermeasure to the power of witches, the false faces provided a religious and cultural remedy that directly addressed the phenomenon of witchcraft fear. By no means were the faces devoted exclusively to combating witchcraft, and indeed they filled other important needs, especially in curative rituals. The fact, however, that a major cultural institution like gagosa was devoted, even in part, to counteracting the perceived effects of witchcraft, is compelling evidence of how widespread and pervasive witchcraft fear had been at one time in the Seneca past. The persistence of witchcraft fear at mid-twentieth century was documented by Annemarie Shimony, among the conservative followers of the Longhouse Religion at the Six Nations Reserve, Grand River, in Canada.[9]

Not surprisingly, the Quakers dismissed out of hand the Seneca beliefs about witches. They chronicled the fears and executions related to witchcraft, but they recorded none of the arcane details about its supposed practice during the years around 1800.[10] For details about specific practices imputed to witches, we must turn to the observations of anthropologists and ethnologists: Lewis Henry Morgan during the 1840s, DeCost Smith during the late 1880s, and Arthur C. Parker during the first decade of the 1900s.

Although the details of witchcraft practice probably changed somewhat over time, we can look at the details of the later periods to get some idea of what the practices might have been like during the last decade of the 1700s and the first decade of the 1800s. For the three periods from which we have some data, the details of witchcraft practices remained quite similar from one period to the next, suggesting that they changed little during the span of seventy years.

From the *Jesuit Relations,* we also have some data on specific practices of alleged witches among the Hurons of the 1640s. The specific practices imputed to witches by Hurons of the seventeenth century bear a remarkable resemblance to those imputed by Iroquois of the mid-nineteenth through early-twentieth centuries. This is not surprising because the Hurons were culturally related to the Iroquois and spoke an Iroquoian language.[11] During the 1650s, a large fraction of the Huron ethnic population was also physically incorporated, as adopted war captives, into the Iroquois population.[12]

Witches could be male or female. They banded together in covens that met secretly at night in the woods, where they initiated and trained new members. As part of the induction rite, the neophyte had to swallow a certain kind of snake and sacrifice a close relative or friend. Witches roamed under the cover of darkness, to cast spells and work charms, sometimes even assuming the guise of animals, such as dogs, hogs, turkeys, or owls, into which they could transform themselves at will. Occasionally they kept their human form at night, and lighted their way through the blackness by shooting flames out of their mouths. The mere sight of mysterious lights moving through the darkened woods, or the sound of howling dogs or hooting owls, were fraught, in some minds, with ominous connotations.[13]

To perform their black magic, witches had at their disposal numerous techniques. They could poison their victim with some magical brew or powder of their own concoction, with which they contaminated the victim's food, or broadcast into his house where he would breath it. Evidently the magical poisons were quite specific, harming only the intended victim, but not the witch or innocent bystanders.[14] Alternatively, a witch could simply cast a spell by reciting an incantation while burning some tobacco. Closely related to the casting of a spell was killing by sheer volition, in which the witch mentally formulated a malediction, pronounced it silently, concentrated, and wished the victim to death.

Witches favoring a more intricate approach could hide a charm near the victim, whose health would then deteriorate until he finally died. Charms varied from simple objects, such as twigs, to malignant perversions of the traditional hunting charm. A twig could be inserted into the soil and left to decay. As the twig decomposed, the victim's health steadily declined. Instead of killing a particular victim, a witch might decide merely to inflict pain. In such a case, he or she could fashion a doll, stick a pin or a rusty nail into the part to be harmed, and bury it near the victim's abode. The victim would then suffer chronic back, hip, or other joint pain.

Hunting charms were originally given to worthy hunters by the spirit forces of the animals they hunted. A hunter who had killed a bear, for example, would soon after have a dream. The spirit force of the prototypical bear, from which the Good Spirit created the earthly bear, would appear in the dream and reveal the secrets of a charm, which had the power to bring the hunter continued success in the future. Three secrets surrounded the charm: whether bone, tooth, or claw was to be used; what specific tobacco-burning ritual the hunter had to perform to release the charm's power; and specifically how the hunter was to fulfill his lifelong obligation to care for the charm ritually.[15]

If the hunter failed to periodically burn tobacco for his charm, offer it thanks, and feed it meat, the charm would turn on him and his family, bringing sickness and death.[16] In this way, the charm would "eat" its way through several members of the family. The malignant power of hunting charms could be deliberately harnessed and directed by witchcraft. Like hunting charms, malignant charms were made of esoteric animal parts, such as mountain lion claws, bear teeth, beaver glands, beetle exoskeletons, or snake vertebrae. The charm was wrapped in buckskin or cloth, and tied into a small bundle.[17] These perverted charms hunted people instead of game animals.[18] Potent and lethal, malignant charms did not have to be placed near the victim to cause harm; from afar, the witch could direct their evil influence to the intended target.[19]

Another witchcraft technique, sometimes called "introjection," was performed by magically projecting a foreign object into the victim's body. Reported to anthropologists during the late-nineteenth and early-twentieth centuries by Iroquois informants, this technique was also reported to the Jesuits as far back as the first half of the seventeenth century by Huron informants. Although a jagged stone fragment or a sharp-edged flint chip would suffice, more elaborate objects were sometimes introjected. The witch might carve a small wooden peg, about the length of a needle but larger in diameter, sharpen it to a point at both ends, and drill a tiny hole through the midpoint of the shank. This hole could be strung with some of the witch's hair, or with a piece of thread tied to a worm or a splinter of bone. Alternatively, the witch might wind some of his or her own hair around a small packet of straws.

The cure for witchcraft by introjection was removal of the foreign object. A shaman could perform this task in a variety of ways. He could decoct and administer an emetic, and then find the pernicious object among the ejected contents of the victim's stomach. Or, especially in cases affecting the victim's limbs, the shaman might apply a poultice of secret ingredients, leaving it bandaged over night. The next morning, while removing the bandages, he could find a pernicious object among them, drawn out of the victim's body by the poultice. The shaman could also use a combination of massaging and hand cupping to withdraw an object from the victim's abdomen.

For deeply embedded objects, a more radical procedure was required. The shaman made a small incision in the victim's side and placed a suction cup over it. The cup consisted of a small cow horn, open at the base with the interior scraped out, and with a small hole drilled into the tapered end. The shaman fitted the base over the incision and provided the suction with his own mouth at the tapered end. After extracting a suitable amount of blood, the shaman would find a pernicious object trapped inside the cow horn.

The following excerpt from the *Jesuit Relations* describes witchcraft practices and techniques as reported among the Hurons during the first half of the seventeenth century.

> The Hurons believe that there is a kind of monstrous serpent . . . which brings with it disease, death, and almost every misfortune in the world. . . . They say that sorcerers use the flesh of that frightful serpent to cause the deaths of those upon whom they cast their spells. With that poisonous flesh they rub some object, a blade of corn, a tuft of hair, a piece of leather or wood, the claw of an animal, or some similar thing. The objects thus rubbed with that ointment derive from it a

malignant efficacy, that causes them to penetrate into a man's entrails, into his most vital parts, and into the very marrow of his bones, carrying with them disease and suffering, which consume and cause to perish those who are attacked by them—unless, through some contrary virtue, means are found to draw out those objects to which the spell is attached. . . .

[T]hose who claim to extract those spells from the bodies of the sick . . . will show some wonderful thing that they pretend to have taken from the most vital parts of a man . . . or, if they really, by means of emetics, produce the ejection of a tuft of hair, a piece of leaf or of wood, or any other similar object accompanying the matter of which nature has relieved itself, they imagine . . . that some spell is connected with that piece of wood or tuft of hair.[20]

Note that the snake still figures in the later Iroquois witchcraft lore: the would-be witch was required to swallow a snake. Thus, in both the Huron and Iroquois cases, the power of witches was traced back to the snake, which in Iroquois cosmology was one of the Evil Twin's masterpieces. In this sense, the power of witchcraft was originally loosed by the Evil Twin, who, after his reformation as Shagodyoweh, helped the Indians ward off the effects of witchcraft through the false faces and their associated rituals.

Inevitably, when a tragedy occurred, such as the inexplicable death of a child, or when a series of premature and untimely deaths all struck in the same family, suspicion of witchcraft arose among some family members. Witchcraft fear also increased when a deadly communicable disease spread through the village.

The Senecas did not automatically attribute all illness to witchcraft; they did recognize that many disorders stemmed from natural, somatic causes. For such disorders, the patient or his family consulted an herbalist, who prepared or prescribed a remedy based on the patient's symptoms.[21] Normally recommended were infusions of medicinal herbs, decoctions of berries, roots, or bark, and poultices. Efficacious for many ailments, the Seneca *materia medica* were, in the hands of knowledgeable and experienced herbalists, probably superior to the purgatives, emetics, and bloodletting frequently used by European-American physicians of the day.[22] Some of Cornplanter's descendants, known as the Cornplanter Senecas, became renowned herbalists, trusted by both Indian and European-American patients well into the twentieth century.[23]

The Senecas understood the efficacy of herbal medicine in terms of the "spirit force" of the plants used.[24] White boneset leaves were steeped to make a tea "for breaking up a bad cold," and purple boneset roots were boiled to make a diuretic. Used to make infusions were: angelica, for pneumonia; various mints, for colds; and self-heal, for biliousness. The leaves, pith, and berries of the elderberry bush had so many uses that elder served "as a whole pharmacy in itself." Red stems of plantain were decocted for treating stomach disorders. Wire Grass was infused to make a muscle liniment—and more: "The old-time lacrosse players used to steep up a big bundle in a kettle. In season they drank it as an emetic in the early morning, and as a tonic during the day, and they bathed their limbs in the solution." Roots of water hemlock were used in poultices, but never in decoctions or infusions, unless one wanted to make a poison. To commit suicide, one had only to "eat of the fatal root."[25]

Cornplanter Seneca herbalists also made a cough syrup of white-pine needles and cherry bark. They pounded the roots of tall white lettuce *(Prenanthes altissima)* into a pulp to poultice snake bites. Infusions from the bark of quaking aspen treated children and dogs for worms, and the red berries of staghorn sumac treated measles and sore throat. They used Christmas fern and fireweed in cures for consumption, and sarsaparilla and spikenard in tonics for the blood. An emetic was concocted from the bark of silky dogwood, and a powerful physic from Culver's Root.[26]

When these remedies failed, the patient or his family enlisted the services of a shaman. His diagnosis and remedy, however, were expected to be less natural and more spiritual. All shamans had at least some knowledge of herbal medicine, but many of the most skillful herbalists were not shamans.

The shaman's repertoire of diagnostic techniques was eclectic. He might inquire after the patient's recent dreams, and identify an unsatisfied wish of the soul, or a spirit, slighted by the patient's failure to perform some obligatory ritual in its honor. The shaman might inhale vapors from a steaming concoction, or smoke from smoldering Indian tobacco *(Nicotiana rustica),* to induce a state of trance and identify a secret wish of the patient's soul, undisclosed in any dream, or the evil influence of a witch. The shaman might drink a magical brew of herbs and roots, and breathe on the patient, who became transparent to the shaman's probing vision, which soon discovered the seat of the disorder.[27]

For unsatisfied wishes of the soul, the shaman was likely to prescribe a sacred bowl game, a game of lacrosse, a feather dance, or a war dance, and, in all cases, a feast to conclude the prescribed doings. If the source of the trouble was a vindictive spirit who felt ritually neglected, he might prescribe the curative rite of one of the medicine societies (False Face, Husk Face, Dew Eagle, Little Water, Dark Dance), or a feast or chant for the dead. For bewitched patients he might recommend a false-face ritual or a chant for the dead. If the shaman determined that the witch was directing the malignant power of a perverted hunting charm, he would usually recommend a ritual by the Medicine Men's Society. If, after rendering the patient transparent, the shaman spotted an introjected object, he could try to remove it.

Possession of the pernicious object gave the shaman some retaliatory power over the witch. He could burn the object or hurl it against a wall, thereby torturing or injuring the witch.[28] If the shaman discovered the identity of the witch, then the witch could be seized and forced, by torture or threat, to confess. A witch who refused to both confess and repent would be killed.

The belief that witches preyed on their victims' loved ones meant that neither the cure nor the death of a bewitched person ended the matter.[29] A family that believed itself bewitched could expect to suffer illnesses, accidents, and deaths, as long as the witch remained alive. The only certain way to break the chain of disasters was to identify and kill the witch who caused them, thereby exacting revenge and protecting the family and the community from the witch's baneful influence.[30] Confession broke a witch's poisons, spells, and charms, but only death guaranteed that he or she would not revert to former practices.[31]

Mary Jemison reported in 1823 that during the thirty years she had lived among the Genesee Senecas, on average, one witch per year had been slain. She personally witnessed two such executions.[32] Morgan reported that as late as 1850, a woman was killed as a witch on the Allegany Reservation. He also asserted that "such instances have been frequent among the Senecas within the last fifty years."[33] In 1888 DeCost Smith repeated versions of a double execution for witchcraft reported to have occurred at Oneida around 1828, and of a man killed as a witch at the Six Nations Reserve in Canada about 1880.[34]

Handsome Lake became a notorious witch hunter. His accusations led to the deaths of at least three people. Ironically, Handsome Lake's witch hunting was brought to an end largely through the efforts of his halfbrother Cornplanter, who had himself been responsible for the witch killing of June 13, 1799.

In the autumn of 1800, another of Cornplanter's daughters—this one named Jiiwi—became ill after giving birth to a daughter.[35] Following a vision, Handsome Lake announced that the spirit messengers had promised him the power "to judge diseases and prescribe remedies," but he was not to exercise that power until the messengers told him he could. Upon hearing this, Cornplanter beseeched the prophet to put his new-found powers to work divining the cause of and cure for Jiiwi's disease. "Why, having the assurance of powers, do you not commence now? . . . My daughter is very sick."[36]

Although Handsome Lake explained that he was not yet authorized to use such powers, Cornplanter eventually prevailed upon the prophet to try to help Jiiwi.[37] Handsome Lake's method was to induce a state of trance within himself by inhaling fumes of smoldering tobacco. "Sometimes sick persons send a shirt or some other article of clothing to the prophet, that he may prescribe a cure. In such a case, he takes two handfuls of tobacco, puts their ends to the fire on the hearth, lies down and covers himself [his head] with a blanket; after he has arisen he prescribes for the disease."[38] In Jiiwi's case, Handsome Lake prescribed that the chants for the dead be sung, indicating, perhaps, that her sister, deceased early in 1799, was feeling neglected or restless.[39]

The chants were sung, but Jiiwi, instead of improving, worsened. Handsome Lake attributed the failure of his prescribed remedy to an incorrect performance of the chants. Amid burgeoning recriminations, Jiiwi's illness dragged on. Handsome Lake was finally persuaded to actually examine the young woman, whereupon he pronounced Jiiwi to be the victim of witchcraft, perpetrated by several of the Cattaraugus Munsees, acting in concert.[40]

The small group of Munsees had been living at Cattaraugus for about a decade when Handsome Lake leveled his accusations against them late in 1800. Though protesting their innocence, the Munsees sent a delegation, including some chiefs, to assist in curing Jiiwi. They proved no more effective than Handsome Lake, however, and the Allegany Senecas suspected bad faith on the part of the Munsees. Believing that one of the visiting Munsee chiefs was the witch primarily responsible for Jiiwi's illness, and that he was willfully withholding a cure, the Allegany Senecas seized him and held him hostage all winter, threatening to kill him if Jiiwi died.[41] It seems inconceivable that the Munsee chief would have been taken captive without Cornplanter's consent.

According to oral tradition, still current among the Cornplanter Senecas during the 1930s and 1940s, the father of Jiiwi's child was a young Munsee chief, named Silver Heels in some versions, John Logan in others, from Cattaraugus.[42] The Cattaraugus Munsees were in the habit of conducting an annual fall hunt through the valleys of Kinzua and Tionesta Creeks, the latter being an area familiar to them from the days when they still lived on the Allegheny River. To hunt in these areas, which were part of the traditional Allegany Seneca hunting grounds, the Munsees had to have Cornplanter's permission, which they customarily obtained during a layover at his village, on their way to the hunt.

In the autumn of 1799 the young Silver Heels was among the Munsee hunters who made the pilgrimage to Jenuchshadago. Cornplanter's permission, largely a formality, was quickly obtained, but the Munsees tarried for about a week. The young chief, quartered in Cornplanter's house, became intimate with Jiiwi. The hunt lasted for several weeks, at the end of which the Munsees headed for home, by way of Jenuchshadago, where they stopped to repay Cornplanter with gifts of venison, for his permission and hospitality. Again, they lingered for a few days; Silver Heels renewed his intimate relationship with Jiiwi. A month or two after the Munsees had returned to Cattaraugus, Jiiwi discovered she was pregnant.

Jiiwi fell ill during the late summer or early fall of 1800, shortly after her daughter's birth. For some reason the Munsees did not return that autumn for a Kinzua-Tionesta hunt. If this oral tradition is true, then the circumstances surrounding Jiiwi's pregnancy afforded Handsome Lake the opportunity to offer a plausible motive for the alleged Munsee witchcraft: to obviate any obligation on the part of Silver Heels to marry Jiiwi.[43]

Whatever were his reasons for ordering or allowing the Munsee chief to be held hostage, Cornplanter soon regretted the action.[44] If Jiiwi died and the Senecas killed their prisoner as a witch, the Munsees might take to the warpath, particularly if they could enlist their Delaware relatives in eastern Ohio as allies. Cornplanter had to find a way to prevent the Munsee captive from being killed, even if Jiiwi died.

He could not look to Handsome Lake for help. Failing to effect a cure, the prophet had salvaged his own reputation by detecting the presence of witchcraft, and by identifying the witches. If Jiiwi lived, Handsome Lake could attribute her survival to the threat of retaliation against the chief witch. If she died, the main culprit could be executed immediately, thereby protecting Cornplanter's family from further depredation. Nor could Cornplanter expect to find much support among his family and relatives. Distraught at Jiiwi's death, and free of the responsibilities of chieftainship, they were not likely to consider the consequences of retaliation.

Cornplanter called a council to discuss what to do with the hostage if Jiiwi died. He invited two of the principal chiefs of the Cattaraugus Senecas, who were in no hurry to go to war with their Munsee neighbors. Unable to reach a consensus on the basic question, the council agreed to seek advice from some friendly European-American leaders in Cussawaga, present-day Meadville, Pennsylvania, with whom Cornplanter had been on excellent terms for years.

The council composed a letter to David Mead, founder of the settlement at Cussawaga, summarizing the situation. The letter paid respect to Handsome Lake, "esteemed by us for his sobriety and knowledge, in many things superior to any of our nation," and recognized his authority as a prophet: "The man we depend on to discover these things is fully capable of explaining how they are contrived and executed, and tells us of many of those dark inventions, which is the present cause of our trouble."

The letter also expressed the utmost confidence in the prophet's integrity: "We think the man we confide in, that professes to search into these things, tells us the truth as far as he sees." But then came the important question: "Yet, Brothers we earnestly request your judgment . . . , whether you think it would be right and consistent with the will of the Great Spirit and the laws of humanity to take life through or by the medium of such proof."[45]

Cornplanter knew what the answer would be. He also knew that it was unnecessary to even mention the word "war"—Mead would quickly grasp that possibility on his own. The letter, however, went on: "It may be that our custom [retaliation] will be fulfilled before we receive your answer, as . . . the woman's life will soon depart from her, and we retain one of the principal persons suspected as a prisoner." The letter was signed by several of the chiefs at Jenuchshadago and by the two chiefs from Cattaraugus. Cornplanter's name stood at the top of the list. Handsome Lake's name was absent.[46]

Mead wrote back immediately, urging the Senecas not to kill the hostage. He then personally carried the council's letter to Governor Thomas McKean at Lancaster, which was, at that time, the state capital of Pennsylvania. Mead's haste was justified. By April 1801 some 200 Munsee and Delaware warriors had massed on the Ohio-Pennsylvania border. A war was in no one's best interest, and the state government sent letters to the Allegany Senecas and the Cattaraugus Munsees, appealing for restraint on both sides and the avoidance of violent conflict.[47]

Cornplanter's plan worked well in terms of precipitating European-American intervention in the dispute, although that intervention was limited to strenuously voiced opinions and exhortations. In the end Jiiwi miraculously survived; the hostage was released; the Ohio warriors went home; Handsome Lake claimed that his stand against Munsee witchcraft had saved Jiiwi's life; and Cornplanter averted war.

Cornplanter tried to reassure the Cattaraugus Munsees that they were still safe and welcome in Seneca country, that "they might lie down in peace—that he had swept their houses clean, that they might live comfortably in them—that he had swept clean before their doors, that they might go out and in, without molestation."[48] Nevertheless, the whole episode permanently soured relations between the Allegany Senecas and the Munsees, though the latter remained at Cattaraugus years afterward—they were still living there in 1810.[49] They eventually emigrated to the Grand River Reserve in Canada.[50]

Henry Simmons, who had left the missions permanently in the autumn of 1799, was not present during any of the dispute over Munsee witchcraft. During the winter of 1800 and 1801, the mission at Genesinguhta was staffed by Joel Swayne, Jacob Taylor, and Jonathan Thomas, none of whom lived in Jenuchshadago. The missionaries, nevertheless, would have become aware of the situation long before the council dispatched its letter to Mead. Unlike Simmons in June 1799, they were not confronted with a *fait accompli,* in which the victim was a friendless old woman of low station, whose passing went unnoticed outside the Allegany Seneca group. They had ample time and opportunity to intervene on behalf of the victim.

The Quakers' silence is explained by two facts: Cornplanter did not solicit their help in the affair, and they were hesitant to the point of paralysis about meddling in it. Late in June 1801 the missionaries wrote to the PYMIC:

> The subject [witchcraft] has afforded us much exercise from time to time, [but circumstances were] so intricately situated as to require much caution had we interfered . . . the distempered state of their minds through the enthusiasm and artful contrivance of their director [Handsome Lake] exceedingly obstructed any counsel or advice from being profitably received. The difficulty originated from an apprehension of injuries sustained by witchcraft . . . not uncommon for these poor natives to be annoyed with.[51]

No lives were lost on account of Handsome Lake's allegations of witchcraft against the Cattaraugus Munsees. Such was not the case, however, when Handsome Lake accused a mother and daughter of witchcraft in 1806 or 1807.[52] This incident occurred at Cold Spring, a new settlement on the west bank of the Allegheny River, in New York State, about twenty miles upriver from Jenuchshadago. Handsome Lake and most of the Allegany Senecas had moved there in 1804, after a falling out with Cornplanter, who was temporarily deposed as chief.[53] Cornplanter wanted to rent his land to European-American farmers, and forbade the resident Senecas to plant on his property. Except for Cornplanter's own family, relatives, and close connections, the group left the grant en masse, most of them settling at Cold Spring.

Although Handsome Lake, serving as both religious and civil leader, held sway at Cold Spring until 1809, there was occasional dissent—such as the time a deranged man stood in the longhouse doorway and, "in the classic Indian gesture of disrespect to a speaker, farted at the conclusion of the prophet's homily."[54] The man then turned away and disappeared. A few days later, a search party found him in a swamp, perched on a nest of branches he had broken and piled up, "devouring snakes." The search party took him back to Cold Spring, where he soon died.[55]

Handsome Lake attributed the man's irreverence to insanity, and blamed the insanity on witchcraft. He charged a woman and her daughter with administering a witch powder. A council of sixteen to twenty headmen decided to punish the women by flogging, with each of the headmen administering one lash to each woman. Handsome Lake later claimed that he had expected the women to survive the whipping; however, they both died.[56]

In 1809 a woman was brought from Onondaga to Cold Spring for trial as a witch. Handsome Lake pronounced her guilty, and she was killed on the spot. Cornplanter, who still resided at Jenuchshadago, let it be known privately that he disapproved of the killing. A few months later, at a council in which a visiting delegation of Quakers also disapproved of the killing, Cornplanter publicly distanced himself from his halfbrother's witch hunts: "I hope we shall be careful in future how we take the lives of any for witchcraft without being sure that they are guilty." He added that witchcraft was "very difficult to prove." He subsequently expressed the opinion that it would make more sense to reserve the death penalty for chiefs who sold any more Indian land, than to impose it on supposed witches, because the one thing could be proved, but "the other he had his doubts about."[57]

WIVES

On the same day that the old woman was killed for practicing witchcraft, Simmons and one of the Senecas intervened to stop an Indian who, while drunk, was beating his wife with his fists. Another reference to wife beating occurred in the young man's dream and confession, recorded in Simmons's journal entry for March 1. These two pieces of anecdotal evidence are in no way sufficient to make a case that wife beating was a common occurrence or a serious social problem. The fact that Handsome Lake addressed the issue in his preaching, however, suggests that the incidence was high enough to merit attention.

> The married often live well together for a while. Then a man becomes ugly in temper and abuses his wife. It seems to afford him pleasure. Neither man nor woman must strike each other.[58]

Handsome Lake called attention to the problem in another way. He specified the punishment that wife beaters would receive in hell.

> Now the master of the house looked about and saw another person. So he said, "Come here, my nephew, I wish to see you flog your wife as was your custom on earth." The punisher then pointed out the image of a woman heated hot with fire, and commanded the man to beat the image. Then the man pleaded with moans to be released from the command, but the punisher forced him to strike the image with his bare hands, and the man fell in agony, prostrate upon the floor screaming.[59]

In both accounts, alcohol seems to have played a role. The young man, who confessed to both drunkenness and wife beating, might very well have been drunk when he beat his wife. It seems probable that alcohol abuse was linked to spousal abuse.

The fact is that we really do not know—and cannot reconstruct—the incidence of domestic violence among the Senecas at the turn of the nineteenth century. Even assuming a low incidence, however, the fact that domestic violence against women was occurring at all indicates some fraying of the social fabric. The ideal model for the relationship between husband and wife in particular, and between the sexes in general, had traditionally been alliance based on reciprocal obligations.[60] We have already seen the importance of alliance in other areas of Iroquois life: in the ritual condolence of the mourning moiety, in the quest of a dreamer's friends to fulfill his wish, in ritual observances dedicated to the dead and other spirit forces in return for their goodwill and assistance. As Elisabeth Tooker phrased it, "[R]elationships between men and women also rested on maintenance of reciprocal obligations."[61]

The alliance between Iroquois men and women allowed for a division of responsibility and labor that was advantageous to all. "Men and women had different roles, neither dominating the other."[62] Women were responsible for affairs in the "clearing," that is, in the houses and the cultivated fields. They gathered firewood, hauled water, cooked and served the meals, took care of the children, and tended the crops. Typically, the only tasks related to the clearing for which men were responsible were house building and field clearing. Men were responsible for affairs in the "forest," which included everything outside the village and its fields. They hunted, trapped, fished, traded, warred, and conducted relations with other villages and nations.[63]

The advantages derived from this division during contact times, up to the reservation period, are demonstrable. With women shouldering all of the responsibility for the clearing, men were free to engage in prolonged, far-ranging hunts to obtain the hides and furs necessary for purchasing European-American manufactured goods. Throughout the colonial era, the fur trade was—with a single exception—the only avenue through which Indians could acquire the goods upon which they had become dependent: blankets, cloth, guns and ammunition, and metal kettles, knives, and hatchets.[64] The only other avenue for acquiring such goods was through gift giving by colonial governments, which, though significant, was unreliable and subject to the political vagaries of colonial and imperial bureaucrats.

Women's role in the clearing and men's role in the forest were equally important to Iroquois survival during the colonial era. Some historians have asserted that the women's contribution to the Iroquois subsistence economy was greater than the men's, or that Iroquois women controlled "the economic organization of their tribe."[65] Such assertions are debatable, even when the notion of subsistence economy is restricted to horticulture, hunting, and gathering, as it was during precontact times. When applied to contact times, such assertions are false because they invariably ignore the importance of trade. [66]

Men cleared the fields and built the houses. Neither task was inconsiderable and both represented essential contributions to subsistence. Field clearing, moreover, the most arduous of all horticultural tasks, was an ongoing project. Nearly every spring, a few new fields were put into service, and a few old ones were abandoned due to declining productivity, which occurred despite the natural fertilization provided by growing beans in association with corn. Bean plants extracted nitrogen from the atmosphere through their leaves, and fixed it in the soil through their roots, making it available to the corn plants. Nevertheless, after a decade or two of incremental declines, a field's productivity had dropped substantially.[67]

It took a year to prepare a new field. In the spring, the men used axes, stone in precontact times, metal in contact times, to girdle the larger trees, chop down the smaller ones, and cut out the underbrush. The girdled trees soon died and were left standing over the winter. The wood dried out considerably, and the following spring the men built a fire at the base of each dead tree, which they tended for days. When enough of the trunk had burned away, the tree could be chopped down.[68]

Much time and effort had to be devoted to house building, too. Though not especially difficult to construct, the longhouses of precontact times were not very durable. Their pole-and-bark construction left them particularly susceptible to wind damage. The absence of any foundation or flooring left the walls resting directly on the soil; eventually the houses rotted at the ground and had to be replaced. Fire was an ever-present danger. The sheets of dried bark used to cover the longhouse could be completely consumed by flames in a matter of minutes.[69]

For a variety of reasons, the village had to move to a new site with new houses every twelve to twenty years. Newly cleared fields were progressively farther from the village. Eventually, the distance between village and field lengthened to the point that it became worthwhile to move the village in the direction of the newest fields. But other factors could also force a move even sooner than declining field productivity would. Wood for fuel and construction in the vicinity of the village was consumed. Food-storage pits became infested with insect pests, and longhouses weathered and rotted at the ground. The women would decide when conditions had become intolerable and it was time to move. The move stretched out over a few years, with lineage after lineage abandoning the old site, as their men built houses at the new site.[70]

Men made a substantial contribution to the Iroquois food supply, although some historians have devalued that contribution. Martha Randle, for example, relegated meat to the status of a "relish," and declared that "hunting was more a prestige and recreation point, than a necessity."[71] Ann Eastlack Shafer was almost as dismissive: "The results of hunting and fishing were valuable additions to the diet but were not essentials."[72] Meat and fish might not have been essential for survival, but one must wonder if the Iroquois, whose diet would otherwise have been limited to corn, beans, and squash, held such a dismissive view of hunting and fishing.

More to the point, the relative contributions of men and women to the food supply did not constitute a basis for women's political influence.[73] Elisabeth Tooker noted that "the contribution of Iroquois men to economic production was perhaps as significant or almost as significant as that of the women . . . therefore Iroquois women cannot be said to have had economic control of the society by virtue of their greater contribution to economic production."[74] Even Judith Brown, who asserted that Iroquois women controlled the economic organization of the tribe, acknowledged that the "role of Iroquois women in politics" could not "be attributed to the size of their contribution to the Iroquois economy."[75]

During contact times, trade for manufactured goods became a crucial element in the Iroquois subsistence economy, as it evolved from self-sufficiency toward integration with the European-American economy.[76] Trade fell almost exclusively within the domain of men.

The single significant circumstance in which Iroquois women were able to engage European Americans in trade was when the latter needed food. Such food sales were limited mostly to persons traveling through or visiting Indian country. Newly arrived pioneers might also have been potential customers, until they harvested their own first crop. But Iroquois men too sold food—in the form of meat taken on the hunt. Sometimes, they did so on a much larger scale than the women could at home in the "clearing." For example, during the early 1790s, Allegany Seneca men supplied the garrison at Fort Franklin with meat, in return for such goods as the garrison could provide.[77]

When European Americans had a sufficient food supply, the only product of the Iroquois economy in which they were interested was fur, which was provided and controlled by men.[78] Men trapped fur-bearers, shot deer for hides, and traded the pelts in exchange for goods or cash. Additionally, they decided which goods to buy or barter, and it remained their decision even if they repeatedly made poor choices, such as alcohol over ammunition or flour.

Thomas Morris, manipulating the Seneca women into agreement on the huge land sale at Big Tree, had appealed to their sense of being disadvantaged, or even neglected, when it came to sharing in the proceeds of the fur trade. He observed that the men tended to supply their own wants first, while the needs of the women and children sometimes went unmet.[79] Pandering to the women, Morris might have exaggerated the men's selfishness in selecting articles for purchase. But even if he did exaggerate somewhat, his observation is inconsistent with the notion that women "controlled the economic organization of their tribe."[80]

It has also been argued that Iroquois women owned, or at least controlled, the "factors of agricultural production," and that this ownership constituted a basis for political influence.[81] These factors of production are generally enumerated as the cultivated fields, the implements of horticulture, such as rakes, hoes, or digging sticks, and the houses with their caches of dried food and seeds.[82] One of the more serious defects in this theory is its reliance on "ownership" of land as a basis for women's political influence. Iroquois land was "owned" communally; land belonged to the nation. Individuals and lineages had no more than a usufruct claim to any particular plot of land,[83] which simply meant that once a woman, or the women from a given lineage, placed a particular field into production, that woman or that lineage had the right to go on using the field. No one else could move in and take it over. A usufruct claim did not entitle the holder to sell the land, or bequeath it outright. A daughter or the next generation in a lineage could maintain the claim only so long as they continued to cultivate the field.

Men had no such claim because, although they cleared the fields initially, they did not use them on a continuous basis.[84] There is no evidence, however, that men desired any such claim, while there is much evidence that they had absolutely no desire to cultivate the fields.

Another serious defect in the factors-of-production theory is the notion that ownership of the implements of horticulture was somehow of economic consequence. Horticultural implements were easily made, quickly worn out, and regularly replaced. Wooden rakes, stone- or wood-bladed hoes, and digging sticks had little inherent economic value. Iron blades for hoes, procured by the men through trade, might have made for a slightly more efficient, and therefore slightly more valuable, cultivating tool. But compared to the implements used in hunting and trapping—

rifles, ammunition, and metal traps and knives—the tools of horticulture were less durable and of less value. As Elisabeth Tooker put it, ownership of agricultural implements "was probably of little economic consequence."[85]

Joy Bilharz too has pointed out that "corn pounders and baskets, although essential, were neither highly valued nor necessarily durable. . . . In contrast, men's implements . . . were both longer lasting and more highly valued."[86] Longhouses, which the women "owned" because they spent more time in them and used them more than the men, "were subject to rot, insect infestations, and fires."[87] Considered as factors of production—as places where women processed, stored, and cooked food—they were, like fields, less durable than analogous factors of production in European-American culture: farmhouses, barns, and gristmills.

Where then can the political influence exercised by Iroquois women be found? Iroquois women—at least certain lineage matrons—seem to have exerted significant political influence. Two factors were the major bases for whatever political influence Iroquois women actually had.[88] The lineage matrons nominated league sachems and had authority to initiate impeachment proceedings against the same, and women had the right to participate on an equal footing with men in the consensus building that was central to all Iroquois politics. The right to participate in the political process through their own institution—the women's council—was probably the most important single factor in giving women a real voice in the political process.

The Iroquois League, or as the Senecas called it, the League of the *Hodeno-saunee,* or Longhouse, was founded to establish and maintain a lasting peace among the Five Nations. The original grand council of the league consisted of fifty peace chiefs, or sachems, drawn unequally from among the Five Nations.[89] The Seneca nation, by far the most populous of the five, had the fewest league sachems—only eight.[90] The league was perpetuated by replacing each peace chief when he died. A condolence ceremony was conducted to mourn his passing, and the name of the deceased was given to his successor. Each name of the original fifty league sachems became, in effect, a title that was passed down, from generation to generation, through the same nation, clan, and lineage to which the original sachem had belonged. Lineages sometimes died out, in which case the league sachems transferred the title to another lineage within the same clan.[91]

A given chiefly title was vested not just in a particular clan, but in a specific lineage within that clan.[92] Each title-owning lineage owned only a single title; no lineage was vested with more than one title.

Although the Seneca nation contained eight different clans, the eight Seneca league-sachem titles were not distributed equally among them.[93] The Beaver, Deer, and Heron clans contained no title-owning lineages; the Wolf, Bear, and Hawk clans each contained one title-owning lineage; the Turtle clan controlled two titles; and the Snipe clan controlled three.[94]

The power to nominate a deceased sachem's successor belonged to the chief matron of the lineage that owned the vacant title.[95] The lineage matrons were the women of the eldest living generation.[96] If the eldest generation contained more than a single surviving female, then the women of the lineage chose one of the survivors to be the "chief matron."[97] The chief matron was ideally supposed to consult the other matrons in her lineage when choosing a nominee. If a suitable nominee could not be found among the men of her lineage, then she was to consider men from the other lineages in her clan, and consult with their matrons. She could even nominate a man from another clan, if necessary. In practice the chief matron often nominated a close male relative, such as her brother or her son, without consulting other matrons.[98]

This power to nominate a male successor was, however, just that—a power of nomination only. The matron's nominee had to be approved through several layers of review.[99] Exactly whose approval was needed depends upon which version of the league "constitution" or tradition is consulted.

According to Seth Newhouse the men of the clan had to approve the nominee. If the clansmen did not approve, they selected an alternative nominee from among their own number. If the clansmen and the matron could not agree on one of the nominees, the final choice was referred to the surviving league sachems of the clan that controlled the title.[100] The nomination was then referred to the other clans for confirmation, and finally to the grand council for ratification.[101]

Newhouse, a Grand River Onondaga, who was also fluent in Mohawk, wrote in what has been referred to as "reservation English" or "Indian English."[102] He completed three different drafts of his "Constitution of the Five Nations:" in 1880, in 1885, and the final draft, which he turned over to anthropologist Arthur Parker, in 1910.[103] Parker then published a heavily edited version of the Newhouse manuscript in 1916.[104]

Another account of the league tradition was written in English and approved by the Grand River chiefs in 1900 as their official version. According to the Chiefs' Version, "[T]he chief matron and the warriors of the family and clan of the deceased lord, shall nominate another lord from the warriors of the family and clan of the dead lord to succeed him. Then the matter will be submitted to the brother lords [league sachems of the same tribal moiety as the bereaved clan]. If they (the brother lords) confirm the nomination, then the matter will be further submitted to their cousin lords [league sachems of the other tribal moiety].[105] And if they also confirm the nomination, then the candidate shall be qualified to be raised by the condolence ceremony."[106]

A forerunner to the Chiefs' Version of the league tradition had been prepared in 1899 by Chief John Gibson, who subsequently had a major hand in the Chiefs' Version too. Gibson, a blind, multilingual Seneca, dictated the oral tradition in Onondaga to ethnologist J. N. B. Hewitt.[107] The Gibson-Hewitt text was later translated into English; much of it has been published in chapter 5 of William Fenton's *The Great Law and the Longhouse,* published in 1998. Not surprisingly, the Gibson-Hewitt text is quite similar to the Chiefs' Version. The clan matron nominates a successor with the consent of the clan's warriors; the nomination is first submitted to the chiefs of their tribal moiety for approval; then to chiefs of the opposite tribal moiety. "Once consensus has been reached within the nation, the candidate is presented to the Condolence Council, where the approval of the Confederacy council is sought."[108]

John Gibson, not entirely satisfied with either the Gibson-Hewitt text or the Chiefs' Version, completed a third version of the league tradition in 1912—this time with the assistance of anthropologist Alexander Goldenweiser, to whom he dictated in the Onondaga tongue. The Gibson-Goldenweiser text was not translated into English until much later; and it was not published until 1992, by Hanni Woodbury.

According to the Gibson-Goldenweiser text, it is the women of the clan who must approve the candidate selected by the matron before the matter goes to the sachems. "Once the chiefs of her nation approve, then the candidate's name is submitted to the chiefs of all the tribes comprising her side of the Confederacy fire."[109] In the grand council the Mohawk, Onondaga, and Seneca sachems all sat on the same side of the council fire; the Oneida and Cayuga sachems sat on the opposite side.[110] During the condolence council, the nominee was "stood up" for final approval by the sachems from the opposite side of the league council fire.[111]

Regardless of which version of the Irquois constitution was actually followed, the nominating prerogative of the lineage matron was subject to several layers of review, including review by men: the lineage warriors, the clansmen, and the league sachems. The matron's nominee could be rejected, and sometimes was.[112]

The matron of a title-owning lineage also had a role to play in any impeachment proceedings against the current holder of her lineage's title. She could sanction impeachment proceedings initiated by others, or she could initiate such proceedings herself. A matron's impeachment powers had significant limitations and were widely shared. And once again, exactly how impeachment was to proceed depends upon which version of the constitution is consulted.

According to the Newhouse text:

> If at any time it shall be manifest that a Confederate Lord has not in mind the welfare of the people, or disobeys the rules of this Great Law, the men or the women of the Confederacy, or both jointly, shall come to the council and upbraid the erring Lord through his War Chief. If the complaint of the people through the War Chief is not heeded the first time, it shall be uttered again; and then if no attention is given [by the erring sachem], a third complaint and warning shall be given. If the Lord is still contumacious, the matter shall go to the council of War Chiefs. The War Chiefs shall then divest the erring Lord of his title.[113]

Before the War Chiefs could actually depose the erring sachem, however, they required the concurrence of the lineage matron. If she sanctioned his removal, then the grand council would sanction it too.[114]

The Newhouse text also gave a title-owning lineage the right to recall the sachem currently wearing its title. The women of the lineage initiated the recall. "If a Lord of the Confederacy should seek to establish any authority independent of the jurisdiction of the Confederacy, . . . he shall be warned three times in open council, first by the women relatives, second by the men relatives, and finally by the Lords of the Confederacy of the nation to which he belongs [i.e., by the other league sachems from his nation]. If the offending Lord is still obdurate, he shall be dismissed by the War Chief of his nation.[115]

The Newhouse text also dealt with the issue of multiple errant sachems, from various lineages, which required a more elaborate procedure. Once again, the lineage matrons initiated the recall proceedings by issuing a series of three warnings to their own respective sachems. If any sachems refused to heed these warning, their cases went to the general council of women of the Five Nations, which issued three warnings of its own. If any sachems refused to heed these warnings, "then the case falls into the hands of the men of the Five Nations," whose council also issued three warnings, delivered through the War Chiefs. If any sachems refused to heed these warning, the men's council could depose or execute them.[116]

In the Chiefs' Version, the erring lord was first approached by the lineage matron, then by a "warrior of his family and clan." If he still refused to reform, the matron and the warrior would go to the chief warrior, who gave the obstinate sachem one final warning before deposing him.[117] This whole procedure seems to have been devised to prevent willful obstruction on the part of a single sachem from deadlocking the grand council, whose every decision had to be unanimous.

The Gibson-Hewitt text contains a similar recall procedure, except that it specifies another layer of review—the league grand council. The matron warned her erring sachem first, a lineage warrior accompanied her for a second warning, and the chief warrior took the case to the grand council, which issued its own warning, and, if necessary, removed the sachem from office.[118] The role of the lineage warrior was to confirm to the chief warrior that the sachem in question was doing something wrong, that the matron had warned him, and that the sachem had persisted in his malfeasance. In certain cases, the chief warrior could remove the sachem from office at this point in the procedure. In other cases, he referred the matter to the league sachems of the clan to which the erring lord belonged, and they made the final decision as to whether he should be removed.[119]

Whether in the Newhouse text or the Gibson tradition, "the power of women to appoint and remove . . . chiefs was not without male review . . . [and the] view of Iroquois women with ultimate political power therefore appears unsubstantiated."[120] Elisabeth Tooker viewed the lineage matron's role in nominating a sachem less as a prerogative to exercise political influence, and more as an obligation to help keep the grand council staffed, and thereby to help perpetuate the league.[121] Based on the Gibson texts and others, William Fenton argued that the matron acted as trustee for her lineage's title. Her role in recalling a sachem was shared by a warrior, "and responsibility ultimately rests with a council of chiefs to whom a head warrior reports the joint findings of matron and warrior."[122]

The matrons' role in nominating and recalling sachems was not unimportant. As Joy Bilharz pointed out with regard to impeachment, a matron's initial warning was probably sufficient to deter her sachem from an improper course.[123] However, the Iroquois cannot be described as a "matriarchy"[124] or a "gynocracy,"[125] as they have been, and still are today in much popular literature.[126] If the Iroquois were not a matriarchy, and if, as Elisabeth Tooker claims, the role of matrons in nominating and recalling chiefs was not primarily "a method by which women exercised political power as has so often been supposed," then how can we account for the political influence that Iroquois women undeniably exerted? The explanation lies mainly in the council of women and, to a lesser extent, in the role of lineage matrons in supporting their local headmen.

The council of women had a well-established place among Iroquois political institutions. Every village had one, along with a council of warriors, the men's council, and the council of headmen, the chiefs' council. The council of warriors caucused on an *ad hoc* basis, as necessary to address specific issues as they arose. The men then advised the chiefs of whatever consensus had emerged among the "warriors." The chiefs' council was composed of any league sachems who resided in the village, the local pine-tree chiefs, who attained positions of leadership through their own accomplishments and merits rather than through lineage-owned titles, war chiefs, spokesmen from each of the lineages in the village, elder men, and any man who had a significant following in the village on a particular issue.[127]

Little is known of the issues addressed in the women's council because European-American observers of the sixteenth, seventeenth, and eighteenth centuries were universally male, and in keeping with their own preconceptions and biases, they paid the women's council little note. It is probable, however, that just as the women of each longhouse were responsible for its day-to-day functioning, so too was the women's council concerned with affairs pertaining to subsistence activities in "the clearing." The women's council did have the right to deliberate on any issue and then advise the chiefs' council of whatever consensus had emerged.[128]

Decisions in the chiefs' council were also reached by consensus. If consensus was not attained, no collective action or decision was possible. Dissidents were free to opt out of the process and go their own way. No part of the political structure had coercive powers over any other part.[129]

The chiefs' council invariably contained several headmen who had emerged as adept consensus-builders by forming alliances based on kinship, persuasion, favors, and largesse. To be influential and effective, a headman had to entertain freely and give gifts liberally. He depended on his lineage matrons to provide feasts for the guests he entertained in large numbers. He therefore required his matrons' unstinting support. A headman could expect the matrons to back him so long as he was successful at securing arrangements in the political arena that redounded in some way to the material benefit or prestige of his lineage.[130]

The formal, institutionalized access to the consensus-building process provided by the women's council was probably the most important source of female influence on Iroquois politics. To a lesser extent, the informal, behind-the-scenes role of lineage matrons in backing and supporting headmen was also a source of political influence. Within Iroquois culture, women's contributions were not only valued and recognized, but reflected as political realities. Consequently, Iroquois women enjoyed a higher status within their society than did European-American women in their own.

CHAPTER TEN

Visions, White Dogs, and Green Corn

Two days after Cornplanter ordered the killing of the old woman accused of witchcraft, Handsome Lake experienced his first vision. The nascent prophet had been seriously ill for weeks, bedridden, and reduced to nothing "but yellow skin and dried bones."[1] On the morning of June 15, 1799, he arose from his sickbed to answer a call. Sensing that something momentous was about to happen to him, Handsome Lake uttered "So be it," as he struggled to his feet. When he emerged from his daughter's house, he beheld the three angels, or messenger spirits, who had called to him. Handsome Lake collapsed into his daughter's arms, "not from any sickness," he would later report, but because he had fallen into a trance.[2]

The messengers, who took the form of mature men, handsome and commanding in appearance, wore brilliant, sky-blue raiment. Each spirit held a bow and arrows—nativist symbols—in one hand and a berry bush in the other. The bushes contained berries of every color, and were symbols of powerful Indian medicine. The messengers bid Handsome Lake to eat of the berries as the first step in restoring his health. They promised that "he would live to see such berries ripe this summer."[3] They said they would instruct Gayantgogwus—his sister—and her husband to make medicine that would continue Handsome Lake's recovery. They explained that the Creator had sent them because of Handsome Lake's changed heart: his repentance and patient suffering, his gratitude at witnessing the marvels of creation, his fervent wish to be whole again.

The messengers declared that the traditional strawberry festival, which the villagers planned to celebrate the following day, must be perpetuated. They then charged Handsome Lake with his mission: "Proclaim the message that we give you and tell it truly before all people."[4] They further promised to "continually reveal things unto you." The messengers explained that four of them had been made by the Creator, and that since the creation of the world they had been charged with a mission of their own, "to watch over and care for mankind."[5] They explained the absence of the fourth messenger. "When we called you by name and you heard, he returned to tell the news. This will bring joy into the heaven-world of our Creator." They told Handsome Lake that he would see the fourth messenger at another time, "and when that time is at hand you shall know."[6]

The spirits reminded Handsome Lake of his sins of drunkenness and profaning sacred songs by singing them while drunk. They insisted that he must repent and reform thoroughly, and refrain from ever drinking another drop of liquor. They warned him against the folly of trying to drink in secret, "because the Great Spirit always knew, not only what people were doing, but also their very thoughts."[7] They further warned him not to refuse or resist his new mission, and that if he did reject it in any way, he would be buried forever in a place that belched forth smoke and steam.

The messengers then proceeded "to uncover the evil upon the earth and show how men spoil" what the Creator had ordained. "Four words tell a great story of wrong and the Creator is sad because of the trouble they bring, so go and tell your people." The four words—drunkenness, witchcraft, love charms, and abortion— summarized the sinful state from which Handsome Lake was being called upon to rescue his people.[8]

Regarding liquor, the messengers said "Alas, many are fond of it and are too fond of it," and all the Creator's Indian children must solemnly vow never to drink it again. The Creator had made whiskey exclusively for his white children. It was never intended for the Indians, for whom it was nothing but destructive.[9]

The messengers said that witches must confess their evil deeds publicly. So evil were the deeds of some witches, however, that it would be impossible to speak of them in public. These witches must confess their crimes privately to Handsome Lake. A few witches, the most evil of all, "must go far out upon an abandoned trail and there they must confess before the Creator alone."[10] The messengers also noted that "there were some very bad ones among them, who would poison others. One of them had lately been killed [the old woman who had been executed for witchcraft]. But there still remained one like her who was a man." Therefore, the threat posed by witches still remained.[11]

In a matter closely related to witchcraft, the messengers spoke of "the secret poisons in little bundles."[12] Charms were feared as the cause of wasting illnesses, and traditional hunting charms were thought to have been perverted in the service of evil. There were other charms, however, that were not intended to sicken or kill others. They were worn during lacrosse games to give speed, agility, and visual acuity to the players. Other charms—love potions and powders—could be used to attract a member of the opposite sex, either to one's self or to a paying client. But love magic too could be unethical, particularly if it was used to induce uncontrollable lust or sexual dysfunction.[13] Handsome Lake especially condemned the use of love charms because they disrupted marriages.

The spirits denounced the practice of abortion, saying it saddened the Creator, who had "created life to live." The Iroquois knew of abortifacient herbs. Sometimes mothers were the primary agents in persuading their daughters to terminate an inconvenient pregnancy, and prepared the abortifacient for them. In the words of the messengers, when a mother did this, "she forever cuts away her daughter's string of children."[14]

That morning, when Handsome Lake fell into his trancelike state, Henry Simmons, Joel Swayne, and Cornplanter had all been about three-quarters of a mile away

from the village. Swayne had come from Genesinguhta to help Simmons construct a
small schoolhouse, and the two were hard at work. Nearby, Cornplanter was supervising some men he had employed to build him a new house. Upon receiving word
that Handsome Lake's condition had suddenly worsened, Cornplanter went "straightway" to his halfbrother's side, where he found their nephew Blacksnake already in attendance. Cornplanter confirmed the warm spot that Blacksnake had discovered on
Handsome Lake's chest; they waited quietly to see if their relative would live or die.

Around noon, after being comatose for about two and a half hours, Handsome
Lake revived and related his vision to those present. Still too weak himself to address the entire village, he asked Cornplanter to call the people together and relay
the message he had received during his vision. He also requested that the villagers
eat strawberries as a sign that they accepted the message from the Creator. All must
eat, even if there was only enough for one berry apiece.[15]

Thus, strawberries became a symbol of the new covenant between the Creator
and his Indian children. The fact that Handsome Lake's first vision occurred on the
eve of the Strawberry Festival strengthened this symbolic association. Simmons continues the narration:

> Handsome Lake's wishes were carried out that very same day. At the request of
> Cornplanter, my companion Joel Swayne and I attended the council . . . During the
> council, I felt the love of God flowing powerfully among us. Near the close, I had to
> communicate some counsel to them, which was, I believe, well accepted. The old
> chief's sister came to us after the council was over, and thanked me for what I had
> said to them.[16]

SKY JOURNEY

Handsome Lake continued in a poor state of health for many weeks after the vision,
despite the magical berries of the messengers, and despite the herbal medicine prepared in accordance with their instructions. He lived in anticipation of a visit from the
fourth messenger, often telling Cornplanter that he expected the visit soon. During the
night of August 7 to 8, the fourth messenger appeared and invited Handsome Lake to
accompany him to an undisclosed destination, "if he was willing to go." The messenger pitied Handsome Lake, who was still suffering from illness, and did not require
an answer at that time, and Handsome Lake did not give one.[17]

But when he awoke on the morning of August 8, Handsome Lake decided that
when the messenger next returned, he would go with him. Expecting the messenger's imminent return, he dressed himself in his best clothes, in preparation for a
journey. Then he sent for Cornplanter. "He was afraid he would not get to see his
brother before he would have to go . . . Cornplanter then came and attended pretty
steadily with Handsome Lake through the course of the day."[18] Simmons continues
the narration:

> That evening, Handsome Lake fainted away, but the fainting spell held him but for
> a short space of time. After recovering, he told Cornplanter that he must go, but not
> forever, he thought, as long as Cornplanter and many more of his people were not
> willing to let go of him. He thought he would be free to return after going some dis-

tance with the man or spirit who had visited him the night before. He told Corn-planter not to put any more clothes on him, nor to move his body, if he did go. Shortly after that, Handsome Lake said he was now going, and although he ex-pected to return, he thought that he should go so far as to see his own son, who had been dead several years, and Cornplanter's daughter, who had been dead about seven months.

Handsome Lake then fainted or fell into a trance, in which posture he remained for about seven hours. His legs and arms were cold; the rest of his body was warm but breathless. He knew not how he went out of the world, but soon perceived that the fourth messenger was going before him as a guide, who appeared to have a bow and one arrow, and was dressed in a clear sky color.[19]

Handsome Lake and his guide watched the great sky road—the Milky Way—descend slowly from the south and touch the earth at their feet. The broad band of stars was believed to be the road over which the souls of the dead journeyed to the next world. The individual stars appeared to Handsome Lake as the footprints of the dead, the "tracks of the human race going in one direction. The footprints were of all different sizes from small to great."[20]

Visual Parables
As his guide led Handsome Lake up the sky road, the two paused at intervals to ob-serve a series of scenes, each of which "Guide" interpreted for Handsome Lake. They saw a grotesquely obese woman sitting and grasping at everything within her reach. Handsome Lake realized that she was so fat, she could not even stand up. Guide told him that she represented the evil of stinginess. "Thus it will be with those who forsake religious teachings and think more of the things of earth than of the new world above. Having glutted themselves with the things of earth, they are unable to stand upon the heaven-road."[21]

At their next stop Handsome Lake beheld three groups of people. Guide told him that the largest group represented those who would hear, but ignore, the Cre-ator's message as delivered by Handsome Lake. A smaller group, containing only half the number of the first, represented those whose response to the message would be half-hearted or lukewarm. The smallest group represented those who would re-pent and truly believe the good news proclaimed by Handsome Lake.[22]

Next the travelers came upon a jail, within which were a pair of handcuffs, a whip, and a hangman's noose. Guide explained that these were the punishments meted out by the white man's law. He noted that some people claimed that the white man's law was better than the Indian's traditional code of behavior. The punishments of the white man's law awaited those who made such claims.[23] Then they came upon a church with a tall spire. A path led to the church but there were no doors or win-dows. "Within was a great noise, wailing and crying, and the house was hot." Guide explained: "It is a hard matter for Indians to embrace these conditions, that is to em-brace the belief of Bible believers."[24] Anthony Wallace has speculated that the closed-up, oppressive church represented the "confining discipline" of Christianity, which Indians found difficult to accept.[25]

One of the parables revisited Handsome Lake's earliest and most persistent theme—temperance. Guide bade Handsome Lake to look earthward, upon Cornplanter's village, where he saw a large number of canoes pulled up at the riverbank. They were loaded with kegs of whiskey, and many of the villagers were drunk and rowdy. An ugly fellow hopped among the whiskey barrels, singing the song of the evil-minded spirit. Guide explained that the ugly man was the punisher or devil, who was delighted "to see the people filled with strong drink."[26] The ugly fellow was very busy, "doing and making all the . . . mischief he could amongst the people."[27]

A few of the scenes foreshadowed concerns that would emerge as major themes in Handsome Lake's preaching. Guide bade Handsome Lake to look earthward upon the Buffalo Creek Reservation, "which seemed honeycombed like ice and covered with a net." Voids form—like honeycombs—in ice as it melts and loses its structural strength. The Great Eaters had ensnared Buffalo Creek in a net. This was, in effect, a prophecy that Buffalo Creek would be lost to the Seneca nation—as indeed it was.[28] Guide pointed out that the chiefs should protect the remaining Indian landholding— not sell it.[29] In a related incident, the travelers saw a white man, angrily prodding the ground with a bayonet, possibly representing the insatiable land hunger of the implacable Great Eaters. Guide said that "the headmen must honestly strive to prevent their followers from helping the frenzied white man."[30]

Historical Figures

As Handsome Lake and Guide continued along the sky road, there appeared a series of three remarkable visual vignettes involving actual individuals. They came to a great mansion suspended halfway between earth and heaven. It was surrounded by a large veranda, enclosed by a railing. Strolling along this porch with a dog was George Washington. Guide said that "he is the only white man so near the new world of our Creator."[31] Washington had won himself this unique spot on the outskirts of heaven during the negotiation and ratification of the Canandaigua Treaty of 1794, which guaranteed the Seneca nation its boundaries and rights to the soil, and marked the high point in state-to-state relations between the Seneca nation and the United States.

The travelers then encountered Jesus Christ, who still bore the scars of crucifixion upon his hands and feet. They found him walking along the sky road without a disciple or a follower in sight. Jesus wanted to know if the Indians were heeding the Seneca prophet's message. Handsome Lake answered that about half his people were listening to him. This evoked a stunning response from Jesus: "You are more successful than I, for some believe in you, but none in me." Jesus then mused, "I am inclined to believe that in the end, it will also be so with you."[32]

Jesus, thoroughly disillusioned with his own followers, told Handsome Lake: "They slew me because of their independence and unbelief. So I have gone home to shut the doors of heaven that they might not see me again until the earth passes away. Then will all the people cry to me for succor, and when I come it will be in this wise: my face will be sober and I shall turn it to my people." He had a final piece of advice for Handsome Lake and the Indians: "Now tell your people that they will become lost when they follow the ways of the white man."[33]

Next, the travelers observed an Indian man "carrying loads of dirt and depositing them in a certain spot. He carried the earth in a wheelbarrow and his task was a hard one." Handsome Lake recognized the man, it was Red Jacket.[34] Guide explained that this was the punishment for those who sold Indian land.[35] Singling out Red Jacket in this way was unfair. Many chiefs and headmen, including Cornplanter, had been involved in land sales. Red Jacket was a convenient and appealing scapegoat because of his animosity toward Cornplanter. His subsequent dismissal of Handsome Lake as a charlatan earned Red Jacket a place of eternal infamy in the Code.[36]

It is possible that this section of the Code was added some time after Handsome Lake's August 1799 vision. It is true that Red Jacket and Cornplanter shared a mutual animosity, and this alone might have prompted Handsome Lake to include the scene when initially reporting his second vision. But Handsome Lake's career as a prophet was only a few months old, and Red Jacket had not yet questioned Handsome Lake's authenticity, so it is also possible that the image of Red Jacket's punishment was not added until later, either by Handsome Lake or by one of the later Longhouse preachers who maintained the Code as an oral tradition.

Anthony Wallace specifically associated Red Jacket's punishment with the sale of the Black Rock corridor in June 1801, along the east bank of the upper Niagara River. Red Jacket favored the sale and Handsome Lake opposed it, although he acquiesced after being politically outmaneuvered by Red Jacket. If Wallace was correct, then that image was a later addition to the Code.[37]

Apocalyptic Sights and Sounds

Interspersed among the scenes of sin and retribution were warnings of imminent world destruction. At one point, Guide showed Handsome Lake two immense balls of liquid suspended in the eastern sky, one red and one yellow. They hung tenuously, poised to fall upon the earth. Should just one of the drops fall, it would wipe out most life on earth. "But," said Guide, "we [the four messengers] are doing our utmost to prevent such an event."[38] At another point, the two sojourners paused and listened. Handsome Lake heard "the wailing of the aged and the crying of children." Guide told him it was the sound of all human life being called back to the Creator. "When this time comes there will be great misery upon the earth."[39]

Guide later pointed out a large, white object that rotated slowly in the western sky. This object was what the Senecas referred to as the "veil over all," a natural phenomenon that regulated "the air over the earth." Guide explained that should the veil ever rotate too quickly, it would bring a disaster to mankind. He added, "Now we are the regulators and watchers of the veil over all."[40]

At the Forks in the Sky Road

At length, Handsome Lake and Guide reached a point in the sky road where a narrow branch veered off to the right toward heaven, and a wide branch ran off to the left toward hell. Here judges awaited the souls of the dead, sending some heavenward, but turning most into the wide road that led to "the great lodge of the punisher." Handsome Lake noticed that the tracks on the road to heaven were mostly those of children. Guide explained that over the course of a lifetime, each person received three chances to repent, and that even a deathbed conversion was sufficient for salvation, because the four messengers were continuously pleading with the Creator to show mercy.[41]

Handsome Lake then noticed a man's breast hanging in the roadside, pierced through the center by a bullet hole. Guide explained that the messengers placed it there as a sign for the man's murderer, who was still alive. When the murderer arrived at the forks, he would be greeted by his handiwork and directed onto the wide road.[42]

Touring the Great Lodge of the Punisher

Guide led Handsome Lake down the wide path to hell. As they moved along, "some great force seemed [to be] pushing them onward," indicating that once one started down this road, it would be impossible to go back. Before they could even see the house of the punisher, Handsome Lake felt heated air invading his lungs and "heard the far away echoes of mournful cries borne on the blasts of hot wind." Even from a distance, Handsome Lake could see that the lodge was constructed of iron, and was very long, extending beyond the eye's reach. Guide removed a crystal from within his garment and held it at arm's length, using it as a spyglass; the iron lodge extended even beyond its range.[43]

Upon entering the lodge, they saw hot vapor rising from fire pits. The damned screamed for help with outstretched arms, but there was nothing Handsome Lake or the four messengers could do for them. Guide said that these tormented souls, when still living upon the earth, had ignored the Creator's message; it was too late to repent now. The master of the house, the punisher, was a shape-shifting monster who continually distorted himself, sometimes exhibiting physical traits strikingly similar to those of the familiar European-American devil. "At times horns shot out from his forehead, at times a cloven foot appeared, and at times a tail was visible."[44]

The punisher excelled in devising uniquely suitable punishments for specific sins. For the alcoholic: "The punisher held a drinking vessel in his hand and within it was molten metal; thrusting it into the hands of the man . . . he said, 'Now warm yourself again as was your custom while upon the earth, for you loved hot drink.' Now the man pleaded but the punisher compelled him to swallow the molten metal. Then the man screamed in a loud voice and fell prone upon the ground, with vapor steaming from his throat." Guide said: "You have seen the manner of punishing those who persist in taking the fiery drink."[45]

A witch was plunged deep into "a great cauldron filled with a boiling liquid." Handsome Lake watched to see if she would come back to the top. "Suddenly she shot to the surface, crying in a strange voice like some unknown animal, and then sank down again." She appeared again, only to be yanked from the cauldron and flung upon the floor, where she became chilled to the bone. Then the punisher threw her back into the cauldron "and immediately her bones rattled to the bottom."[46] A woman who had used love charms to attract men was forced to go naked. She could no longer powder her cheeks, now sallow and sunken to the bone. Where once she had parted her hair, the flesh now rotted away, "and in all the hair of her body were writhing serpents."[47]

A wife beater was forced to strike the red-hot effigy of a woman.[48] Couples who had quarreled continually on earth were compelled to do so again—until their eyes bulged from their heads, their tongues lolled out, and flames shot from their genitals."[49] An adulteress was penetrated with red-hot penes, until "she cried aloud in agony and . . . fell with steam issuing from her body."[50] A fiddle player was forced to use a hot iron bar as a bow, and saw away at the sinews of his own arm, as if they were musical strings.[51]

Card players were forced to shuffle red-hot iron cards "until their flesh was eaten away and the meat fell off."[52]

After witnessing these torments of the damned, Handsome Lake and Guide retreated to the fork in the sky road.

On the Heaven Road

Guide now led Handsome Lake onto the narrow road, where floral fragrances greeted them, delicious fruits grew along the wayside, and "every kind of bird flew in the air above them."[53] Soon they came to a place of rest and refreshment, where issued a fount of clear water. Guide withdrew a bottle from inside his garment, dipped it into the spring, and gave it to Handsome Lake. As they took turns drinking, the water did not become depleted and never had to be replenished.[54] Not long after they had resumed their journey, a white dog ran up to them, wagging its tail. It sprang into Handsome Lake's arms, and he recognized it as the dog he had prepared for sacrifice at the last Midwinter Rites. The animal still wore its decorations: daubs of red paint on its cheeks, a collar of white wampum around its neck, and ribbons of various colors around its legs, snout, body, and tail. Guide explained that this happy reunion attested to the Creator's pleasure at the white-dog sacrifice.[55]

They soon encountered the souls Handsome Lake was hoping to meet: Cornplanter's daughter and Handsome Lake's son. They were dressed in heavenly sky-blue robes, similar to Guide's. Handsome Lake embraced them, and they sat down to talk. Simmons recorded the conversation in some detail:

> Cornplanter's daughter expressed her sorrow that her brother Henry frequently disputed with her father. Sometimes their arguments were so heated that they became very angry at each other. Her brother always thought he knew more than his father, whose advice he would never take. Henry always insisted on having his own way, which was very wrong.[56]

Guide interjected that "she had spoken correctly in describing Henry's abuse of their father Cornplanter. Henry should obey his father for as long as Cornplanter continued to live."[57]

> Handsome Lake was then addressed by his own son, who was concerned that Handsome Lake had suffered so much. He was also concerned that Handsome Lake's other son, who was still living, had taken so little care of their father. Quite to the contrary, the living son would go out of his way when his father grew worse, for fear of having to take some trouble on his father's account. The dead son thought the living son had no sense in so doing. Guide said every son ought to do good for his father.[58]

Handsome Lake parted with his son and niece, and Guide led him onward for a short distance. Then Guide stopped and said they had arrived at the point where Handsome Lake must go back. "Here there is a house prepared for your eternal abode, but should you now enter a room, you could never go back to the earth-world."[59] Before sending Handsome Lake back, however, Guide gave him some instructions. He reiterated the need for temperance.

> Guide told him that it was very often the case that people were apt to take too much strong drink. The Great Spirit made strong drink to use, he did not make it to hurt people; although the Indians did not keep from injuring themselves greatly by it. If they continued to get drunk, abuse themselves, and injure others, they need not expect to come to the happy place that Handsome Lake was visiting now.[60]

Guide also dealt with the cult of dreams and the need to discern the moral impetus behind dreams—did a particular dream come from a good or an evil source?

> Guide told him that the Indians dreamed a lot. And, sometimes their dreams were true, having come from the Great Spirit. But, often, when a dream was true, the Indians would not believe that it had come from the Great Spirit. Instead, they would think it had come from the devil. And, when the devil told them something in a dream, they often believed that the message had come from the Great Spirit. This confusion resulted in more people doing the work of the devil, which meant that the devil had the most people on his side. This pleased the devil because it made him seem greater than the Great Spirit, and more honored.[61]

Guide also addressed the presence of the Quaker missionaries, stressing that above all it must not be allowed to divide the people.

> Guide further told him that white people had come into the Indian towns to instruct their children. This would be all right, provided that all the Indians agreed to it. If they did not all agree, and if many of them wanted to keep to their old habits of living, well that might be right too. But, if they wanted to keep to their old ways, then they had no business drinking whiskey because that belongs to white people and was not made for Indians.[62]

Returning finally to the apocalyptic theme, Guide warned of a great sickness that would soon befall Cornplanter's village, unless the people "did amend their ways, and think more upon the Great Spirit, who might then perhaps see cause to forestall the sickness." As a sign of their repentance, they should immediately sacrifice and consume a white dog.[63] Then he sent Handsome Lake home.

Handsome Lake's first two visions were preoccupied with the imminence of world destruction (in the absence of repentance and reform), the definition of sin, and the prescription for salvation. Apocalyptic predictions permeate the Code; a string of eschatological prophecies precedes the sky journey, but could easily have been a part of it originally, so consistent are they with the vision of the prophet's journey. The prophecies foretell the signs of the end-time: factionalism will rule the day among chiefs, headmen, and even religious officials; crops will fail; plagues will kill many; witches will practice their craft in broad daylight; false prophets will

Handsome Lake Preaching at Tonawanda Longhouse. Painting by Ernest Smith.
ROCHESTER MUSEUM & SCIENCE CENTER, ROCHESTER, NEW YORK.

arise; and the poisonous monsters of the underworld will be loosed upon mankind. The powers of nature will finally be suspended, the earth and the heavens will stop, and the world will be destroyed by fire.[64] Those who accept Handsome Lake's gospel, however, will be spared these horrors. They will die peacefully in their sleep and go straight to heaven. Only the unrepentant and the unreformed—though they be the majority of mankind—will have to endure the terrors of the end-time and suffer an eternity of punishment.[65]

The definition of sin formed the basis for a subsequent phase of Handsome Lake's revelation, his social gospel, which he enunciated gradually from 1800 onward. The four great sins all had social implications: drunkenness, witchcraft, love magic, and abortion. Other sins enumerated in the Code had similar social consequences; marital infidelity, gossip, jealousy, spousal abuse, cruelty to children, neglect of the elderly, greed, and thievery. The prescription for salvation was to take Handsome Lake's message to heart, confess one's sins, and desist from all evil practices and deeds. The prophet said, "If all the world would repent, the earth would become as new again."[66] It was also necessary to worship the Great Spirit in the traditional Indian way, by participating in the annual cycle of religious ceremonies.[67]

WHITE DOGS

Sometime before dawn on August 9, the prophet came out of his trance. He related the entire experience to Cornplanter, who immediately called a council. Simmons continues the narration:

> In the morning Cornplanter sent his son to tell me to attend the meeting, which I did. I listened to them retell the whole story. Then, they asked me to tell them whether I believed it to be true. I told them there had been instances of the same kind among white people, even among the Quakers. Someone would fall into a trance, and see both the good place and the bad place and many other wonderful sights. I believed these visions. And, I told them I could see no reason why it should not be the case with the Indians also, as we are all of one flesh and blood made by the Great Spirit. Although there appeared no reason in my view why it should not be true, yet perhaps, because there was so much of it, Handsome Lake might not have recollected enough so as to tell it exactly as he had seen and heard. I said more to the same purport, and they appeared satisfied.
>
> That afternoon they prepared a white dog to eat, and burned his skin to ashes, during which time a number of them circled around the fire—singing, shouting, and dancing greatly. After which, they all partook of their delicious dish of dog meat.[68]

White-Dog Sacrifice

The sacrifice of the white dog as practiced among the Allegany Senecas at the turn of the nineteenth century took the following ceremonial form. A single white dog was ritually strangled and then decorated with red paint, ribbons of various colors, and a collar of white wampum. The dog was strangled because "a wound on the animal or an effusion of blood would spoil the victim and render the sacrifice useless."[69] Similar care was taken that none of the dog's bones should be broken.[70] Once decorated, the dog was hung upon the wooden statue of Tarachiawagon, where it remained on displayed for a period of hours or days, depending on the occasion. The animal was then taken down and burned to ashes on a pyre kindled near the statue while a religious official threw handfuls of tobacco on the fire, and worshipers sang and danced around the wooden image, praising and thanking the Good Spirit. The tobacco used in the sacrificial rite, probably *Nicotiana rustica,* was "of a particular kind, rubbed fine, which they consider as peculiarly agreeable to the Great Spirit." The ascending tobacco smoke accompanied the prayers and aspirations directed to the Good Spirit, and made them more pleasing.[71]

At some point in the ceremony, while the dog was still burning, the official recited a lengthy prayer to the Creator acknowledging favors received, giving thanks for preservation in times past, and seeking continued care and protection. The official also addressed the assembled worshipers, "advising them how they ought to conduct [themselves], and pointing out some of the prominent evils which they ought to avoid."[72]

Halliday Jackson reported that "on some extraordinary occasions they eat the flesh of the dog."[73] The sacrifice offered at Cornplanter's village following Handsome Lake's second vision was one of those occasions,[74] offered specifically in response to the spirit guide's injunction that the "people must collect together in worship, and cook a white dog, from which they must all eat." Aside from such special occasions, the Allegany Senecas at the turn of the nineteenth century performed the white-dog sacrifice twice a year, during the Midwinter Rites and the Green Corn Festival.[75]

The specifics of the white-dog sacrifice, recorded by observers during the first three decades of the nineteenth century, varied with time and place. At Seneca villages where there was no large outdoor statue, the slain and decorated dog was hoisted on a pole, ten to twenty feet above the ground. Some accounts say the dog was strangled the evening before it was hung up for display; others, that it was killed at sunrise on the same day. In some villages the dog was decorated before it was strangled. Decorations varied too, and could include feathers and purple (black) wampum, which was used alone or mixed with white. Sometimes a bundle of tobacco was tied to the dog. In one case mint was thrown into the fire, instead of tobacco. In another ceremony, the ashes of the cremated dog were collected, carried through the village, and sprinkled at the door of each house. At different times several groups sacrificed two dogs: one burnt to ashes, the other eaten. Sometimes the dog was partially roasted, then boiled with vegetables in a soup; at other times, both dogs were incinerated.[76]

When Morgan described[77] the white-dog sacrifice at mid-nineteenth century, it had changed little from the turn-of-the-century practice.[78] Morgan's description provides some insight into the spiritual beliefs that surrounded the sacrifice. According to Morgan, the offering was not made to expiate or atone for the sins of the people, nor did the animal serve as a scapegoat upon which the guilt of all could be heaped. The spirit of the white dog was offered simply as a gift that would please the Creator and dispose him toward accepting the people's prayers of praise, thanksgiving, and petition. In this sense, the spirit of the white dog served the same purpose as the smoke of tobacco burned as incense. The dog had to be burned, because the Iroquois believed that the spirit of the dog lingered near the body until the flames sent it heavenward.[79] Morgan explained why the white dog was thought to be such a pleasing gift to the Creator:

> The fidelity of the dog, the companion of the Indian as a hunter, was emblematic of their fidelity. No messenger so trusty could be found to bear their petitions to the master of life. The Iroquois believed that the Great Spirit made a covenant with their fathers to the effect that, when they should send up to him the spirit of a dog of a spotless white, he would receive it as the pledge of their adherence to his worship, and his ears would thus be opened in a special manner to their petitions.[80]

No longer practiced, the white-dog sacrifice began to decline in the 1880s. By the end of the nineteenth century, the New York Iroquois had virtually abandoned it. At the Six Nations reserve in Canada, the practice survived on an irregular basis into the twentieth century. The reason customarily given by Indian informants of the late-nineteenth and early-twentieth centuries for the demise of the practice was that the special breed of dog needed for the ritual had become extinct, hybridized, or simply too rare. Pressure from the Canadian government and, in the United States, the negative opinion of European Americans regarding animal sacrifice might have contributed to the lapse of this ritual. The possibility that the white-dog ritual might some day be revived cannot be ruled out.[81]

According to a tradition that was still current at the Six Nations reserve at mid-twentieth century, Handsome Lake himself declared that the white-dog sacrifice must cease based on a revelation from the messengers.[82] This revelation, absent from the Edward Cornplanter version of the Code, was part of a version obtained by William Beauchamp in 1894, in which the messengers told Handsome Lake, "you must not burn the dog as you have been doing."[83] If the prophet did disclose such a revelation, his followers ignored it for the next seven or eight decades.[84]

The notion that they would disregard one of the prophet's teachings is not at all improbable. Handsome Lake tried to suppress the medicine societies, but his people refused to give them up and started practicing them in secret.[85] The societies flourish to this day—especially among ardent adherents of the Longhouse Religion. It is improbable, however, that Handsome Lake's followers would ignore one of his teachings for seventy or eighty years and then start to heed it. It seems more likely that they discontinued the white-dog sacrifice for other, more practical, reasons.

Approbation and Equivocation

Simmons's endorsement of Handsome Lake's second vision was fairly straightforward. His reply was completely consistent with Quaker beliefs regarding the inner light, the seed of salvation placed by Christ in every human heart, and the Holy Spirit's ongoing work in the form of immediate revelation.

Simmons's approbation of Handsome Lake's message seems to have been sincere, although missionaries from other Christian denominations thought that Native American religious experience was invalid, and rarely hesitated to tell the Indians so. Even other Quaker missionaries merely tolerated the Handsome Lake phenomenon, and did so largely as an expedient necessary for continuing their mission to civilize the Indians before all else. Once the Indians were civilized, they would be able to see past the superstition and idolatry of their native religion, and begin to accept the precepts of Christianity. Only Simmons seems to have credited the workings of the Holy Spirit, both in Handsome Lake's message and in the people's response to it.[86]

Even Simmons hedged a bit: "Although there appeared no reason in my view why it should not be true, yet perhaps, because there was so much of it, Handsome Lake might not have recollected enough so as to tell it exactly as he had seen and heard." Simmons might have felt the need to question Handsome Lake's competence in case the prophet's nativism, still quite moderate, became too extreme. Simmons and the Quakers could then challenge that nativism on the basis that Handsome Lake had simply misconstrued the Good Spirit's message, without having to challenge the validity of Native American religious experience.

Simmons was not the only one equivocating in the wake of Handsome Lake's August vision. Cornplanter began to reassess the time frame needed for the Allegany Senecas to adopt elements of European-American culture and modify their own way of life. On the morning of August 10, Simmons went to Cornplanter's house to make a written record of Handsome Lake's sky journey, while it was still fresh in the prophet's memory. Handsome Lake, now much recovered from his illness, was able to recount his vision to Simmons through an interpreter—probably Cornplanter's son, Henry. During the visit, Cornplanter told Simmons that "he liked some ways of the white people very well, and some ways of the Indians also. He thought it would take some length of time to lead his people out of all their own customs."[87]

Cornplanter seems to have sensed that the Allegany Senecas had crossed a threshold, that his half brother's spiritual message was beginning to resonate with the people, and that it had the potential for developing into an Indian religious revival. Cornplanter himself supported Handsome Lake's prophetic mission. He told Simmons that the Allegany Senecas intended to keep up their worship dances. "They could not read, so they knew of no other way in which to worship the Great Spirit. If they gave up their sacred dances, they would have no manner of worship at all."[88]

Then Cornplanter expressed the idea that conversion to Christianity was unnecessary for the Indians, that they were saved under a different dispensation granted especially for them. Simmons probably would not have objected to the idea that Indians could be saved without converting to Christianity—to his way of thinking the Indians simply were not ready for Christianity. God would not damn the Indians just because they were not yet prepared for Christianity. But Simmons was offended at the way Cornplanter voiced his opinion.

After pointing out that the Indians had no means of worship other than their traditional forms, Cornplanter said that "it was the white people who had killed our Savior." He seems to have meant that, because the Indians and their ancestors had had nothing to do with the crucifixion of Christ, they were exempt from the penitence, discipline, and regulation that, to many Indians, appeared as the central core of Christianity. Cornplanter may have confused original sin with the crucifixion, but Simmons did not try to clarify the point. He instead launched into one of his tirades.

> How he had heard about our Savior, I know not. But, it seems he had. I told him it was the Jews who crucified or killed him, and whether they were white, red, or black or what color they were of, I knew not. Neither did I know but that the Indians were their descendants, for many of the Indians' habits were similar to those practiced by the Jews in former days. Yet I told him that, nevertheless, we were all still crucifying and killing him—whenever we were doing wickedly. He said that was very true, very true. Several other Indians were also present. Thus matters ended at that time.[89]

Simmons's association of the Indians with the Jews was one made quite often by European Americans during the nineteenth century. The Indians' ancestors were believed by some to be of the lost tribes of Israel, and this was thought to explain certain superficial similarities between the religious practices of the Indians and those of the ancient Hebrews such as animal sacrifice, and dancing and feasting as forms of worship.[90] Cornplanter was content to leave the matter there.

GREEN CORN

"Today a proclamation was issued by order of the chiefs for all their people, many of whom were dispersed through the forests at their hunting quarters, to repair home to their village in fourteen days. At that time, they will hold a council and worship dance, agreeable to their ancient custom. By then, their corn will be ripe or fit for boiling."[91] Thus was the 1799 Green Corn Festival announced. Communications and travel being slow, it was seventeen days before the last band of hunters—together with their wives and children—straggled into Cornplanter's village. On August 28 a council designated thirty men to participate in a special hunting party that was immediately dispatched to obtain meat for the feasting that would accompany the festival. The hunters returned the next day with seventeen deer, "after which a great deal of cookery was carried on by some men and some women who had been appointed for that purpose."[92]

That year the Green Corn Festival lasted for three and a half days. Simmons described it in more detail than he usually devoted to native religious practices; nevertheless his account is lamentably sketchy. From the limited description he did give, however, it appears that the 1799 celebration was remarkably similar to those witnessed by Morgan at Tonawanda during the 1840s and by Fenton and Kurath at the Allegany Reservation around mid-twentieth century.[93]

Simmons mentioned three activities on August 30, the first day of the 1799 festival, that are clearly recognizable as the same activities reported later by Morgan and Fenton: the first stage of the white-dog sacrifice; the feather dance; and the communal feast at the end of the day's activities.[94]

Simmons reported that the "wooden image . . . had a white dog hanging on it. The dog had been painted and was draped with wampum and ribbons." He recorded that the dancing started about noon on the first day and alternated with intervals of preaching until about sundown. At mid-twentieth century at the Coldspring Longhouse on the Allegany Reservation, the sacred dancing was performed in the morning and concluded before noon.[95] Additionally, at Coldspring, the first day—actually a preliminary to the festival proper—was devoted to the "boiling of the babies." This curious appellation was derived from two concurrent but separate activities: boiling the feast soup and naming the babies born since Midwinter. The soup was eaten in celebration after the babies were named. As Anthony Wallace drolly pointed out, boiling was not the fate of the babies, even symbolically. [96]

Simmons's description of the first-day dancing certainly seems to be that of the feather dance, which was also featured during Coldspring's first day of the festival proper. Coldspring also included a thanksgiving prayer addressed to the Creator and delivered by one of the faithkeepers.[97] One or more of the intervals of preaching between dance heats mentioned by Simmons were probably devoted to thanksgiving prayer.

Because the first-day dancing in 1799 continued, at intervals, until about sunset, it is virtually certain that other dances besides the feather dance were performed. Because the Three Sisters—the spirits of corn, beans, and squash—were closely associated with women, it is possible that one of the other dances performed in 1799 was something like the traditional women's dance performed at Coldspring. As the women danced, carrying ears of corn, the Three Sisters—also known as Our Life Supporters—were believed to join in the dance. The songs that accompanied the women's dance described "the planting, germination, and successive growth of the corn, to the time it ripens, is harvested, and put away in the fall."[98]

Morgan's mid-nineteenth-century description of the first-day activities at Tonawanda also included the thanksgiving address with the burning of tobacco, the feather dance, and three or four other dances. Morgan included an example of a combined thanksgiving prayer and tobacco invocation recited on the first day of Green Corn.

> Great Spirit in heaven, listen to our words. We have assembled to perform a sacred duty, as you have commanded. This institution has descended to us from our fathers. We salute you with our thanks, that you have preserved so many of us for another year, to participate in the ceremonies of this occasion.
>
> Great Spirit, continue to listen. We thank you for your great goodness in causing our mother, the earth, again to bring forth her fruits. We thank you that you have caused our Supporters [our Life Supporter, the Three Sisters: corn, beans, and squash] to yield abundantly.
>
> Great Spirit our words still continue to flow towards you. (Throwing on tobacco.) Preserve us from all danger. Preserve our aged men. Preserve our mothers. Preserve our warriors. Preserve our children. We burn this tobacco: may its smoke arise to you. May our thanks, ascending with it, be pleasing to you. Give wisdom to the keepers of the faith, that they may direct these ceremonies with propriety. Strengthen our warriors that they may celebrate with pleasure the sacred dances of your appointment.
>
> Great Spirit, the council here assembled, the aged men and women, the strong warriors, the women and children, unite their voice of thanksgiving to you.[99]

The communal feast at the end of each day's activities was reported by all observers, except that Morgan, writing about Tonawanda at mid-nineteenth century, reported that "the Iroquois at the present day . . . do not sit down together to a common repast, except at religious councils of unusual interest. The feast, after being prepared at the place of council, is distributed at its close, and carried by the women, in vessels brought for the purpose, to their respective homes, where it is enjoyed by each family at their own fireside. But when the people feasted together after the ancient fashion, as they still do occasionally, they selected the hour of twilight."[100] As Simmons put it: "About sundown they concluded their dancing and preaching, and they all partook of their cookery."[101]

Of the second day of Green Corn, Simmons wrote: "The next day went on much as the day before, though to a greater strain of vanity and idolatry. And they burned the dog to ashes."[102] This leaves much to be filled in. Morgan and Fenton both reported that the thanksgiving dance was performed on the second day, and that this was the day for burning the white dog. Fenton also reported that the individual chants of personal thanksgiving were given on this day at Coldspring. These chants were spontaneously sung out by individuals ranging from the faithkeepers and headmen to the humblest villager. Thanks could be sung to the Creator or any of the lesser spirits for virtually any blessing or favor, and could even be directed to other members of the congregation.[103] Morgan reported that the personal chants were sung not on the second, but on the third day of Green Corn at Tonawanda, and that the fourth day was devoted to the sacred bowl game.

The bowl game was the final major event in the Green Corn celebration. In 1799 the bowl game started on the third day and was resumed on the fourth day, continuing until noon, when the festival was formally concluded.[104] At Tonawanda it began after the personal chants on the third day.[105] At Coldspring it also began on the third day of the festival proper.[106] The bowl game came last because it was played until one of the two moieties won, which could take days.

A rousing fifty-gun salute closed the Green Corn Festival at Cornplanter's village. "When I arrived, they were then closing the scene, which they did by shooting guns. About fifty men stood in a longitude direction, opposite their wooden image, and shot twice or thrice up toward the sun. Their minister shot first, and so on."[107]

Simmons's Farewell Address

On the evening of the second day of the Green Corn Festival, Simmons let Cornplanter know that he was "desirous of speaking to them in council, at a convenient opportunity, before they separated and repaired to their respective habitations." Cornplanter "proposed letting me know when their business, then in agitation, was gone through."[108] On the fourth and last day of the festival, after the bowl game had ended, Simmons received word that the Indians were about ready to meet him in council. He arrived "just before they closed the business," in time to witness the concluding volley of rifle fire.[109]

> After which, as many as could fit into Cornplanter's house entered therein. This left numbers of men, women, and children gathered round, outside the house. Cornplanter and their minister made two pretty lengthy speeches, advising them to be still and attentive to what I had to say. And, for the most part, they were very quiet and solid. Indeed, I felt the divine power spread over the gathering, in a very conspicuous manner, to the washing of my face with tears.
>
> I first opened to them my prospect of leaving them in a few weeks hence, to return home to my native land. And, because I did not know whether I should be favored with such another opportunity of meeting so many of them together, I wanted to use this occasion to drop some advice to them, and to take them by the hand and part with them in an affectionate and brotherly way.
>
> I encouraged them to press forward toward happiness, not only in this life, but in that which is to come. I also set forth my disunity with their vain and idolatrous way of worshiping the Great Spirit. I fully believed that the manner in which they acted was displeasing to him—even though it was their forefathers' custom. I believed there was a loud call to them to come forth and learn better.
>
> Now, they had remarked that it was given to their forefathers so to worship, and they thought it right for them to keep it up in remembrance of their aged fathers. But, they had also honestly acknowledged to me that they had changed their manner

of worship to a more profligate way and did not hold it so solemn as their forefathers used to do.

So, I queried them as to why they were so unwilling to part with some parts of their forefathers' mode of life and yet had taken so readily to some new ways, so very injurious to them, such as that of strong drink. I also mentioned their present habits of decking and adorning themselves with such very extravagant, superfluous, and expensive clothes, and of wearing such an abundance of silver ornaments about themselves, neither of which their forefathers were accustomed to. But rather, I believed, their forefathers were glad to get skins to cover themselves with. At this some of them laughed.

I strenuously pressed them to lay out their money for such articles as would be useful to them, and not to spend it for naught.

After a pause, they expressed great thankfulness for what I had mentioned to them. They acknowledged that they could not say it was not true. I had been with them a long while, and they believed I was a good man. I had always been willing to do what was right among them. But as I was now about to leave them, they felt thankful that I and my companions had been so favored with good health, ever since we came among them. And they desired that the Great Spirit might conduct me safe home, to see my relations and Friends there. They told me I must write back, to let them know how I got along, etc.

They then took me by the hand and we parted like brothers. At the conclusion of this council, Halliday Jackson, one of my companions, came down from the farm at Genesinguhta and tarried with me until the next day [September 3].[110]

This farewell address expressed all of Simmons's conflicting emotions toward the Indians: his affection for them, his intuitive trust in their capacity for authentic religious experience, his prejudice against native culture, his sectarian bias against native religious practices and customs, and his impatience and frustration with the "slow progress of civilization among them." And, of course, he delivered the whole address in vintage Simmons's style: passionate, sincere, blunt, and tactless. The Senecas, as ever, made a gracious reply, thanked Simmons, and wished him well.

CHAPTER ELEVEN

Motives and Agendas

A little more than a week after his farewell address, Henry Simmons was occupied at his new schoolhouse, when he received some surprise visitors. The small schoolhouse, located some three-quarters of a mile from Cornplanter's village, had been erected over the course of the summer by Simmons and Joel Swayne, with the assistance of Seneca labor, for which the Quakers paid by plowing some of the Indians' fields. By September, or perhaps even earlier, Simmons had taken up residence in the schoolbuilding. Nearby, a new house that Cornplanter was having built remained unfinished, although it too had been under construction in mid-June.[1]

About an hour before sunset September 11, a delegation from the Indian Committee in Philadelphia suddenly appeared, unannounced and unexpected. Simmons was delighted to see Joshua Sharpless and three other Friends: "Their arrival was to us a time of mutual heartfelt joy."[2] Sharpless was one of the two Quaker elders who had traveled from Philadelphia in the spring of 1798 to oversee the establishment of the mission. Accompanying him on this trip were Isaac Coats, Thomas Stewardson, and James Cooper. In addition to inspecting the mission farm, touring Cornplanter's village and its environs, and conferring with the Indians, the delegation was also tasked with organizing a new monthly meeting among some sixty Quaker families in upper Canada.[3]

The visitors spent the night in the schoolhouse; and, despite the lateness of the hour, Cornplanter and some of the headmen came to greet them briefly. In the morning, Cornplanter "and some of his connections" returned to the schoolhouse, remaining long enough only to deliver some food. After breakfast, Simmons and the delegates boarded canoes and poled their way about a mile up the Allegheny to Cornplanter's village, where they stopped and arranged for a council to be held on the fourteenth.[4] The delay would allow time for Indian runners to carry word of the council to the headmen who were out with hunting parties.[5]

The Quakers proceeded upstream to Genesinguhta, where the delegates spent the next day touring the model farm and some nearby Indian homes. In his journal Isaac Coats recorded his opinion of "the improvements made by our young Friends in this wilderness country, which appear considerable; their corn and buckwheat are good; they have pretty good oats, a considerable quantity of hay, a large garden of good vegetables, and about five acres of ground cleared and plowed, ready to sow wheat. They have a comfortable two-story house to live in and several other necessary buildings."[6]

On the morning of September 14 the Quaker delegation floated back down the Allegheny to Jenuchshadago. They spent about an hour touring the village before "something like a French horn was blown in order to collect the chiefs and others to the council." The Quakers and about thirty headmen assembled shortly in Cornplanter's house, with Cornplanter's son Henry again serving as interpreter.[7] The Quaker delegation presented its credentials in the form of a certificate from the Indian Committee of the Philadelphia Yearly Meeting, which was read aloud. Also read was a written address containing the delegates' observations on the Indians' "progress," and inviting comment on the mission's usefulness and the missionaries' service to date.

> Now brothers, we should like to hear from your own mouths whether or not you are entirely satisfied with our young men being among you. They came here with a hope of being useful by instructing you in a better way of managing your land and providing for yourselves and your cattle. We desire you to speak freely.
>
> Brothers, it has been of some satisfaction to us, in riding through your town, to see marks of industry taking place; to see that you are building better and warmer houses to live in; and to see that so much of your cleared land is planted with corn, potatoes, beans, squashes, cucumbers, etc. And, to see these article kept in good order.[8]

The delegates also observed that where the Indians' new houses were being built, "the timber is very much cut off, opening a rich flat, which we encourage you to clear and make fit for plowing. We believe it to be very good land for wheat as well as corn." The Indians had increased their stock of cattle and were pasturing the animals in the rich bottoms along the river. The delegates recommended that some of the bottomland be set aside for producing hay to help feed livestock over the long, cold winters. Given the lateness of the current season, however, they suggested a stopgap measure: "As you gather your corn, cut the stalks close at the ground, bind them up in small bundles, and put them in stacks, as our young men do. These stalks will keep the cattle part of the cold weather." The Quakers urged more men to participate in agricultural tasks and applauded the Indians' efforts to keep alcohol out of the village, pointing out that money not spent on whiskey could be used "instead to buy clothes and to buy oxen and plows with which to work your land."[9]

Before responding to the Quaker speech, Cornplanter wished to know if Henry Simmons still intended to leave the mission. Simmons explained that he had yet to consult with the delegates on that particular matter. He encouraged the Indians to answer the delegates' question regarding "their satisfaction with our being among them, and I desired that they might not hide anything from them." Cornplanter replied:

> They had made strict inquiry among themselves about us but could not find any fault against us. Rather, we were always doing what was right among them, etc. Cornplanter said I had been a great help to him, particularly in endeavoring to prevent so much whiskey from coming into their town, and if I went away he would have nobody there to help him.[10]

The council then recessed so that the Quakers could discuss Simmons's future in private. The delegates expressed their wish that Simmons would remain in his post through the upcoming winter, but left the decision to him. Simmons reaffirmed his determination to go home. The council reconvened and Quaker elder Joshua Sharpless informed Cornplanter of Simmons's decision.[11]

> Cornplanter replied that he had nothing more to say about it. It might be the best thing for me to go and see my parents and Friends. Cornplanter said he would accompany me through the Indian settlements as far as Canandaigua on the route that I had proposed for traveling. He then expressed satisfaction that the business was gone through. So we took each other by the hands, all round.
>
> After which, we took a bite of bread and butter, took leave, and returned to Genesinguhta that same day.[12]

The Quakers got back to the farmhouse just before sunset. During the night Joshua Sharpless, while returning to his bed after visiting the "necessary" house, fell through an open trapdoor, into the cellar. He hit his head on one of the floor joists and was knocked unconscious. His companions, roused by the noise, rushed to his aid. After a few minutes, he regained consciousness, but could not remember what had happened to him. The next day was First Day, and the Friends held a worship meeting at the farmhouse, where the delegates decided to remain until Sharpless recovered.[13]

On Monday morning, a half dozen headmen came from Jenuchshadago and from a few locations on the Allegheny River above Genesinguhta, to spend some more time with the visitors. Cornplanter arrived at about noon, bearing gifts—a quarter of venison and two pigeons. He offered to provide guides to conduct the Quaker delegation as far as Buffalo. The Quakers declined, explaining that, in light of Joshua Sharpless's condition, they did not know when they would be able to travel. The Indians stayed until midafternoon.[14]

The following morning, September 17, Sharpless pronounced himself ready to travel. The delegation delayed its departure long enough for Simmons, Jackson, and Swayne to write letters to their families back home—to be delivered by the delegates. At midmorning the party set out for upper Canada, accompanied by Halliday Jackson, who had been as far as Buffalo once before, and by an Indian named Sunfish, who guided the travelers. The Quakers were surprised to discover that the Indians had opened and widened the path for several miles, "just on our account."[15]

Simmons returned to his schoolhouse; but he would remain there for only three more weeks, before setting out for home. This delay allowed Jackson to return from upper Canada and resume his post at the mission before Simmons left.

MOTIVES

Both the Senecas and the Quakers had underlying motivations for establishing a mission among Cornplanter's people. Certain items on the Quaker agenda set up a conflict between European-American and Seneca cultural values that produced tensions between the Senecas and the Quakers, and within the Seneca community itself.

Cornplanter's Motives

Cornplanter had two fundamental motives in requesting the Quaker mission. The Quakers would help open and expand economic opportunities for his people, by providing access to the agrarian milling and smithy technologies of the day and by demonstrating the techniques of plow agriculture and animal husbandry. The Quakers would also serve as political and legal advocates, who could be counted upon absolutely to help protect the remaining Indian landholding against scheming land companies and aggressive squatters. Quaker advocates could help win compensation at the state and federal levels, for legitimate Seneca grievances that were left unresolved, or simply ignored, by the local American justice system.

Quaker Motives

In establishing the mission, Friends had several discernible motives. They had a sense of moral indebtedness and obligation to the Indians for that part of the North American continent that had already been taken from them. The Quakers realized that the Indians had been dispossessed of their lands with very little compensation, usually against their will, and often through the use of force. The Quakers also recognized that the Indians, as well as the frontier settlers, had suffered much through the unending cycles of retaliatory bloodshed. This awareness of the history between Indians and European Americans contributed to the Quaker sense of moral obligation, which expressed itself as benevolence toward the Indians.

In extending consideration to American Indians, Friends were not moved by feelings of personal or collective guilt. Rather they were prompted by their own experience, during the Revolutionary War years, of persecution on account of their peace testimony, which was sufficient to give them some insight into what it was like to be vulnerable to an overwhelmingly superior force that had the power to exercise cruelty or mercy, according to whim.

The Quakers also hoped to influence the government and the public toward an Indian policy that recognized and respected Indian rights, as a matter of justice. They preferred to bear witness through deeds, and to lead by example as in the matter of slavery and abolition. Their Society's long history of humane and just dealings with the Indians gave them the moral authority to call upon the government and its citizens to improve relations with the Indians by treating them fairly and decently.

Some historians have asserted that Quaker benevolence toward American Indians was motivated by a desire to refurbish the Society's image, which had been tarnished by charges of Toryism and disloyalty during the Revolution. This assertion is highly questionable, however, given the virulent hatred of Indians harbored by many Americans. That Friends wanted their philanthropic initiatives among the Indians to come to the attention of their fellow citizens does not necessarily mean that they were involved in a selfserving public-relations campaign.

Friends were not promoting their own image; they were promoting a concept of relations with the Indians based on peace, justice, and humanitarianism. To help turn this vision into a reality, Friends did work to influence the government and to find a role for themselves in Indian policy. Playing such a positive role gave them a powerful voice in support of their ideal.

The Quakers also sought to "civilize" the Senecas. Although they did see civilization as a prerequisite for Christianizing the Senecas, Friends also felt that improving the Indians' standard of living was a worthwhile goal in its own right. The Quakers held very strong opinions about what constituted civilization, and about the path the Indians should follow to material security and prosperity. Their prescription, like the government's, was one of radical acculturation, in which the Senecas would abandon many traditional ways and replace them with European-American practices. Although Friends were not religious proselytizers, they were very definitely cultural proselytizers.

AGENDAS

On both sides, motivations translated into specific agendas, which at times converged to some degree, and at times diverged to the point of conflict.

Quaker Agenda

Schooling for the Indian children was near the top of the Quaker agenda. It was not a high priority, however, among the Allegany Senecas—at least not at the dawn of the nineteenth century. With a few notable exceptions such as Cornplanter, most of the Senecas saw no practical benefit from classroom instruction. Some—the nativists in particular—perceived a threat to Indian cultural identity and values.

The gratifying attendance at his school reported by Simmons during the first half of February 1799 was short-lived. Late in February he complained that the children had deserted his classroom to prepare for a dance frolic. Early in March Cornplanter and his supporters promised Simmons that their children would "attend the school steadily," clearly implying that other children did not.[16] After recording this promise, Simmons never mentioned school attendance again. His little school was simply overtaken by the seasonal cycle of subsistence activities.[17] Seneca families were off to their sugar camps, pigeon roosts, and trout streams, summer hunting trips, and winter hunting camps. The schoolhouse was built that summer, but according to Halliday Jackson, the children "were very irregular in their attendance, and no great progress in learning was made." After Simmons went home, one of the two Friends at Genesinguhta taught school there during the winter of 1799 to 1800. "A number of children attended and made some progress."[18]

The cause of education was dealt a severe blow by the strong nativist sentiment in Handsome Lake's teachings. In 1801 the prophet told his followers they should "not allow their children to learn to read and write."[19] He soon recognized, however, that some Senecas would have to become educated, if his nation was to deal effectively with European-American businessmen, lawyers, politicians, and judges. Accordingly, he declared that two persons from each of the Six Nations should be educated. "So many white people are about you that you must study to know their ways."[20] In time, he relaxed his opposition even more, and the Quakers were able to provide limited instruction informally.[21]

A decade-long hiatus in formal schooling came to an end in 1811, when the Quakers—at the Indians' request—opened a school at Cold Spring on the reservation. Formal schooling was interrupted again by the turmoil surrounding the War of 1812. In 1816, however, the school at Cold Spring was reopened.[22] By the following year, the Quakers were beginning to achieve the results they desired.

> Nearly twenty lads attended, divers [several] of whom could read and write the English language, and had otherwise made satisfactory progress in learning. The cleanliness of their persons, their order in the school and general deportment, appeared to be encouraging.[23]

Progress continued throughout the following decade. In 1822 the school was moved to Tunesassa, where in addition to classroom instruction the boys received training in the mechanical arts. A school for Seneca girls was opened in 1826.[24]

The Quaker agenda also called for the Senecas to adopt European-American agrarian technology: plow agriculture, animal husbandry, gristmilling, lumber milling, and blacksmithing. On these points, there was a good deal of overlap between the Quaker and Seneca agendas, especially with respect to technology transfer in the form of mills and smithies. The Senecas needed no convincing of the benefits of such technology. Cornplanter, in a display of considerable entrepreneurial skill, had organized the construction and operation of his own private sawmill as early as 1795, four years before the Quakers arrived.

The main Seneca problem in relation to obtaining their own mills and smithies was a lack of capital. Friends were willing to go only so far to help the Senecas in this regard. They wanted to see the Indians form habits of thrift, and feared that simply giving them everything they needed would be counterproductive. The Quakers sought to impress upon the Indians the value of saving their annuity money and applying it to capital improvements.[25] In May 1798 Joshua Sharpless and John Pierce promised the Allegany Senecas half the money for construction of a gristmill during the summer of 1799, provided that the Indians raised sufficient grain to warrant it and that they put up the other half of the money.

The Senecas, always in debt to traders, were unable to save the $400 needed for their half.[26] In 1804 the Quakers paid for the construction of a gristmill,[27] which was erected on a 700-acre piece of property they had purchased next to the reservation, on Tunesassa Creek—present-day Quaker Run. During 1803 and 1804, the Quakers moved their entire mission to Tunesassa and built a new farm there,[28] leaving all the improvements they had made at Genesinguhta to the Indians, as had been originally agreed. Although the Indians did not get their own gristmill, they could use the Quaker mill. The Quakers ground all of the Indians' grain free for the first two years, and charged a nominal fee thereafter.[29]

The Quakers also erected a sawmill at Tunesassa, which became the source of some friction. The Quaker missionaries viewed the sawmill as a means of generating revenue to help defray the costs of the mission. They cut timber on their own land, then milled and sold it at Tunesassa, to Indians and non-Indians alike, though they gave the Indians a 50 percent discount. Additionally, the Quakers agreed to saw timber that the Senecas cut on the reservation and hauled to Tunesassa. The Quakers sawed the first 10,000 board feet free of charge, after which they "sawed it for the halves," keeping half the boards produced as payment for the milling.[30] This was standard practice among European Americans at the time[31]; but some of the Allegany Senecas felt the Quakers were taking advantage of them.

From the Quakers' point of view, boards cut and sold to the Senecas at a 50 percent discount constituted a cheap, convenient source of lumber for the Indians. The Quakers made allowance for the fact that the Indians were often strapped for cash by letting them bring their own logs to the mill, to be sawed for the halves. This arrangement ensured that the supply of lumber available for Seneca use was inexpensive—at least in terms of cash outlay. The Indians only needed money to cover half the market price for boards they purchased, and none at all for their own timber.

Some of the Allegany Senecas, nevertheless, resented the commercialization of the Quaker sawmill, feeling that the mill should have been dedicated for Indian use. Some felt the Quakers derived a huge benefit from sawing Seneca lumber to the halves. This benefit came at Seneca expense, in terms of timber and the labor involved in cutting it and hauling it to the mill. It was not long before the Indians were clamoring for a sawmill of their own, located on reservation land and owned by the Allegany Seneca community.[32]

Cornplanter's sawmill did not meet these specifications, and the community had a falling-out with Cornplanter involving this sawmill. In 1804 he wanted to relocate his mill to a better site on the reservation; however, he wanted to continue operating it as his own private enterprise. The community decided that most of the proceeds from any sawmill located on the reservation should go to the group. Cornplanter told them that if that was the way they felt, he would lease his land to white farmers so that he could collect rent. He then forbade the Senecas from planting on his property. During the ensuing ruckus, most of the Allegany Senecas moved off the grant and onto the reservation. Cornplanter was even deposed as chief, temporarily; and although subsequently reinstated, he never did win permission to move his sawmill onto the reservation.[33]

In 1807 the Quakers acquiesced to the demand for a Seneca sawmill. The missionaries explained their recommendation to the Indian Committee as follows:

> The disaffected part of the Indians have frequently labored to propagate a belief that *our* sawmill was erected with a view of accumulating an interest out of them—stating they had been informed it was intended for *their* use, but they found it quite otherwise. These and other similar ideas by being artfully insinuated we perceived had gained considerable ascendancy over some of those who had appeared well disposed.[34]

The Indian Committee agreed to contribute $300 toward the construction of a sawmill for the Indians, provided the Senecas supplied the construction labor.[35] The Seneca sawmill was completed in the autumn of 1808, and the millwright was retained for several months to work the mill and train some of the Indian men in its operation and management.[36] In 1811 when lumber prices were low and the Quaker sawmill was idle, the Senecas leased their mill to two European Americans, while still bearing the maintenance costs.[37] By 1812 the Indians were running it again.[38]

Beyond filling the need for lumber on the reservation, the Indian mill never had much business. During the second decade of the 1800s, the practice of rafting unmilled logs down the Allegheny River to Warren, Franklin, and Pittsburgh effectively bypassed both sawmills for all but local purposes. In 1820 the Seneca sawmill irons were sold, and the mill passed into oblivion.[39]

The transfer of blacksmith technology appears to have been both less contentious and more successful. In 1799 the Quakers set up a forge at the Genesinguhta farm for repairing their own tools and those they had loaned to the Indians. In September 1801 Vincent Wiley, a young Quaker blacksmith, arrived at Genesinguhta to provide skilled smithy services for the Quaker-Seneca community, and to teach his craft to two Indian boys. He stayed for one year. His apprentices were capable enough, but illness and family problems conspired to interfere with their becoming truly adept before Wiley went home.[40] By 1803 the Senecas were expressing dissatisfaction with the limited range of blacksmith services the Indian apprentices could provide.[41] Another Quaker blacksmith came along during the summer of 1803 and provided additional training for the Indian smiths, which helped quite a bit.[42]

The Quaker agenda called for the Indians to learn animal husbandry, and the Senecas took to this agrarian pursuit with great enthusiasm—eventually with more enthusiasm than the Quakers would have preferred. The Quakers encouraged the Indians to procure the draft animals—oxen and horses—that were essential to plow agriculture.[43] Teams of oxen were very expensive, so the Allegany Senecas purchased and used them communally, paying for them out of the annuity funds.[44] Horses, cows, pigs, and chickens, however, were privately owned.

The Allegany Senecas increased their stock of farm animals through breeding and yearly purchases.[45] By 1803 they had increased their herd of cattle beyond their capacity to feed them through the winter. The Indians turned to the Quakers, who felt compelled to provide them with fodder, to the extent possible without endangering their own animals.[46] In 1805 the Quakers reported that the Indians had "a number of fat cattle to sell this fall and hogs in abundance."[47] By the following summer the Senecas had increased their stock of cattle and oxen even further. There were still too many wolves, however, to allow the introduction of sheep.[48]

Animal husbandry suffered a setback during the winter of 1806 and 1807, when much livestock perished in the cold weather while the Indians were away on an extended hunt.[49] The Senecas grew insufficient fodder to carry their livestock through the winter, and they had not yet constructed adequate winter shelter for all their animals. The heavy loss of livestock must have opened the Indians' eyes to their husbandry shortcomings, because in 1808 the Quakers remarked that they were taking better care of their animals.[50] Halliday Jackson reported that in 1814 the Allegany Senecas "continued to increase their stock of cattle, horses, and swine, quite equal to their means of supporting them through the winter."[51] The Senecas also started raising horses to supply their own needs and to sell.[52] By 1817 the Allegany Senecas had, in the Quakers' opinion, "more horses than is of any advantage to them."[53]

The most problematic item on the Quaker agenda was an ambitious and comprehensive program to restructure Seneca society. The Seneca men were to desist from hunting as a livelihood and take up farming to raise cash crops such as wheat and rye.[54] The production of cash crops required the introduction of plow agriculture because traditional hoe horticulture, although sufficient for raising subsistence crops, was too inefficient. Plow agriculture meant that men would have to replace women in the fields because, supposedly, a man's physical strength was needed to handle a plow and its team of horses or oxen. Seneca women were to stay home and practice domestic crafts such as spinning, knitting, weaving, and soap- and candle-making.[55]

This program's basic premise—the raising of cash crops as the Senecas' primary source of income—was flawed. A cash crop required a market where it could be sold. But the nearest market of any size was Pittsburgh, 207 miles downriver. Bulky cereal grains could be transported on the river in barges or keel boats, but the shipping costs would make Seneca grain more expensive than that grown locally in the Pittsburgh region, where there were already sufficient farms to supply local needs.[56] Lumber, however, could be transported without the use of European-American river vessels. The Senecas simply rafted their lumber together, piled their pelts, deerskins, and canoes on top, and floated the whole load to Pittsburgh, avoiding freight charges completely. Thus, although the Senecas could not be competitive in the distant Pittsburgh grain market, they could and did trade successfully in the Pittsburgh market for lumber and deer hides.[57]

Seneca men did start plowing fields, but not as fulltime farmers raising cash crops. And before they took to plowing, they satisfied themselves that the results would justify the effort and the capital investment in plows and draft animals. In the spring of 1801, the Allegany Senecas conducted an agricultural experiment.

> Several parts of a large field were plowed, and the intermediate spaces [were] prepared by their women with the hoe, according to former custom. It was all planted with corn; and the parts plowed (besides the great saving of labor) produced much the heaviest crop; the stalks being more than a foot higher and proportionally stouter than those on the hoed ground.[58]

The Seneca men sowed oats, hay, and field corn, which they used to over-winter their livestock. They also plowed fields for corn, beans, squash, potatoes, and other vegetables, but these crops were planted and tended by the women. The introduction of plow agriculture did not drive Seneca women from the fields as the Quakers had intended. Rather, women continued to raise subsistence vegetables, while men grew fodder crops and some grains for human consumption such as spring wheat and buckwheat.[59] The association of certain crops with women and others with men still persisted on the Six Nations Reserve in Canada at mid-twentieth century.[60]

Conflicting Cultural Values

The reordering of Seneca society that the Quakers had in mind went far beyond the revision of gender-based economic roles. The model that the Quakers and the government had in mind was European-American agrarian society, as it existed at the end of the 1700s. That society was based on private property, a dispersed settlement pattern, and the profit motive. Seneca society at that time was based on communal ownership of land, organized around village life, and operated on the principle of reciprocal sharing.

Seneca land was owned by the nation. Specific plots in cornfields, specific maple-sugar groves, specific hunting-camp sites, etc., were assigned to specific extended families. But the family had only the right to use the plot, grove, or campsite. They did not own it, and could not sell it. It was not their exclusive property, although they did own the corn, sugar, or meat produced from the land by their labor.

Seneca life centered on the village, which was not just a place, but a coherent political, religious, and social unit. Seneca politics were consensual, and local politics were concerned with such a wide range of issues that councils had to be called frequently. Some of these were general councils, attended by the whole village. Many more were councils of the chiefs or headmen. Even the chiefs' councils were often preceded by councils of the warriors and of the women, during which these constituencies decided what they wanted their headmen to say. Sometimes a chiefs' council was followed by meetings of warriors and women, during which the headmen explained the decisions of the chiefs' council. Local Seneca politics depended on the logistical advantages offered by having most of the body politic live in the same village.

Several times a year, the Allegany Senecas celebrated religious festivals, which not only took place in the village, but in which all villagers participated. The Midwinter Rites and the Green Corn Festival were multiple-day celebrations. At Midwinter, the dream-guessing rites and medicine-society rituals required much house-to-house visiting. These religious rites and social activities were greatly facilitated by the fact that virtually every family had its primary residence in the village.

Seneca people spent a much greater portion of their time socializing than did their European-American contemporaries who lived on isolated farmsteads. Men did most of their socializing with each other, playing sports ranging from archery to lacrosse, and smoking together. Women did most of theirs while they worked together in the fields, gathered firewood, and hauled water. They worked at their own pace, which was not taxing and provided ample opportunity for sharing confidences, news, and gossip. The entire community frequently joined together for communal meals, social dances, and storytelling, especially during the long winter evenings. The ability to engage in these frequent and prolonged social contacts depended on regular and lengthy periods of village habitation.

The centrality of the village to so many aspects of Seneca life was just the expression of more fundamental cultural phenomenon—the comparatively extensive degree to which membership in the extended family, the clan, and the village contributed to an individual's sense of personal identity. The extent of personal identity derived from group membership helps explain how, in a noncoercive society, these entities were able to make demanding claims on individual behavior. Participation in the political, religious, and social activities of the village reinforced group identity and provided such a sense of personal fulfillment that to live apart from the village was to stop living as a Seneca.

Sharing and reciprocity were deeply embedded Iroquois cultural values. Between Indians, economic exchanges took the form of reciprocal gift-giving. Although there was an expectation of a rough parity in the exchange, it would not be correct to characterize reciprocal gift-giving as a form of barter. Reciprocation might occur at a considerable time after the receipt of a gift. The exchange also served as much to reinforce a sense of mutual reliance and obligation as it did to satisfy a specific economic requirement. Food was shared with families who did not have enough, with no expectation of anything in return—except that, if fortunes reversed in the future, similar gifts would be bestowed upon today's givers. Reciprocity permeated all relationships and activities. When women went to work in the fields, they did not go separately to their individual plots and labor only there. They went in groups, working all together, tending to each individual's plot in turn.

The Quaker program called for radical acculturation. Neither the Quakers nor the government expected an immediate transformation of Seneca society. They were patient and willing to start with what they believed were small steps, such as getting Seneca men to work in the fields. But the ultimate goal was to recast Seneca culture in the likeness of an idealized European-American agrarian society.

Reciprocity was the first cultural value to trip up the Quakers, and it proved to be an ongoing source of tension, in two respects. The Quakers were reluctant to practice it themselves, fearing that to do so would retard both self-sufficiency and development of the profit motive among the Indians. The Quakers, moreover, tried to get the Senecas to stop practicing it with one another. From the very outset of the mission, however, the Quakers found themselves entangled in a reciprocal relationship. When the Quakers first arrived in May 1798, they lacked food, tools, and seeds until their supply boat came up from Pittsburgh. The Indians offered the Quakers what they needed as gifts. The Quakers tried to minimize their indebtedness by paying cash for as much as the Indians would let them, but there were limits to how much Seneca generosity the Quakers could refuse without seeming to reject Seneca friendship.[61]

When negotiating the ground rules for operation of the demonstration farm at Genesinguhta, the Quakers made a series of promises that heightened Seneca expectations about what the missionaries would do for them. They promised to give one-quarter of any surplus grain to the elderly and infirm, to plow fields for the Indians until they were equipped to do it for themselves, to lend tools from a collection that would be reserved for Indian use and left with the Indians when the Quakers departed, to set up a blacksmith shop at Genesinguhta where they would mend the Indian tools as well as their own, and to put up half the cost of building a gristmill on the farm, provided the Indians came up with the other half.[62] The Quakers kept all these promises but regarded the measures as temporary expedients to help the Indians get started on the road to civilization. Their goal was to wean the Indians from any dependency on such services and to assist them in becoming self-sufficient. Many of the Indians, however, regarded the promises as part of an ongoing reciprocal relationship in which the Quakers would perform these services in return for using the Indian land to farm.

The Quakers had no problem with continuing to help the elderly and infirm, and after a few years the Indians were plowing their own fields.[63] The Indians were unable to come up with their half of the cost for a gristmill, but the Quakers built the mill at Tunesassa in 1804. The Indians must have been satisfied with this arrangement, because unlike the case with the Quaker sawmill, they never complained about the nominal fee for the gristmill. Tool lending and mending, however, became something of a nuisance for the Quakers.[64]

The tool collection consisted of farming implements such as plow irons, hoes, shovels, spades, axes, and scythes, and of carpenter, mason and cooper tools. Because they were used by the whole village, these tools saw very hard service. The Quakers had to keep the tools repaired until Indian blacksmiths could be trained. The missionaries complained to the Indian Committee that if they did not attend to each and every Indian demand, recriminations would quickly follow.[65] The Indians, unsatisfied for a time with their own newly trained blacksmiths, continued to make demands on the Quakers. Given that the Genesinguhta farm was located on the reservation and operated at the sufferance of the Allegany Senecas, the missionaries felt compelled to comply with those demands.

By the end of 1802 the missionaries believed the only way to extricate themselves from the reciprocity relationship, which they believed was retarding Indian progress, was to move the mission farm off the reservation. To the committee in Philadelphia, they wrote of the Indians that "settlements made on their lands for their benefit may for a seasonable time have a good effect," but because the Indians did not understand the Quaker goal of Indian self-sufficiency, such settlements led to "dependence that evidently obstructs their own advancement." As the demonstration farm prospered, the Indians seemed to feel that the missionaries were under even more of an obligation to "gratify every request . . . which are often very unreasonable and improper to grant and if not complied with," brought from the Indians the retort that "we enjoy such and such benefit from their land. . . . This at times reduces us to a compliance that tends to retard their advancement and renders our influence of less avail in many things" than perhaps might be the case "if we were situated more independent of them."[66]

Corn pounder (originally published by Morgan in 1851). Wooden mortar two feet in diameter and wooden pestle four feet in length, used to grind dried corn into meal. The Allegany Seneca women greatly appreciated the gristmill erected by the Quakers at Tunesassa in 1804, where they could get their corn ground for a nominal fee. Prior to that, women and girls had spent hour after hour, pounding corn into meal. DARLINGTON LIBRARY, UNIVERSITY OF PITTSBURGH.

During the winter of 1802 to 1803 the Indians obtained an emergency supply of animal fodder from the Quakers. The Quakers feared that in some future winter Indian needs might exceed their ability to supply them without jeopardizing their own animals. Refusal to help the Indians in a crisis might lead to an irreparable breach, especially if the Quakers were still working the farm on the reservation.[67]

Thus in 1803 the Quakers began their relocation to Tunesassa; they finished moving in 1804. In September 1803 the missionaries turned the tools over to the Indians, suggested that a chief be placed in charge of lending them, and declared that they themselves were done with tool lending.[68] Not wishing to discourage the Indians, however, the Quakers promised to keep a sufficient inventory of tools at Tunesassa from which they could sell to any Indians who wanted to buy.[69]

In 1806 an Indian Committee delegation making an inspection visit tried to break certain Seneca expectations about Quaker behavior—expectations that stemmed from Seneca notions about reciprocity.

> As our Friends at Tunesassa have the mills and farm to attend to themselves, you cannot expect them to do a great deal of work for you. But if at any time you want instruction about fencing your farms, building your houses, laying out roads, etc., apply to them and they shall always be willing to give you such counsel as they may think best.[70]

The delegates found that "some little uneasiness had got into a few of the Indians' minds with respect to our Friends not lending them tools and working for them as much as they formerly did."[71] The Quakers addressed the issue in a council with the Indians.

> If you wish us to send on any more tools for our Friends to sell to you, we hope you will tell us your minds. As you know, we told you before that we would send on a few scythes, sickles, augurs and some such tools for our Friends to sell to such of you as might want to buy, but that they should leave off lending. And we hope your blacksmiths will be industrious and make you what tools they can."[72]

One of the Indians claimed that they could find tools at prices cheaper than those charged by the Quakers, who replied that they sold at cost and could go no lower.[73] Less than four months later the Senecas again requested that the missionaries keep a stock of tools for sale to Indians.[74] The Quakers were not consistent, however, in refusing to lend tools. When the staffing at the mission changed, tool lending was resumed.[75]

Whenever the Quakers had come into the village or Indian homes, the Senecas had always extended their hospitality by offering food. This was a universal custom among the Indians, and the Senecas seem to have expected the same when they visited the Quakers, especially after women were added to the mission staff in 1805. In 1806 some of the Allegany Senecas complained that Friends were not feeding them when they went to Tunesassa on business.[76] The Quakers answered bluntly:

> We now want you to understand plainly that our Friends at Tunesassa are not come there to feed you. There is a great many of you and but one family of them, and if they always entertained you . . . it would take our women most of their time . . .

they would have no time to instruct the Indians in useful things. . . . You know there are some of your people who do not like work very well. These might go and stay several days, living on our Friends. This would be unreasonable. You say it is a common thing for you to entertain one another. This is very good. You may also understand it is a common thing among your Friends the Quakers to entertain one another whenever they go to see each other and stand in need of victuals. And if any of you will visit us in our settlements, we will entertain you freely. But we don't wish you to give our Friends at Tunesassa any trouble about giving victuals.[77]

The Senecas reiterated that sharing food was an Indian custom and they would continue to practice it among themselves, although they no longer expected the Quakers to do so.[78] Despite Quaker advice that the Indians at least scale back their observance of this custom, Handsome Lake upheld it.

The Creator made food for all creatures and it must be free for all. He ordained that people should live in communities. Now when visitors enter a lodge the woman must always say, 'come, eat.' Now it is not right to refuse what is offered. The visitor must take two or three bites at least.[79]

This sentiment was typical of the attitude that continued to prevail among the Senecas regarding reciprocity. Handsome Lake tried to reinforce this cultural value, telling his followers that "they might farm a little and build houses, but must not sell anything which they raised on their land." Instead they must "give it away to one another, especially to their old people." They should "enjoy all things in common."[80]

Later, he became a bit more accommodating of the trend toward accumulation of material resources within individual families. He said there were three things that the white man did right. He worked a tract of cultivated land and harvested food, built a warm house, and raised livestock—all for his family. Even if he died, his family would still have the benefit of these resources. Therefore, there was nothing wrong with accumulating them, provided they did not become a source of pride and selfishness. Handsome Lake insisted that charity must still be given to the poor, especially to poor children and the elderly.[81]

The Senecas also resisted Quaker pressure to take up a more dispersed settlement pattern. When the Quakers first arrived in 1798, they found the Allegany Senecas settled in three locations: Cornplanter's village on the grant where most of the population resided, Genesinguhta some nine miles upriver where only a few families remained and where the Quakers themselves originally settled, and an unnamed "upper settlement" another ten miles upriver where an unspecified number of families lived.[82] At that time inhabitants of Genesinguhta and the upper settlement went to Cornplanter's village for councils and religious feasts.[83]

The Quakers reported that the houses in the upper settlement were spread out more than those in Cornplanter's village. Its more dispersed settlement pattern might be explained by the fact that it was a satellite community whose inhabitants had to repair to the main village for councils and feasts. In 1803 the Quakers reported that the upper settlement split into two parts when several families moved about two miles farther upriver.[84]

Until the mass exodus from the grant in 1804, few Indian families built houses very far from Cornplanter's village. Most of the people who moved off the grant settled at Cold Spring, a newly constructed, tightly clustered village on the reservation. A few families did move onto separate farmsteads in the general vicinity of Genesinguhta.[85] They seem to have exchanged support from the village for support from the Quakers, who were quite pleased with these families but much less so with those who settled in Cold Spring.

> Several other families have fixed on spots of land up the river to build on, detached from their little town. . . .These . . . are taking hold of the right end of things and the nearest road to distinct property. To these our advice flows freely and [is] generally acceptable to them. The other party that are huddling together in the town are Indians yet and [are] not beginning right in our view.[86]

"The nearest road to distinct property" was indeed the road the Quakers wanted the Allegany Senecas to take because, in the prevailing European-American view, "a love for exclusive property" lay at the heart of civilization.[87] Just as the Quakers urged the Indians to abandon reciprocity in favor of the profit motive, they promoted private Indian ownership of land over communal landholding. This meant that someday the reservation would have to be divided into individually owned plots.

From the inception of the mission, much of the advice and instruction given by the Quakers regarding the fencing of fields, dispersing onto individual farmsteads, making improvements thereon, and accumulating capital had been aimed at evoking a desire within Indian individuals to own their land separately and privately. The Quakers saw these steps as beneficial in their own right, apart from whatever effect they might have to stimulate an appetite within the Senecas for private property. As long as the Quakers observed Seneca progress through these intermediate steps, they were content to let the Indians make the leap to private property in their own good time.

This attitude changed after the War of 1812, when the Ogden Land Company—holder of the preemption rights to the Allegany Reservation land—began pressing the Senecas to sell their land.[88] In response, the Quakers began pushing the idea of dividing the reservation into lots that would be held in severalty. The Quakers thought that giving Indian families their own private parcels of land "would attach them more generally to the true value of it and would not leave the decision of their property as much to the chiefs."[89] Chiefs, after all, had been susceptible to bribery by land speculators in the past. The Quakers argued that severalty would forestall the kind of wholesaling of Indian land that had occurred at Big Tree.

Although severalty might indeed prevent such wholesaling, it would not necessarily have prevented the Indian landholding from being retailed away. The Senecas realized that the preemption-right holder could pressure individuals into selling, especially if the individuals were in debt and their creditors had a claim on their private property. Private Indian land might also be taxed, and if the owner was unable to make the payments, the land could be seized and sold. It would be difficult if not impossible to force troublesome European Americans off land they had leased from individual Indian landowners, even if they were doing something damaging to the Indian community, such as selling liquor.[90]

The Senecas also questioned the practicality of dividing the reservation into allotments. Their usufruct plots were so intermixed that it would be almost impossible to run boundary lines.[91] By the late 1810s many Allegany Senecas were participating in a postwar lumber boom, and would lose their free access to reservation timber not on their allotted plots. These individuals did not look favorably on a plan that could have put them out of business.[92]

Nevertheless, from 1817 through 1820 the Quakers strenuously pushed for severalty. They tried to overcome Seneca objections by including restrictions that would prevent reservation land from being sold or leased to non-Indians. Halliday Jackson summed up the Quaker proposal.

> With a view of setting them in a more permanent possession of the soil, [the Indian Committee] recommended a division of their land into lots, suitable to accommodate each family, to be held under such regulations that it might descend from parent to children . . . and under such restrictions as would debar individuals from selling, leasing, or transferring it in any way to white people.[93]

What the Quakers proposed here was not true private property because the individual property holder did not have the right of alienation, nor did the Seneca nation have the right to sell or lease an individual plot without the consent of the property holder. The plan was really a covenant between the Seneca nation and its constituent property holders to provide a form of guaranteed use that could be transmitted to heirs, while at the same time limiting the ability of the chiefs to sell Indian land.[94]

This plan, which the Quakers presented to President James Monroe, met their twin goals of accelerating the development of civilization among the Indians and affording increased protection for the Indian landholding.[95] It did not address the Seneca concerns about the feasibility of disentangling their improvements on the reservation so that internal boundary lines could be run, nor about continued access to dispersed, communal resources such as timber. The Senecas were not convinced that the Quaker-proposed covenant could legally protect the reservation. They knew of no precedent in European-American law for property that was private in some respects but communal in others. They feared that land speculators might find a way to exploit any legal weakness in such a strange kind of property.[96]

At Cattaraugus in 1817 a council of delegates from all the Seneca reservations considered the Quaker proposal. The council agreed that, on an experimental basis, the Allegany Reservation could be surveyed into lots. The Senecas could then better assess the potential results of dividing the reservation.[97] The Allegany Senecas, however, were not entirely comfortable with being the guinea pigs for an experiment in land division. The following year they asked the Quakers to act on their behalf in obtaining from President Monroe an official title or deed to their reservation. They also wanted to know what the president thought of the Quaker plan.[98] These requests indicate a concern that dividing the reservation might somehow lead to losing it.[99]

In August 1818 when the surveyor showed up on the Allegany Reservation to start laying out individual lots, he was met by Cornplanter and some other chiefs who firmly refused to allow the survey to proceed. They politely asked the surveyor and Jonathan Thomas, the Quaker missionary accompanying him, to leave the reservation.[100] In June 1819 word came from Monroe that he recommended the Quaker plan.[101] But there was no title or deed for the reservation. By this time the Allegany Senecas had split into two factions over the issue of dividing the reservation into individual lots.[102] Those opposed ultimately prevailed.

Indian Agenda

Cornplanter wanted the Quakers to help protect the Indian landholding. It is uncertain whether their recommendation to subdivide the reservation was, from the perspective of preserving the land base, good advice or not. But once a Seneca faction coalesced around opposition to severalty, the Quakers ceased to actively push the idea. They did not want to promote factionalism among the Senecas, which they perceived as a threat to the Seneca land base, and they did not want to risk an irreparable breach with a significant portion of the Allegany Seneca population.

After the Senecas rejected the severalty proposal, Friends assisted the Senecas in legally defending their land throughout the nineteenth century and beyond the middle of the twentieth.[103] Even with the help of Friends, however, the Senecas were unable to prevent such disasters as the complete loss of the Buffalo Creek Reservation by mid-nineteenth century and the government's taking of one third of the Allegany Reservation for the Kinzua Dam Reservoir in the early 1960s.

Cornplanter also wanted the Quakers to act as a buffer against those elements of European-American society inclined to cheat and prey upon his people. In an 1803 conference with Friends, he stated:

> When I was at Philadelphia a long time ago, the Indians and white people at that time continued to kill each other. I then heard of the Quakers that they were a peaceable people and would not fight or kill anybody. I inquired of the President of the United Sates about them, whether or no this account was true, he said it was true enough they were such a people. I then requested him to send some of them to live among the Indians, expecting they would be very useful to us. . . . You have lived peaceably among us, and no difficulty has happened between you and our people. We now want you to stay with us, and stand between us and the white people, and if you see any of them trying to cheat us, we wish you to let us know of it. Or if you see any of our people trying to cheat the white people, we wish you to let it be known also, as we confide in you that you will not cheat us.[104]

The Quakers filled this role admirably. After missionary Jacob Taylor, who had learned to speak the Seneca language, announced that he was planning to go home, some Seneca chiefs wrote to the Indian Committee:

> You know our Friend has been with us a great while and we are well satisfied with the aid he has given us. We have always found him very useful in assisting us in cases of difficulty. We wish him to be here to assist us about our sawmill, and in dif-

ficulties which frequently occur between us and the white people, who are now settling round our land. . . . We think another person, a stranger to us and not acquainted
with Indians, could not render us the same service.[105]

When the Quakers were preparing to open a demonstration farm at Cattaraugus,
the Senecas from that reservation expressed great eagerness for Friends to do so, "as
they hope it might be a means of preventing bad white people from imposing on
them."[106]

Cornplanter's people were most vulnerable to fraud and theft when they went to
Franklin or Pittsburgh to trade. In 1790 the situation in Pittsburgh was so bad that
Cornplanter addressed the Pennsylvania Supreme Executive Council and asked it to
appoint an official interpreter who would reside at Pittsburgh to "take care of me and
my people." He recommended his personal interpreter Joseph Nicholson to serve in
this capacity, which would be that of a state Indian agent. Cornplanter explained his
extraordinary request to the council.

> My reasons for wishing an interpreter to be placed there are that often times, when
> my hunters and people come there, their canoes and other things are stolen, and
> they can obtain no redress, not having any person there upon whom they can rely to
> interpret for them and see justice done to them.[107]

A possible solution to this problem was for Friends to keep a trading post and
store as part of their mission. Halliday Jackson suggested as much, although he was
more concerned about the Senecas being exposed to alcohol when they visited distant markets. Jackson's concern was not entirely different from Cornplanter's, however, because the Allegany Senecas were most vulnerable to theft and fraud when
they were drunk in a distant market. Jackson wrote:

> A trade upon benevolent principles would be advantageously opened by Friends
> with the Natives, giving them more for their peltries than others, and thus super-
> seding the necessity of their going to a distant market. It should be a barter with
> *useful* supplies.[108]

Handsome Lake was quite specific in expressing his desire that the Quakers
keep a store for the Allegany Senecas.

> I myself have been advising our people to pursue the course of life you recommend
> to us, and we have fully concluded to follow habits of industry. But we are only just
> beginning to learn, and we find ourselves at a loss for tools to work with. We now
> request you to bring on plenty of all kinds you think will be useful, then such of our
> people as are able to buy for themselves [may do so]. . . . We also want you to bring
> on useful clothes and sell to us, that we may get some necessary things without hav-
> ing to go so far for them.[109]

With the exception of keeping some farming implements and tools on hand for
sale to the Indians, the Quakers refused to keep a store for the Allegany Senecas.

> We do not want to keep a store of goods among you, we think it will be best not
> [to]. But we intend to send a few scythes, sickles, augurs, and some such tools to

sell to such of you as may want to buy. But if any of your people buy from them and then sell to white people, they are not to sell any more to such as do so.[110]

This left the Allegany Senecas with no choice but to continue trading at Pittsburgh, the best market in the region. The Senecas took this disappointment in stride and tried to make the most of their relationship with the Quakers in other areas.

One of the first things the Indians wanted the Quakers to do was help them build better houses. Jackson reported that during the summer of 1798:

Divers [several] of the Indians early manifested a disposition to have better houses to live in; and being furnished with the necessary tools, they were also afforded the requisite assistance and instruction. Several of them constructed in the course of this summer much better houses than they had been accustomed to, and manifested a considerable share of ingenuity in the use of the carpenter's tools.[111]

The following year Jackson reported that " many of the Indians had by this time built good log houses, and generally covered them [the roofs] with shingles."[112] By 1803, seventeen new houses had been built just at the upper settlement alone. "These had shingled roofs, were . . . neatly built with square logs, most of them two stories high with stone chimneys and glass windows."[113] A whole new village was constructed at Cold Spring in 1804, and in 1806 Jackson reported:

Near 100 new houses have been built since the committee visited them three years ago, most of them well put up with hewn logs, very neatly notched in at the corners, many of them covered with shingles and have panel doors and glass windows. Their improvements in divers respects since I left them have rather exceeded my expectation and [are] quite equal to any improvement I have observed in any of the new settlements made by whites in the same length of time.[114]

When the Senecas could not get what they felt they needed from the Quakers, they charted an independent course, even if it conflicted with Friends' advice, as in their continued pursuit of hunting as a livelihood and their transition to lumbering. Friends encouraged the Indians to desist from these activities because, in the Quaker view, they retarded the Indians' advancement in civilization by taking them away from farming and sending them to distant markets, where they were exposed to the temptation of alcohol. Economic necessity persuaded the Senecas to ignore Quaker admonitions, and many Allegany Senecas still found it more profitable to hunt than to farm.

A trade embargo enacted prior to the War of 1812, however, made it difficult to export goods to Europe. Fur prices crashed, and hunting temporarily ceased to be worthwhile as a cash-producing pursuit.[115] The Allegany Senecas continued to hunt for food, however. In 1816 when an unusually early frost killed most of the corn crop, they retired to the woods and subsisted throughout the winter on hunting alone.[116] They also took furs and hides to Pittsburgh that year, which indicates that the fur trade had revived after the war.[117]

The Allegany Senecas were rafting timber to Pittsburgh as early as 1809.[118] But it was not until after the War of 1812 that the lumber business on the upper Allegheny started to boom. The Senecas participated in this boom too. Several of them spent the summer of 1814 "in squaring timber for the Pittsburgh market and took it down in the fall." That winter there was more industry than usual "in making shingles and squaring timber."[119] The Senecas probably used their sawmill to prepare some of their lumber for the Pittsburgh market. In 1817, the heavy involvement of the Allegany Seneca men in the lumber business brought the following rebuke from a visiting Quaker delegation:

> You are very capable to calculate what is for your advantage and what is not. We therefore desire you would take into consideration whether you would not have been in a better situation generally if you had employed the same time which you have spent in cutting and rafting timber in cultivating your good land.[120]

Obviously the Allegany Senecas felt they were in a better situation, having spent the summer lumbering instead of farming to raise a cash crop for which there was no market. Timber was their cash crop. One of the missionaries explained the Seneca perspective on this matter:

> They see many sawmills down the river below their reservation that will purchase their logs and pay cash for them, or saw them into boards and give the Indian half for himself to run to market. Often [he] gets a return for his labor in a few weeks. Many of their young men have served a sort of apprenticeship to the business. Understanding it, they follow it of choice for interest rather than the labor of the field . . . The men [are] not so much accustomed to clear land. . . . It takes time and attention to chop, burn, fence, and prepare it for crops. The crops [are] often light, oxen not owned by all. Many tools wanted [are] not within the reach of some with the means they have to procure. . . . [When] hunting and cutting logs present themselves, they choose these rather than the improvements of a new farm.[121]

"Today I took my final farewell of many of the Indians at Cornplanter's village, some of whom appeared very sorry about my departing from them," Henry Simmons wrote on Sunday, October 6, 1799.

> I set forward in a canoe up the river about nine miles to Genesinguhta, our settlement, where my companions resided. Some of the principal men came there to see me start in the morning.

The next day he left for home.

> After taking solemn leave of my two companions, Halliday Jackson and Joel Swayne, and of the Indians who had come to see me off, I set out with Cornplanter and several others. . . .

Cornplanter had business in Canandaigua, New York, with Israel Chapin, the federal superintendent of Indian affairs for the Six Nations. He accompanied Simmons that far, thereby escorting the missionary through the wildest country he would encounter on his trip home. While at Canandaigua, Cornplanter dictated to Chapin a letter for the Indian Committee of the Philadelphia Yearly Meeting.

> I thank the Great Spirit for his protection in preserving me and my Friend whom I have accompanied to this place. I hope the Great Spirit will still preserve my Friend on his journey to Philadelphia, and every evening when night shall overtake him, that the Great Spirit will spread over him the curtain of safety, that he may again meet the Society that sent him among us for the purpose of teaching us the useful arts of the white people. And that he may return to them my kind thanks for the kind offices they are disposed to bestow on us. I cannot omit this favorable opportunity to inform Friends that I believe the young men placed at the Allegheny have discharged the trust committed to them in endeavoring to do the best they could for our advantage.[1]

Simmons completed his journey home to Bensalem in early November 1799.[2] In December he attended a meeting of the Indian Committee in Philadelphia and resigned from missionary work.[3] Sometime during 1800, he started courting Rachel Preston. They announced their betrothal in appearances before Rachel's monthly meeting, which met alternately at New Garden and West Grove, Chester County, Pennsylvania[4] and they were married on October 8, 1800 at the West Grove meeting-house.[5] Henry officially transferred his membership from Middletown to New Garden-West Grove in March 1801.[6] Rachel gave birth to their first child in July 1801; they had three more children.[7]

Not much further is recorded in the Quaker records about Henry. He served on a temperance committee[8] and assisted in maintaining the New Garden monthly meeting records.[9] In 1805, Rachel was recognized as a minister by the New Garden monthly meeting.[10] In early September 1807 she applied to New Garden for permission to attend the yearly meeting, which was to be held in Baltimore that year.[11] Her application was approved and the customary "minute" was issued to her, but in early November she returned her minute, explaining that she would not be able to go to the yearly meeting on account of her husband's illness.[12] Henry Simmons died on November 24, 1807, at age 39. His last child—a daughter—was born six months later. Rachel named her Henryetta.[13]

Cornplanter was slowly but steadily eclipsed in the political sphere during the first two decades of the 1800s, initially by his older half brother Handsome Lake, and subsequently by a new generation of Seneca leadership. In 1802 he was part of a Seneca delegation that visited President Jefferson in the new capital city of Washington—but the delegation was headed by Handsome Lake. Cornplanter was deposed as a chief in 1804 during the dispute over his sawmill and his plans to lease fields on the grant to European-American farmers. Most of the Allegany Senecas settled in Cold Spring, where Handsome Lake exercised undisputed spiritual authority and increasing political leadership. Cornplanter was reinstated as a chief in 1807, but only as one among several. In 1809 he spoke out publicly against Handsome Lake's witch-hunting. This helped precipitate the collapse of Handsome Lake's political power at Cold Spring, but not of his moral authority within the Seneca nation. The prophet, feeling unwelcome in his own land, went to Tonawanda for a while and Cornplanter resumed his former role as chief headman of the Allegany Senecas.[14]

During the War of 1812 Cornplanter supported the American cause, but only on the basis that the Senecas would be well compensated for their military efforts. Handsome Lake opposed any participation by Indians in European-American wars, however, and his influence curtailed American mobilization of Seneca warriors, especially from the Allegany and Tonawanda Reservations. But other Senecas and New York Iroquois did join the fight in significant numbers, given their limited populations. In 1814 they and their Canadian relatives who fought on the British side slaughtered each other at the Battle of Chippawa on the Niagara frontier between Canada and the United States.[15]

After the war Cornplanter gradually withdrew from active political life, although he continued occasionally to step forward on certain issues, as he did in 1818 when he intervened to prevent the surveying of lots on the reservation. In 1823 he accompanied Red Jacket to Washington to protest a proposal for removing the Senecas from New York and resettling them in Wisconsin.[16]

In 1814 a visiting Quaker delegation paid Cornplanter a visit that seemed friendly enough. The very next year, however, the Western Missionary Society opened a school on the grant at Cornplanter's request, a development indicative of growing disaffection between him and the Quakers. The rift was caused in part by Cornplanter's keeping a store of whiskey on the grant for sale to European Americans traveling on the Allegheny River. The Quakers disapproved, and Cornplanter resented their public rebukes. Although the proposal to hold the reservation in severalty had interested him initially, he eventually came to fear that dividing the reservation might be but a prelude to losing it.[17]

His resentment and suspicion led him into a nativistic period of his own in which he rejected all things European-American from animal husbandry to education. He revolted against the notion of Indians serving as pawns in white men's wars and burned all his war trophies: flags, medals, belts, his sword, and his captain's commission that had been issued to him during the War of 1812. Starting in December 1820, he experienced a series of visions that essentially recapitulated the teachings of Handsome Lake. During this period, the Warren County commissioners levied a tax on the grant. When tax collectors appeared on the grant, Cornplanter and his kin brandished rifles and sent them packing. Eventually he gave his note to cover the tax, but he never had to pay the note because the state legislature subsequently exempted his grant from taxation. Cornplanter lived on the grant unmolested by European-American authorities for the rest of his life. He died there on February 18, 1836, at age 83.[18]

Handsome Lake continued in his role of religious prophet and social reformer until his death in 1815, but his career was not without controversy. In the wake of his Delaware witchcraft accusations, Handsome Lake clashed with Red Jacket over the Black Rock issue. During a Seneca national council at Buffalo Creek in June 1801, he accused Red Jacket of witchcraft. Red Jacket was tried and acquitted, but the council approved of Handsome Lake's opposition to witchcraft, banned the use of liquor, and appointed Handsome Lake as moral censor of the Seneca nation.[19] In this exalted status, he led the Seneca delegation to Washington in 1802. President Jefferson endorsed his program of moral and social reform, which only added to Handsome Lake's stature among the Senecas. The following year Handsome Lake, then at the zenith of his political power, succeeded for a time in having the council fire of the Six Nations moved from Buffalo Creek to Cornplanter's village.[20]

When the Allegany Senecas left Cornplanter's grant in 1804, Handsome Lake went with them to Cold Spring. There he persecuted more people as witches. Critics charged that he made such accusations to eliminate political opponents and those who doubted the authenticity of his visions. In his zeal to eradicate witchcraft, Handsome Lake even attacked a fundamental Seneca religious and cultural institution— the medicine societies. To him, their rituals smacked of witchcraft, and he declared that the societies should disband and desist from their practices. When sickness broke out in 1807, people blamed Handsome Lake's suppression of the medicine societies, and they defiantly continued the rituals.[21]

Unrest over this issue combined with Cornplanter's public criticism of witch-hunting in 1809 undercut Handsome Lake's political control at Cold Spring. The prophet went into a self-imposed, short-lived exile at Tonawanda. Upon his return, he found that the council had decided that no more lives should be taken on account of witchcraft accusations. Handsome Lake was still a member of the chief's council, but Cornplanter was once again the chief headman of the Allegany Senecas.[22]

After 1809 Handsome Lake stayed out of politics, except for his opposition to Indian participation in the War of 1812, for which he became known as the "peace prophet."[23] He dedicated the remainder of his life to promoting moral and social reform. Every year he traveled a circuit through the reservations in western New York, preaching his message of temperance, social unity within the Indian community, peace between different peoples, preservation of the Indian land base, and material progress that did not overrun Indian cultural values.[24] While on one of these tours, Handsome Lake died at Onondaga on August 15, 1815, at age eighty.

Henry Simmons's 1799 Journal

Original Version	Edited Version
The beginning of the Second Book Conishcotago 1799	The beginning of the second book[A] Cornplanter's village, 1799
Second Month 3rd This morning being the first day of the week	*February 3, Sunday*
When in Cornplanter's house, His son Henry, and about a dozen of his people being present, several of them petty Chiefs; Who wanted me to tell them how the World, and things therein were Created at first.	I was in Cornplanter's house with the chief and his son, Henry. About a dozen other Indians, some of them petty chiefs, were also present. They wanted me to tell them how the world and things therein were created in the beginning.
I immediately apply'd my Heart with fervent breathings to the Lord for His aid and support, in this Question; and found him a present help. I told them it was a hard Question, I understood it better than I was able to explain it to them. but I would endeavour to satisfy them. And told them, there is a Certain good Book, called the Holy Scriptures, which very few, who can Read, will dare to deny its being true, which gives us an account, of the World being made (and of all living Creatures both in Water and on Land) by the great Spirit, and also the first man & Woman whom the great Spirit created of the dust of the Earth, and breathed into them the breath of Life, and they became living Souls, who had two Sons, one of them was a good man, and the other Wicked who kiled his Brother, because he was more righteous than himself. and askt them if they did not see it so now a days; that wicked people envy'd good ones, and at times were ready to take their Lives.	I immediately applied my heart with fervent breathings to the Lord for his aid and support in this question. I found him to be a present help. Then, I told them it was a hard question, that I understood it better than I was able to explain it to them, but that I would endeavor to satisfy them. I told them there is a certain good book, called the Holy Scriptures. Very few people who can read will deny the truth of this book. It gives us an account of the world being made (and of all living creatures both in water and on land) by the Great Spirit, who also made the first man and woman from the dust of the earth, and breathed life into them. Thus, they became living souls. They had two sons; one was a good man; the other was wicked. The wicked son killed his brother, because he knew his brother was more righteous than himself. I asked them if they did not see it so nowadays—that wicked people envied good ones, and at times were ready to take their lives.
I told them that the great Spirit, made all these things, in Six days, and on the Seventh day He rested, from all His Labour the day we now rest	I told them the Great Spirit made all things in six days, and on the seventh day he rested from his labor. Accordingly, we now keep First Day, on

---

[A] The first book was a letter book Simmons kept from 1798 to 1799. He was in the habit of copying letters that he sent and received into a sewn manuscript booklet. After starting his 1799 journal, he continued copying letters into the first book. Thus, the journal became his "second book."

Original Version

from our Labour to serve and Worship him, where in he blessed us, and made us happy, insomuch that we hold two days in the week for to Worship him, and in so doing, he Comforts our Hearts, and preserve us in Love and Unity with one another. I desir'd it might be the Case with them.

I supposed some of them doubted our knowing these Holy wrightings to be true, and told them, that the way I had to know it was, by reading of them, and as the great Spirit pleased to make them manifest in the secret of my heart, teling me they are true, and making me sensible of it, even to that degree at times, of causeing tears to flow from mine Eyes, when I have read them; and told them it was the only way I had to know when I was doing right or wrong, by strictly attending to the great Spirit in my heart, and asked them, if this was not the case, when they thought of doing something which they ought not to do, whether they did not feel something pricking at there Hearts, and telling them not to do so.

Several of the Chiefs, Cornplanter for one; confest it was the very truth, they had experienced it so. I told them it was the great Spirit that thus pricked, and tells us not to do so, and it is the Devil that urges us to do it.

I then told them, here would be an advantage to their Children, in learning to read, as the great Spirit plased to enlighten their understandings and make them Sensible of this good Book; as well as many other benefits which will be likely to attend their Children, thus being Educated.

After some time they informed me, that there was not one of them who had any objections to what I had said, but were satisfied, and thought if I would mention it to the rest, it might be of some use to them; as there were some of them, who were averse to their Children being Educated.

After this Meeting my School was much Larger than before, between 20 & 30, several of them Men grow, and some of them anxious to learn, though many of them very tedious, which kept me so faithful in Teaching them, that at times I have been almost weary in well doing.

Cornplanter inform'd me that when a young Man, he was a great Hunter, and often thought of the great Spirit, who made the Wild beasts, and all things, and to be sure he had always very good luck, he said. I told him that was the only way to

Edited Version

which we rest from our labor, to serve and worship him. Because of this and because we worship him on an additional day during the week, he has blessed us and made us happy. He comforts our hearts, and preserves us in love and unity with one another. I told them I desired that the same might be the case with them.

I supposed some of them doubted the truth of the holy writings. So I told them how I know the Scriptures to be true, which is by reading them and by waiting on the Great Spirit to manifest their truth in the secret of my heart. The Great Spirit makes my heart sensible of their truth, even to the extent that, sometimes when I read the Scriptures, tears flow from my eyes. And I told them that this was also the only way I could tell whether I was doing right or wrong. That is, by strictly attending as the Great Spirit spoke to my heart. I asked them if this was not also the case with them, when they thought of doing something wrong. Did not they too feel something pricking at their hearts, and telling them not to do it?

Several of the chiefs, including Cornplanter, confessed it was the very truth; they had experienced it so. I told them it is the Great Spirit who pricks our hearts and tells us not to do wrong. It is the devil who urges us to do wrong.

I told them this was one of the advantages of their children learning to read. They would be able to read the good book for themselves. Then, as it pleased the Great Spirit to enlighten their understanding, they would sense the truth of the good book. Many other benefits would also derive from their children being educated.

After a while, they informed me that none of them had any objection to what I had said. They were satisfied. They suggested that it might be helpful if I would repeat the same to the rest of the Indians, because some of their people were averse to their children being educated.

Later, after this meeting, my school was much larger than before, between twenty and thirty scholars, several of them grown men. Some of them are anxious to learn, though in many cases instructing them is very tedious. But this keeps me faithful in teaching them, so much so that at times I have been almost weary in well doing.

While we were still at the meeting in his house, Cornplanter informed me that when he was a young man, he was a great hunter. He said his good luck was due to the fact that he often thought of the Great Spirit, who made the wild beasts, and

Original Version	Edited Version

receive a blessing, by thinking of, and returning thanks to the great Spirit, even the Farmers, were then blest with better Crops of Grain.

all things. I told him that was the only way to receive a blessing, by thinking of, and returning thanks to the Great Spirit. Even the farmers who did so were then blest with better crops of grain.

February 11, Monday

2nd Mo. 11th Second day of the Week, Cornplanter & two of his Sons came up early in the Morning, to the house where I lodged. Who told me he had something particular to communicate which was thus, they had lately received an Express from the Buffalo Indians; that one of their little Girls had Dreamed, that the Devil was in all white people alike, and that the Quakers were doing no good among them, but otherwise, and it was not right for their Children to learn to read & write. Wherefore they had held a Council yesterday on the Subject; And many of his people were so foolish as to believe it was true, for many of them put great confidence in their Dreams. but he did not believe it, and had got very tir'd of hearing so much noise about their Dreams. He wished me not to be discouraged, for he intended to make his people do better.

Cornplanter and two of his sons came up early in the morning, to the house where I lodged. Cornplanter said they had come to talk about something in particular, which was as follows. They had lately received an express from the Buffalo Indians regarding a dream that one of their little girls had had. She had dreamed that the devil was in all white people alike, and that the Quakers were doing no good among them, but otherwise. She had also related that it was not right for the Indian children to learn to read and write. Cornplanter and his people had held a council yesterday on the subject. And many of his people were so foolish as to believe the dream was true, for many of them put great confidence in their dreams. But he did not believe it, and had got very tired of hearing so much noise about their dreams. He wished me not to be discouraged, for he intended to make his people do better.

I told him I did not feel uneasy at all about it; for I thought I knew from whence it had originated, I knew that Farmers Brother and others of the Buffolo Indians were much Injured & set against the Quakers, through the instigation of some bad white people about them he said that was very true.

I told him I did not feel at all uneasy about the dream because I thought I knew from whence it had originated. I knew that Farmer's Brother and others of the Buffalo Indians were much injured and set against the Quakers by the instigation of some bad white people at Buffalo. Cornplanter said that was very true.

I told him it was certainly a very good work from the great Spirit; therefore I knew the Devil would use his utmost endeavors to lay it waist, for I had experienced from a very little Boy, that he is always seeking and ready to distroy all that is good. but as it is a Work from the great Spirit, I believed, He would support and carry it on to his own Glory.

I told him our work was certainly a very good work from the Great Spirit. Therefore I knew the devil would use his utmost endeavors to lay it waste. It had been my experience, from the time I was a very little boy, that he is always seeking and ready to destroy all that is good. But, as our work is a work from the Great Spirit, I believed he would support and carry it on to his own glory.

He said, that some of the White people were as much to blame, as the Indians; which was the reason the Devil came so often; for when they wanted to get their Land, they would go to some of the worst among them, and make a bargain first, and afterwards apply to the Chiefs. I believed that to be true. I told him I would continue teaching them that would come. And as for the rest, we would let them Quietly alone. perhaps the Great Spirit would open their Eyes, and enlighten their understanding, so they might behold the nonsensicalness of such Dreams and Stories, Who could if he pleased, change their thoughts, in an hour's time.

Cornplanter said that some of the white people were as much to blame as the Indians for the devil's frequent interference. When these white people wanted to get Indian land, they would go to some of the most dissolute and disreputable Indian individuals, and make a bargain with them first, and afterwards apply to the chiefs to honor the deal. I believed that to be true. I told him I would continue teaching those who would come. And, as for the rest, we would let them quietly alone. Perhaps the Great Spirit would open their eyes and enlighten their understanding, so they might behold the nonsense of such dreams and stories. After all, the Great Spirit could, if he pleased, change their thoughts in an hour's time.

Original Version	Edited Version
The School was a little smaller for one day. But afterward was Larger than it had been at all.	The school was a little smaller for one day. But afterward was larger than it had ever been.

February 27, Wednesday

2nd Mo. 27th This Day proved a very trying and painful one, to my Soul, by reason of a prospect of an Approaching Dance & Frolick among the Indians, Some of which I had beheld before with great grief. tho' not too so great a degree as at this time. they had been in the practice for many Weeks back every two or three Days or nights; And at this time were preparing in Cornplanter's House (where I was employ'd teaching the Children) two Large Kettles of provisions for the purpose, which would hold near or quite a Barrel apiece; and while I was thus engaged, a person informed the Scollars thereoff which put them in such an agitation I was scarcely able to teach them at any rate, Some of them left the School and went home to prepare for the Dance; this being the Second time of my being so served.	This day proved a very trying and painful one to my soul, by reason of the prospect of an approaching dance and frolic among the Indians. I had beheld some of these before with great grief, though not to so great a degree as at this time. They had been having such frolics every two or three days or nights for many weeks back. I conduct the school in one half of Cornplanter's house, which is actually two houses, close-by each other, with the space in between them roofed over. In the other half of Cornplanter's house, two large kettles, each capable of holding near or quite a barrel apiece, were being prepared with provisions for the upcoming frolic. While I was helping one of the scholars, someone informed the others about the planned frolic. This put them in such a state of agitation that I was scarcely able to teach them at any rate. Some of them left the school and went home to prepare for the dance. This was the second time of my being so served.
After I let out School, I went into the Woods and fell several large Trees, for the Women for fire Wood, which had been my frequent practice During the Winter, when I returned to the house, by this time they had got into the Career of their folly a Large Concourse of Men & Boys Dancing and Shouting in an astonishing manner, with some Musical Instruments some of which were Large Water Tortals Dried with the Entrails taken out, and Corn put in the place thereoff the neck stretched which serves for a handle. Divers Women were Collected, who appear'd only as Spectators, Cornplanter having two Long buildings like under one roof which were Occupi'd as Dwellings.	After I let out school, I went into the woods and felled several large trees for the women to use as firewood, which had been my frequent practice during the winter. By the time I returned to Cornplanter's house, they had got into the career of their folly, with a large concourse of men and boys dancing and shouting in an astonishing manner. Their musical instruments were large water turtles that had been dried after the entrails had been taken out and replaced with corn kernels. The neck was stretched to serve for a handle. Several women had collected, but appeared only as spectators. Cornplanter had two long, parallel buildings with the space between them roofed over.
I entered into the most vacant one, where I found him, his Son Henry & most of his Family were sitting. I acquainted him, of the painful exercises which I had Laboured under at various times, on account of their many Danceing Frolicks, and it had appeared much more exerciseing to me that Day than it had hitherto I endeavour'd to assert to him the Evil thereoff and that it was Certainly the Devils works; and they who did so, were serving of him, and told him, I thought, every Man had a right to be Master of his own House, and before I would suffer such doings in mine, I would burn it to Ashes & live in a Cave, and did hope I might never see any more of it amongst them; further told him, what made it more painful to me was, they Collected the inocent Children and were bringing them up in their footsteps, in doing that which was so very wicked, when it ought to be	I entered the half of Cornplanter's house where he, his son Henry, and most of his family were sitting. I acquainted Cornplanter with the painful exercises under which I had labored at various times, on account of their many dancing frolics. I told him that it had appeared much more exercising to me that day than it had hitherto. I endeavored to assert to him the evil of these dancing frolics, which were certainly the devil's works. Those who participated were serving the devil. I told him I thought every man had a right to be master of his own house, and before I would suffer such doings in mine, I would burn it to ashes and live in a cave. I hoped that I might never see any more of it among them. I further told him that what made it more painful to me was the fact that they collected the innocent children and were bringing them up in their footsteps, in doing that which was so very wicked, when it

Original Version	**Edited Version**
otherwise & more I said to him, nearly to the same purport; in a very broken manner to the amazement (I believe) of many of the Spectators. He told me he could not say much about it, at the present; but would converse on the Subject the next Day; I then retir'd to my house of lodging.	ought to be otherwise. And more I said to him, nearly to the same purport, in a very broken manner, to the amazement, I believe, of many of the spectators. He told me he could not say much about it at the present, but would converse on the subject the next day. I then retired to my house of lodging.

February 28, Thursday

And on the Morrow, I went as Usual, in order to teach School where I found a Large number of them Collected in Council, in the very house, I entered into the other apartment, and as I sat the Subject Poor Mordicai was livingly brought to my remembrance, when as he sat at the Kings gate waiting to see how the matter would go; after a while I was Called in, and went with great willingness, tho' in much fear,	And on the morrow, I went as usual in order to teach school and found a large number of adults collected in council in that half of Cornplanter's house that I used for the school. I entered into the other apartment and waited for them to call me to the council. As I sat there, the subject of poor Mordecai, sitting at the king's gate waiting to see how the matter would go, was vividly brought to my remembrance. After a while I was called in, and went with great willingness, though in much fear.
Cornplanter informed me they had been counciling on the Subject, which I had mentioned the evening before, and had concluded, (although they did not all see alike) to quit such Dancing Frolicks for some of them thought it must be wicked, because they had Learned it of white people, as well as that of drinking Rum or Wisky & geting Drunk, which they knew was Evil, but they had a Hussleing kind of play and Dance too twice a year of their own production Originally, which they thought to continue in the practice off.	Cornplanter informed me they had been discussing the subject that I had spoken about the evening before, and had concluded, although they did not all see alike, to quit such dancing frolics. Some of them thought it must be a wicked habit because they had learned it of white people, as well as that of drinking rum or whiskey and getting drunk, which they knew was evil. However, they had a hustling kind of play and dance too twice a year of their own production originally, which they thought to continue in the practice of.
They asked me several Questions. 1st Whether I thought it was right for Indians & White people, to mix in marrying, I told them it was a bad Question. It might be right for some to marry so, but thought it would not be right for me. 2nd Whether Indians & White people, went together to the same place after Death. I told them there was but two places, a place for the Good, and a place for the Bad, of all Nations of People & 3rd Whether all would be of one Language, When there, I answered yes. They seemed satisfied.	They asked me several questions. First, whether I thought it was right for Indians and white people to mix in marrying. I told them it was a bad question. It might be right for some to marry so, but thought it would not be right for me. Second, whether Indians and white people went together to the same place after death. I told them there were but two places, a place for the good and a place for the bad of all nations of people. Third, whether all would be of one language when in that place after death. I answered yes. They seemed satisfied.
They informed me of one of their Women who had a Child by a White Man who then resided at Pittsburgh, and never came to see anything about his Child. They thought the Great Spirit intended that every Man should take care & maintain his own Children.	They informed me of one of their women who had a child by a white man who then resided at Pittsburgh, and never came to see anything about his child. They thought the Great Spirit intended that every man should care for and maintain his own children.
I arose (the Interpreter also) and made a long Speech to them, Opening more clearly the Evil of many Customs prevailing among them particularly that of Dancing, & Shouting, in such a hideous manner which they are accustomed too. As there were many then present who did not hear me the Evining before; while thus engaged I experienced	I, along with the interpreter, arose and made a long speech to them, opening more clearly the evil of many customs prevailing among them, particularly that of dancing and shouting in such a hideous manner, which they are accustomed to. I did this because there were many then present who did not hear me the evening before. While thus engaged, I

Original Version	Edited Version

the God of Israel, to be my present help, who brought me into such a broken State, that I believe Some then present were fully Convinc'd, and many of their Dark Hearts, more enlightened. The council continued until Dark, I then returned to my house of Lodging.

experienced the God of Israel to be my present help. He brought me into such a broken state that I believe some of them present were fully convinced and many of their dark hearts, more enlightened. The council continued until dark. I then returned to my house of lodging.

March 1, Friday

On the preceding morning, the Old Chief, two of his Sons & Divers others, Came to my lodging abode, who informed me he came on purpose to tell me something particular which he did not the day before; as some of his People did not see & think as he did, as for his own part he had a great regard for the Quakers, and could find no fault with me, or my companions, but felt happy we were among them, and had before several times, express'd a gladness of my being with him, and he hoped we might live a long while together. He also said, that when he first saw us comeing to his house he was glad and thanked the Great Spirit at that time, whom he thought must have brought us thither.

The next morning the old chief, two of his sons, and several others, came to my lodging abode. Cornplanter informed me he had come for the express purpose of telling me something particular that he had not wanted to bring up the day before because some of his people did not see and think as he did. As for his own part, he had a great regard for the Quakers and could find no fault with me or my companions, but felt happy we were among them. He had several times before expressed his gladness at my being with him, and he hoped we might live a long while together. He also said that when he first saw us coming to his house, he was glad and thanked the Great Spirit at that time, whom he thought must have brought us thither.

He further said there was a number of Boys, & some Girls, some of whom were then present, whom they intended should attend the School steadily, and would give up the Boys into my care to do by them, as I would by my own Son, he wish me to learn them to work, and correct them as they deserved, even his own Children. And also if I wanted any of the young Men, to go to Genesinguhtau or do any business, which I thought would be of advantage to them, I should Command them, and he mentioned one or too who were then present, for that purpose. Thus he seemed in a manner willing to resign his own Commission to me. I acknowledged his love and tender regard towards me, And felt truly thankful to the Lord, for these Favours.

He further said there was a number of boys and some girls, some of whom were then present, whom Cornplanter and his supporters intended should attend the school steadily. They would give up the boys into my care, for me to do by them as I would by my own son. He wished me to help them learn to work and to correct them as they deserved, including his own children. And, also, if I wanted any of the young men to go to Genesinguhta or do any business thatI thought would be of advantage to them, I should command them. He mentioned one or two, who were then present, upon whom I could call when I needed them. Thus, he seemed, in a manner, willing to resign his own commission to me. I acknowledged his love and tender regard toward me. I felt truly thankful to the Lord for these favors.

In this Council, a Young Man informed the Company of a Dream which he Drempt a few nights before, when out in the Woods Hunting, in Company with a Lad. He thought an Indian Struck him twice with a Knife, when he fell, and thought he must Die, but soon appear'd to asscend upwards, some distance along a narrow path, in which appeared many tracks of People all going up some barefoot and some not; at length he came to a house, and the Door opened, for him to go in, which he did, where he beheld the beautifulest Man sitting that ever he saw in his Life; Who invited him to sit down, which he endeavoured to do, but could not, and tried to stop, & to talk, but could do neither. So passed on, out at a Door opposite to the one he came in at,

In this council, a young man informed the company of a dream that he had a few nights before, when out in the woods hunting, in company with a lad. He thought an Indian struck him twice with a knife; he fell and thought he must die. But soon he appeared to ascend upwards, some distance along a narrow path, in which appeared many tracks of people, all going up, some barefoot and some not. At length he came to a house and the door opened for him to go in, which he did. The most beautiful man whom ever he had seen in his life was seated inside. The man invited him to sit down and he endeavored to do so, but he could not sit down. He tried to stop moving and he tried to talk to the man. But, he could do neither. Unable to stop moving, he passed on and went out through a door,

Original Version	Edited Version
	opposite to the one he had come in at. And so, he found that he had both come and gone before he could even utter a word to the beautiful man.
when out, he heard a great noise and after travilling some distance he came to another building, which had an uncommon Large Door, Like a Barn Door, in which a man met him, who looked very dismal, his Mouth appear'd to move in different shapes, from one side of his Face to the other, this person Conducted him in, where he beheld numbers like Indians who seemed to be Drunken & very noisy, and looked very Distressed, some of whom he knew, who had been Dead several years.	When outside again, he heard a great noise and, after traveling some distance, he came to another building, which had an uncommon large door, like a barn door. Standing in the doorway to meet him, was a man who looked very dismal and whose mouth appeared to move in different shapes, from one side of his face to the other. This person conducted him inside where he beheld numbers of like Indians who seemed to be drunken and very noisy, and who looked very distressed. He knew some of them, but they had been dead several years.
Amongst them was one very old white headed Woman, whom they told him was dying, and when she went, the World would go too. there appeared to be a fire place on the ground, although he could not discern anything but smoke & Ashes, of which their hair on their heads were Covered, He soon found he could sit and talk fast enough in this House, which he could not do in the other.	Among them was one very old white-headed woman whom they told him was dying, and when she went, the world would go too. There appeared to be a fireplace on the ground, although he could not discern anything but smoke and ashes, with which the hair on their heads was covered. He soon found he could sit and talk fast enough in this house, which he could not do in the other.
The person who conducted him in, who appear'd to be their Officinator, gave him some stuff to Drink, Like melted Pewter, which he told him he could not take, but he insisted he should, by telling him he could Drink Wiskey & get Drunk, and that was no worse to take than it, he then took it, which he thought burnt him very much, He then took a chain & bound round him, he asked him what that was for, he told him to prevent him from going after Women & other Men's Wives, He then told him to go strike a Woman, who was sitting there, which he attempted to do, but could not for his arms were off, He told him the reason of his loosing his arms, was because he had often been guilty of striking his Wife, And if he would entirely quit that practice, he should have his arms made whole again, and if he forsook all other Evil practices which he had be guilty of, he should have a Home in the first House which he enter'd.	The person who conducted him in, who appeared to be their official, gave him some stuff to drink, like melted pewter. He told the official that he could not take it down. But the official insisted he should, by telling him he could drink whiskey and get drunk, and that was no worse than to take this drink. He then took it, which he thought burned him very much. The official then took a chain and bound it round him. He asked what that was for, and the official told him it was to prevent him from going after women and other men's wives. The official then told him to go strike a woman who was sitting there, which he attempted to do, but could not because he suddenly discovered that his arms were off. The official told him the reason he had lost his arms, which was because he had often been guilty of striking his wife. And, if he would entirely quit that practice, he should have his arms made whole again. And, if he forsook all other evil practices, which he had been guilty of, he should have a home in the first house he had entered.
He was then bid to go home, when he awoke he found himself Crying, & could not tell his Dream for some time after, for Crying, for he knew it was true, And confest in the Council that he had been guilty of all those actions above mentioned.	He was then bade to go home. When he awoke he found himself crying. He could not tell his dream for some time afterward because he would cry so much and because he knew it was true. He confessed in the council that he had been guilty of all those actions above mentioned.
After I had considered the matter well, I told him, I believed his Dream was true, and hoped he would remember it as long as he lived Etc. He said he intended to try to do better than he had done, and intended to learn to read.	After I had considered the matter well, I told him I believed his dream was true and that I hoped he would remember it as long as he lived, etc. He said he intended to try to do better than he had done, and he intended to learn to read.

Original Version	Edited Version
I told them, (respecting the old grey headed Woman) I thought She was the Mother of wickedness and as they had been so long in a Dark & Evil State, I thought She must be white Headed. and did hope She was Dying from among them, and when She was Dead, the Worldly Spirit would go too.	Regarding the old gray-headed woman, I told them that I thought she was the mother of wickedness, and as they had been so long in a dark and evil state, I thought she must be white-headed. And I hoped that she was dying from among them because when she was dead, the worldly spirit would go too.
Cornplanter, Said the Devil would Die, if they tryed to do good.	Cornplanter said the devil would die if they tried to do good.
	March 26, Tuesday
3rd Month 26th Corn Planter sent 9 of his Men to Buffolo to receive money, their Anuity who returned, in 14 Days, with one Thousand five Hundred and Sixty Dollars, (and some Goods which they receive early of the British as a favour for their adherence in the time of War, between the Brittish & Americans).	Cornplanter sent nine of his men to Buffalo to receive their annuity money. They returned in fourteen days with $1,560. They also brought back some goods, which they receive yearly from the British as a favor for the Seneca adherence to the British side during the war between the British and Americans.
In a few days after their return the money & Goods were divided, and a Council held, at which they requested me to attend, in order to read some writing to them, which I did, and was pressed in Spirit, to Caution them against Spending their money for Strong drink and other unnecessary Articles; but to purchase Cloatheing to keep them Warm in the Winter and other useful things Etc.	A few days after the men returned, the money and goods were divided and a council was held. I was asked to attend because they had something that they wanted me to read for them. After reading what they wanted me to, I was pressed in Spirit to caution them against spending their money for strong drink and other unnecessary articles. I encouraged them to purchase clothing with which to keep them warm in the winter and other useful things, etc.
	Mid-May 1799: the Quakers decide to intervene
5th Month. About the middle of the same, the Indians returned from Pittsburgh, with a quantity of Wisky, which caused much Drunkenness amongst them which lasted for several weeks and was the means of some of their deaths. One old Woman perished out of doors in the night season with a bottle at her side; numbers of them going about the village from morning till evening and from evening untill morning, in a noisy distracted condition sometimes fighting each other, and entering into the houses in a detestable manner, ready to pull others out of their Beds, even in the very house where I lodged myself, in the dead of the night also.	About the middle of May, a party of Cornplanter's Indians returned from Pittsburgh with a quantity of whiskey that caused much drunkenness among them, which lasted for several weeks and was the means of some of their deaths. One old woman perished outdoors in the night season with a bottle at her side. Numbers of them would go about the village, from morning until evening and from evening until morning, in a noisy distracted condition, sometimes fighting each other. They would enter other people's houses in a detestable manner, ready to pull others out of their beds. They even did so in the very house where I myself lodged— and in the dead of the night too!
There deplorable condition by reason of that distructive Article of Strong drink, greatly augmented our concern and exercise for the promotion of their present and future happiness, insomuch, that we were desirous of having them Collected in Council, and a day being agreed upon, for that purpose I informed my Companions thereof, where we all attended, and was (I think I may say) divinely favoured to communicate some pertinent & juditious Counsel to them on various Subjects, to the furtherance of Civilization and their future well being;	Their deplorable condition by reason of that destructive article of strong drink greatly augmented our concern and exercise for the promotion of their present and future happiness. So much so, that we were desirous of having them collected in council. And a day being agreed upon for that purpose, I informed my companions thereof. All three of us attended. I was—I think I may say—divinely favored to communicate some pertinent and judicious counsel to them on various subjects, to the furtherance of civilization and their future well-being.

Original Version	Edited Version
	Several days later the Indians respond
And after several days deliberation thereon, a large number of them assembled in Council, and made reply on each subject which we had spoke to them upon; Myself only being present, I was not capable of retaining their Speech in memory, (made by Cornplanter) so as to commit the one half to paper but only the Contents; which is thus.	The Indians spent several days deliberating the issues we had raised. Then, a large number of them assembled in council and made reply on each subject that we had spoken to them upon. By this time, my companions had returned to Genesinguhta and I was the only one still present. Thus, I was not capable of retaining in memory the speech made by Cornplanter. In fact, I cannot write down even one-half of it on paper. But I do remember the main contents, which were as follows.
They had made enquiry and conversed with each other about us, and said they could not find any fault with us, but found we were just and upright in all our ways & proceedings amongst them Etc. and that the fault and bad conduct lay on their own side, and wished us to be easy in our minds, for they would take our advice and try to do better, they had concluded with a resolution not to suffer any more Wisky to be brought amongst them to sell, and had then Chosen two young men as petty Chiefs, to have some oversight of their people in the promotion of good among them, and that they intended to take up Work, and do as we said, would assist their Wives and Women on the Labour of the Field Etc.	They had made inquiry and conversed with each other about us, and said they could not find any fault with us, but found we were just and upright in all our ways and proceedings among them, etc. And that the fault and bad conduct lay on their own side. They wished us to be easy in our minds, for they would take our advice and try to learn to do better. They had concluded with a resolution not to suffer any more whiskey to be brought among them to be sold. Then, they had chosen two young men as petty chiefs, to have some oversight of their people in the promotion of good among them. They intended to take up work, and do as we said, and would assist their wives and women on the labor of the field, etc.
After a pause, I arose on my feet, and told them I had paid great attention to their words, and thought I should remember them a great while, for which I felt my heart truely thankful to the Great Spirit, and was renewedly encouraged to persevere in every branch of good instruction to them I was capable of, with an earnest hope of seeing their own words verifi'd, which would more and more encourage us among them, and also our Friends at home, to whom we wrote frequently letting them know what progress is makeing among our Indian Brethren Etc. Cornplanter said we will now cover the Council Fire. Thus it ended.	After a pause, I arose on my feet and told them I had paid great attention to their words, and thought I should remember them a great while. I felt my heart truly thankful to the Great Spirit for their new resolve. And I felt newly encouraged to persevere in every branch of good instruction to them that I was capable of. Also, I had an earnest hope of seeing their own words verified, which would more and more encourage us who were working among them. I told them that if they lived up to their words, it would also encourage our Friends at home, to whom we wrote frequently letting them know what progress is being made among our Indian brethren, etc. Cornplanter then covered the council fire. Thus it ended.
	Some days after the Indian response
Some days henceforward they held a Worship dance, Men, Women, and Children, having on their best apparel were engaged round their Wooden Image, or God, in a true circle, no set number, but those who have a mind to step into the ring, does so, their faces being towards the Image, two men were seated flat on the ground face to face within the circle, engaged with musical instruments such as Gourd Shell and Water tortal dried with the entrails out, and Bullets, Shot, or Corn in the place thereof, which they beat on a Dear Skin lying on the Ground, which makes a very great rattle, the	Some days after the council, the Indians held a worship dance. Men, women, and children wearing their best apparel were dancing in a circle around their wooden image, or God. There seemed to be no designated dancers. Those, who had a mind to step into the ring, did so, facing toward the image. Two men were seated flat on the ground, face to face within the circle, engaged with musical instruments. Their instruments were gourd shell and water turtle, dried with the entrails out, and bullets, shot, or corn in the place thereof. They beat these on a deerskin lying on the ground, making a very great rattle. The

Original Version	Edited Version

men in the circle dance and shouts greatly still moveing a Slow pace round the Womens motion is chiefly, by moveing their feet, set close together sideways, first the toes then the heels moving round with the men also, but are Silent, After they had taken two heats at dance, their minister (who was a very lusty Indian) said it was enough, and thanked them, and shortly after addressed them with a long speech by way of advice, after which they concluded the business with eating which had been prepared the fore part of the same day.

men in the circle, always moving round at a slow pace, dance and shout greatly. The women dance chiefly by keeping their feet set close together and moving them sideways, first the toes and then the heels, as they move round with the men. The women, however, remain silent. After they had taken two heats at dance, their minister, who was a very lusty Indian, said it was enough, and thanked them. Shortly after that, he addressed them with a long speech by way of advice, after which they concluded the business by eating some food, which had been prepared the fore part of the same day.

About a week after the dance

About a week after they made a great feast, after their antient custom, by way of remembrance of their Dead, for such are their strange Ideas that they apprehend their deceised ones will receive with them some benefit thereby: the present one being made on the account of the old Chiefs Daughter who had been dead upwards of 4 months. They prepared much food of different kinds and took it to a cabin near their Burying ground where they eat, old and young a very great number, their Custom is that each one must tast the others Dish.

About a week after the worship dance, they had a great feast as a form of remembrance of their dead, which was according to their ancient custom. They have such strange ideas. They believe that they and their deceased ones will receive some benefit on account of their holding the feast. The present one was being held on account of the old chief's daughter, who had been dead upwards of four months. They prepared much food of different kinds and took it to a cabin near their burying ground where they ate it. They were, old and young, a very great number. Their custom is that each one must taste the other's dish.

June 13

6th Mo. 13th By Command of the Old Chief 3 of his men took the Life of a Woman, with knives, one whom they supposed to be a Witch or that She had poisoned others, and threatened the day before to do the like again which reached Cornplanters Ears, However worther of death She might have been, I know not, but I took her to be a bad Woman. The same day, I, with the assistance of an Indian, rescued a Woman, whose Husband was beating her with his fist in a Cruel manner, he being somewhat intoxicated.

By command of the old chief, three of his men took the life of a woman, with knives. They supposed that she was a witch or that she had poisoned others, and that she had threatened the day before to do the like again. This threat reached Cornplanter's ears. However worthy of death she might have been, I know not, but I took her to be a bad woman. The same day, I, with the assistance of an Indian, rescued a woman whose husband was beating her with his fist in a cruel manner, he being somewhat intoxicated.

June 15

Sixth Month 15th the Cornplanter being from home about ¾ of a mile, where he had men employ'd to build him a house, and where we were engaged in Erecting a Schoolhouse, an express came to him that his Brother or Step Brother was dying, (who had been on the decline of Life for several years) he straightway went, and found a number of his people conven'd and his Brother laying breathless for the Space of half an hour, but in about 2 hours after he came to himself again, and informed his Brother how he was and what he had seen, which was thus, as he lay or sat in the house he heard some body call to him out of the house, he immedi-

Cornplanter was about three-fourths of a mile from his home, where he had men employed to build him a house, and where we were engaged in erecting a schoolhouse. An express came to him that his brother or step brother was dying, who had been on the decline of life for several years. Cornplanter went straightway and found a number of his people convened where his brother had been lying breathless for the space of half an hour. But about two hours later, his brother came to himself again and told Cornplanter how he was feeling and informed him of what he had seen, which was as follows. As he lay or sat in the house, he heard somebody call

Original Version

ately arose and went out, his daughter seeing him askt where he was going he told her he would soon be back, and as he stood without, he saw three men by the side of the house, he then fainted and fell gently to the ground without being any Sick, the men had Bushes in their hands with berries on them, of different kinds, who invited him to take some and eat, and they would help him, and that he would Live to see such like berries ripe this Summer. he thought he took one berry off of each mans bush. They told him the great Spirit was much displeased with his people's getting drunk, and other gross Evils which they were guilty of, but as to himself they could not charge him with any thing, except sometimes geting drunk, but as he had been Sick a great while, he had thought more upon the great Spirit, and was preserved from drinking Strong drink to excess, and if he got well he must not take to it again for the great Spirit knew (not only what people were always doing) but also their very thoughts, and that there was some very bad ones among them, who would poison others, but one of them was lately killed, yet there still remained one like her who was a man. He requested his brother, to Call his people in Council, and tell them what he had said to him, and if they had any Dri'd Berries amongst them, he wished all in the Council might take if it was but one apiece,

which was done accordingly the same day, where myself and Companion (Viz) Joel Swayn, attended, at the request of Cornplanter when a large number of them assembled with shorter notice than ever I had seen them before, men Women & Children, many of whom appear'd Solid and weighty, wherein I felt the love of God flowing powerfully amongst us, and near the close had to communicate some Council to them, which was (I believe well accepted, the old Chiefs sister came to us after the Council was over, and thanked me for what I had said to them.

Note: The three persons afforesaid told him there was four of them, but one did not come, expecting to see him time hence. And he often told his Brother Cornplanter, he expected that person would soon come. As he continued in a poor state of Health for many Weeks after, One night he Drempt the absent person came (who appear'd like the Great Spirit) and askt him if he did not remember the three men who came to him some time before, and told him there was four of them altogether, but

Edited Version

to him from outside. He immediately arose and went out. His daughter saw him and asked him where he was going. He told her he would soon be back. As he stood outside, he saw three messengers by the side of the house. He then fainted and fell gently to the ground, but not from any sickness. The men had in their hands bushes with different kinds of berries on them. They invited him to take some and eat. They said the berries would help him and he would live to see such berries ripe this summer. He thought he took one berry off each man's bush. They told him the Great Spirit was much displeased with his people's getting drunk and with other gross evils of which they were guilty. But, in his own particular case, they could not charge him with anything except sometimes getting drunk. Because he had been sick a great while, he had thought more upon the Great Spirit, and was preserved from drinking strong drink to excess. And, if he got well, he must not take to drinking again because the Great Spirit always knew, not only what people were doing, but also their very thoughts. And, there were some very bad ones among them, who would poison others. One of them had lately been killed. But there still remained one like her who was a man. Handsome Lake told Cornplanter all this and asked him to call his people together in council and tell them the same thing. And, if they had any dried berries among them, Handsome Lake wished all in the council might take and eat, even if there was only enough for one berry apiece.

Handsome Lake's wishes were carried out that very same day. At the request of Cornplanter, my companion Joel Swayne and I attended the council, for which a large number of them assembled with shorter notice than ever I had seen them before— men, women, and children—many of whom appeared solid and weighty. During the council I felt the love of God flowing powerfully among us. Near the close, I had to communicate some counsel to them, which was, I believe, well accepted. The old chief's sister came to us after the council was over, and thanked me for what I had said to them.

August 7

Note: The three messengers mentioned above, who revealed themselves to Handsome Lake in the sixth month, told him then that they had a fourth companion who had not come at that time because he expected to see Handsome Lake some time hence. Handsome Lake often told Cornplanter he expected that person would soon come. For many weeks after the visitation of the messengers with the berry bushes, Handsome Lake continued in a poor state of health. One night [April 7, 1799] he

Original Version

one of them staid behind, and intended to come some time after, and he was the very one, now come to take him along if he was willing to go as he pitied him seeing he had suffered very much; He did not give him any answer, whether he would go with him or not,

but in the morning when he awoke he said he would go and put on his best Clothes, then wished to see his Brother, and was affraid he should not get to see him before he would be gone, as he was some distance off, a messenger went immediately to inform his brother thereof, who when he came, attended pretty steadily with him through the course of the day,

and about evening he fainted away, which held him but for a short Space of time, after recovering he told his Brother, he must go, but not forever he thought, as long as he and many more of his people was not willing to let him go, and that Man or Spirit was free to let him return, after going some distance with him. He told his Brother not to put any more Clothes on him, or move him, if he did go, Soon after said he was now going, and he expected to return, but thought he should go so far as to see his Son who had been dead several years, and his brothers Daughter who had been dead about Seven months.

He then fainted or fell into a Trance in which posture he remained about Seven hours, his Legs & arms were cold, his body warm but breathless, he knew not how he went out of the World, but soon perceived a guide going before him, who appear'd to have a Bow and one Arrow, and was dressed in a Clear Sky Couler, his guide told him to look forward, when he did, behold the two deceased ones before noted, was comeing to meet them, dressed in the manner of his Guide, and after embraceing eachother they turned aside to sit down to converse together

wherein the Daughter exprest her sorrow, in frequent hearing her father (viz) Cornplanter and brother Henry disputing together some times so

Edited Version

dreamed that the absent messenger finally came, who appeared like the Great Spirit and asked Handsome Lake if he remembered the three messengers who had come to him some time before. This new visitor announced that he was the fourth messenger, who had stayed behind last time, but now had come to take Handsome Lake along with him, if he was willing to go. The messenger pitied Handsome Lake, seeing that he had suffered very much. Handsome Lake did not give him any answer, whether he would go with him or not.

August 8

But in the morning, when he awoke, Handsome Lake said he would go with the messenger and put on his best clothes. Then, Handsome Lake wished to see his brother, Cornplanter, who was some distance away. He was afraid he would not get to see his brother before he would have to go with the messenger. So, one of the Indians was immediately sent to fetch his brother. Cornplanter then came and attended pretty steadily with Handsome Lake through the course of the day.

That evening, Handsome Lake fainted away, but the fainting spell held him but for a short space of time. After recovering, he told Cornplanter that he must go, but not forever, he thought, as long as Cornplanter and many more of his people were not willing to let go of him. He thought he would be free to return after going some distance with the man or spirit who had visited him the night before. He told Cornplanter not to put any more clothes on him, nor to move his body, if he did go. Shortly after that, Handsome Lake said he was now going, and although he expected to return, he thought that he should go so far as to see his own son, who had been dead several years, and Cornplanter's daughter, who had been dead about seven months.

Handsome Lake then fainted or fell into a trance, in which posture he remained for about seven hours. His legs and arms were cold; the rest of his body was warm but breathless. He knew not how he went out of the world, but soon perceived that the fourth messenger was going before him as a guide, who appeared to have a bow and one arrow, and was dressed in sky blue. His guide told him to look forward. When Handsome Lake did so, he beheld the two previously mentioned deceased ones coming to meet them, dressed in the manner of his guide. After embracing one another, they turned aside to sit down and converse together.

Cornplanter's daughter expressed her sorrow that her brother Henry frequently disputed with her father. Sometimes their arguments were so heated

Original Version	Edited Version
high as to get very angry at each other, her brother thinking he knew more than his father, and would not take his advice, but must have his own way, which was very wrong, the guide then told her to stop, He would speak, and said it was true what She had said about her brother abusing his Father, for he ought to obey him, as long as he lives	that they became very angry at each other. Her brother always thought he knew more than his father, whose advice he would never take. Henry always insisted on having his own way, which was very wrong. The guide then told her to stop because he wanted to say something. He said that she had spoken correctly in describing Henry's abuse of their father, Cornplanter. Henry should obey his father for as long as Cornplanter continued to live.
The young man then addressed his Father (in this way) being concerned that he had suffered so much and that his own Son then living had taken so little care of him, but would go out of the way when his father grew worse for fear of having some trouble, he thought he had no Sense in so doing. Guide, said every Son ought to do good for their father	Handsome Lake was then addressed by his own son, who was concerned that Handsome Lake had suffered so much. He was also concerned that Handsome Lake's other son, who was still living, had taken so little care of their father. Quite to the contrary, the living son would go out of his way when his father grew worse, for fear of having to take some trouble on his father's account. The dead son thought the living son had no sense in so doing. Guide said every son ought to do good for his father.
further said, he was glad he had told the truth to his people of what the three men had said to him some time before. they told him they had come in a hurry, and the reason of that was, on account of his Sickness & long suffering and he had thought much of the great Spirit, who knew not only what people was doing but also their thoughts, Guide said to him, the three men invited him to eat of their Berries which would help him, and that he would live to see such berries ripe the ensueing Summer, which he saw had come to pass. and that their was two people who had lived in their Town who was disposed to hurt others. but one was now dead, the other yet living.	Guide further said he was glad that Handsome Lake had told the truth to his people regarding what the three men had said to him some time before. Guide briefly restated their message to Handsome Lake. They told him they had come in a hurry because of Handsome Lake's sickness and long suffering. And, also, because Handsome Lake had thought much of the Great Spirit, who knew not only what people were doing but also their thoughts. Guide continued with his retelling. The three men invited Handsome Lake to eat of their berries, which would help him. They promised Handsome Lake that he would live to see such berries ripe the following summer. Guide pointed out that this promise had been kept. Finally, Guide concluded his summary of the message the three men had delivered to Handsome Lake. They had told him that there were two people who had lived in their town who were disposed to hurt others. One of them was now dead, but the other was yet living.
They mentioned one fault they had against him, that of getting Drunk, time back, but as he had declined it, and concluded if he got well to do so no more; they would forgive him, and he must quit all kinds of frolicks & dancing, except their Worship dance, for that was right, as they did not make use of any liquor at the time Etc.	They mentioned one fault they had against Handsome Lake and that was his habit of getting drunk, which he had practiced some time ago. But, they would forgive him because he had now declined liquor for some time and because he had resolved that if he got well, he would never touch the stuff again. However, he must also quit all kinds of frolics and dancing, except their worship dance. To dance in worship was right because the people did not make use of any liquor during worship dance, etc.
Guide, told him that it was very often the case that people were apt to take too much Strong drink, it's the great Spirit who made it to use but did not make it to hurt people and the Indians did not keep from injureing themselves greatly by it, and if they	Guide told him that it was very often the case that people were apt to take too much strong drink. The Great Spirit made strong drink to use, he did not make it to hurt people; although the Indians did not keep from injuring themselves greatly by it. If they

Original Version	Edited Version

do still get drunk, abuse themselves and injure others they need not expect to come to that happy place. Guide told him to look round towards the river, which he did, and saw many canoes loaded with Kegs of Wisky, and also saw an ugly fellow whom the guide told him was the D.l. going about very busy doing and making all the noise and mischief he could among the people.

Guid—Told him they often drempt, and some times their dreams were true from the great Spirit; but they would not believe it was from him, but from the Devil, and when the D.l. have told them something, they have concluded it was the great Spirit, and that pleases the D.l. he being thought the greatest and most honored, having the most people on his side.

Further told him, that White people were come into their Towns to instruct their Children, and that is right if they can all agree to it, but many of them are not willing, but will keep to their old habits of living, well that may be right too, but if they do they must not drink Wisky for that belongs to white People, and was not made for Indians.

Guide, said many people thinks the great Spirit knows not what they are doing of, but He sees & knows all things and nothing is hid from Him.

Guide mentioned one circumstance which he was very Sorry for, that was, their would be Shortly great sickness in their Village, unless they did amend their ways, and think more upon the great Spirit, who might then perhaps see cause to remove it. And that his people must collect together in Worship, and Cook a white Dog and every one eat thereof, as a preventative against the Sickness,

Guide, told him he might soon get well if his people took care of him & gave him Medicine. Then told him to return; and that he would not see them any more untill he Died, and perhaps not then, except he did that which was right & good as long as he lived, which would be untill the hair on his head was about half gray, then he must leave the World, and never return any more.

---

continued to get drunk, abuse themselves, and injure others, they need not expect to come to the happy place that Handsome Lake was visiting now. Guide told him to look toward the river, which Handsome Lake did. There he saw many canoes loaded with kegs of whiskey. He also saw an ugly fellow, whom the guide told him was the devil, going about very busy doing and making all the noise and mischief he could among the people.

Guide told him that the Indians dreamed a lot. And, sometimes their dreams were true, having come from the Great Spirit. But, often, when a dream was true, the Indians would not believe that it had come from the Great Spirit. Instead, they would think it had come from the devil. And, when the devil told them something in a dream, they often believed that the message had come from the Great Spirit. This confusion resulted in more people doing the work of the devil, which meant that the devil had the most people on his side. This pleased the devil because it made him seem greater than the Great Spirit, and more honored.

Guide further told him that white people had come into the Indian towns to instruct their children. This would be all right, provided that all the Indians agreed to it. If they did not all agree, and if many of them wanted to keep to their old habits of living, well that might be right too. But, if they wanted to keep to their old ways, then they had no business drinking whiskey because that belongs to white people and was not made for Indians.

Guide said that many people think the Great Spirit does not know what they are doing. But he sees and knows all things; nothing is hid from him.

Guide mentioned a circumstance that was causing him great sorrow. Shortly, there would be great sickness in Cornplanter's village, unless they did amend their ways, and think more upon the Great Spirit, who might then perhaps see cause to forestall the sickness. Furthermore, Handsome Lake's people must collect together in worship, and cook a white dog, from which they must all eat, as a preventative against the sickness.

Guide told Handsome Lake he might soon get well, if his people took care of him and gave him medicine. Guide then told him to return. He also said that Handsome Lake would not see the four messengers again until he died, and perhaps not then, unless he did that which was right and good for the rest of his life, which would last until the hair on his head was about half gray. At that point, Handsome Lake must leave the world, and never return to it again.

Original Version	Edited Version
After his Brother heard those Sayings he called a Council the same evening,	Cornplanter, after hearing what Handsome Lake had to say upon waking up, called a council that very same night [night of August 8 to 9].

August 9

and sent his Son for me to attend in the morning which I did, and heard them rehearse the matter, after which they requested me to tell them whether I believed it to be true. I told them there had been Instances of the same kind amongst White people even of the Quakers, falling into a Trance, and saw both the good place, and bad place, and seen many Wonderful sights, which I did believe. And told them I could see no reason why it should not be the case with them, as we are all of one Flesh & Blood made by the great Spirit; although there appeared no reason in my view why it should not be true, yet perhaps, as there was so much of it, the man might not have recollected so as to tell it exact as he seen or heard, it. more I said, to the same perport, and they appear'd satisfied.	In the morning Cornplanter sent his son to tell me to attend the meeting, which I did. I listened to them retell the whole story. Then, they asked me to tell them whether I believed it to be true. I told them there had been instances of the same kind among white people, even among the Quakers. Someone would fall into a trance, and see both the good place and the bad place and many other wonderful sights. I believed these visions. And, I told them I could see no reason why it should not be the case with the Indians also, as we are all of one flesh and blood made by the Great Spirit. Although there appeared no reason in my view why it should not be true, yet perhaps, because there was so much of it, Handsome Lake might not have recollected enough so as to tell it exactly as he had seen and heard. I said more to the same purport, and they appeared satisfied.
The afternoon of the same day they prepar'd a white Dog to eat, and burnt his Skin to ashes During which time it was burning a number of them were Circled around the Fire, Singing Shouting & dancing greatly; after which they all partook of their Delicious dish, of Dog Meat Etc.	That afternoon they prepared a white dog to eat, and burned his skin to ashes, during which time a number of them circled around the fire—singing, shouting, and dancing greatly. After which, they all partook of their delicious dish of dog meat, etc.

August 10

The morning following I went to Cornplanters in order to make a note of the Sick Man sayings, (who had then much recover'd of his sickness) at the same time the old Chief said he liked some ways of the white people very well, and some ways of the Indians also, and he thought it would take some length of time, to lead them out of all their own Customs, & as to their Worship Dance which they hold twice a year, they intended to keep it up, as they could not read, they knew of no other way of Worshiping the great Spirit, if they declined that they would have no manner of worship at all.	The next morning [August 10] I went to Cornplanter's house in order to make a note of the sick man's sayings. Handsome Lake had, by then, much recovered from his sickness. While I was there, the old chief said he liked some ways of the white people very well, and some ways of the Indians also. He thought it would take some length of time to lead his people out of all their own customs. And, as to their worship dance, which they hold twice a year, they intended to keep it up. They could not read, so they knew of no other way in which to worship the Great Spirit. If they gave up their sacred dances, they would have no manner of worship at all.
further said it was the white people who kill'd our Saviour how he had heard about our Saviour I know not, but it seems he had. I told him it was the Jews, who Crucify'd or kill'd Him, and whether they were white, red, or black or what couler they were of I knew not, neither did I know but Indians were their descendants; for as many of their habits were Semilar to the Jews, in former days. Yet nevertheless, I told him we were all still, Crucifying & killing Him, while we were doing Wickedly. He said that was very true, very true. Several other Indians being present. Thus matters ended at that time.	Cornplanter further said it was the white people who had killed our Savior. How he had heard about our Savior, I know not. But, it seems he had. I told him it was the Jews who crucified, or killed, him, and whether they were white, red, or black or what color they were of, I knew not. Neither did I know but that the Indians were their descendants, for many of the Indians' habits were similar to those practiced by the Jews in former days. Yet I told him that, nevertheless, we were all still crucifying and killing him—whenever we were doing wickedly. He said that was very true, very true.

Original Version	Edited Version
	Several other Indians were also present. Thus matters ended at that time.
	August 11
Eight Mo. 11th Proclamation Issu'd by order of the Chiefs, for all their People to repair home to their Village, from their Hunting Quarters, in fourteen days, in order to hold a Council, and Worship Dance, agreeable to their antient custom; as their Corn then would be ripe, or fit for boiling.	Today a proclamation was issued by order of the chiefs for all their people, many of whom were dispersed through the forests at their hunting quarters, to repair home to their village in fourteen days. At that time, they will hold a council and worship dance, agreeable to their ancient custom. By then, their corn will be ripe or fit for boiling.
	August 28
8 Mo. 28th Numbers of them assembled in Council, and agreed that such a number should turn out to Hunt, in order to get some Meat to furnish their feast Table, Accordingly upwards of 30 men set out and returned the day following with 17 dear, after which great Cookery being carried on, by some men, & some Women, apointed.	Many of the Indians assembled in council and agreed that certain of their number should turn out to hunt, in order to get some meat to furnish their feast table. Accordingly upwards of thirty men set out and returned the day following [August 29] with seventeen deer. After which, a great deal of cookery was carried on by some men and some women who had been appointed for that purpose.
the preceding day of course about noon their dance Commenc'd near if not quite two Hundred, Men, Women, & Children dancing, (I suppose not much Short, if any, of one Hundred as spectators) in several circles round their Wooden Image, which had a white dog hanging on it, with some Wampum, Ribands & paint about him,	The next day, August 30, at about noon, their dance commenced. Nearly, if not fully, two hundred men, women, and children were dancing. I suppose the spectators numbered not much short, if any, of one hundred. They danced in several circles round their wooden image, which had a white dog hanging on it. The dog had been painted and was draped with wampum and ribbons.
two men were seated on a Deer Skin just at the foot of the Image, who had each of them a Water Tortal Shell, with Corn, or Shot, within, which they beat on the Skin, as Musick to the dancers, who also made Changeable noises by way of Song, at which the dancers paid great attension as the sound of their Musick and tone of their Song chang'd, so did their dancing, twisting their arms, Heads, bodies, yelling & Shouting, Change also— which would be very astonishing to those who had never beheld Indians.	Two men were seated on a deerskin just at the foot of the image. Each of them had a water turtle shell, with corn or shot within, which they beat on the deerskin so as to make music for the dancers. The men on the deerskin also made changeable noises by way of song. The dancers paid great attention to the sound of the music and the tone of the song, and as these changed, so did their dancing. They changed the twisting of their arms, heads, and bodies; they also varied their yelling and shouting. All of which would be very astonishing to those who had never beheld Indians.
Many of the men almost naked, and painted greatly round their Bodies, arms, & about their Heads, in different coulars and in various figures, most of the men & Boys were painted, little or much, and many of them were dressed in a very Superfluous manner, as also were the Women array'd to that degree that some of their Strouds or Petticoats have cost them twenty dollars, which are overlaid with Silk Ribands of diverse coulars. The females way of dance, is, by moveing their feet sideway when set close together, and also motioning their Hands over each other, moving gently	Many of the men were almost naked and painted greatly round their bodies, arms, and about their heads, in different colors and in various figures. Most of the men and boys were painted, a little or a lot. And many of them were dressed in a very superfluous manner, as also were the women arrayed. The women's manner of dress was superfluous to such a degree that some of their strouds, or petticoats, must have cost them twenty dollars. Their petticoats were overlaid with silk ribbons of diverse colors. The females' way of dance was by keeping their feet set close together and moving them side-

Original Version	Edited Version
round in the Circles with the Men, & Boys, who look very steadfastly to the ground, but are silent.	ways. They also motioned their hands over each other, moving gently round in the circles with the men and boys. The women look very steadfastly to the ground and are silent.
at certain intervals, of their dances, some of the fore rank of men made Speeches to the company, by way of Preaching, especially one who was particularly called their Minister. About Sundown they concluded and all partook, of their Cookery.	At certain intervals, between dances, some of the high-ranking men made speeches to the company, by way of preaching. One man in particular, whom they called their minister, preached a lot. About sundown they concluded their dancing and preaching, and they all partook of their cookery.
The next day went on much as yesterday tho' to a greater strain of vanity & Idolitry and burnt the dog to ashes. In the evening of the same I informed the old Chief, Cornplanter, I was desirous of speaking to them in Council, at a convenient opportunity before they seperated & repair'd to their respective Habitations, he immediately addressed the company with my words, and proposed leting me know when their business then in agitation was gone through.	The next day [August 31] went on much as the day before, though to a greater strain of vanity and idolatry. And, they burned the dog to ashes. That evening, I informed the old chief, Cornplanter, that I was desirous of speaking to them in council, at a convenient opportunity, before they separated and repaired to their respective habitations. He immediately addressed the company with my words, and proposed letting me know when their business, then in agitation, was gone through.
The day following they were engaged in a Husleing or Lottery Play, and the day preceding that till about noon, During which time they were engaged they yeled most Horribly.	The day after that [September 1], they were engaged in a hustling or lottery game, which they continued to play into the next day [September 2], until about noon. While playing this game, they yelled most horribly.
just before they closed the Business, they sent me word, that they were about ready to meet me in Council, when I came they were then closeing the Scene which was done by Shooting Guns, about 50 Men stood in a Longitude direction opposite their Wooden Image & shot twice or thrice up towards the Sun, their Minister Shot first, and so on.	Just before they closed the business, they sent me word that they were about ready to meet me in council. When I arrived, they were then closing the scene, which they did by shooting guns. About fifty men stood in a longitude direction, opposite their wooden image, and shot twice or thrice up toward the sun. Their minister shot first, and so on.
After which they entered the house, as many as could get in, and numbers of Men, Women, & Children, outside round the house. Cornplant & their Minister, made two pretty lengthy Speeches, to them by way of advice, to be still and attentive to what I had to say to them and for the most part were very Quiet & Solid. Indeed I felt the Divine Power spread over the gathering, in a very Conspicuous manner, to the Washing of my face with Teers	After which, as many as could fit into Cornplanter's house entered therein. This left numbers of men, women, and children gathered round, outside the house. Cornplanter and their minister made two pretty lengthy speeches, advising them to be still and attentive to what I had to say. And, for the most part, they were very quiet and solid. Indeed, I felt the divine power spread over the gathering, in a very conspicuous manner, to the washing of my face with tears.
I first opened to them, my prospect of leaving them in a few weeks hence, and return home to my Native Land, and not knowing that I should be favoured with such another opportunity of meeting so many of them together, was willing to drop some advice to them, and take them by the Hand & part with them in an affectionate & Brotherly way,	I first opened to them my prospect of leaving them in a few weeks hence, to return home to my native land. And, because I did not know whether I should be favored with such another opportunity of meeting so many of them together, I wanted to use this occasion to drop some advice to them, and to take them by the hand and part with them in an affectionate and brotherly way.

Original Version	Edited Version
inviting to press forward towards a happy Life, not only the present one, but that which is to come, I also set forth my disunity, with their vanity & Idolitrous way of Worshiping the Great Spirit; in a full belief that it was displeasing to Him, the manner they acted, although it were their fore-Fathers Customs, I believed there was a loud Call to them to come forth & Learn better,	I encouraged them to press forward toward happiness, not only in this life, but in that which is to come. I also set forth my disunity with their vain and idolatrous way of worshiping the Great Spirit. I fully believed that the manner in which they acted was displeasing to him—even though it was their forefathers' custom. I believed there was a loud call to them to come forth and learn better.
but as they had remarked that it was given to their fourfathers so to Worship and thought it right for them to keep it up in remembrance of their aged Fathers. but Honestly acknowledged they had changed it to a more profligate way & did not hold it so Solemn as their forefathers used to do.	Now, they had remarked that it was given to their forefathers so to worship, and they thought it right for them to keep it up in remembrance of their aged fathers. But, they had also honestly acknowledged to me that they had changed their manner of worship to a more profligate way and did not hold it so solemn as their forefathers used to do.
I queried with them why they were so unwilling to part with some of their forefathers mode of Life and had taken so readily to other some, so very Injurious to them; that of Strong drink, and that of decking & adorning themselves with such very extravigant superfluous & expencive Clothes, as also such an abundance of Silver ornaments about them, which their fore fathers were not accustomed to, but, I believed, were glad to get Skins to cover themselves with. at this some of them Laughed.	So, I queried them as to why they were so unwilling to part with some parts of their forefathers' mode of life and yet had taken so readily to some new ways, so very injurious to them, such as that of strong drink. I also mentioned their present habits of decking and adorning themselves with such very extravagant, superfluous, and expensive clothes, and of wearing such an abundance of silver ornaments about themselves, neither of which their forefathers were accustomed to. But rather, I believed, their forefathers were glad to get skins to cover themselves with. At this some of them laughed.
I streeniously pressed them to lay out their Money for such articles as would be useful to them, not to spend it for nought.	I strenuously pressed them to lay out their money for such articles as would be useful to them, and not to spend it for naught.
After a pause, they expressed great thankfulness for what I had mentioned to them, and said they could not say it was not true for as I had been with them a long while, they believed I was a good Man, and had always been willing to do that that was right amongst them,	After a pause, they expressed great thankfulness for what I had mentioned to them. They acknowledged that they could not say it was not true. I had been with them a long while, and they believed I was a good man. I had always been willing to do what was right among them.
but as I was now about to leave them, they felt thankful, that I & my Companions had been so favour'd with good health, ever since we came amongst them, and Desir'd that the Great Spirit might conduct me safe home, to see my relations & Friends there, and that I must Write back, to let them know how I got along Etc.	But as I was now about to leave them, they felt thankful that I and my companions had been so favored with good health, ever since we came among them. And they desired that the Great Spirit might conduct me safe home, to see my relations and Friends there. They told me I must write back, to let them know how I got along, etc.
They then took me by the hand and we parted like Brothers. About the conclusion, one of my Companions (Viz) Halliday came down, & tarried with me until the morrow	They then took me by the hand and we parted like brothers. At the conclusion of this council, Halliday Jackson, one of my companions, came down from the farm at Genesinguhta and tarried with me until the next day [September 3].

Original Version	Edited Version
	September 11
9 Mo. 11th 99 Then arrived at Coniscotago, some of our Friends from Philadelphia & parts adjacent very unexpected to myself, not having heard anything about their comeing before. Which was to us a time of mutual heart felt joy, whose names hereafter will be mentioned.	Then arrived at Cornplanter's village some of our Friends from Philadelphia and parts adjacent, very unexpected to myself, not having heard anything about their coming before. Their arrival was to us a time of mutual heartfelt joy. I will list their names later.
	September 12
12th I accompanied them to Genesinguhta, where my Companions resided. where they tarried till the 14th.	I accompanied our Friends to Genesinguhta, where my companions resided. We all tarried there till the fourteenth.
	September 14
We then proceeded down the river back to Coniscotago, in a Canoe, in order to sit with the Indians in Council. When assembled Cornplanter & Son Henry Interpretter, stood up, and expressed thankfulness, for our being thus favoured in Health, as to meet each other again in Council, and was then ready to hear what friends had to Deliver. They first produced & read their Certificate. which was as follows,	We then proceeded down the river back to Cornplanter's village, in a canoe, in order to sit with the Indians in council. When the Indians were assembled, Cornplanter and his son Henry, who served as interpreter, stood up and expressed thankfulness for our being favored in health such that we were able to meet each other again in council. Cornplanter and his people were then ready to hear what the Friends had to deliver. Our Friends from Philadelphia first produced and read their certificate, which was as follows:
To the Indians at Genesinguhta and the Neighbourhood thereof.	To the Indians at Genesinguhta and the neighborhood thereof.
Brothers, It is now a considerable time since three of our young Men, from a desire to be serviceable to you, in instructing you in farming, and such other useful ways of the White people, as would enable you to live comfortably on the Lands, which the Good Spirit has permitted you to enjoy, left their comfortable homes, kind & beloved Connections and Friends, and settled amongst you in the Wilderness.	Brothers, it is now a considerable time since three of our young men settled among you. They came here because of a desire to be serviceable to you, to instruct you in farming and such other useful ways of the white people as would enable you to live comfortably on the lands which the Good Spirit has permitted you to enjoy. To do this, they left behind their comfortable homes, kind and beloved connections, and friends. They came here to live with you in the wilderness.
Brothers, To see how our Young Men fair and what progress you make in learning from them, Our Friends, Joshua Sharpless, Isaac Coats, Thomas Stewardson & James Cooper, propose visiting you Now Brothers,	Brothers, to see how our young men fare and what progress you make in learning from them, our Friends, Joshua Sharpless, Isaac Coats, Thomas Stewardson, and James Cooper, propose visiting you now, Brothers.
As these our Brethren are true men, beloved by us, and have your Welfare much at Heart, we hope you will receive them as such and attend to what advice they may give you.	As these our brethren are true men, beloved by us, and have your welfare much at heart, we hope you will receive them as such and attend to what advice they may give you.
Signed on behalf of the people Called Quakers of Pennsylvania, New Jersey, etc. By your Friends and Brothers.	Signed on behalf of the people called Quakers of Pennsylvania, New Jersey, etc. By your Friends and Brothers.

Original Version		Edited Version	
John Biddle	David Bacon	John Biddle	David Bacon
John Smith	John Parrish	John Smith	John Parrish
Peter Barker	John Drinker	Peter Barker	John Drinker
John Elliott	Oliver Paxson	John Elliott	Oliver Paxson
Henry Drinker	William Savery	Henry Drinker	William Savery
Saml. Emlen Junr	John Staples	Saml. Emlen Junr	John Staples
Thomas Wistar	Thomas Fischer	Thomas Wistar	Thomas Fischer
	Thomas Harrison		Thomas Harrison
	John Hunt		John Hunt
	Ellis Yarnal		Ellis Yarnal

The second address to them, which was in Writing also. Is as follows

Brothers, You have now heard that our comeing here, was to see how you, and our young Men who live amongst you, are getting along, We are glad the Good Spirit has favoured us to meet you in Health, and given us this opportunity of takeing you by the hand, and brightening the Chain of Friendship.

Now Brothers, We should like to here from your own mouths, if you are quite satisfied with our Young Men being amongst you, they came here with an hope of being useful, by instructing you in a better way of manageing your Land, and providing for yourselves and your Cattle, We desire you to speak freely.

Brothers, It has been some satisfaction to us, in riding through your Town to see marks of Industry taking place, that you are building better & Warmer Houses to live in, and that so much of your Clear'd Land is planted with Corn, Potatoes, Beans, Squashes, Cucumbers Etc. and to see these article kept in good order.

Brothers, We observe where your new Houses are building that the Timber is very much Cut off, a rich flat, which we wish you encouraged to clear, and make it fit for Ploughing, we believe it to be very good Land for Wheat as well as Corn, and as the White People are settling around you, the Deer and other Game will grow Scarcer, and more difficult to be taken, we therefore hope that more of your Men will assist in Clearing Land, fencing it, planting it with Corn, & sowing it with wheat, you will then have a Supply of Provision more Certain to depend upon than Hunting

The second address to the Indians, which was also in writing, read as follows:

Brothers, you have now heard that our coming here was to see how you and our young men, who live among you, are getting along. We are glad the Good Spirit has favored us to meet you in health, and [has] given us this opportunity of taking you by the hand, and brightening the chain of friendship.

Now brothers, we should like to hear from your own mouths whether or not you are entirely satisfied with our young men being among you. They came here with a hope of being useful by instructing you in a better way of managing your land and providing for yourselves and your cattle. We desire you to speak freely.

Brothers, it has been of some satisfaction to us, in riding through your town, to see marks of industry taking place; to see that you are building better and warmer houses to live in; and to see that so much of your cleared land is planted with corn, potatoes, beans, squashes, cucumbers, etc. And, to see these article kept in good order.

Brothers, we observe where your new houses are being built that the timber is very much cut off, opening a rich flat, which we encourage you to clear and make fit for plowing. We believe it to be very good land for wheat as well as corn. And, as the white people are settling around you, the deer and other game will grow scarcer and more difficult to be taken. We, therefore, hope that more of your men will assist in clearing land, fencing it, and planting it with corn, and sowing it with wheat. You will then have a supply of provisions more certain to depend upon than hunting.

Original Version	Edited Version
Brothers, we were pleased to see your Stock of Cattle increased, the rich bottoms on the river, will be plenty for them to live on in the Summer Season, but as your Winters are long & Cold, it will require something for them to live on in the Winter, now the White People keep their Cattle on Hay, on Straw, and on Cornfodder, Straw you cannot get, until you raise Wheat, or other Grain, the rich bottoms if they were put in order would produce a great deal of Hay, but for an immediate supply, we think if as soon as you gather your Corn, you would cut the Stalks close at the Ground, bind them up in Small bundles, and put them in Stacks, as our Young Men do, they would keep the Cattle part of the Cold Weather.	Brothers, we were pleased to see your stock of cattle increased. The rich bottoms on the river will be plenty for them to live on in the summer season. But, as your winters are long and cold, it will require something more for them to live on in the winter. Now, the white people keep their cattle on hay, on straw, and on corn fodder. However, straw you cannot get until you raise wheat, or other grain. The rich bottoms, if they were put in order, would produce a great deal of hay. But for an immediate supply, we suggest this. As you gather your corn, cut the stalks close at the ground, bind them up in small bundles, and put them in stacks, as our young men do. These stalks will keep the cattle part of the cold weather.
Brothers, We are pleased to see a quantity of new fence made this Summer near where our young Men live, and we would not have you get discouraged at the Labour it takes, for if you will clear a little more Land every Year, and fence it, you will soon get enough to raise what Bread you want, as well as some for Grass to make Hay for Winter.	Brothers, we are pleased to see a quantity of new fence made this summer near where our young men live. We would not have you get discouraged at the labor it takes. If you will just clear a little more land every year, and fence it, you will soon have enough to raise what bread you want, as well as some for raising grass to make hay for winter.
Brothers, We understand you are desirous to discourage Whiskey from being brought amongst you, with which we are much Pleased, and should be glad you could entirely keep it away, for to get it, you give your Money, which you should have to buy Clothes with, and to buy Oxen and Ploughs with, to Work your Land; and it does not do you any good.	Brothers, we understand you are desirous to discourage whiskey from being brought among you, with which we are much pleased, and should be glad you could entirely keep it away. For, to get whiskey, you give your money, which you should use instead to buy clothes and to buy oxen and plows with which to work your land. And, besides, the whiskey does not do you any good.
After the aforesaid was delivered, Our friend Isaac Coats, offered some pertinent & judicious Council, to them Verbally. But before they could make reply to us, on what had been communicated to them, they wished to know, whether I was still in the determination of returning home.	After the aforesaid was delivered, our friend Isaac Coats offered some pertinent and judicious council to them, verbally. But before they could make reply to us on what had been communicated to them, they wished to know whether I was still in the determination of returning home.
I told them I believed it was as right for me to return in a short time, as it were for me to come amongst them, yet nevertheless, as our Friends had come forward, we did intend to consult each other about it, after the Council, for as they were older than myself, and sometimes old people knew better than young ones. but I told them they could give our friends an answer, in respect to their satisfaction with our being amongst them, and desired they might not hide anything from them,	I told them I believed it was right for me to return in a short time, as it had been for me to come among them. Yet, nevertheless, as our Friends had come forward from Philadelphia, we did intend to consult each other about it after the council. They were older than myself, and sometimes old people knew better than young ones. But I told them they could give our Friends an answer, in respect to their satisfaction with our being among them, and I desired they might not hide anything from them.
they then began, and said, they had made strict enquiry amongst themselves, about us but could not find out any fault against us, but that we were always doing what was right among them Etc. Cornplanter said I had been a great help to him, particularly in endeavouring to prevent so much Whiskey from comeing into their Town, and if I went away he would have no body there to help him.	They then began, and said they had made strict inquiry among themselves about us but could not find any fault against us. Rather, we were always doing what was right among them, etc. Cornplanter said I had been a great help to him, particularly in endeavoring to prevent so much whiskey from coming into their town, and if I went away he would have nobody there to help him.

Original Version	Edited Version
We then requested the Indians to seperate from us a few minutes that we might have a little opportunity by ourselves, and after a pause, friends exprest a wish, that I could have felt easy to remain in my present Post during the ensueing Winter, but believed it right to leave the matter pretty much to myself. I then exprest how Important the Concern had been with me and that I stood fully resign'd to the divine will, either to go, or to stay long, had at times no choice in it, but as I had been favoured to see Latterly, & at that present time, pretty clearly, that it was my Duty to return home.	We then requested the Indians to separate from us a few minutes that we might have a little opportunity by ourselves. And, after a pause, our friends expressed a wish that I could have felt easy to remain in my present post during the upcoming winter, but believed it right to leave the matter pretty much to myself. I then expressed how important the concern had been with me and that I stood fully resigned to the divine will, either to go or to stay long. At times I had no choice in it. But, lately and at that present time, I had been favored to see pretty clearly that it was my duty to return home.
Some of the Indians then assembled again and our friend Joshua Sharpless, informed them, that it were their wishes I could have felt contented to stay a little while longer, but thought they must leave it to myself, and that I thought, it was my Duty to return home or words to the same purport.	Some of the Indians then assembled again, and our Friend Joshua Sharpless informed them that the elder Friends wished that I could have felt contented to stay a little while longer, but thought they must leave it to myself, and that I thought it was my duty to return home or words to the same purport.
Cornplanter, repli'd he had nothing more to say to it, but, that it might be right for me, to go and See my Parents, & Friends, & that he should accompany me through the Indian settlements as far as Cannadarque on the way which I had proposed going, he then expressed satisfaction, that the business was gone through, So took eachother by the hands round.	Cornplanter replied that he had nothing more to say about it. It might be the best thing for me to go and see my parents and Friends. Cornplanter said he would accompany me through the Indian settlements as far as Canandaigua on the route that I had proposed for traveling. He then expressed satisfaction that the business was gone through. So we took each other by the hands, all around.
After which, We took a bite of Bread & Butter, took leave, & returned to Genesinguhta the same day; where our Friends remained, till the 17th	After which, we took a bite of bread and butter, took leave, and returned to Genesinguhta that same day, where our Friends remained until the seventeenth [September].
	September 17
then takeing our Solemn leave of each other, they set out for Canada, in order to visit the Scattering members their who were under appointment to that purpose from the Yearly Meeting held in Philadelphia.	We and our Friends from Philadelphia took solemn leave of each other. Then they set out for Canada in order to visit the members of our Society scattered there. Our Friends were under appointment to that purpose from the Yearly Meeting in Philadelphia.
	October 6, Sunday
10th Month 6th 1799—first day of the week, now taking a final farewell of many of the Indians at Coniscotago Village some of whom appear'd very Sorry of my departing from them. I set forward up the river in a Canoe, to Genesinguhta about 9 miles, our Settlement where my Companions resided and where some of the principal Men came to see me start in the morning,	Today I took my final farewell of many of the Indians at Cornplanter's village, some of whom appeared very sorry about my departing from them. I set forward in a canoe up the river about nine miles to Genesinguhta, our settlement, where my companions resided. Some of the principal men came there to see me start in the morning.
	October 7, Monday
2nd day 7th After taking solemn leave of my two Companions, (viz) Halliday Jackson, and Joel Swayne and the Indians, Set out with Cornplanter & several others.	After taking solemn leave of my two companions, Halliday Jackson and Joel Swayne, and of the Indians who had come to see me off, I set out with Cornplanter and several others. . . .

NOTES

Prologue

1. Near present-day Warren, Pennsylvania.
2. Probably about 9:30 A.M.
3. To construct this account of Handsome Lake's hunting trip, illness and first vision, and of the mid-May disturbances at Cornplanter's village, the following sources were consulted: Parker 1913, 20–30; Simmons 1799 Journal: mid-May and June 15 entries; Abler 1989, 210–12; and Wallace 1972, 239–42.
4. In Edward Cornplanter's version of the Code of Handsome Lake, given in Parker 1913, the daughter and her husband determined that Handsome Lake was dead immediately upon his collapse outside their house. They carried his body back into their house and dressed it for burial—before Blacksnake arrived. When Blacksnake arrived and examined his uncle, he discovered the warm spot on the chest almost right away. In Blacksnake's version of these events, dictated to Benjamin Williams, a literate Seneca, many years after they occurred and published in Abler 1989, Handsome Lake was still lying outdoors when Blacksnake arrived. The nephew determined that the uncle was not breathing and enlisted the help of some neighbors in moving the body back inside the house. While handling the body, Blacksnake subsequently discovered the warm spot.
5. Parker 1913, 20.
6. Ibid., 20–21.
7. Simmons 1799 Journal: mid-May entry. Further quotations attributed to Henry Simmons are taken from his 1799 journal, unless specifically noted otherwise.
8. PA 1896, 2-4: 537; see also Hough 1861, 171.
9. Letter from Henry Simmons to Israel Chapin, dated March 25, 1799, as found in PA State Archives, RG 5, Kent-Barnard Collection, series 3, general correspondence, LC box 3 and 4, 1799–1924.
10. This chapter's account of the late-May or early-June temperance council and the Indians' decision to ban alcohol from Cornplanter's village is based on Simmons 1799 Journal: entries for mid-May 1799 and following.
11. Parker 1913, 27.
12. Simmons 1799 Journal: June 15 entry.

Chapter One

1. PCR 1838–53, 16: 496–97; PA 1896, 2-4: 537; records of the Pennsylvania state government show that Cornplanter had arrived in Philadelphia by November 23, 1790, and that he was still in the city on February 7, 1791. A letter from Cornplanter to the children of the Friends of Onas dated February 10, 1791 (found in Barton 1990, 1 and frontispiece; also in PYMMS Minutes 1791 for April 21), was almost certainly written and dispatched in Philadelphia. (Fenton 1998, 200; Richter 1992, 388 n. 49; Jennings 1984, 231 n. 19). The children of the Friends of Onas were the Quakers of the Philadelphia Yearly Meeting (PYM) of the Religious Society of Friends (RSF).
2. PCR 1838–53, 16: 357, 497, 501–8; PA 1896, 2-4: 527–37; Hough 1861: 161 n, 171 n; letter from Cornplanter to the Quakers of Philadelphia, dated February 10, 1791, as found in Barton 1990, 1 and frontispiece; also in PYMMS Minutes for April 21, 1791; PA 1896, 2-4: 536; Hough 1861, 170 n, 171 n.
3. Baldwin 1791: letters dated April 9 at Fort Franklin and May 12 at "Obeal's Town," Cornplanter's village; Proctor 1791, journal, 468.
4. Deardorff 1951: 84; Baldwin 1791: letters dated April 19 at Fort Franklin, May 12 at "Obeal's Town," May 25 at Chemung, and September 14 at Newtown; Baldwin 1791: letter dated April 9 at Fort Franklin; diary entries from November 3 through November 14 cover his final visit to Cornplanter's village, diary entries after November 14 show that he did not return to Cornplanter's village.
5. PCR 1838–53, 16: 505; PA 1900, 4-4: 164–65; on October 29, 1790 Cornplanter and other Seneca chiefs petitioned the government of Pennsylvania for compensation to the Seneca nation in the amount of $830. On February 1, 1791 the governor of Pennsylvania signed an act of the General Assembly granting $800, in trust for the Seneca nation, to Cornplanter and two other chiefs, Big Tree and Half Town.
6. James 1963, 300; Kelsey 1917, 92–93; PYMMS 1791, minutes: February 18, April 21, May 19, June 16, October 20.
7. Barton 1990, 82.
8. Graymont 1972, 220.
9. Ibid., 216.
10. Cook 1887, 174.
11. Ibid., 159.
12. Graymont 1972, 217–18; later, the Seneca villages of Big Tree and Little Beard's Town grew up on or near the site of the old Genesee

Castle, Geneseo; Sullivan Papers [1779–95] 1930–39, 3:131.

13. Cook 1887, 188.

14. Sullivan Papers [1779–95] 1930–39, 3:134.

15. The Munsee were a tribe that had been displaced from their homeland on the upper Delaware River; PA 1855–56, 1-12: 156–57.

16. Chazanof 1970, 18–23; Wallace 1972, 183.

17. Ellicott 1937, I: 41; also, PYMIC Collection, reel I, box 2, general description of the Allegany Reservation by an unidentified Quaker visitor written shortly after 1804.

18. Hough 1861, 165 n, 170 n, 171 n; PA 1896, 2-4: 532, 536.

19. Downes 1940, 309.

20. PCR 1838–53, 16: 501–2; PA 1855–56, 1-10: 510; PA 1855–56, 1-11: 509.

21. PA 1896, 2-6: 780.

22. Wilkinson 1953, 267.

23. All-river route distances on the Allegheny are taken from Kussart 1938, 4-5; Cornplanter's village was five miles upstream from the mouth of Kinzua Creek, on the opposite, or west, side of the river, near the mouth of Cornplanter Run. See also Fenton 1998, 104.

24. Jackson 1830b, 34; Jackson 1830a, 22; Norton [1816] 1970, 9.

25. Wallace 1972, 185–86, 215; Norton [1816] 1970, 9, 11.

26. ASPIA 1832–61, 1: no. 4; communication from Secretary of War Henry Knox to President George Washington and the Congress of the United States, dated July 7, 1789; see also Harmon 1941, 10–19.

27. Ricciardelli 1963, 311–12; Snow 1994, 156–57.

28. Hough 1861, 167 n; PYMIC Collection, 1791–1802, reel I, box 1, letter "To Our Indian Brethren of the Six Nations" from "your old Friends the people called Quakers in Pennsylvania, New Jersey and parts adjacent," dated January 5, 1796. Manuscript copy of Timothy Pickering's letter to the Six Nations, dated February 15, 1796, as found in Simmons 1797 Letter Book; see also PYMIC Collection, 1791–1802, reel I, box 1, February 15, 1796.

29. Hough 1861, 165 n; also, PA 1855–56, 2-4: 532.

30. Hough 1861, 165 n, 170 n, 171 n; see also, PA 1855–56, 2-4: 532, 536, 537.

31. Information pertaining to the walking purchase of 1737, including details of the walk itself, are drawn from Wallace 1949, 25–29, 132–35; James 1963, 182–85; Jennings 1984, 329–39, 388–97.

32. According to historian Francis Jennings, the entire transaction of 1737—not just the walk itself—was based on deception. In 1735 the Penns claimed that the purchase had been negotiated and consummated by their father in

1700. They claimed in 1737 that the purchase had occurred in 1686. In *The Ambiguous Iroquois Empire,* Jennings presents evidence that William Penn had negotiated a tentative agreement in 1700 to purchase a small fraction of the land eventually purchased in 1737. The agreement was never consummated in a deed and no compensation was ever paid. The 1686 agreement cited by the Penns had nothing to do with the lands in question. The maps that were shown to the Indians in 1737 used false labels. The Penns, in short, used false documents to maneuver the Indians into making the 1737 agreement; they then used doctored maps to further defraud the Indians during negotiation of the agreement; and finally they cheated during implementation of the agreement—during the walk. (Jennings 1984, 329–39, 388–97.)

33. The Association had a lengthy and descriptive Quaker title, which was "the Friendly Association for Regaining and Preserving Peace with the Indians by Pacific Measures." The PYM's Indian Committee, formed in 1795, was officially titled "the Committee for the Gradual Civilization and Improvement of the Indian Natives"; James 1963, 99, 178–92; Marietta 1984, 188–89.

34. James 1963, 99, 178–92; Kelsey 1917, 68, 77–78.

35. James 1963, 300–301; Wallace 1972, 220.

36. For substantiation of this assertion see the following sources: letter dated August 12, 1790, from Seneca chiefs to governor of Pennsylvania, in vol. 6 of the O'Rielly Collection of the New-York Historical Society, as found in Wallace 1972, 172 [this letter was probably transmitted to Pennsylvania by Oliver Phelps in a letter of his own dated August 14, 1790]; PCR 16: 439–40, 505; PA 1896, 2-4: 533; Hough 1861, 165 n; PA 1896, 2-6: 707, 759, 765–66. Documentary evidence that originated as official correspondence and reports of European-American civil and military authorities reveals three representative cases. The Pine Creek murders of June 1790: PCR 16, 397–99, 417–18, 422, 437–39, 440, 442, 483–84, 497, 508; PA 1855–56, 1-11: 709–10, 714–15, 719–21, 730, 744–46; PA 1855–56, 1-12: 8–9. The Big Beaver Creek murders of March 1791: PA 1896, 2-4: 545–50. The Fort Franklin murder of May 1794: PA 1896, 2-6: 701–02, 706–07, 709, 729, 787–88.

When it came to unpunished "white-on-Indian" murder, Cornplanter's personal experience was probably all too typical of Senecas during the period 1784 to 1789. Between 1786 and 1790, his nephew and his brother-in-law were both killed by European Americans who were neither tried nor charged for their crimes. [PCR 16: 504-05.] In 1789, while traveling up the Ohio River on his way home from the Treaty of Fort Harmar, Cornplanter and his party were fired upon by three white men. Only the poor marksmanship of the shooters saved Cornplanter and his people from additional casualties. [PCR 16: 503.]

37. Wallace 1972, 152; PA 1899, 2-4: 533, 549, 551, 555–57; PA 1896, 2-6: 733–34, 740, 752, 778.

38. Fort Franklin was located in northwestern Pennsylvania at the confluence of French Creek and the Allegheny River, about 80 miles by river, 65 miles overland, below Cornplanter's village and about 127 miles by river, 85 miles overland, above Pittsburgh.

39. European Americans of the day frankly acknowledged that cheating Indians by white traders was customary. [See PA 1855–56, 1-11: 732–33.]

40. This definition of acculturation portrays the acculturation process as a one-way street, ignoring traffic going from Native-American to European-American culture. It also ignores the fact that the Indians had the viable option of modifying and adapting selected European-American cultural elements.

41. PYMIC Collection, 1791–1802, reel I, box 1, November 3, 1795–March 8, 1796.

42. PYMIC Collection, 1791–1802, reel I, box 1, letter "To Our Indian Brethren of the Six Nations" from "your old Friends the people called Quakers in Pennsylvania, New Jersey, and parts adjacent," dated January 5, 1796.

43. Manuscript copy of Timothy Pickering's letter to the Six Nations, dated February 15, 1796, as found in Simmons 1797 Letter Book; see also, PYMIC Collection, reel I, box 1, February 15, 1796.

44. PYMIC Proceedings 1806, 10–11; this explanation for the closing of the Oneida mission is repeated in Kelsey 1917, 95–96 and in Barton 1990, 4.

45. PYMIC Collection, 1791–1802, reel I, box 1, March 17, 1797.

46. The two islands in the Allegheny River, which accounted for an additional 119 acres, brought the grant total to 779 acres. (Pierce 1798, journal entry for May 17.) Sharpless records a total of "near 800 acres" (Sharpless 1798, journal entry May 21.) but seems to have taken fewer pains to be exact than Pierce, who reported three constituent acreages (west bank and two islands). Pierce is confirmed, as well, by Deardorff. (Deardorff 1941, 11.) (Deardorff 1941, 22.)

47. Deardorff 1941, 8–10.

48. Sharpless 1798, journal entry for May 30 (p. 17 of Times-Mirror extracts reprint; ninety-fourth leaf of manuscript book); see also,

Pierce 1798, journal entry for May 29 (p. 23 of manuscript; forty-first leaf of typescript).

49. Deardorff and Snyderman 1956, 588; *Jenuchshadago* (variously spelled): "there a house was burned," i.e., Burnt House. The spelling of Jenuchshadago used here is one of the variant spellings used in Wallace 1972.

According to the Reverend Timothy Alden, founder of Allegheny College who visited Cornplanter's village in 1816, "burnt house" was a reference to a former settlement on the site, which had been burned by Col. Daniel Brodhead's troops during the Revolutionary War in 1779. According to Merle Deardorff, however, the settlement torched by Brodhead had already been called "burnt house." (Deardorff 1951, 83; Fenton 1945c, 89, 93.) If Deardorff is correct, the name *Jenuchshadago* turns out to have been prophetic as well as retrospective.

50. *Genesinguhta:* Through the Houses? Through the Hills? The meaning is uncertain. The spelling of Genesinguhta used here is one of the variant spellings used by the Quaker missionaries in their letters and journals. The meaning is unclear. It probably meant "where they go through the houses," or, possibly, though much less probably, "through the hills." [Deardorff and Snyderman 1956, 599–600.]

51. Sharpless 1798, journal entry for May 21 (p. 8 of Times-Mirror extracts reprint; fiftieth leaf of manuscript book).

52. Sharpless 1798, journal entry for May 30 (p. 17 of Times-Mirror extracts reprint; ninety-fourth leaf of manuscript book); see also, Pierce 1798, journal entry for May 29 (pp. 12, 23 of manuscript; twenty-second, forty-first leaves of typescript).

53. Deardorff 1941, 10–11; 1951, 81.

54. Pierce 1798, journal entry for May 19 (p. 8 of manuscript; sixteenth leaf of typescript); see also, Sharpless 1798, journal entry for May 23 (p. 9 of Times-Mirror extracts reprint; fifty-fourth leaf of manuscript book).

55. Pierce 1798, journal entry for May 21 (p. 11 of manuscript; twenty-second leaf of typescript).

56. Ibid., journal entry for May 11 (p. 3 of manuscript; sixth leaf of typescript).

57. Pierce 1798, journal entry for May 28 (pp. 19 and 20 of manuscript; thirty-fifth and thirty-sixth leaves of typescript); see also, Sharpless 1798, journal entry for May 28 (p. 14 of Times-Mirror extracts reprint; seventy-eighth and seventy-ninth leaves of manuscript book).

58. Pierce 1798, journal entry for May 28 (p. 19 of manuscript; thirty-fifth leaf of typescript); see also, Sharpless 1798, journal entry for May 28 (p. 14 of Times-Mirror extracts reprint; seventy-seventh and seventy-eighth leaves of manuscript book).

59. Jackson 1830b, 32–33; Jackson 1798–1800 Journal, 133; Wallace 1972, 227.
60. Jackson [1798–1800] 1952, 134; see also, letter dated July 29, 1798, from Simmons, Jackson, and Swayne at Genesinguhta to the Indian Committee in Philadelphia, as found in Simmons 1798–99 Letter Book.
61. Letter dated July 29, 1798, from Simmons, Jackson, and Swayne at Genesinguhta to the Indian Committee in Philadelphia, as found in Simmons 1798–99 Letter Book.
62. Letter dated November 16, 1798, from Simmons, Jackson, and Swayne at Genesinguhta to the Indian Committee in Philadelphia, as found in Simmons 1798–99 Letter Book.
63. Jackson [1798–1800] 1952, 138.
64. Halliday Jackson reports that he was on a trip to Buffalo when the council occurred. He records leaving Genesinguhta on November 9, 1798. He does not record the date of his return, but it appears he returned on November 17. He then learned of the council, which had been held in his absence. (Jackson [1798–1800] 1952, 138–41.)
65. Jackson [1798–1800] 1952, 141.
66. Letter dated January 23, 1799, from Simmons, Jackson, and Swayne at Genesinguhta to the Indian Committee in Philadelphia, as found in Simmons 1798–99 Letter Book.

Chapter Two

1. Sharpless 1798, journal entry for May 18 (p. 6 of Times-Mirror extracts reprint; forty-first leaf of manuscript book); see also, Deardorff and Snyderman 1956, 601.
2. The Quakers of that era did not use the common names for the days of the week because they were holdovers from pagan mythology. Rather, Sunday was called First Day, and so on through Saturday, or Seventh Day. For the same reason, they called the twelve months of the year First, Second, etc., starting with January. Thus, Sunday, February 3, 1799, was First Day, Second Month, Third, 1799.
3. The chiefs might have allowed Simmons to remain in their presence while they deliberated, but they probably retired elsewhere or allowed Simmons to excuse himself. The Quakers were aware of the long-established diplomatic protocol that the European-American negotiators withdrew from the council house or council fire while the Indians debated issues among themselves. After the Indians reached a decision, they sent for the negotiators and delivered their answer.
    See Kent and Deardorff 1960, 312–13; see also Proctor [1791] 1896, 479; see additionally, Pierce 1798, journal entries for May 18 and May 19 (pp. 8–9 of manuscript; fif-

teenth–seventeenth leaves of typescript) and Sharpless 1798, journal entries for May 18 and 19 (pp. 6–7 of Times-Mirror extracts reprint; forty-third–forty-fifth leaves of manuscript book).
4. Richter 1992, 8–11.
5. Morgan 1851, 156, 161–63; Wallace 1972, 85–91.
6. Sipe [1927] 1998, 465–66; PA 1896, 2-6: 729.
7. Philadelphia was the state capital until 1799, when the state government transferred its seat to Lancaster, where it remained until 1812, when Harrisburg became the capital.
8. The other chiefs, including Big Tree and Half Town, may or may not have recognized Cornplanter as the "head" of the Seneca delegation; but the Americans did. (See Washington's reply of December 29, 1790, to the Seneca speech that had been delivered December 21, as found in Hough 1861, 166, 168.) On this trip to Philadelphia and on many other occasions Cornplanter relied on the services of Joseph Nicholson as interpreter.
9. Written speech of Cornplanter, Half Town, and Big Tree to President Washington, delivered in Philadelphia on January 10, 1971, as found in Hough 1861, 170–71; see also PA 1896, 2-4: 536.
10. Letter from Cornplanter to the Quakers of Philadelphia, dated February 10, 1791, as found in Barton 1990, 1 and frontispiece; see also PYMMS Minutes for April 21, 1791.
11. Deardorff 1999, 1756–57; Deardorff and Snyderman 1956, 601 n 29.
12. Reply of Red Jacket to Reverend Cram, 1805, in Drake 1837, 98–100.
13. Broom et al. 1954, 987.
14. Wallace 1972, 167, 205.
15. Ellicott 1937, 41.
16. Evans [1924] 1979, 193–94; Ellicott 1937, 41, 52, 74, 90.
17. Ellicott 1937, 37.
18. Iroquoian is the name given to a group of related American Indian languages and peoples. The Iroquoian group includes not only the individual languages of the six Iroquois nations but also the languages of numerous other nations. These include the Hurons, Eries, and Susquehannocks. Some Iroquoians also exhibited similar cultural traits, such as hoe horticulture, adoption of war captives, and belief in the significance of dreams for health and fortune.
19. *Jesuit Relations* 54: 97, 99.
20. Ibid., 1: 259.
21. Wallace 1958, 236; St. John 1989, 137.
22. *Jesuit Relations* 33: 191, 193.
23. Wallace 1958, 237–38.
24. Ibid.
25. Ibid., 241.
26. *Jesuit Relations* 42: 165–67.

27. Biographical information about Adlum as well as the account of his canoe trip up the Allegheny from Fort Franklin to the Seneca towns is taken from Kent and Deardorff 1960, 273–74 and 294–302.
28. Way 1942, 98–99.
29. In writing "Towns" plural, Adlum was referring to both Cornplanter's village and Genesinguhta. In 1794 a sizable native population still resided at Genesinguhta.
30. Kent and Deardorff 1960, 444–45.
31. Morgan 1851, 193; Fenton [1936] 1970, 8; Wallace 1972, 55.
32. Simmons and the other missionary schoolmasters who followed him were plagued with erratic attendance by their pupils, until a boarding school was established near the reservation in 1854, guaranteeing the Quaker teachers a "captive" audience.
33. Sharpless 1798, journal entry for May 23 (p. 9 of Times-Mirror extracts reprint; fifty-fifth–fifty-sixth leaves of manuscript book).
34. When the Iroquois were still actively fighting to hold off the European Americans, captured white women were sometimes taken as permanent wives by Indian men. But, for the Senecas, the wars were over by this time.
35. Written speech of Cornplanter, Half Town, and Big Tree to President Washington, delivered in Philadelphia on January 10, 1791, as found in Hough 1861, 170 n; see also, PA 1896, 2-4: 536.
36. PA 1900, 4-5: 368–69.
37. Fenton 1951, 40.
38. Richter 1992: 105, 114, 116–20, 128, 133–34, 141–48, 155–63, 173–74, 178–80, 185–215.
39. The fighting in America effectively ended in 1760 with the fall of Montreal to the British. The Treaty of Paris, which officially ended what was known in England as the Seven Years' War, was not signed until 1763.
40. On occasion, Iroquois warriors would find themselves directly facing each other on the eve of battle, as at Lake George in 1755 when New York Mohawks confronted a group of Canadian Mohawks allied with the French. The Iroquois would then go out of their way to avoid combat with each other. (Snow 1994, 143–44.)
41. Wallace 1972, 114.
42. Graymont 1972, 34, 66, 69, 101, 112.
43. Wallace 1972, 125–34.
44. Letter from Cornplanter to Maj. Isaac Craig dated December 3, 1795, as found in Sipe [1927] 1998, 465–66. Some anthropologists restrict the use of the term acculturation, applying it to cultures but not to persons. (See Broom et al. 1954, 974–75.) Here there is no need for such a fine, technical distinction; I apply the term acculturation to both person and culture.

45. Sipe [1927] 1998, 465. According to the Warren Centennial of 1897, the first white sawmill in Warren County was built on Jackson Run in 1800.
46. Letter from Cornplanter to Maj. Isaac Craig dated December 3, 1795, as found in Sipe [1927] 1998, 465–66.
47. Deardorff 1951, 85.
48. Pierce 1798, journal entry for May 12 (p. 4 of manuscript; eighth leaf of typescript); see also letter from Gen. Richard Butler to Governor Thomas Mifflin of Pennsylvania dated March 23, 1789, in PA 1855–56, 1-11: 562–63.
49. Sharpless 1798, journal entry for May 28 (p. 13 of Times-Mirror extracts reprint; seventy-fifth leaf of manuscript book. [Note: in this case there is a slight discrepancy between the Times-Mirror extract and the manuscript book. The manuscript reads "had cost Cornplanter more than 200 dollars." The extract reads "had cost Cornplanter $200."]).
50. Kent and Deardorff 1960, 465–66.
51. Belknap and Morse [1796] 1955, 17.
52. Broom et al. 1954, 979.
53. Richter 1992, 79.
54. Ibid., 83–84.
55. Wallace 1972, 25.
56. Hultkrantz 1997, 30–31, 49, 51, 52, 61–62, 94, 95, 107, 108, 118; Pomedli 1991, 43–83; Parker 1913, 61 n. 1.
57. Hamlet, act 2, scene 2.
58. Simmons 1799, journal entry for March 1 (forty-eighth leaf of manuscript book).

Chapter Three

1. Fenton 1998, 200; Richter 1992, 388 n. 49; Jennings 1984, 231 n. 19.
2. Marietta 1984, xi–xv, 125.
3. James 1963, 247–51; Frost 1973, 57–58; Marietta 1984; 55–56.
4. Marietta 1984, 55, 234.
5. Ibid., 50, 55.
6. Ibid., 4, 55, 67, 127.
7. Frost 1973, 54–56; Marietta 1984, 5–8.
8. Marietta 1984, 58–70, 72.
9. BCCR 1994, 2: 287, men's minutes of the Middletown Monthly Meeting, minute dated March 9, 1772, Henry Simmons, Sr., acknowledged his impudent conduct in charging Martha Harper with stealing without any evidence.
10. James 1963, 12, 31, 82, 119, 130; Frost 1973, 4, 221.
11. Information on the structure and organization of the RSF and the PYM is drawn from Eckert 1989, vii–xi; James 1963, 6–16; Marietta 1984, 5; Frost 1973, 3–5, 53; Woody [1920] 1969, 17–19.
12. Quaker meetings required to keep minutes as formal records were called meetings of record;

however, not all gatherings were meetings of record. Subordinate to each monthly meeting were a number of "preparative" meetings that carried on day-to-day business between sittings of the monthly meeting. (James 1963, 7; Frost 1973, 3; Woody [1920] 1969, 19–20.)

13. Tolles 1948, 7; James 1963, 10–11; Frost 1973, 4.
14. James 1963, 9.
15. Marietta 1984, 3–4, 6–9, 17.
16. Frost 1973, 54–56; Marietta 1984, 10.
17. James 1963, 13–14, 51; Frost 1973, 177–78, 183; Marietta 1984, 28–30, 38.
18. James 1963, 9, 11; Frost 1973, 56–57; Marietta 1984, 54, 78.
19. PYMIC Collection, reel I, box 1, October 2, 1795.
20. James 1963, 5–6; Frost 1973, 35–39, 44.
21. Frost 1973, 25, 35.
22. James 1963, 14; Frost 1973, 3, 40, 52–53.
23. Ibid.
24. Eighteenth-century Friends did not use the term "inner light." (Frost 1973, 15.) They spoke instead of "an evangelical and saving light and grace in all." (Barclay [1678] 1908, 17.) Or, of the "Light" that "enlightens the hearts of all . . . to salvation." (Barclay [1678] 1908: 110) Or, they said that "a divine, spiritual, or supernatural light is in all men." (Barclay [1678] 1908, 141.)
25. Barclay [1678] 1908, 137–39, 141–42.
26. James 1963, 281.
27. Barclay [1678] 1908, 121–22, 132, 164–65, 262–63.
28. Barclay [1678] 1908, 94.
29. Fox [1694] 1906, 12; Frost 1973, 152–53, 167.
30. Barclay [1678] 1908, 28, 72.
31. Ibid., 54, 78.
32. Marietta 1984, 169.
33. Ibid., 170.
34. James 1963, 91.
35. Ibid., 142–43; Marietta 1984, 136–37.
36. Tolles 1948, 18–19; James 1963, 156; Marietta 1984, 154.
37. Marietta 1984, 137; Matthew 22: 21 King James Version.
38. Marietta 1984, 140–41, 151–53.
39. Ibid., 131–49.
40. James 1963, 165–66; Frost 1973, 191; Marietta 1984, 154–55, 170–74.
41. Tolles 1948, 26–27; James 1963, 167; Marietta 1984, 156, 158, 164.
42. Marietta 1984, 158.
43. Marietta 1984, 165; Tolles (1948, 28) says that these four had been "elected against their wishes and refused to claim their seats."
44. Tolles 1948, 231–32; James 1963, 156; Marietta 1984, 131–35.
45. James 1963, 165; Marietta 1984, 140–41, 146, 151–53, 156.

46. Marietta 1984, 144–46, 159–61.
47. James 1963, 167; Marietta 1984, 5, 147.
48. Tolles 1948, 235; Marietta 1984, 164–65.
49. Marietta 1984, 103–4, 170.
50. James 1963, 177–78.
51. James 1963, 166; Marietta 1984, 131–32, 155, 171.
52. Frost 1973, 191, 202; Marietta 1984, 171–72, 174.
53. Marietta 1984, 174–75.
54. Tolles 1948, 235; James 1963, 167; Marietta 1984, 78, 116, 178–79.
55. Marietta 1984, 179–82.
56. James 1963, 178–81, 190.
57. James 1963, 181–92.
58. James 1963, 191.
59. Marietta 1984, 188–95.
60. Marietta 1984, 222.
61. Romans 13:1 KJV.
62. James 1963, 243–44; Marietta 1984, 264, 266, 268–69.
63. Marietta 1984, 203–4, 209–13, 222–24.
64. Ibid., 225.
65. Frost 1973, 191, 202; Marietta 1984, 258, 261, 266, 278.
66. Marietta 1984, 227–28, 236.
67. Marietta 1984, 231–32.
68. Ibid., 236–37.
69. Marietta 1984, 237; Frost 1973, 190–91.
70. Tolles 1948, 8.
71. Matthew 5:34–37 KJV.
72. James 1963, 245; Marietta 1984, 237, 269.
73. Marietta 1984, 237–39.
74. James 1963, 245; Marietta 1984, 239–42.
75. Marietta 1984, 244–45.
76. Ibid., 247–48.
77. Ibid., 19–21, 105, 107–8.
78. Ibid., 108.
79. James 1963, 255–57, 271; Marietta 1984, 108.
80. James 1963, 119–27; Frost 1973, 218; Marietta 1984, 112–13.
81. Marietta 1984, 114, 116; James 1963, 127–28.
82. James 1963, 218–19; Marietta 1984, 78, 116–18.
83. James 1963, 219; Marietta 1984, 118.
84. James 1963, 225–27; Marietta 1984, 119–20.
85. James 1963, 227–28; Marietta 1984, 120.
86. Marietta 1984, 111.
87. James 1963, 96.
88. Tolles 1948, 65; James 1963, 58.
89. Tolles 1948, 65–69; James 1963, 34, 44–59.
90. James 1963, 8, 23.
91. Ibid., 52.
92. Ibid., 46.
93. Ibid., 48–50.
94. Ibid., 52, 55–56; Frost 1973, 60.
95. James 1963, 194.
96. Ibid., 58.
97. Tolles 1948, 69–73.
98. James 1963, 76–83.

99. Ibid., 172–73, 178, 182–83, 184–85.
100. Ibid., 183–86.
101. Ibid., 186–89.
102. Ibid., 178.
103. Ibid.
104. Ibid., 100–2.
105. Tolles 1948, 72; James 1963, 201–4.
106. James 1963, 238–39; Marietta 1984, 273.
107. James 1963, 231–34.
108. Ibid., 234–38.
109. Ibid., 259–63; Marietta 1984, 273.
110. James 1963, 298–99; Marietta 1984, 278; Jackson 1830b, 22–27.
111. It is not clear whether Cornplanter met with Friends or just sent them a letter upon his departure from Philadelphia. In either case, he definitely reached out to them in a letter dated February 10, 1791. (Letter from Cornplanter to the Quakers of Philadelphia, as found in Barton 1990, 1 and frontispiece; see also PYMMS Minutes for April 21, 1791.) Cornplanter asked Philadelphia Friends to take in and to educate his son Henry, another boy, and the son of Cornplanter's interpreter, Joseph Nicholson. The Quakers agreed to take the boys. Cornplanter, however, had also approached the new federal government during his Philadelphia visit. Before the Quakers responded to his request, President Washington had dispatched Waterman Baldwin to Cornplanter's village, to serve as schoolteacher. Cornplanter deferred sending the children to Philadelphia, explaining in a letter to the Quakers that "as General Washington had sent a schoolmaster amongst us, Mr. Baldwin . . . we mean to let him teach them a little first and then take your offer and will send them down." (Deardorff and Snyderman 1956, 584.)
112. James 1963, 300–1.
113. Ibid., 301–5.
114. Marietta 1984, 24; Friends Historical Library, Swarthmore College, microfilm MR-Ph305, Middletown MM, men's minutes, February 5, 1801. Also, microfilm MR-Ph304, Middletown MM, men's minutes, March 5, 1801.
115. James 1963, 8, 226; Marietta 1984, 5.
116. BCCR 1994, 3: 46, men's minutes of the Wrightstown MM, minute dated March 5, 1757; BCCR 1994, 2: 276, men's minutes of the Middletown MM, minute dated July 7, 1757.
117. BCCR 1994, 2: 214, Middletown MM births and deaths, listed by parents and their children, including marriage date of parents.
118. Frost 1973, 158–59; Marietta 1984, 56, 62.
119. Frost 1973, 154–55.
120. Marietta 1984, 10–19.
121. Frost 1973, 155, 159–60.
122. James 1963, 8; Frost 1973, 172–73, 183; Marietta 1984, 58.

123. Frost 1973, 173–74, 183; Marietta 1984, 58.
124. Frost 1973, 173–74, 183.
125. Marietta 1984, 61–62, 67.
126. Information on the family visitation program is drawn from Tolles 1948, 239; James 1963, 174; Frost 1973, 53–54; and Marietta 1984, 75, 259.
127. Mary Paxon Simmons died on July 5, 1769. (BCCR 1994, 2: 214, Middletown MM births and deaths.)
128. BCCR 1994, 2: 214, Middletown MM births and deaths.
129. Ibid., 286, men's minutes of the Middletown MM, minute dated February 7, 1771.
130. Two of Henry Simmons's brothers died in early childhood, one his full brother, the other his half brother. (BCCR 1994, 2: 214, Middletown MM births and deaths.)
131. The discussion on Henry Simmons's education, on the problems typical of late-eighteenth-century rural Quaker education, and on the eventual educational reforms is informed by the following sources: Woody [1920] 1969, 22–23, 92–95, 104, 167–71; James 1963, 65, 72–75, 253–55; Frost 1973, 97–98, 101–2, 105, 108, 111, 123, 129.
132. The discussion on Friends' city schools is informed by the following sources: Woody [1920] 1969, 41–84; James 1963, 65–69; Frost 1973, 101.
133. Frost 1973, 56–57; Marietta 1984, 6–7.
134. Marietta 1984, 22.
135. Tolles 1948, 75–77, 251–52; Frost 1973, 49, 200–1.
136. Marietta 1984, 5; Tolles 1948, 58–59, 73–74; Frost 1973, 199–200.
137. Tolles 1948, 74–75; Frost 1973, 201; Marietta 1984, 23–24.
138. Tolles 1948, 8–9, 135, 137, 138, 186–87, 208–9; Frost 1973, 207–9.
139. Certificate issued by Middletown MM, dated May 5, 1796, as found in Simmons 1796–97 Journal.
140. PYMIC Minutes, minute dated December 21, 1799, copied and endorsed on reverse side of Simmons's certificate of approval from Middletown, which was found in Simmons 1796–97 Journal.
141. Deardorff and Snyderman 1956, 586; Snyderman 1957, 568; Barton 1990, 4.
142. Wallace 1972, 221; Deardorff and Snyderman 1956, 587; PYMIC Collection, reel I, box 1, letter from Henry Simmons to PYMIC, dated May 23, 1797.
143. Snyderman 1957, 568; Barton 1990, 4; Wallace 1972, 221; for more details on Henry Simmons's missionary background prior to his arrival at Cornplanter's village, see PYMIC Minutes, microfilm MR-Ph490,

roll 8, where Henry Simmons, Jr., is indexed as follows:

144. Emlen [1794] 1965, 299–300.
145. PYMIC Proceedings 1806, 5; James 1963, 94–95, 305, 311–12, 314, 328, 331, 332.
146. Sharpless 1798, journal entry for May 30 (p. 17 of Times-Mirror extracts reprint).
147. Jackson 1830b, 79.
148. Ibid., 83–84.
149. James 1963, 1, 2, 21, 22, 247, 330, 333.
150. Ibid., 266–67.
151. Ibid., 86–87.
152. Marietta 1984, xv, 113–14, 122–28, 273, 309.
153. Woolman [1794] 1909, 265.
154. Emlen [1794] 1965, 313.
155. James 1963, 89, 99–100, 298, 317, 331–32.

Chapter Four

1. Richter 1992, 20.
2. Ibid.,11, 14, 21; Tooker 1984, 111.
3. Richter 1992, 14–15.
4. Ibid., 21.
5. Ibid., 21, 39.
6. Fenton [1936] 1970, 13, 16; Beauchamp 1896, 269, 270; Boyle 1898, 128.
7. Sagard [1636] 1866, 243–45; *Jesuit Relations* 1896–1901, 10: 187–89, 17: 201–5; Perrot 1911, 101–2; Charlevoix [1744] 1761, 2: 12–16; Loskiel 1794, 106–7; Morgan 1851, 307–11; Beauchamp 1896, 270–71; Boyle 1898, 126–28; Culin 1975, 112, 118.
8. Beauchamp 1896, 270–71.
9. Stone [1838] 1864, 449.
10. Beauchamp 1896, 273.
11. Lahontan 1735, 2: 20; Morgan 1851, 294; Hewitt 1892, 190; Eyeman 1964, 18; Oxendine 1988, 41; Stone [1838] 1864, 447–48.
12. Morgan 1851, 294; Culin 1975, 594. Lacrosse stick length varied. Specimens held in museum collections and described by contemporaneous observers range in length from 3.5 to 5 feet. The Seneca stick described by Lewis Henry Morgan in 1851 was 5 feet long. Morgan reported that this type of stick had been in use among the Senecas for so long "that they have lost the date" (Morgan 1851, 298). The long, 5-foot stick was probably the type in use around the year 1799.
13. Hewitt 1892, 189. In the 1500s, the 1600s, and the 1700s, the ball was made from a knot of wood, obtained from a rotted tree, and rounded by carving. The twisted grain of the wood made the ball tough. (Perrot 1911, 93; Morgan 1851, 298; Oxendine 1988, 42, 44.) Sometime around the end of the 1700s, American Indians started making lacrosse balls of sewn buckskin. (Oxendine 1988, 44.) It is thus possible that during the 1790s, the Senecas were still using wooden lacrosse balls.
14. Oxendine 1988, 44; Culin 1975, 592.
15. Stone [1838] 1864, 448; Morgan 1851, 295; Vennum 1994, 247.
16. Catlin [1841] 1973, 2: 126; Hewitt 1892, 190.
17. Morgan 1851, 297; Catlin [1841] 1973, 2: 126.
18. Stone [1838] 1864, 447; Morgan 1851, 294; Hewitt 1892, 189–91; Vennum 1994, 248.
19. Morgan 1851, 297.
20. Catlin [1841] 1973, 2: 126.
21. Vennum 1994, 186.
22. Ibid.,186.
23. Stone [1838] 1864, 448.
24. Morgan 1851, 295; Hewitt 1892, 191; Vennum 1994, 46. Ritual preparation might also have included abstinence from sex. Sexual abstinence was definitely part of the Cherokee pre- and postgame ritual. (Vennum 1994, 218.) The Cherokees were Iroquoian, so other Iroquois players might have observed similar ritual restrictions. Any such restrictions among the Iroquois, however, are undocumented, which is not to say they did not exist.
25. Hewitt 1892, 191; Eyeman 1964, 18; Vennum 1994, 41, 170.
26. Hewitt 1892, 191; Vennum 1994,166–67.
27. Vennum 1994, 170–71; Mooney 1890, 122.
28. Vennum 1994, 38, 169.
29. Ibid.,40–41.
30. Mooney 1890, 108–9; Vennum 1994, 28–29.
31. Hewitt 1892, 191; Vennum 1994, 28.
32. Hewitt 1892, 191.
33. Oxendine 1988, 31; Vennum 1994, 107.
34. *Jesuit Relations* 1896–1901, 10: 185.
35. Perrot 1911, 94.
36. Stone W [1838] 1864, 446–47; Hewitt 1892, 191.
37. Oxendine 1988, 31; Vennum 1994, 110.
38. Lahontan 1735, 2: 20; Vennum 1994, 108, 109; Stone W [1838] 1864, 447.
39. Morgan 1851, 293.
40. Vennum 1994, 110.
41. Stone W [1838] 1864, 447; Vennum 1994, 113.
42. Mooney 1890, 114–19; Vennum 1994, 41–43.

43. Converse [1908] 1981, 146; Hewitt 1892, 191; Speck 1949, 118; Morgan 1851, 269.
44. *Jesuit Relations* 1896–1901, 10: 185–87.
45. Perrot 1911, 96.
46. Sagard [1636] 1866, 243; Perrot 1911, 96–101.
47. Wallace 1972, 319; Vennum 1994, 222; Eyeman 1964, 19.
48. *Jesuit Relations* 1896–1901, 14: 47; Speck 1949, 117–18; Eyeman 1964, 18.
49. Eyeman 1964, 19; Vennum 1994, 222.
50. *Jesuit Relations* 1896–1901, 10: 185; Shimony [1961] 1994, 278; 1994, Eyeman 1964, 19; Wallace 1972, 245, 247.
51. *Jesuit Relations* 1896–1901, 13: 131.
52. Richter 1992, 25, 29.
53. Ibid., 10, 24.
54. Jennings 1985, 116.
55. Vennum 1994, 38–41.
56. Richter 1992, 24–25.
57. Mooney 1890, 111; Vennum 1994, 28.
58. Vennum 1994, 213.
59. Ibid., 220–21.
60. Ibid., 234.
61. Ibid., 229.
62. Ibid., xiv.
63. Ibid.,112.
64. Ibid.,112, 231.
65. Ibid., 231.
66. Tooker 1970, 105.
67. Ely S. Parker was Morgan's primary informant and his major source of ethnographic detail. Parker was a Tonawanda Seneca sachem who later served on the military staff of Gen. Ulysses S. Grant. By the end of the Civil War Parker had risen to the rank of lieutenant colonel, subsequently becoming a brigadier general. The amazing extent of Morgan's reliance on Parker is revealed in Fenton (1941b, 147–58). Morgan dedicated *The League of the Iroquois* to Parker with the following inscription: To Hasanoanda (Ely S. Parker), a Seneca Indian, this work, the materials of which are the fruits of our joint researches, is inscribed in acknowledgment of the obligations and in testimony of the friendship of the author.

Chapter Five

1. Fewer than 100 Senecas emigrated to Canada during and after the American Revolution. (Public Archives of Canada, Haldimand Papers, B 103, 457, found as exhibit B19, *A Census of the Six Nations on the Grand River, 1785,* in Johnston 1964, 52.) In 1792 the United States prepared a census return that reported a Seneca population of 1,700 persons. (Henry O'Reilly Collection, New York Historical Society, Papers Relating to the Six Nations Indians, VIII—as cited in Johnston 1964, introduction, xli, n. 15.) Ten years later,

Harm Jan Huidekoper estimated the combined population of Buffalo Creek, Tonawanda, and Cattaraugus to be between 1,400 and 1,500. (Tiffany and Tiffany 1904, 72.) The approximately 360 people at Cornplanter's village would bring the total to between 1,760 and 1,860 persons by the year 1802. For additional estimates of Seneca population during the 1790s, see Fenton 1998, 629, 688–89.

2. Letter from Henry Simmons at Jenuchshadago to Israel Chapin, U.S. Agent to the Six Nations at Canandaigua, N.Y., dated March 25, 1799, as found in PA State Archives, in RG5, Kent-Barnard, series 3, general correspondence, LC box 3 and 4, 1799–1924.

3. Memorandum containing the speech of Capt. J. Bruff and the replies of Red Jacket and Farmer's Brother. (Henry O'Reilly Collection, New York Historical Society, Papers Relating to the Six Nations Indians, XV—as quoted and cited in Wilkinson 1953, 257.)

4. Densmore 1999, 91.

5. Sosin 1961, 106.

6. Ibid., 45–46, 169; Van Every 1961, 315–16.

7. McConnell 1992, 48–50; Van Every 1961, 34–35.

8. McConnell 1992, 238–39, 243–44; Van Every 1961, 258, 528–29; Downes 1940, 135–38; Sosin 1961, 109–10.

9. McConnell 1992, 248; Sosin 1961, 106; Downes 1940, 136, 138–40.

10. McConnell 1992, 248; Marshall 1967, 163, 165–66; Sosin 1961, 163, 169–72; Billington 1944, 182–83.

11. McConnell 1992, 248, 250–51. Ten years earlier the British had constructed Fort Stanwix to guard the portage route between the upper Mohawk River and Wood Creek, between waters that flow into the Atlantic Ocean and those that flow into Lake Ontario. After their victory in the French and Indian War, the British abandoned the post in 1766 as an economizing measure, leaving only a groundskeeper-caretaker. (PSWJ 1921–65, 7: 328, 335.)

12. DRCHSNY 1853–57, 7: 728. Peter Marshall has pointed out that the Six Nations made this outlandish proposal only after Johnson had rejected their proposal for a line that ran northeast from present-day Harrisburg, Pennsylvania to Fort Edward, located on the Hudson about 50 miles upriver from Albany, New York. [Marshall 1967, 163.] They had offered the Fort Edward-Harrisburg line knowing full well that Johnson would reject it. The Six Nations wanted to dramatically emphasize their discontent over what was happening to the Mohawks, who were about to be cheated out of 800,000 acres—their last major landholding—around Kayaderosseras Creek by a fraudulent land patent. Johnson responded that he had been

working diligently for a long time to annul the Kayaderosseras patent and was confident the Mohawk complaint would be redressed. He said it was unfortunate that the Six Nations had decided to interpose Kayaderosseras as an impediment to delineating a realistic boundary. In reply, the Six Nations delegates said: "We hope our behavior on this occasion will have a proper effect upon the Great King, and induce him to hearken to our complaints." They then offered the sweeping cession of northeastern and southwestern Pennsylvania, West Virginia, and Kentucky. (DRCHSNY 1853–57, 7: 726–28.)

Johnson noted that their second proposal did not address the issue of where the line should fall across New York. This section of the line was critical to the Six Nations because it would define the eastern border for their homelands. The Iroquois told Johnson they had decided to leave the matter open for the time being, because it was so complicated. (DRCHSNY 1853–57, 7: 729–30) While there is no doubt that Sir William Johnson exerted tremendous influence over the Iroquois, it seems that the idea of opening Kentucky to settlement originated with the Six Nations. There is nothing in Johnson's reports or correspondence to suggest otherwise. For background on the Kayaderosseras patent, see DRCHSNY 1853–57, 7: 576–77 and PSWJ 1921–65, 4: 360, 749; 11: 712–13. For corroboration that Johnson viewed the Fort Edward-Harrisburg proposal as a form of Iroquois protest over the Kayaderosseras patent, see PSWJ 1921–65, 4: 746–47; 11: 714, 747–48.

13. McConnell 1992, 250, 257; Wallace 1972, 122; Van Every 1961, 281, 283; Brewster 1954, 145; Billington 1944, 186.

14. Downes 1944, 121–22, 134; McConnell 1992, 137–38, 235–37, 245–47; Marshall 1967, 163.

15. McConnell 1992, 246–47, 252.

16. Ibid., 250; Sosin 1961, 172–73, 176; Billington 1944, 184.

17. Sosin 1961, 163, 169, 171.

18. Marshall 1967, 160–61. As Marshall points out, Johnson also had his own speculative interests in New York lands. (See Marshall 1967, 158–60.)

19. For background on Johnson's links to George Croghan, Samuel Wharton, the "suffering traders" of Pennsylvania, and the Indiana Land Company, see Marshall 1967, 161–62, 164, 169, 172–73, 177–79 and Billington 1944, 189–91.

20. Marshall 1967, 178; Billington 1944, 192–93. If the Virginia speculators had not been satisfied, they could have obstructed efforts by several of Johnson's associates to obtain a land grant in present-day West Virginia.

21. McConnell 1992, 243–44.

22. SCP 1930–33, 1: lxxii, lxxxiv; Brewster 1954, 38.

23. Marshall 1967, 160, 171–72.

24. Donehoo 1926, 509–46.

25. McConnell 1992, 48–49, 253. Even Sir William Johnson doubted the validity of the Iroquois claim (Billington 1944, 187).

26. McConnell 1992, 251; Marshall 1967, 176; Van Every 1961, 283; Brewster 1954, 144–45; Buck and Buck [1939] 1979, 114.

27. Downes 1940, 17; Jennings 1984, 135–36, 140, 229–30, 321; Richter 1992, 98, 102, 114–15, 136, 150; McConnell 1992, 5–7. Listed according to present-day state, the Ohio Country watersheds were as follows. Ohio: Muskingum, Scioto, Miami, and Cuyahoga. Western Pennsylvania: Allegheny, Monongahela, and Beaver. Northern West Virginia: Cheat and Youghiogheny.

28. Jennings 1984, 351.

29. McConnell 1992, 9–20; Downes 1940, 18; Snow 1994, 115; Hunt 1940, 92–94.

30. McConnell 1992, 62.

31. Ibid., 15, 19–20, 62, 210.

32. Ibid., 80; Richter 1992, 256; Jennings 1984, 308.

33. McConnell 1992, 58–60, 71, 77–80, 106–7, 236, 246–48.

34. Kelsay 1984, 46–48.

35. Ibid., 48, 78–79; Nammack 1969, 53–54. Nammack's chapter 4, "The Kayaderosseras Grant," thoroughly covers the history of this lengthy and nearly intractable patent dispute to its resolution in 1768 (Nammack 1969, 53–69).

36. McConnell 1992, 256; Downes 1940, 135, 143–44.

37. Graymont 1972, 48, 58, 66, 72, 80, 91, 94–95, 103, 107–8.

38. Ibid., 60, 64, 67, 86–87, 91, 94–95.

39. Ibid., 74–79.

40. Also spelled Kahnawake. The Caughnawagas were a mixture of American Indian nationalities, including Huron, Oneida, and Onondaga, but most Caughnawaga residents were of Mohawk descent. All the Caughnawagas were Roman Catholics—their ancestors had converted during the 1600s, influenced by French Jesuit and other French Catholic missionaries. To escape the factional disputes with native traditionalists and to have access to Catholic priests, the ancestors of the Caughnawagas emigrated to Canada during the 1660s and 1670s. Because Mohawks were the dominant element, their settlement—a mission called Saint Francois Xavier du Sault—on the Saint Lawrence River opposite Montreal came to be known as Caughnawaga, after the name of the easternmost Mohawk town in New York. (Snow 1994, 121–22; Richter 1992, 119–20; Graymont 1972, 59.)

41. Guy Johnson was both nephew and son-in-law of Sir William Johnson, who had been the royal superintendent of the northern Indian district until his death in 1774, when Guy succeeded him. (Graymont 1972, 49–50.)
42. Graymont 1972, 60, 66–69, 75–78, 85, 94, 100.
43. Ibid., 75, 94, 117.
44. Ibid., 61, 89, 104.
45. Ibid., 98–99, speeches of Kayashuta (Guyasuta) and Flying Crow.
46. Kirkland began his missionary work among the Oneidas in 1766. Prior to that he had worked among the Senecas for almost two years. (Graymont 1972, 34–40.)
47. Graymont 1972, 111.
48. Ibid., 58. Graymont found the quoted material in the Kirkland Papers at Hamilton College and gave the following citation: "Speech of Oneida to Gov. Trumbull, March 1775 (misfiled in 1777 folder)."
49. Graymont 1972, 106.
50. Wallace 1972, 130.
51. In 1775 the Second Continental Congress appointed Philip Schuyler as one of several Indian commissioners, whose task, initially, was to secure Iroquois neutrality. Schuyler quickly emerged as the leading commissioner. He headed the American delegation at the Albany neutrality conference in August 1775, until he was called away to command the American military expedition into Canada. Illness forced him to relinquish command before Montreal was captured by the Americans. After convalescing in New York, Schuyler was given command of the northern military department, which post he held until relieved by Gen. Horatio Gates just before the battle of Saratoga in 1777. Schuyler's views on Indian policy subsequently influenced Henry Knox and George Washington.
52. Graymont 1972, 95.
53. Ibid., 71–73; Wallace 1972, 129–30.
54. Graymont 1972, 82–83; 92–94.
55. Ibid., 106–8.
56. Ibid., 101, 111–12.
57. Ibid., 91–92.
58. Ibid., 73, 87–90, 92, 107–8.
59. Ibid., 99, 120, 122–24, 164.
60. Tory luminaries such as Guy Johnson, who organized the Indians for the successful royalist defense of Canada, and John Johnson, who organized a loyalist fighting force that was often augmented by Iroquois warriors, certainly did their part for the king's cause. But no one else incessantly wooed the Iroquois to the British side as did John Butler, for which he was awarded a promotion to the rank of lieutenant colonel.
61. Graymont 1972, 94–99, 126–28.
62. Ibid., 108–11.
63. Ibid., 56–57, 60, 62, 65–66, 100–1, 112–13.
64. Ibid., 52, 103, 110.
65. King William's War (1689–97), also known as the War of the League of Augsburg; Queen Anne's War (1702–13), also known as the War of the Spanish Succession; King George's War (1744–48), also known as the War of the Austrian Succession; and the French and Indian War (1754–63), also known as the Seven Years' War (because war was not formally declared in Europe until 1756).
66. War chiefs had traditionally arranged the terms of cease-fire agreements. Iroquois thinking seems to have been that warriors had conducted the fighting and only they could end it, with warriors on both sides agreeing to a termination of hostilities. Larger issues relating to reparations, land cessions, and other matters that might be included in an actual peace treaty were beyond the purview of the war chiefs. With their enhanced influence, however, war chiefs began not only to negotiate the terms of treaties involving these larger issues, but also, abetted by European-American negotiators, to commit to obligations on behalf of their nations.
67. Graymont 1972, 280.
68. Ibid., 163.
69. Ibid., 113; Wallace 1972, 132.
70. Graymont 1972, 120–28, 165.
71. Ibid., 135, 142, 146–47.
72. Wallace 1972, 140–41.
73. Graymont 1972, 192–94.
74. Ibid., 196; Wallace 1972, 141–42.
75. Graymont 1972, 206; Wallace 1972, 142.
76. Wallace 1972, 143.
77. Ibid., 143.
78. Graymont 1972, 220, 222–23, 229–41; Wallace 1972, 144–48.
79. Graymont 1972, 245; Wallace 1972, 146.
80. Graymont 1972, 254–56; Downes 1940, 281.
81. Downes 1940, 276.
82. Ibid., 277–78.
83. Kelsay 1984, 366; Manley 1932, 92; Graymont 1972, 297–98; Densmore 1999, 129–30.
84. Graymont 1972, 298; Densmore 1999, 130.
85. Downes 1940, 278.
86. Graymont 1972, 241; Wallace 1972, 148–49; Densmore 1999, 15; Downes 1940, 252–53, 259–60, 287.
87. Downes 1940, 280–81, 283; Manley 1932, 21; Graymont 1972, 276–78.
88. They came close once, during the summer of 1794. Cornplanter, disillusioned with the Americans and impressed by the military successes of the Western Confederates, was on the verge of opening hostilities with the United States, when news of Anthony Wayne's victory over the Western Confederates at Fallen Timbers deterred him from the warpath.

89. I have dated the Constitution according to the year in which it was ratified—1788.
90. Buck and Buck [1939] 1979, 205.
91. Wallace 1972, 211.
92. Ibid., 155, 212; Buck and Buck [1939] 1979, 207–8.
93. Buck and Buck [1939] 1979, 205–6.
94. Ibid., 208–9.
95. The Trans-Appalachian West includes those lands between the Appalachian Mountains and the Mississippi River, south of the Great Lakes, and north of the two Spanish Floridas (East and West Florida).
96. Downes 1940, 284–85.
97. Prucha 1994, 50 n. 21.
98. Manley 1932, 21; Kelsay 1984, 351, 363; Graymont 1972, 284.
99. Except for Red Jacket, who suffered several failures of nerve. Unlike Cornplanter and Brant, Red Jacket was never a war chief; his talent was that of orator.
100. Manley 1932, 73.
101. Downes 1940, 289–90; Manley 1932, 73–75.
102. Graymont 1972, 273, 278; McConnell 1992, 250–51; Manley 1932, 87.
103. Downes 1940, 282; Manley 1932, 19.
104. Sword 1985, 13; Graymont 1972, 259–60; Downes: 283–84, 287; Manley 1932, 17–18.
105. Sword 1985, 20; Graymont 1972, 277–78; Calloway 1995, 277.
106. Treaty of Fort Stanwix, 1784, found as appendix A in Graymont 1972, 297–98, and as appendix A in Densmore 1999, 129–30; also in Prucha 1990, 5.
107. Manley 1932, 10, 49, 82, 96, 100; Graymont 1972, 278.
108. Manley 1932, 78–81; Graymont 1972, 273–74.
109. Downes 1940, 290; Manley 1932, 90–91, 93.
110. Manley 1932, 89–90; Graymont 1972, 279–80.
111. Manley 1932, 91–92; Graymont 1972, 281–82.
112. Manley 1932, 92, 96–97, 101–4; Graymont 1972, 282.
113. Manley 1932, 101; Graymont 1972, 282.
114. Fenton 1998, 610; Manley 1932, 60.
115. Manley 1932, 72; Fenton 1998, 620.
116. Kelsay 1984, 367; Graymont 1972, 283. The official Pennsylvania records, however, show that, prior to the treaty, $9,000 was authorized for expenditure on treaty goods (PA 1855–56, 1-10: 317) and £3,375 was actually spent (PCR 14: 186). The records show that, after the treaty, an additional $1,000 was authorized and spent on treaty goods. The expense of transporting the goods to the treaty site was funded separately in the amount of £600 (PA 1855–56, 1-10: 333). See also PCR 14: 186–87, 205; PA 1855–56, 1-10: 317–19, 333, 489, 496, 610.

117. PA 1855–56, 1-11: 507–9.
118. Graymont 1972, 266; Manley 1932, 48; Jennings 1985, 201; Calloway 1995, 286.
119. Lord Dunmore's War culminated a conflict over possession of Kentucky that had been raging for years between the Virginians and the Shawnees, who did not want to surrender their Kentucky hunting grounds. (McConnell 1992, 268–81.)
120. Wallace 1972, 154; McConnell 1992, 268–79.
121. The Erie Triangle is easily discerned on a modern map of Pennsylvania. The eastern boundary of the triangle is the western boundary of New York, extending southward from the south shore of Lake Erie. The triangle's southern boundary is an imaginary westward extension of the northern boundary of Pennsylvania, which coincides with the forty-second parallel (42° north latitude), extending westward to the southern shore of Lake Erie. The third side of the triangle is the southern shore of Lake Erie between the intersection of the forty-second parallel with the southern shore of Lake Erie and the northern terminus of the western boundary between Pennsylvania and New York.
122. Fenton 1998, 685, 692–95.
123. Most of the Seneca homelands lay west of a longitudinal line that in 1785 would become known as the "preemption line." The line ran from Sodus Bay on the south shore of Lake Ontario, southward through Seneca Lake, to the eighty-second milestone on the northern boundary of Pennsylvania. The Seneca territories east of the preemption line were dwarfed by their homeland territories on the west side of the line, which comprised about 6 million acres within the present-day state of New York. In 1784 at second Stanwix, however, the United States had annexed roughly a million acres of this territory, leaving the Senecas in possession of roughly 5 million acres of their ancestral homelands.
124. Second Stanwix in 1784; the Treaty of Fort McIntosh, near present-day Beaver, Pennsylvania, concluded in 1785 with some "representatives" of the Delawares and the Wyandots of Ohio; and the Treaty at the Mouth of the Great Miami River, concluded in 1786 with representatives from some of the Shawnees of Ohio.
125. Cornplanter, himself one of the signatories of second Stanwix, and other Iroquois headmen did repeatedly register their protests with American officials about the inequity of the 1784 treaty, until the Treaty of Canandaigua restored a measure of fairness to the relationship between the United States and the Six Nations in 1794.
126. Downes 1940, 294; Sword 1985, 28.

127. Downes 1940, 297; Sword 1985, 30.
128. The Shawnee nation had traditionally comprised five tribes, the Chalahgawthas, the Thawegilas, the Maykujays, the Kispokothas, and the Piquas. Having endured a century-long diaspora from their territory in present-day southern Ohio and northern Kentucky, all five tribes had reassembled in the Scioto River watershed of present-day Ohio by about 1750. In 1774, however, at the conclusion of Lord Dunmore's War—which was the culmination of a vicious cycle of revenge and retaliation between Shawnees and Virginians—most of the Thawegilas left Ohio and once again moved south, seeking refuge among the Creek Indians of present-day Alabama. In 1779 during the fighting with the United States, most of the Kispokotha and Piqua tribes abandoned Ohio and moved into Spanish territory along the border between present-day Missouri and Illinois. (Edmunds 1983, 7–12.)
129. Sword 1985, 29; Wallace 1972, 158.
130. Wallace 1972, 163–65.
131. Henry Knox was secretary of war from 1785 to 1789 under the Articles of Confederation and from 1789 to 1794 under the Constitution. During the Revolutionary War, he had served as Washington's chief of artillery and risen to the rank of major general. He retired from government service in 1794.

    Timothy Pickering served as postmaster general from 1791 to 1795, during which time he doubled as commissioner of Indian affairs under Knox. He succeeded Knox as secretary of war in 1795 until becoming secretary of state from 1795 to 1800. Later he served as a U. S. senator from Massachusetts from 1803 to 1811 and a U. S. congressman from 1813 to 1817. During the Revolutionary War he had been Washington's quartermaster general.
132. Sword 1985, 67; Wallace 1972, 156, 160, 176–77; Harmon 1941, 10–19; Manley 1932, 54–57; Prucha 1994, 54, 89–91.
133. Manley 1932, 31, 44–47; Graymont 1972, 264, 287, 290; Sword 1985, 27, 83; Horsman 1967, 6–9. Even Thomas Jefferson subscribed to this theory. See his letter to William Henry Harrison, dated February 27, 1803, as found in Prucha [1975] 1990: 22–23, and also in the *Writings of Thomas Jefferson,* edited by Andrew A. Lipscomb [Washington, D.C.: Thomas Jefferson Memorial Association, 1903–04], 10: 369–71.
134. Letter from George Washington to Congressman James Duane, dated September 7, 1783, as found in Manley 1932, 47; Horsman 1967, 9; and Prucha 1990, 2. This lengthy letter touched the salient points of Indian policy. The

influence of Philip Schuyler's opinions on Washington is clear. (See the letter from Schuyler to the president of the Second Continental Congress dated July 29, 1783, as found in Horsman 1967, 6–7 [Manley 1932, 31, 44].) Washington's letter is also in *The Writings of George Washington from the Original Manuscripts, 1745–1779,* edited by John C. Fitzpatrick (Washington, D.C.: U.S. Government Printing Office, 1931–44), 27: 133–40. Schuyler's letter is in the papers of the Second Continental Congress, 1774–89, item 153, III, 601–7, National Archives.
135. Horsman 1967, 38, 42, 44–45; Prucha 1994, 54–55; Sword 1985, 60–61, 65–67.
136. Sword 1985, 74–75; Wallace 1972, 158–59.
137. Prucha 1994, 56–58.
138. Silverberg 1971, 24–25; Philbrick 1965, 114–20.
139. Previously, Virginia had also claimed territories that included the Erie Triangle, but it ceded those claims to Pennsylvania in 1779 in a bilateral arrangement that fixed both the western extent of Pennsylvania's southern boundary and its western boundary. The western end of Pennsylvania's southern boundary was not surveyed until 1784, and the state's western boundary was not surveyed until 1786. (Rieseman 1943, 1: 210–12.)
140. PA 1855–56, 1-11: 526–28, 530–31; PA 1855–56, 1-12: 103; PA 1855–56, 1-12: 103.
141. Rieseman 1943, 1: 210–15; PA 1855–56, 1-11: 251–52, 308–11, 313–14, 387–91; PA 1855–56, 1-12: 100–1; PA 1896, 2-6: 672; PCR 15: 530–31.
142. PA 1855–56, 1-11: 528–33; PA 1855–56, 1-12: 100–4; PCR 15: 553–55, 604–5; PCR 16: 36–37.
143. Sword 1985, 86–116, 171–91.
144. Ibid., 79–200.
145. Ibid., 203–4.
146. Ibid., 201–37.
147. Sword 1985, 247; Horsman 1967, 42–43.
148. Sword 1985, 238–46; Kelsay 1984, 488–90, 496–504; Philbrick 1965, 155–56; Fenton 1998, 638.
149. Calloway 1995, 287–88.
150. Sword 1985, 246–98; Prucha 1994, 91–92. In violation of the 1783 Treaty of Paris between Great Britain and the United States, the British had failed to evacuate their garrisons from the forts on the American side of the Great Lakes: Oswego, Niagara, Detroit, and Michilimackinac. Belatedly realizing their blunder in giving up the whole Trans-Appalachian West, the British held on to these lakeside posts as a means of preserving their influence among Indian tribes in the area, and of perpetuating their control of the lucrative fur trade. They surrendered the posts in 1796

to the U.S. Army in compliance with Jay's Treaty, negotiated by U.S. commissioner John Jay in London in November 1794.
151. Sword 1985, 299–329; Philbrick 1965, 157–59; Prucha 1994, 92–93; Jennings 1985, 203.
152. PA 1855–56, 1-11: 562–63, 566–67; PA 1855–56, 1-12: 85–86; Deardorff 1941, 8–13, 22; Pierce 1798, journal entry for May 17 (at p. 7 of manuscript, thirteenth leaf of typescript); Sharpless 1798, journal entry for May 21 (at p. 8 of Times-Mirror extracts reprint; forty-ninth leaf of manuscript book).
153. PA 1855–56, 1-11: 733; PA 1855–56, 1-12: 321; PA 1896, 2-4: 555, 569–70; Kent 1974, 101–3, 112–13; Reynolds 1938, 32–33, 35, 37.
154. Proctor [1791] 1896, 485; PA 1896, 2-4: 569–70; Wallace 1969/1972: 163–164, 169.
155. The Munsee Indians (known variously as the Minsi, Minisink, Minising, or Muncy Indians) originally lived on both sides of the Delaware River in the region where the present-day states of Pennsylvania, New Jersey, and New York converge. Often referred to as a division of the Delawares, the Munsees were in fact an ethnically distinct group, who maintained their own sociopolitical organization and managed their own affairs with European Americans, although they frequently cooperated with the Delawares, to whom they were closely related culturally. (Jennings 1984, 27–28, 28 n. 6, n. 7, n. 8; McConnell 1992, 12, 225, 226.)
156. Wallace 1972, 163–64; Kent 1974, 103.
157. Abler 1989, 184; Wallace 1972, 164–65; PCR 16: 497.
158. PA 1855–56, 1-11: 709–10.
159. PCR 16: 397–99; PA 1855–56, 1-12: 8–9.
160. The following sources informed the presentation of the Treaty of Canandaigua: Fenton 1998, 622–706; Campisi and Starna 1995, 467–90; Campisi 1988, 60–64; Emlen [1794] 1965, 296–329.
161. The Tuscaroras, the "sixth" nation, did not join the Iroquois confederacy until the eighteenth century. In confederacy councils and league ceremonies, they were represented by the Oneidas, who had made some of their land in Iroquoia available for Tuscarora settlement.
162. Jennings 1985, 203; Prucha 1994, 96.
163. Emlen [1794] 1965, 329.
164. Treaty of Canandaigua, 1794, found as appendix B in Densmore 1999, 131–34.
165. The Buffalo Creek meridian is the line of longitude (78.88° west, i.e., 78 degrees and 53 minutes west longitude) extending from the mouth of Buffalo Creek at present-day Buffalo, New York, southward to the northern boundary of Pennsylvania.
166. The Senecas had still held 5 million acres at the conclusion of second Stanwix in 1784. In 1788, however, they sold 2 million acres east of the Genesee River to Oliver Phelps and Nathaniel Gorham, leaving the Senecas with 3 million acres west of the Genesee and east of the Buffalo Creek meridian. The 1 million acres restored to the Senecas at Canandaigua, which consisted of the lands in the southwestern angle of New York State west of the Buffalo Creek meridian plus the southern two-thirds of the Niagara strip, thus brought the total in their possession at the end of 1794 to 4 million acres—all of it west of the Genesee River.
167. Federal Nonintercourse Act of 1790, "An Act to Regulate Trade and Intercourse with the Indian Tribes", section 4, as found in Prucha 1990, 15.
168. The transaction at Big Tree was a private one between Robert Morris and the Seneca nation, not a treaty in the usual sense of the word. The requirements for the appointment of a federal commissioner and for Senate ratification, however, led to the settlement at Big Tree being referred to as a "treaty."
169. Chazanof 1970, 18–19; Campisi 1988, 49, 52, 58.
170. The preemption line was, more precisely, a longitudinal line drawn due north from the eighty-second milestone on the northern boundary of Pennsylvania, which coincides with the forty-second parallel (latitude 42° north). The preemption meridian was close to the seventy-seventh meridian (longitude 77° west), somewhat to the east. From Pennsylvania, it ran north through Seneca Lake, to Sodus Bay on the south shore of Lake Ontario.
171. Chazanof 1970, 19.
172. Ibid., 19–20; Kelsay 1984, 417.
173. PA 1896, 2-4: 530; see also, Hough 1861, 163 n; Wallace 1972, 153–54, 173–74.
174. Chazanof 1970, 20.
175. Ibid., 20; Wilkinson 1953, 258–59; Wallace 1972, 180.
176. Chazanof 1970, 21; Wilkinson 1953, 259–60.
177. Chazanof 1970, 21; Evans [1924] 1979, 177, 186; Wilkinson 1953, 265.
178. Wilkinson 1953, 261–62; Evans [1924] 1979, 186–87; Densmore 1999, 49.
179. Wilkinson 1953, 261; Evans [1924] 1979, 186.
180. Wilkinson 1953, 260, 262.
181. Ibid., 262–63; Wallace 1972, 180.
182. Wilkinson 1953, 263–65.
183. Wilkinson 1953, 276.
184. Robert Morris's speech, August 1, 1799, New York Historical Society O'Rielly Collection, XV, as quoted and cited in Wilkinson 1953, 265.

185. Wilkinson 1953, 265.
186. Ibid., 266; Chazanof 1970, 21; Evans [1924] 1979, 189.
187. Wilkinson 1953, 271; Chazanof 1970, 22; Evans [1924] 1979, 190.
188. Thomas Morris's speech of August 30, 1797, New York Historical Society O'Rielly Collection, XV, as quoted and cited in Wilkinson 1953, 267.
189. Wilkinson 1953, 265–66; Evans [1924] 1979, 188–89; Wallace 1972, 180.
190. Letter from Robert Morris to Theophile Cazenove, dated September 14, 1799, as quoted from Robert Morris's private Letter Book and cited in Wilkinson 1953, 268.
191. Chazanof 1970, 22; Evans [1924] 1979, 189–90.
192. Wilkinson 1953, 268–69; Evans [1924] 1979, 190–91; Wallace 1972, 181.
193. Wilkinson 1953, 269.
194. Ibid.
195. Ibid., 269–70; Evans [1924] 1979, 191.
196. Wilkinson 1953, 270–71; Evans [1924] 1979, 191; Wallace 1972, 182.
197. Wilkinson 1953, 271; Wallace 1972, 183; Densmore 1999, 54.
198. Wilkinson 1953, 272.
199. Densmore 1999, 51; Wilkinson 1953, 272–73.
200. Wallace 1972, 181; Evans [1924] 1979, 190; Densmore 1999, 51.
201. Wallace 1972, 181.
202. Evans [1924] 1979, 193–94; Chazanof 1970, 23.
203. Wilkinson 1953, 266; Evans [1924] 1979, 194.
204. Wallace 1972, 214.

Chapter Six

1. Fenton gives the first day of the Midwinter Rites as five days after the first new moon following the zenith of the Pleiades. (Fenton [1936] 1970, 7,10.)
2. Jackson 1830a, 26; [1798–1800] 1952, 135.
3. Jackson 1830a, 23–24.
4. Morgan 1851, 208, 187–88.
5. Ibid., 208–10; Fenton [1936] 1970, 4–5, 10–11, 11 n. 20.
6. Tooker 1970, 132–33.
7. Morgan 185, 211–12.
8. Sixty-five years after the fact, Jemison recollected the identity of her captors as Shawnee. (Seaver [1824] 1982, 34.)
9. Tooker 1970, 127; Seaver [1824] 1982, 18–19, 22–25, 34, 38.
10. The general reliability of Seaver's appendix titled "Of Their Religion, Feasts, and Great Sacrifice" is called into question by several improbable assertions. For example, he claimed that during Thanks-to-the-Maple the Indians were required to walk heel-to-toe

along a half-inch wide straight line laid out by the chiefs for distances of up to ten miles. (Seaver [1824] 1982, 163–64.) In his description of the Midwinter Rites, however, Seaver cites Jemison as his source, and his description is consistent with other contemporaneous accounts of Midwinter.
11. Tooker 1970, 128.
12. Ibid., 83–84, 149.
13. Seaver [1824] 1982, 165.
14. Tooker 1970, 133.
15. Morgan 1851, 212; Jackson 1830a, 24; Seaver [1824] 1982, 165; Tooker 1970, 131, 133.
16. The Allegany Senecas sometimes referred to snapping turtles as mud turtles. (Conklin and Sturtevant 1953, 264.) The snappers *(Chelydra serpentina)* lived in the Allegheny River.
17. Jackson 1830a, 24.
18. Morgan 1851, 212–13; Seaver [1824] 1982, 165–66; Tooker 1970, 134.
19. Jackson [1798–1800] 1952, 142–43; Jackson 1830a, 25; Seaver [1824] 1982, 166; Tooker 1970, 133–34; Fenton [1936] 1970, 11–12.
20. Morgan 1851, 215; Tooker 1970, 135.
21. Parker 1913, 102–3.
22. Ibid., 101–3; Wallace 1972, 51, 55.
23. Wallace 1972, 56.
24. Morgan 1851, 196.
25. Wallace 1972, 56. For berries and fruits used by the Iroquois, see Parker 1910, 94–99.
26. Among the Tonawanda Senecas, specific maple groves and sugar camps were preempted year after year by the same extended families (Fenton 1945a, 109). It is possible that the custom of families returning annually to tap the same grove and occupy the same camp was also practiced among the Allegany Senecas.
27. Proctor [1791] 1896, 473–75.
28. The descriptions and observations attributed to various white captives throughout this work do not necessarily contain the captives' exact words. Rather the quoted material comes from narratives compiled and published by authors who interviewed former captives or edited written accounts provided by them.
29. Walton [1784/1848] 1975, 67, 152, 153.
30. Jackson 1830a, 16.
31. Wallace 1972, 55–56.
32. Fenton and Deardorff 1943, 292–93.
33. It took a few days to build a nest, and a few more to produce an egg. Then it took two weeks for the eggs to hatch and two more weeks for the squabs to fledge. (Todd 1940, 269.)
34. Fenton and Deardorff 1943, 294–95.
35. Harris 1903, 449–50. (Fenton and Deardorff 1943, 294–95.) (Todd 1940, 269.)
36. Fenton and Deardorff 1943, 294–95.
37. Cornplanter's father was a Dutch trader named John Abeel, who had operated out of Albany,

New York. English speakers frequently angli-
cized Abeel to O'Beel or O'Bail, sometimes
imputing Irish ancestry to Cornplanter. Captain
was a courtesy title widely applied to Cornplanter as recognition for his stature among his
own people and for his pivotal role in relations
between American Indians and European
Americans. It was not a military rank, but like
the title of colonel that was once applied to notable Southern gentlemen, simply a mark of
courtesy and respect.

38. Proctor [1791] 1896, 499.
39. Fenton and Deardorff 1943, 290, 291, 300.
40. Harris 1903, 450–51; Walton [1784/1848]
    1975, 67, 153–54.
41. Walton [1784/1848] 1975, 67, 153.
42. Gunn 1903, 517.
43. Sharpless 1798, journal entries for May 18
    and 28 (pp. 6 and 13 of Times-Mirror extracts
    reprint; forty-first and seventy-fifth leaves of
    manuscript book).
44. Jackson 1830a, 17.
45. Parker 1913, 25, 25 n. 1; Wallace 1972, 13.
46. Wallace 1972, 56.
47. Ibid., 228; Kent and Deardorff 1960, 294–96.
48. Jackson 1830a, 21.
49. Fenton 1942a, 48–51.
50. Wallace 1972, 58.
51. Ibid.
52. Ibid., 58–59.
53. Jackson 1830a, 21–23.

Chapter Seven

1. See also Wallace 1972, 199–200.
2. Jackson 1830a, 33.
3. It is possible that Simmons went to the model
   farm at Genesinguhta to consult with his fellow missionaries, before approaching Cornplanter about calling a general council.
   Simmons could easily have traveled to the
   farm, conferred with Jackson and Swayne,
   and returned to Cornplanter's village, in one
   day. His use of the words "our" and "we" in
   the following passage is suggestive of such
   prior consultation. "Their deplorable condition
   by reason of that destructive article of strong
   drink greatly augmented our concern and exercise for the promotion of their present and
   future happiness. So much so that we were desirous of having them collected in council."
4. Jackson [1798–1800] 1952, 144–45. It is not
   absolutely certain that the first council held
   on May 15, 1799, was a general assembly of
   the entire village. It might have been a meeting between the Quakers and the Allegany
   Seneca leadership, similar to the second
   meeting that Jackson described for that day.
   Jackson (1830b, 35) states that "their chiefs
   and principal men collected in council."

It does seem that the leadership arrived at
the decision to ban alcohol on May 15, and,
during the second meeting that day, conveyed
to the Quakers their intent and determination
to do so. The leadership, nevertheless, would
have had to forge a consensus among the general populace. This explains why Jackson
([1798–1800] 1952, 145) recorded the Seneca
reply as coming on the same day as the temperance council, whereas Simmons recorded
it as coming several days after the temperance
council of May 15. Thirty years after the
event, Jackson too wrote that the formal answer came "a few days after" the temperance
council of May 15. (Jackson 1830b, 35–36.)
5. Mancall 1995, 56, 85, 111, 114–15, 166.
6. Ibid., 50–51, 101–2, 110–23; Richter 1992,
   263–66.
7. PCR 3: 274.
8. DHSNY 1849, 2: 627–28.
9. Ibid., 591–92.
10. PSWJ 1921–65, 10: 69.
11. Ibid., 7: 348.
12. In 1701 from Shemekenwhoa of the Shawnees
    (PCR 2: 33); in 1704 from Oretyagh of the
    Conestogas on the lower Susquehanna River
    (PCR 2: 141); in 1715 from Sassoonan of the
    Delawares on the Susquehannna (PCR 2: 605);
    in 1729 from Tawenna and Civility of the Con-
    estogas (PCR 3: 361–65); in 1731 from Sas-
    soonan of the Susquehanna Delawares again
    (PCR 3: 405–6), and also from Shickellamy of
    Shamokin, the Six Nations' resident superin-
    tendent over the external affairs of the
    Delawares and the Shawnees living on the
    Susquehanna River (Sipe [1927] 1998, 124);
    in 1732 from some chiefs of the Delawares on
    the Allegheny River at Kittanning (Sipe [1927]
    1998, 72); in 1733, 1734, and 1738 from chiefs
    of the Shawnees at various locations within the
    Allegheny watershed (PA 1855–56, 1-1:
    549–52; Sipe [1927] 1998, 72–73, 119); in
    1741 from some chiefs of the Mingos and the
    Shawnees on the Allegheny River (PCR 4:
    502); in 1745 from Shickellamy of Shamokin
    again (PCR 4: 758); in 1753 from Scaroyady,
    the Six Nations' resident superintendent of the
    Shawnees living in the Ohio Valley (PCR 5:
    676; Sipe [1927] 1998, 217); in 1766 from
    New Comer of the Delawares on the Musk-
    ingum and Tuscarawas Rivers in Ohio (Beatty
    [1766] 1962, 66); in 1767 from a chief of the
    Miamis of Ohio (PSWJ 1921–65, 12: 558); in
    1768 from Benewisco of the Ohio Shawnees,
    speaking also for the Mingos and the Delawares
    of the Ohio Country (PSWJ 12: 635); in 1771
    from some chiefs of the Shawnees on the
    Scioto River (PSWJ 12: 914–15); in 1773 from
    a Huron (Wyandot) chief attending a confer-
    ence at Pittsburgh (PSWJ 12: 1035).

13. Proclamations regulating the Indian rum trade were issued by Pennsylvania governors in the following years: 1701 (PCR 2: 21); 1715 (PCR 2: 604); 1731 (PCR 3: 411–12); 1736 (PCR 4: 86–87); 1745 (PCR 4: 759–61); 1747 (PCR 5: 193–96); 1749 (PCR 5: 397–98); 1758 (PCR 8: 172; PA 1855–56, 1-3: 437, 519).
14. Mancall 1995, 162–63.
15. Ibid., 43, 110, 122–23, 163; Richter 1992, 265; White 1991, 187, 264, 497–98.
16. PCR 3: 275; Richter 1992, 265.
17. PA 8-1: 12, 34.
18. PCR 2: 105; PA 8-1: 50, 57, 119.
19. PCR 2: 21, 42–43.
20. Mancall 1995, 52–57, 163, 211 n. 108; PSWJ 1921–65, 4: 559.
21. Mancall 1995, 54, 211 n. 108; PSWJ 1921–65, 12: 273.
22. Mancall 1995, 163.
23. PCR 2: 604.
24. Ibid., 3: 275–76.
25. PCR 3: 363. Tawenna might or might not have been correct about this, although I suspect he was right. We do know that William Penn told Conestoga chief Oretyagh in 1701 that if traders brought any rum among the Indians, they should "not buy it but send the person who brought it back with it again." Additionally, the Indians should "give information thereof to the government that the offenders might be duly prosecuted." (PCR 2: 43.)
26. PA 1855–56, 1-1: 551.
27. Mancall 1995, 119.
28. PSWJ 1921–65, 12: 915.
29. Ibid.
30. PCR 3: 275.
31. Ibid., 365.
32. PSWJ 1921–65, 10: 73.
33. Richter 1992, 263–64.
34. Mancall 1995, 57–61, 125–26; White 1991, 497, 498.
35. Mancall 1995, 99–100, 102, 119, 123–25, 129.
36. DRCHSNY 1853–57, 5: 863–66.
37. DHSNY 1849, 2: 591.
38. PCR 5: 676.
39. Ibid., 3: 405.
40. Ibid.
41. Ibid., 405–6.
42. Mancall 1995, 160–61.
43. Kenny [1758–59] 1913, 429.
44. Journal of George Croghan, 1765, as found in *Early Western Travels, 1748–1846* (32 vols.), edited by Reuben G. Thwaites, (Cleveland, 1904–7), 1: 158–59, and as cited and quoted in Mancall 1995, 126.
45. Frazier 1992, 199.
46. DRCHSNY 1853–57, 5: 796–97.
47. PA 1855–56, 1-1: 261.
48. Mancall 1995, 99–100.
49. PSWJ 1921–65, 12: 1035.
50. PCR 3: 274.
51. Ibid., 275.
52. PA 1855–56, 1-1: 265–66.
53. Ibid., 549–51.
54. Peter Bard to Governor Denny, July 1, 1758, in Manuscript Papers of the Indian and Military Affairs of the Province of Pennsylvania, 1737, 1775, 593–94, American Philosophical Library, Philadelphia, as cited in Mancall 1995, 59, 213 n. 127.
55. Kenny [1761–63 Journal] 1913, 14, 16, 17.
56. See chapter 5, note 155 above.
57. Zeisberger 1768–69 Journal, 73–74.
58. Ibid., 68.
59. Ibid., 91.
60. PSWJ 1921–65, 7: 348.
61. Mancall 1995, 89; White 1991, 334; PCR 3: 365, 406.
62. Beatty [1766] 1962, 67.
63. Zeisberger [1780] 1910, 90.
64. Mancall 1995, 128–29, 170.
65. Ibid., 42, 46, 49, 162.
66. Ibid., 43.
67. Ibid., 39, 47, 48–49, 57.
68. Ibid., 48; White 1991, 335.
69. Mancall 1995, 158–59.
70. Ibid., 43, 55; Richter 1992, 264.
71. Petition of merchants of Albany to Lords of Trade, March 1764, *New York Colonial Documents* 7: 613–15, as cited and quoted in Mancall 1995, 161, 241 n. 21.
72. Johnson to Lords of Trade, October 1764, *New York Colonial Documents* 7: 665, as cited and quoted in Mancall 1995, 162, 241 n. 22; see also White 1991, 479–80 for a specific example of the importance of rum in the fur trade at Michilimackinac during the first five years of the 1800s.
73. Mancall 1995, 13, 26, 159.
74. Ibid., 85–86; Richter 1992, 266–77; White 1991, 343.
75. Mancall 1995, 93–95; Richter 1992, 264.
76. Mancall 1995, 94; White 1991, 497.
77. Mancall 1995, 95; White 1991, 498.
78. Mancall 1995, 67, 79–82; Richter 1992, 265; McConnell 1992, 18.
79. Mancall 1995, 80, 94.
80. Ibid., 86–89; McConnell 1992, 18.
81. Mancall 1995, 113–14; Zeisberger [1780] 1910, 90; Richter 1992, 266.
82. Mancall 1995, 89.
83. Ibid., 91–92, 100.
84. Ibid., 91–93; Richter 1992, 266; White 1991, 322.
85. Mancall 1995, 96–98; Richter 1992, 266–68; White 1991, 322.
86. In his book, *Deadly Medicine: Indians and Alcohol in Early America,* Peter C. Mancall has carefully examined the documentary record and arrived at some valuable insights as to

why eighteenth-century Indians drank as they did. The discussion presented here and in the following paragraphs is based on Mancall's findings.
87. Mancall 1995, 67–70, 72; Richter 1992, 265.
88. Mancall 1995, 69–70.
89. Ibid., 67, 74.
90. Ibid., 68–70, 75, 83.
91. Ibid., 69.
92. Ibid., 74–75.
93. Ibid., 75; McConnell (1992, 18) expresses the opposite view. But, in this case, Mancall's familiarity with and citation of the medical literature outweighs McConnell's opinion about "dream states" and "vision quests." See Mancall 1995, 4–7, including the notes on pp. 193–97. In fairness to McConnell, note that the physiological effects of excessive alcohol consumption were not a subject of his research and study, as they were for Mancall. Michael N. McConnell's *A Country Between: The Upper Ohio Valley and Its Peoples, 1724–1774,* is an excellent work, which I found to be indispensable in connection with other topics.
94. Mancall 1995, 14–15, 163.
95. Ibid., 14.
96. Ibid., 79.
97. Ibid., 72–73; White 1991, 498.
98. Mancall 1995, 68.
99. Ibid., 76–78; White 1991, 498.
100. Mancall 1995, 77, 83; Zeisberger 1768–69 Journal, 85.
101. Mancall 1995, 82.
102. Ibid., 7–8.
103. Jackson 1830b, 37.
104. Ibid., 38.
105. Ibid., 40.
106. Ibid., 41.
107. Ibid., 44.
108. Ibid., 45–46.
109. Unsigned letter, dated January 18, 1802, from a Friend at Genesinguhta; from the Historical Society of Pennsylvania, Logan Papers, vol. 11, p. 70, as cited and quoted in Wallace 1972, 304, 365 n. 4.
110. PYMIC Collection, box 2, 1803–15, Letter of August 30, 1803, as cited and quoted in Wallace 1972, 307, 365 n. 15.
111. *Massachusetts Missionary Magazine,* 1804, vol. 1, pp. 68–69, as cited and quoted in Wallace 1972, 307, 366 n. 16.
112. Clark 1849, 105.
113. Ibid., 105–6.
114. Ibid., 106.
115. Jackson 1830b, 51.
116. Deardorff 1941, 17.
117. Jackson 1806 Journal, 582.
118. Jackson 1830b, 51.
119. Philips [1806] 1956, 602.

120. Ibid., 604; see also Jackson 1806 Journal, 579.
121. Jackson 1806 Journal, 585–86; see also Philips [1806] 1956, 608.
122. Jackson 1830b, 53.
123. See note 56 above.
124. Jackson 1806 Journal, 588; see also Wallace 1972, 310. Wallace or his assistant (Sheila C. Steen) seems to have been able to read parts of the manuscript that Snyderman found illegible and represented with empty brackets. One or both might have been working from a manuscript copy of the original journal, which might differ slightly from the original. In any case, Wallace filled in many of Snyderman's empty brackets. The Wallace and Snyderman transcriptions of this passage from the Jackson 1806 Journal differ in other, minor respects as well.
125. PYMIC Collection, reel 1, box 2, 1803–15, Speech to Indian Committee by Conudiu et al., November 6, 1807.
126. Journal of Isaac Bonsal, 1806–7, entry for September 18, 1807, as cited and quoted in Wallace 1972, 305, 365 n. 9.
127. Journal of William Allinson, 1809, book 1, pp. 26–27, entry for September 17, 1809.
128. Ibid., book 3, p. 7, entry for September 29, 1809.
129. Ibid., book 2, p. 31–32, Taylor's letter of September 19, 1809, copied in Allinson's journal entry for September 21, 1809.
130. Wallace 1972, 306.
131. Ibid., 309. White, too, noted the correlation between the proximity of Indian villages to European-American settlements and the prevalence of intemperance in those villages. (White 1991, 497–98.)
132. Wallace 1972, 308–9.
133. Benn 1998, 64–65; Jackson 1830b, 60–61.
134. Benn 1998, 64, 65; Jackson 1830b, 62.
135. Jackson 1830b, 62.
136. Address of visiting delegation from PYMIC to the "Chiefs and Others Residing on the Allegheny River," dated September 23, 1814 (PYMIC Collection, 1803–15, reel I, box 2).
137. Jackson 1830b, 63.

Chapter Eight

1. Jackson 1830a, 24.
2. Proctor [1791] 1896, 475.
3. Jackson 1830a, 25–26.
4. Morgan 1851, 261; Kurath 1964, 73–74.
5. Morgan 1851, 260, 279; Fenton 1942b, 12; Kurath 1964, 52.
6. Morgan 1851, 191, 193, 194, 195, 199, 206, 212, 221; Kurath 1964, 4. It is inferred from Morgan that the feather dance was performed at all the major religious celebrations. Kurath

(1964) did not include Thanks-to-the-Maple and Harvest Feast when listing major celebrations of the Coldspring Longhouse on the Allegany Reservation, at which the feather dance was performed. Kurath made some observations of her own during a monthlong visit to Allegany in the summer of 1948 and during a few other brief visits. But, for the most part, she relied on the notes and sound recordings made by William N. Fenton at Coldspring between 1933 and 1951, as well as on Fenton's published works. Morgan wrote at mid-nineteenth century, based on observations he made, mostly at the Tonawanda Reservation, during the 1840s. Morgan mentions the feather dance specifically in connection with Thanks-to-the-Maple. (Morgan 1851, 191, 193.) Fenton mentions it specifically in connection with the Harvest Feast. (Fenton [1936] 1970, 13.)

7. Morgan 1851, 282–83; Fenton 1942b, 14; Kurath 1964, 50.
8. Morgan 1851, 264; Fenton 1942b, 11–12.
9. Jackson 1830a, 14, 24; Morgan 1851, 263–67, 279, 282.
10. Jackson 1830a, 24; Morgan 1851, 282.
11. Morgan 1851, 279–83; Fenton 1942b, 13; Kurath 1964, 4–5, 51.
12. Morgan 1851, 280–81; Fenton 1942b, 12–14; Kurath 1964, 4–5, 51.
13. Fenton 1942, 13; Kurath 1964, xi–xiii, 4–5, 51.
14. Jackson 1830a, 24; Fenton 1942b, 12; Kurath 1964, 4, 45.
15. Morgan 1851, 280–82; Fenton 1942b, 14.
16. Fenton 1942b, 14; Kurath 1964, 4. Kurath, herself a professional dancer (modern dance), also gave a very technical description of the men's feather-dance step at mid-twentieth century. (Kurath 1964, 57.)
17. Morgan 1851, 283; Fenton 1942b, 14; Kurath 1964, 4. Kurath also gave a technical description of the women's feather-dance step at mid-twentieth century. (Kurath 1964, 57.)
18. Jackson 1830a, 15.
19. Seaver [1824] 1982, xi–xii.
20. Jackson 1830a, 15; see also Wallace 1972, 191–92.
21. Morgan 1851, 384–86.
22. Ibid., 201–2, 221. The drum dance was originally a war dance. Handsome Lake is sometimes credited with replacing war songs with thanksgiving chants; however, the change could have begun before his ministry. See Tooker 1970, 104–6; Shimony [1961] 1994, 190; Fenton 1941b, 155 n. 20.
23. Morgan 1851, 283. Kurath gave a summary description of the thanksgiving (drum) dance at mid-twentieth century. (Kurath 1964, 5, 57.)
24. A more complete version can be found in Morgan 1851, 219–21; see also Fenton [1936] 1970, 14.

25. Morgan 1851, 202–3.
26. Ibid., 201; Conklin and Sturtevant 1953, 279; Kurath 1964, 5. In connection with Morgan's report of turtle-shell rattles being used in the thanksgiving dance, the dance described by Simmons and Jackson at Cornplanter's village during Green Corn, may not have been a feather dance, but a thanksgiving dance, with rattles instead of a drum. Deardorff (1951, 92), however, agrees with identification of the August 1799 dance described by Simmons and Jackson as the feather dance. See also Fenton 1941b, 147.
27. Jackson 1830a, 24.
28. Fenton 1942b, 9; Conklin and Sturtevant 1953, 275.
29. Kent and Deardorff 1960, 448–53; Emlen [1794] 1965, 297; Morgan 1851, 268–79; Fenton 1942b, 27–28; Kurath 1964, 8, 52, 57.
30. Morgan 1851, 268; Emlen [1794] 1965, 297; Kent and Deardorff 1960, 448–53.
31. Kent and Deardorff 1960, 448.
32. Morgan 1851, 270 n, 271 n.
33. Morgan mentioned "a change in the music" partway through a war-dance song, involving a brief relaxation in dance intensity, followed by a resumption with "more animation than before." (Morgan 1851, 270, 272–73.) Adlum too noted a shift to "quick time." (Kent and Deardorff 1960, 448.)
34. Kurath 1964, 52. Kurath gave a summary description of the war (brag) dance at mid-twentieth century. (Kurath 1964, 8, 57.)
35. Kent and Deardorff 1960, 448–49.
36. Ibid. Morgan reported that each speaker, at the conclusion of his delivery, was obligated to give a present, either to the dancers or to the person addressed in his speech. (Morgan 1851, 273.) Emlen observed a similar practice, in which a bottle of rum was given as a present. (Emlen [1794] 1965, 297.)
37. Kent and Deardorff 1960, 452–53.
38. Ibid., 453.
39. Emlen [1794] 1965, 297.
40. Ibid.
41. Jackson 1830a, 27–28.
42. Fenton and Kurath 1951, 160–64.
43. Ibid., 145.
44. Morgan 1851, 174, 287; Fenton and Kurath 1951, 145, 147, 153.
45. Fenton and Kurath 1951, 145–47, 153–58.
46. Morgan 1851, 164; Fenton and Kurath 1951, 147–53, 158–60.
47. For a discussion of Iroquois mortuary practices from Early Woodland times through the mid-1600s, see Richter 1992, 13–15, 81–83, 320–21 n. 8.
48. Jackson 1830a, 27.
49. Morgan 1851, 174–76; Wallace 1972, 98–99.

Chapter Nine

1. John Pierce and Joshua Sharpless both reported that by June 6, 1798, Cornplanter's daughter was suffering from a life-threatening illness. (Pierce 1798, journal entry for June 6 [p. 27 of manuscript; forty-eighth and forty-ninth leafs of typescript]; Sharpless 1798, journal entry for June 6 [p. 18 of Times-Mirror extracts reprint; one-hundred and third leaf of manuscript book].)
2. Simmons 1799 Journal, undated entry prior to entry for June 13—"The present one [dead feast] was being held on account of the old chief's daughter, who had been dead upwards of four months." The dead feast occurred in late May or early June, Cornplanter's daughter must have died in late January or early February 1799.
3. Jackson 1798–1800 Journal, 145.
4. Seaver [1824] 1982, 143; Morgan 1851, 165; Wallace 1972, 26, 85; Shimony [1970] 1989, 146.
5. Seaver [1824] 1982, 143, 173–75; Wallace 1972, 84–85, 201, 254.
6. Parker 1913, 29 n. 3; Wallace 1972, 56–57, 79.
7. Based on his 1946 interview with the Cayuga sachem Deskaheh, Alexander General, at the Six Nations Reserve, Grand River, in Canada, Anthony F. C. Wallace identified Shagodyoweh, the Great World Rim Dweller and patron of the false faces, as being the Evil Twin of the creation story. (See Wallace 1972, 345–46 n. 6.) Having asserted the functional equivalence between Tawiskaron and Shagodyoweh, Wallace hastened to add the following insightful comment. "All efforts to 'identify' the characters in myths by making this sort of logical equation are, in one sense, wasted because myths are like dreams, not only in their fantastic content, but also in their variability from one version to the next." (Wallace 1927, 346 n. 6.) For an Onondaga version of the false-face tutelary spirit, see Smith (1889, 278–79).
8. Wallace 1972, 89–91, 345–46 n. 6; Fenton [1941] 1984, 24–25.
9. Shimony [1961] 1994, 262–63, 264, 266–67, 267–68, 271–72, 273–74, 285–88; Shimony [1970] 1989, 143–44, 146, 155, 159–60.
10. Jackson 1830b, 42–43; Journal of William Allinson, 1809, book 1, entry for September 17, 1809, as cited and quoted in Wallace (1972, 293, 364 n. 39).
11. Richter 1992, 15, 65.
12. Jennings 1984, 95, 99–100; Richter 1992, 61–62, 65–66.
13. The description of witchcraft practices given in this chapter is a composite picture drawn from the following sources, with emphasis on the older sources: Morgan 1851, 164–66; Smith 1888, 184, 186–87; Smith 1889, 277–78; Parker 1913, 27–29 n. 3, 46 n. 1, 119; Shimony [1961] 1994, 287–89; Wallace [1969] 1972, 84–85, 254; Shimony [1970] 1989, 145, 148, 150–53, 158, 160.
14. Shimony ([1961] 1994, 287) wrote that broadcast poison droplets "affect anyone in the room." Later, Shimony ([1970] 1989, 148) wrote that exposing a handkerchief, previously soaked in the poison, disseminates the unseen poison "about the room and contaminates the victim."
15. Parker 1913, 40 n. 1; Shimony [1961] 1994, 285.
16. Parker 1913, 40 n. 1.
17. Thus, in addition to being a perversion of the hunting charm tradition, the witchcraft charm is also corruption of the medicine-bundle tradition. [Shimony [1961] 1994, 286; Shimony [1970] 1989, 164 n. 6.]
18. Shimony [1970] 1989, 152.
19. Shimony ([1961] 1994, 287) wrote that a beetle charm "affects a person who steps on it."
20. *Jesuit Relations,* 33: 217–19.
21. Parker 1909, 184.
22. Wallace 1972, 209.
23. Fenton 1945b, 46.
24. Shimony [1961] 1994, 263–67.
25. Fenton 1945b, 46–47.
26. Ibid., 48–50.
27. Wallace 1972, 254.
28. Parker 1913, 28 n. 3.
29. Ibid., 29 n. 3.
30. Wallace 1972, 255.
31. Ibid., 254–55.
32. Seaver [1824] 1982, 174.
33. Morgan 1851, 165 n. 1.
34. Smith 1888, 184–85.
35. Wallace 1972, 255.
36. Code 1913, 49–50.
37. Ibid., 50.
38. *Evangelical Intelligencer,* vol. 1, 1807, 92–93, as quoted and cited in Wallace (1972, 254, 360 n. 13).
39. Code 1913, 50.
40. Wallace 1972, 255–56.
41. HSP PA, letter from Cornplanter to Mead, circa January 1801; letter from Munsee chiefs to Mead, dated April 11, 1801. The author used typewritten copies of these letters found in the Warren County (Pa.) Historical Society's files on chief Cornplanter.
42. Wallace 1972, 256.
43. Fenton 1946, 53–54; Wallace 1972, 256.
44. Deardorff and Snyderman 1956, 592, incl. n. 27; Mead's reply to Cornplanter was dated February 2, 1801, indicating that the letter sent to Mead by Cornplanter's council must have been written in late January.
45. The distinctly European-American turn of phrase employed here is the result of the let-

ter having been taken down by an amanuensis, Henry York.

46. HSP PA, letter from Cornplanter to Mead circa January 1801.
47. HSP PA, letter from Munsee chiefs to Mead, dated April 11, 1801; letter from Mead's associates to the governor, dated April 14, 1801; Jackson 1830b, 42–43.
48. Jackson 1830b, 43.
49. Ibid., 57.
50. Fenton 1946, 54; Wallace 1972, 261.
51. PYMIC Collection, reel I, box 1, June 28, 1801.
52. The Code does not specify the date, so it must be inferred from other events in the Code, for which dates are known. It is difficult to narrow the date any further than 1806 to 1807.
53. Jackson 1830b, 49.
54. Wallace 1972, 291.
55. Code 1913, 46–47; Wallace 1972, 291.
56. Code 1913, 46; Wallace 1972, 291.
57. Wallace 1972, 293.
58. Code 1913, 32.
59. Ibid., 72.
60. Tooker 1984, 118–20.
61. Ibid., 119.
62. Bilharz 1995, 103.
63. Fenton 1998, 26; Richter 1992, 23; Tooker 1984, 119; Hertzberg 1966, 23–30; Wallace 1952, 24–28.
64. Bilharz 1995, 103.
65. Brown 1970, 164.
66. Rothenberg 1980, 67, 70–71; Richter 1992, 75–87, especially 87, 268–69.
67. Richter 1992, 23, 297 n. 31.
68. Tooker 1984, 115.
69. Ibid., 114–15; Richter 1992, 23–24.
70. Richter 1992, 23–24; Fenton 1998, 23.
71. Randle 1951, 139.
72. Shafer 1941, 80.
73. Tooker 1984, 115.
74. Ibid., 115.
75. Brown 1970, 164.
76. Rothenberg 1980, 67, 70–71; Bilharz 1995, 103.
77. Kent 1974, 103.
78. There was one exception to exclusively male participation in the fur trade. Sometimes, Indian women imported alcohol into their villages and traded it to the men for pelts, which they then sold to European-American traders. (Zeisberger 1768–69 Journal, 68, 91; PSWJ 7 1921–65, 348; Mancall 1995, 89; White 1991, 334.)
79. Wallace 1972, 182.
80. Brown 1970, 164.
81. Brown 1970; 159–60.
82. Ibid., 159; Tooker 1984, 115; Bilharz 1995, 103.
83. Tooker 1984, 116–17; Bilharz 1995, 102.
84. Tooker 1984, 116.
85. Ibid.
86. Bilharz 1995, 103.
87. Ibid.
88. Tooker 1984, 112–14; Bilharz 1995, 105–7.
89. One sometimes encounters forty-nine as the number of league sachems, instead of fifty. This discrepancy stems from a controversy over the number of distinct titles actually possessed by the Onondagas. The Cayugas alleged that two of the league sachem titles claimed by the Onondagas were really two different names for the same peace chief, and that the Onondagas, therefore, hold thirteen, not fourteen, titles. (Fenton 1998, 169–70, 192–94.)
90. Eight of the fifty league sachems were Senecas, nine were Mohawks, nine were Oneidas, ten were Cayugas, and fourteen were Onondagas. (Fenton 1998, 193–94.)
91. Parker 1916, 43; Shimony [1961] 1994, 27.
92. Fenton 1998, 25, 29, 197, 199–200, 203, 215; Richter 1992, 42–43; Tooker 1984, 114; Parker 1916, 97.
93. The Seneca nation contained segments of eight different clans, Wolf, Bear, Beaver, Turtle, Deer, Snipe, Heron, and Hawk. (Morgan 1851, 79.)
94. League sachem titles were divided among the clans of the Seneca nation as follows, Snipe clan, three titles; Turtle clan, two titles; Wolf, Bear, and Hawk clans, one title each; Beaver, Deer, and Heron clans, no titles. (Snow 1994, 64; Tooker 1984, 114.)
95. Richter 1992, 39; Woodbury 1992, xxvii, xxxi; Snow 1994, 62; Fenton 1998, 29, 100, 199, 215, 216; Parker 1916, 107.
96. Richter 1992, 20.
97. Ibid., 42.
98. Ibid., 43; Tooker 1984, 114.
99. Fenton 1998, 30.
100. In this context, it seems that "clan" referred not to a national clan segment, such as the Seneca Hawk clan, but to the transnational clan that encompassed all national segments of that clan. For example, the transnational Hawk clan encompassed two national segments, the Seneca Hawks and the Onondaga Hawks. The transnational Wolf, Bear, and Turtle clans were each composed of groups from all of the original Five Nations.
101. Parker 1916, 44; Bilharz 1995, 105.
102. Seth Newhouse (1842–1921). His mother was an Onondaga of the Hawk clan; his father was a Mohawk. An accomplished orator, he spoke for the warriors and women as a political partisan of the Mohawk warrior party. He could write in both English and Mohawk. His 1885 manuscript, which he kept revising until 1898, was rejected by the Grand River

chiefs, in part, because it overemphasized the Mohawk role in the league tradition. (Fenton 1998, 80, 81, 82; Fenton 1968, 39; Weaver 1984, 166.) The Mohawk council of women did approve his manuscript, however. (Fenton 1998, 82.)

103. Weaver 1984, 175.

104. Fenton 1998, 81; Weaver 1984, 180.

105. Generally speaking, sachems from a given nation who sat on the same side of their national or tribal—not league—council fire were "brothers " to each other and "cousins" to those who sat on the opposite side of the national council fire. (Fenton 1998, 25–27, 102, 213–14; Richter 1992, 45.)

Additionally, each of the Five Nations defined kin relationships among its own league-sachem titles. The Mohawks and the Oneidas both employed the relationships of brother and cousin. The Onondagas used the relationships of brother, cousin, and uncle. The Cayugas used the relationships of brother, cousin, father, and son. The Senecas used the relationship of cousin exclusively. (Shimony [1961] 1994, 101–16.)

106. Parker 1916, 107.

107. John A. Gibson (1849–912). His mother was a Seneca of the Turtle clan; his father was an Onondaga. Blinded at the age of thirty-one by a lacrosse injury, Gibson was fluent in Onondaga, Cayuga, and English; he also spoke Seneca, Oneida, and some Tuscarora. Additionally, he was a preacher of the Code of Handsome Lake and a Seneca sachem of the Grand River league. (Woodbury 1992, xii.) Following the emigration of so many Iroquois to Canada after the American Revolution, the Iroquois League was replicated in Canada. There, thus, were two parallel Iroquois leagues, one in New York and one in Canada at Grand River. (Shimony [1961] 1994, 103.)

108. Woodbury 1992, xxxi n. 67.

109. Ibid., xxxi.

110. Fenton 1998, 27–28, 212–14.

111. Woodbury 1992, xxxi.

112. Fenton 1998, 167.

113. Parker 1916, 34.

114. Ibid., 34.

115. Parker 1916, 37.

116. Ibid., 46.

117. Parker 1916, 106.

118. Fenton 1998, 219 n. 4.

119. Ibid., 219–21.

120. Bilharz 1995, 107.

121. Tooker 1984, 114.

122. Fenton 1998, 223.

123. Bilharz 1995, 106.

124. Murdock 1934, 302.

125. Allen 1986, 32.

126. The findings of more-recent, nontendentious studies confirm the view that the Iroquois were not a matriarchy or a gynocracy: Elisabeth Tooker, *Women in Iroquois Society* (1984); Joy Bilharz, *First Among Equals? The Changing Status of Seneca Women* (1995); William Fenton, *The Great Law and the Longhouse, A Political History of the Iroquois Confederacy* (1998), pp. 222–23; Dean Snow, *The Iroquois* (1994), p. 65. Even Judith Brown, who made fairly extravagant claims about women controlling the Iroquois economy, acknowledged that the Iroquois were not a matriarchy. (Brown 1970, 155.) (See also Wallace [1969] 1972, 28–30.)

127. Richter 1992, 43; Fenton 1998, 29, 359, 715.

128. Richter 1992, 43; Fenton 1998, 359.

129. Richter 1992, 44–45.

130. Ibid., 44.

Chapter Ten

1. Code 1913, 22.

2. The account of Handsome Lake's first vision presented here is a synthesis of different accounts: one account, based on an oral tradition that was committed to writing early in the twentieth century, is found in Edward Cornplanter's version of the Code of Handsome Lake (Code 1913, 22–30); the second account is from Simmons (1799 Journal, entry for June 15); the third account is Halliday Jackson's gloss of the Simmons account, printed in Wallace (1952, 341–42); the fourth—and least detailed—account is found in Jackson ([1798–1800] 1952, 146).

3. Simmons 1799 Journal, entry for June 15.

4. Code 1913, 26.

5. Ibid., 25.

6. Ibid., 25–26; Simmons 1799 Journal, entry for June 15.

7. Simmons 1799 Journal, entry for June 15.

8. Code 1913, 27.

9. Ibid., section 1.

10. Ibid., 28, section 2.

11. Simmons 1799 Journal, entry for June 15.

12. Code 1913, 29, section 3.

13. Ibid., 72, section 104; Wallace 1972, 85, 241, 245; Shimony [1961] 1994, 217.

14. Code 1913, 30, section 4; Parker 1913, 30 n. 3; Shimony [1961] 1994, 208.

15. Simmons 1799 Journal, entry for June 15.

16. Ibid.

17. Ibid., entry for August 7.

18. Ibid., entry for August 8.

19. Ibid.

20. Code 1913, 62, sections 82 and 83.

21. Ibid., 62–63, section 84.

22. Ibid., 63, section 85.

23. Ibid., 63–64, section 86.
24. Ibie., 64, section 87.
25. Wallace 1972, 243.
26. Code 1913, 61–62, section 81. In Edward Cornplanter's version of the Code, as edited and published by Arthur Parker in 1913, this visual parable precedes the sky journey. Simmons included it, however, in his account of the August 8 vision. (Simmons 1799 Journal, entry for August 8.)
27. Simmons 1799 Journal, entry for August 8.
28. The Code represents an oral tradition that was not captured in writing until early in the twentieth century, so it is possible that this prophecy was added after the Buffalo Creek Reservation had been sold by the chiefs in 1838, or after it had been irretrievably lost in 1842. (Wallace 1972, 332–36, 368 n. 63; Hauptman 1999, 176–77.)
29. Code 1913, 64, section 88.
30. Ibid., 65–66, section 91.
31. Code 1913, 66, section 92.
32. Ibid., 67–68, section 94.
33. Ibid.
34. See Parker 1919, 260; Deardorff 1951, 100–1.
35. Code 1913, 68, section 95.
36. Wallace 1972, 260.
37. Ibid., 259–60, 265.
38. Code 1913, 64–65, section 89.
39. Ibid., 65, section 90.
40. Ibid., 67, section 93.
41. Ibid., 69, section 96.
42. Ibid., 69, section 97.
43. Ibid., 70, sections 98, 99, 100.
44. Ibid., 70–71, sections 100, 101.
45. Ibid., 71, section 102.
46. Ibid., 71, section 103.
47. Ibid., 72, section 104.
48. Ibid., 72, section 105.
49. Ibid., 72–73, section 106.
50. Ibid., 73, section 107.
51. Ibid., 73, section 108.
52. Ibid., 73–74, section 109.
53. Ibid., 74, section 112.
54. Ibid., 74–75, section 113.
55. Ibid., 75, section 114.
56. Simmons 1799 Journal, entry for August 8.
57. Ibid.
58. Ibid.
59. Code 1913, 76, section 118.
60. Simmons 1799 Journal, entry for August 8.
61. Ibid.
62. Ibid.
63. Ibid.
64. Code 1913, 58–59, sections 69–77.
65. Ibid., 59, section 75.
66. Ibid., 43, section 38.
67. Ibid., p. 41, section 31; 42, section 35; 51, sections 54 and 55; 54, sections 60 and 61.
68. Simmons 1799 Journal, entry for August 9.

69. Seaver [1824] 1982, 164–65.
70. Morgan 1851, 210.
71. Jackson 1830a, 25.
72. Ibid., 25–26.
73. Ibid., 25.
74. Simmons 1799 Journal, entry for August 9.
75. Jackson 1798–1800 Journal, 135, 142; 1799 Journal, entries for August 30 and 31.
76. Seaver [1824] 1982, 164–65, 166; Tooker 1970, 116–17, 120–21, 131–34.
77. See chapter Four, note 67.
78. Morgan 1851, 210–11, 217–21.
79. Ibid., 216–17.
80. Ibid., 216–17; see also Blau 1964, 115 n. 31.
81. Blau 1964, 113 n. 2, n. 7; Shimony [1961] 1994, 185; Tooker 1965, 130; Tooker 1970, 152–53; Fenton [1936] 1970, 11; Fenton 1942b, 17.
82. Fenton [1936] 1970, 12; Shimony [1961] 1994, 185.
83. Beauchamp 1897, 175; Tooker 1970, 118.
84. Tooker 1970, 151.
85. Code 1913, 39–40, section 29; 50–51, sections 52 and 53; Wallace 1972, 252, 292.
86. Halliday Jackson did not voice his doubts about Handsome Lake, but he did confide them to his journals. (Jackson 1830b, 42, 50.) Although harboring suspicions about the authenticity of Handsome Lake's visions and personal mission in particular, Jackson does seem to have recognized the validity of Native American religious experience in general. (Jackson 1830a, 26.)
87. Simmons 1799 Journal, entry for August 9.
88. Ibid., entry for August 10.
89. Ibid.
90. Blau 1964, 109.
91. Simmons 1799 Journal, entry for August 11.
92. Ibid., entries for August 28 and 29.
93. Morgan 1851, 198–205; Fenton [1936] 1970, 9, 13–17; Fenton 1942b, 18–20; Fenton 1963, 20–22; Kurath 1964, xiii, 16–17.
94. The white-dog sacrifice described in Fenton (1942b, 17) is not a contemporaneous event. Fenton included the description to provide historical and cultural context for religious songs that were still being sung during Longhouse ceremonies. One of Fenton's informants, Joseph Logan, an Onondaga chief at the Six Nations reserve in Canada, knew the traditions that had surrounded the white-dog sacrifice, and he had witnessed the sacrifice when it was still being performed among the Six Nations Onondagas. (Fenton 1942b, 8, 17.)
95. In 1965 the council fire of the Coldspring Longhouse was ceremonially moved to the new Steamburg Longhouse, also on the Allegany Reservation because of impending inundation by the waters of the new Kinzua dam. (Abrams 1967, 23.)

96. Fenton [1936] 1970, 9; Wallace 1972, 52, 58.
97. Fenton [1936] 1970, 14.
98. Ibid., 16–17; Kurath 1964, 16–17.
99. Morgan 1851, 200.
100. Ibid., 205.
101. Simmons 1799 Journal, entry for August 30.
102. Ibid., entry for August 31.
103. Morgan 1851, 203; Fenton [1936] 1970, 13, 16.
104. Simmons 1799 Journal, entries for September 1 and 2.
105. Morgan 1851, 204–5.
106. Fenton [1936] 1970, 9, 13.
107. Simmons 1799 Journal, entry for September 2.
108. Ibid., entry for August 31.
109. Ibid., entry for September 2.
110. Ibid., entries for September 2 and 3.

Chapter Eleven

1. Simmons 1799 Journal, entries for June 15 and September 11; Coats 1799, journal entry for September 11; Jackson 1830b, 36.
2. Simmons 1799 Journal, entry for September 11.
3. Simmons 1799 Journal, entry for September 17; Coats 1799, journal entries for September 22 through October 2; The Pelham Monthly Meeting in upper Canada was established on October 2 under the care of the Philadelphia Yearly Meeting.
4. The documentary evidence indicates that the school was located close to the river, about a mile downstream from Cornplanter's village. (Coats 1799, journal entries for September 11 and 12.)
5. Coats 1799, journal entry for September 12.
6. Ibid., September 13.
7. Ibid., September 14.
8. Simmons 1799 Journal, entry for September 14.
9. Ibid.; Coats 1799, journal entry for September 14.
10. Simmons 1799 Journal, entry for September 14; Coats 1799, journal entry for September 14.
11. Simmons 1799 Journal, entry for September 14; Coats 1799, journal entry for September 14.
12. Simmons 1799 Journal, entry for September 14.
13. Coats 1799, journal entry for September 15.
14. Ibid., September 16.
15. Coats 1799, journal entry for September 17; Simmons 1799 Journal; entry for September 17.
16. Simmons 1799 Journal, entries for February 27 and March 1.
17. Jackson 1806 Journal, 587; Mush's speech to the Quaker delegation.
18. Jackson 1830b, 34, 39.
19. Jackson 1830b, 43, 45.
20. Code 1913, 38, section 26.
21. Jackson 1830b, 50, 54.
22. Ibid., 57, 67.
23. Ibid., 69.
24. Ibid., 88–89.
25. Sharpless 1798, journal entry for May 28.
26. PYMIC Collection, reel I, box 1, February 28, 1801.
27. Jackson 1830b, 49.
28. Jackson 1830b, 46–47; in 1806 Joseph Ellicott of the Holland Land Company forwarded to the PYMIC a deed for 692 acres on Tunesassa Creek, purchased for $860. (PYMIC Collection, reel I, box 2, December 5, 1806.)
29. PYMIC Collection, reel I, box 2, January 7, 1805. The Quakers originally intended to grind Seneca grain free for only the first year of operation. But in December 1805 they decided to continue the practice for an additional year. In 1814 they again suspended grinding fees to encourage the Indians back to agricultural pursuits, which had been disrupted by the War of 1812. (PYMIC Collection, reel I, box 2, September 23, 1814.)
30. Jackson, 1806 Journal, 572–78; Philips [1806] 1956, 602; PYMIC Collection, reel I, box 2, January 7 and June 26, 1805.
31. PYMIC Collection, reel II, box 3, March 17, 1819.
32. Ibid., reel I, box 2, August 21,1807.
33. Ibid., February 2,1804, April 21, 1804; Wallace 1972, 287–88; Barton 1990, 7–8.
34. Ibid., October 16, 1807.
35. Jackson 1830b, 53.
36. PYMIC Collection, reel I, box 2, October 28, 1808.
37. Ibid., February 12, 1811.
38. Ibid., March 20, 1812.
39. Ibid., reel II, box 3, December 3, 1820.
40. Jackson 1830b, 36, 42, 44, 46.
41. PYMIC Collection, reel I, box 2, September 24, 1803.
42. Jackson 1830b, 48; 1806 Journal, 573.
43. Sharpless 1798, journal entry for May 19; Pierce 1798, journal entry for May 19; PYMIC Collection, reel I, box 1, July 28, 1798; Jackson 1830b, 41.
44. PYMIC Collection, reel I, box 2, February 12, 1811.
45. PYMIC Collection, reel I, box 1, August 3, 1801; Jackson 1830b, 36, 41.
46. Jackson 1830b, 46.
47. PYMIC Collection, reel I, box 2, November 2, 1805.
48. Jackson 1830b, 52.
49. PYMIC Collection, reel I, box 2, February 3, 1807.
50. Ibid., July 16, 1808.

51. Jackson 1830b, 64.
52. Jackson 1830b, 52.
53. PYMIC Collection, reel II, box 3, October 16, 1817.
54. PYMIC Collection, reel I, box 1, January 5 and February 15, 1796; Sharpless 1798, journal entry for May 28.
55. PYMIC Collection, reel I, box 2, September 25, 1806, March 21, 1810, February 12, 1811.
56. Kaufman 1964, 446.
57. PYMIC Collection, reel I, box 2, March 15, 1815; Wrenshall 1942, 81, 83.
58. Jackson 1830b, 43.
59. PYMIC Collection, reel I, box 2, June 16, 1810, March 20, 1812; Jackson 1806 Journal, 582; 1830b, 52, 56, 85–88.
60. Shimony [1961] 1994, 154–55.
61. Sharpless 1798, journal entries for May 22, May 23, May 27; Pierce 1798, May 19, May 22, May 24, May 27, May 31; Jackson 1830b, 32–33.
62. Sharpless 1798, journal entries for May 18, May 19, May 28; Pierce 1798, May 19, May 28; Jackson 1830b, 30–31.
63. Jackson 1830b, 36, 39, 43.
64. PYMIC Collection, reel I, box 2, September 24, 1803.
65. Ibid., box 1, November 11, 1802.
66. PYMIC Collection, reel I, box 1, December 11, 1802.
67. Jackson 1830b, 46.
68. PYMIC Collection, reel I, box 2, September 24, 1803.
69. PYMIC Collection, reel I, box 2, December 14, 1803.
70. Jackson 1806 Journal, 577.
71. Ibid., 573.
72. Ibid., 576.
73. Ibid., 579–80.
74. PYMIC Collection, reel I, box 2, January 31, 1807.
75. Ibid., May 10, 1812.
76. Jackson 1806 Journal, 579.
77. Ibid., 580–81.
78. PYMIC Collection, reel I, box 2, January 31, 1807.
79. Code 1913, 35, section 20.
80. Jackson 1830b, 43.
81. Code 1913, 35, section 19; 36, sections 21 and 22; 38, section 25.
82. Sharpless 1798, journal entry for May 21.
83. Jackson 1800 Journal: March 1.
84. Jackson 1830b, 44, 48.
85. Ibid., 49.
86. PYMIC Collection, reel I, box 2, April 21, 1804.
87. The phrase "a love for exclusive property" originated with Henry Knox, but the Quakers agreed with the notion that private property was the basis of civilization. (Jackson 1803b, 33.)
88. PYMIC Collection, reel II, box 3, June 29, 1816; Jackson 1830b, 58, 67.
89. PYMIC Collection, reel II, box 3, June 29, 1816.
90. Ibid., November 21, 1824.
91. Ibid., March 17, 1819; Jackson 1830b, 72.
92. PYMIC Collection, reel II, box 3, March 17, 1819; Jackson 1830b, 73.
93. Jackson 1830b, 68.
94. PYMIC Collection, reel II, box 3, October 16, 1817.
95. Jackson 1830b, 68–69.
96. PYMIC Collection, reel II, box 3, November 21, 1824.
97. Jackson 1830b, 69; PYMIC Collection, reel II, box 3, October 16, 1817.
98. Jackson 1830b, 72.
99. These requests were made by a group of chiefs who favored dividing the reservation. They hoped that a positive response from the president would help quiet the opponents of division, who objected on the basis that division might eventually cost them the reservation. (PYMIC Collection, reel II, box 3, August 24, 1818.)
100. PYMIC Collection, reel II, box 3, August 11, 1818.
101. Ibid., January 15, 1819; Jackson 1830b, 74, 77.
102. Ibid., August 24, 1818; Jackson 1830b, 72, 74, 77.
103. Hauptman 1999, 154–61, 175–220; 1986, 85–122.
104. PYMIC Collection, reel I, box 2, August 30, 1803.
105. Ibid., June 11, 1807.
106. Ibid., June 8, 1808.
107. PCR 16: 504.
108. Jackson 1810 Journal, n. 122.
109. PYMIC Collection, reel I, box 2, August 30, 1803.
110. PYMIC Collection, reel I, box 2, December 14, 1803.
111. Jackson 1830b, 33.
112. Ibid., 36.
113. Ibid., 48.
114. Jackson 1806 Journal, 582.
115. Jackson 1830b, 56.
116. Ibid., 67.
117. Wrenshall 1816, 128.
118. Norton [1816] 1970, 9.
119. PYMIC Collection, reel I, box 2, March 15, 1815.
120. PYMIC Collection, reel II, box 3, October 16, 1817.
121. Ibid., March 17, 1819.

Epilogue
1. Jackson 1830b, 37.
2. Simmons 1799 Journal, entry for November 7.

3. PYMIC Minutes, minute dated December 21, 1799, copied and endorsed on reverse side of Simmons's certificate of approval from Middletown for mission duty, which was found in Simmons's 1796–97 Journal.
4. FHL, microfilm MR-Ph340, New Garden MM, men's minutes, 1790–1802, p. 324, September 1800.
5. Ibid., microfilm MR-Ph345, New Garden MM, record of marriage certificates, 1800–27, p. 1, October 8, 1800.
6. Ibid., microfilm MR-Ph340, New Garden MM, men's minutes, 1790–1802, p. 337, March 1801.
7. Ibid., New Garden MM births and deaths; children of Henry Simmons and Rachel Preston: Deborah July 11, 1801, John September 3, 1803, Hannah February 18, 1806, Henryetta May 23, 1808.
8. Ibid., microfilm MR-Ph340, New Garden MM, men's minutes, 1790–1802, p. 366, September 1802.
9. Ibid., microfilm MR-Ph340, New Garden MM, men's minutes, 1802–12, p. 33, January 1804.
10. Ibid., microfilm MR-Ph344, New Garden MM, women's minutes, 1804–22, p. 29, December 5, 1805.
11. Ibid., microfilm MR-Ph344, New Garden MM, women's minutes, 1804–22, p. 63, September 10, 1807.
12. Ibid., microfilm MR-Ph344, New Garden MM, women's minutes, 1804–22, p. 66, November 5, 1807.
13. Ibid., New Garden MM births and deaths.
14. Philips [1806] 1956, 603; Jackson 1830b, 53. Wallace 1972, 287–89, 291–94.
15. Benn 1998, 131–32, 148, 166; Wallace 1972, 294–96; Sipe [1927] 1998, 466–67; Densmore 1999, 80–87.
16. Densmore 1999, 105.
17. Jackson 1830b, 63–64; PYMIC Collection, reel I, box 2, March 15, 1815; Wallace 1972, 322, 327; Sipe [1927] 1998, 467.
18. Wallace 1972, 327–29; Deardorff 1941, 18; Sipe [1927] 1998, 467–72; Cornplanter was born during the summer of 1752 (Deardorff and Snyderman 1956, 600 and n. 27).
19. Wallace 1972, 259–60; Densmore 1999, 57–58; Code 1913, 53, section 58.
20. Wallace 1972, 266–72; 285–86.
21. Ibid., 252, 289–92.
22. Ibid., 294.
23. Ibid., 294–96.
24. Ibid., 278–80.

Abler 1989
Thomas Abler, ed. *Chainbreaker: The Revolutionary War Memoirs of Governor Blacksnake, as Told to Benjamin Williams*. Lincoln: University of Nebraska Press.

Abrams 1967
George Abrams. Moving the Fire: A Case of Iroquois Ritual Innovation. In *Iroquois Culture, History, and Prehistory: Proceedings of the 1965 Conference on Iroquois Research*, edited by Elizabeth Tooker. Albany: University of the State of New York.

Alden 1827
Rev. Timothy Alden. *An Account of Sundry Missions Performed among the Senecas and Munsees: In a Series of Letters*. New York: J. Seymour.

Allen 1986
Paula G. Allen. *The Sacred Hoop: Recovering the Feminine in American Indian Traditions*. Boston: Beacon Press.

Allinson 1809
William Allinson. Manuscript journal describing a visit to New York Indians in 1809. Quaker Collection, Haverford College, Allinson Collection, Box 116.

ASPIA 1832–61
American State Papers: Documents, Legislative and Executive. . . . 2 vols. Indian Affairs Series. Washington, D.C.: Gales & Seaton.

Axtell 1978
James Axtell. The Ethnohistory of Early America: A Review Essay. *William and Mary Quarterly* 25: 110–44.

Axtell 1981
James Axtell. *The European and the Indian: Essays in the Ethnohistory of Colonial North America*. New York: Oxford University Press.

Axtell 1985
James Axtell. *The Invasion Within: The Contest of Cultures in Colonial North America*. New York: Oxford University Press.

Baldwin 1791
Waterman Baldwin. Letters and Diary. Merle H. Deardorff Collection, MG-220, box 1, State Archives of Pennsylvania, Harrisburg.

Barclay [1678] 1908
Robert Barclay. *Apology for the True Christian Divinity: Principles and Doctrines of the People Called Quakers*. Philadelphia: William H. Pile's Sons. Translated from the Latin by Barclay.

Barton 1990
Lois Barton. *A Quaker Promise Kept: Philadelphia Friends Work with the Allegany Senecas, 1795–1960*. Eugene, Oreg.: Spencer Butte Press.

BCCR 1994
Anna Miller Watring and F. Edward Wright, eds. *Bucks County Church Records of the 17th and 18th Centuries*. 3 vols. Westminster, MD.: Family Line Publications.

Beatty [1766] 1962
Guy Soulliard Klett, ed. *Journals of Charles Beatty, 1762–1769*. University Park: Pennsylvania State University Press.

Beauchamp 1896
William M. Beauchamp. Iroquois Games. *Journal of American Folk-Lore* 9, no. 35: 269–77.

Beauchamp 1897
William M. Beauchamp. The New Religion of the Iroquois. *Journal of American Folk-Lore* 10: 169–80.

Belknap and Morse [1796] 1955
Jeremy Belknap and Jedidiah Morse. Report on the Oneida, Stockbridge, and Brotherton Indians, 1796. Reprinted in *Museum of the American Indian*. Notes and Monographs no. 54. New York: Heye Foundation.

Benn 1998
Carl Benn. *The Iroquois in the War of 1812*. Toronto: University of Toronto Press.

Berkhofer 1965a
Robert F. Berkhofer, Jr. *Salvation and the Savage: An Analysis of Protestant Missions and American Indian Response, 1787–1862*. Lexington: University of Kentucky Press.

Berkhofer 1965b
Robert F. Berkhofer, Jr. Faith and Factionalism among the Senecas: Theory and Ethnohistory. *Ethnohistory* 12, no. 2: 99–112.

Bilharz 1995
Joy Bilharz. First Among Equals? The Changing Status of Seneca Women. In *Women and Power in Native North America*, edited by Laura F. Klein and Lillian A. Ackerman. Norman: University of Oklahoma Press.

Billington 1944
Ray A. Billington. The Fort Stanwix Treaty of 1768. *New York History* (April): 182–94.

Blau 1964
Harold Blau. The Iroquois White Dog Sacrifice: Its Evolution and Symbolism. *Ethnohistory* 11, no. 2: 97–119.

Boyle 1898
    David Boyle. The Pagan Iroquois. *Annual Ar-chaeological Report for 1898* (Ministry of Education, Toronto): 54–196.
Brewster 1954
    William Brewster. *The Pennsylvania and New York Frontier: Its History from 1720 to the Close of the Revolution.* Philadelphia: George S. Mac-Manus.
Broom et al. 1954
    Leonard Broom, Bernard J. Siegel, Evon Z. Vogt, and James B. Watson. Acculturation: An Exploratory Formulation. *American Anthropologist* 56: no. 6 (December): 973–1000.
Brown 1970
    Judith K. Brown. Economic Organization and the Position of Women among the Iroquois. *Ethnohistory* 17, nos. 3, 4: 151–67.
Buck and Buck [1939] 1979
    Solon J. Buck and Elizabeth H. Buck. *The Planting of Civilization in Western Pennsylvania.* Pittsburgh: University of Pittsburgh Press.
Calloway 1995
    Collin G. Calloway. *The American Revolution in Indian Country: Crisis and Diversity in Native American Communities.* Cambridge: Cambridge University Press.
Campisi 1988
    Jack Campisi. From Satnwix to Canandaigua: National Policy, States' Rights, and Indian Land. In *Iroquois Land Claims,* edited by Christopher Vecsey and William A. Starna. Syracuse: Syracuse University Press.
Campisi and Starna 1995
    Jack Campisi and William A. Starna, On the Road to Canandaigua: The Treaty of 1794. *American Indian Quarterly* 19, no. 4: 467–90.
Catlin [1841] 1973
    George Catlin. *Letters and Notes on the Manners, Customs, and Conditions of the North American Indians.* 2 vols. Reprint, New York: Dover Publications.
Charlevoix [1744] 1761
    Pierre de Charlevoix. *Journal of a Voyage to North-America.* Translated from the French. 2 vols. R. and J. London: Dodsley.
Chazanof 1970
    William Chazanof. *Joseph Ellicot and the Holland Land Company: The Opening of Western New York.* Syracuse: Syracuse University Press.
Clark 1849
    Joshua V. H. Clark. *Onondaga Reminiscences.* Syracuse, N.Y.: vol. 1. Stoddard and Babcock.
Coats 1799
    Isaac Coats. Manuscript journal kept during a two-month sojourn to visit Indians in the western parts of Pennsylvania and New York and Friends in upper Canada, August 23 through October 27, typed transcript of this journal, Warren

Public Library, Pennsylvania Room, Ref. 970, In 2, v: 1.
Code 1913
    Edward Cornplanter's. Code of Handsome Lake. In *The Code of Handsome Lake, the Seneca Prophet,* New York State Museum Bulletin 163, ser. ed. Arthur C. Parker. Albany.
Conklin and Sturtevant 1953
    Harold C. Conklin and William C. Sturtevant. Seneca Indian Singing Tools at Coldspring Longhouse: Muscial Instruments of the Modern Iroquois. *Proceedings of the American Philosophical Society* 97, no. 3: 262–90.
Converse [1908] 1981
    Harriet Maxwell Converse. *Myths and Legends of the New York State Iroquois.* Edited by Arthur C. Parker. New York State Museum Bulletin 125, Albany.
Cook 1887
    Frederick Cook, ed. *Journals of the Military Expedition of Major General John Sullivan against the Six Nations of Indians in 1779.* Auburn, N.Y.: Knapp, Peck, and Thomson Printers.
Culin 1975
    Stewart Culin. *Games of the North American Indians.* Originally published as the Twenty-Fourth Annual Report of the Bureau of American Ethnology to the Smithsonian Institution, 1902–1903. Washington, D.C.: Government Printing Office 1907. Reprint, New York: Dover.
Deardorff 1941
    Merle H. Deardorff. The Cornplanter Grant in Warren County. *Western Pennsylvania Historical Magazine.* 24: 1–22.
Deardorff 1946
    Merle H. Deardorff. Zeisberger's Allegheny River Indian Towns: 1767–1770. *Pennsylvania Archaeologist* 16, no. 1 (January): 2–19.
Deardorff 1951
    Merle H. Deardorff. The Religion of Handsome Lake: Its Origin and Development. In *Symposium on Local Diversity in Iroquois Culture,* edited by William Fenton. Bureau of American Ethnology Bulletin no. 149. Washington, D.C.: Smithsonian Institution.
Deardorff 1999
    Merle H. Deardorff. Henry Obail, 1774–1832: The Young Cornplanter. *Stepping Stones* (Warren County [Pa.] Historical Society) 14, no. 3 (September 1970). Reprint, *Stepping Stones,* 43, no. 2 (May) 1756–61 and 1770.
Deardorff and Snyderman 1956
    Merle H. Deardorff and George S. Snyderman, eds. A Nineteenth-Century Journal of a Visit to the Indians of New York, *Proceedings of the American Philosophical Society* 100, no. 6 (December): 582–612.
Densmore 1999
    Christopher Densmore. *Red Jacket: Iroquois*

Diplomat and Orator. Syracuse: Syracuse University Press.

DHSNY 1849
Documentary History of the State of New York. Edited by E. B. O'Callaghan. Vol. 2. Albany, N.Y.: Weed, Parsons.

Donehoo 1926
George P. Donehoo, ed., *Pennsylvania—A History.* Vol. 1. New York: Lewis Historical Publishing.

Downes 1940
Randolph C. Downes. *Council fires on the Upper Ohio: A Narrative of Indian Affairs in the Upper Ohio Valley until 1795.* Pittsburgh: University of Pittsburgh Press.

DRCHSNY 1853–57
Documents Relative to the Colonial History of the State of New York. Edited by E. B. O'Callaghan. 15 vols. Albany, N.Y.: Weed, Parsons.

Eckert 1989
Jack Eckert, compiler. *Guide to the Records of the Philadelphia Yearly Meeting.* Records Committee of the Philadelphia Yearly Meeting.

Edmunds 1983
R. David Edmunds. *The Shawnee Prophet.* Lincoln: University of Nebraska Press.

Ellicott 1937
Joseph Ellicott. *Reports of Joseph Ellicott as Chief of Survey (1797–1800) and as Agent (1800–1821) of the Holland Land Company's Purchase in Western New York.* Buffalo Historical Society Publication no. 32, vol. 1, ser. ed. R. W. Bingham. Buffalo.

Emlen [1794] 1965
William N. Fenton, ed. The Journal of James Emlen Kept on A Trip to Canandaigua, New York. *Ethnohistory* 12, no. 4: 279–342

Evans [1924] 1979
Paul D. Evans. *The Holland Land Company.* N.J., 1979 Buffalo Historical Society Publication no. 28. Buffalo. Reprint, Fairfield, N.J.: Augustus M. Kelley Publishers.

Eyeman 1964
Frances Eyeman. Lacrosse and the Cayuga Thunder Rite. *Expedition* 6, no. 4 (Summer): 15–19.

Fenton [1936] 1970
William N. Fenton. *An Outline of Seneca Ceremonies at Coldspring Longhouse.* No. 9, Yale University Publications in Anthropology. Reprint, New Haven, Conn.: Human Relations Area Files Press.

Fenton [1941a] 1984
William N. Fenton. *Masked Medicine Societies of the Iroquois.* Annual Report of the Board of Regents of the Smithsonian Institution for 1940, publication 3606. Washington, D.C.: Government Printing Office. Reprint, Ohsweken, Ontario: Iroqrafts.

Fenton 1941b
William N. Fenton. *Tonawanda Longhouse Ceremonies: Ninety Years after Lewis Henry Morgan.* Bureau of American Ethnology, Bulletin no. 128, Anthropological Papers no. 15. Washington, D.C.: Smithsonian Institution.

Fenton 1942a
William N. Fenton. Fish Drives among the Cornplanter Seneca. *Pennsylvania Archaeologist* 12, no. 3 (July–October): 47–52.

Fenton 1942b
William N. Fenton. *Songs from the Iroquois Longhouse: Program Notes for an Album of American Indian Music from the Eastern Woodlands.* Bureau of American Ethnology, Publication no. 3691. Washington, D.C.: Smithsonian Institution.

Fenton 1945a, b, c, d
William N. Fenton. Place Names and Related Activities of the Cornplanter Senecas. *Pennsylvania Archaeologist* 15, no. 1: 25–29; no. 2: no. 3: 88–96; no. 4: 108–18 (a, b, c, and d, respectively).

Fenton 1946
William N. Fenton. Place Names and Related Activities of the Cornplanter Senecas. *Pennsylvania Archaeologist* 16, no. 2: 1946.

Fenton 1951
William N. Fenton. Locality as a Basic Factor in the Development of Iroquois Social Structure. In *Symposium on Local Diversity in Iroquois Culture.* Bureau of American Ethnology, Bulletin no. 149, edited by William N. Fenton. Washington, D.C.: Smithsonian Institution.

Fenton 1963
William N. Fenton. The Seneca Green Corn Ceremony. *The New York State Conservationist* 18, no. 2 (October–November): 20–22.

Fenton 1968
William N. Fenton, ed. *Parker on the Iroquois: Iroquois Uses of Maize and Other Food Plants, The Code of Handsome Lake, The Constitution of the Five Nations.* Syracuse: Syracuse University Press.

Fenton 1998
William N. Fenton. *The Great Law and the Longhouse: A Political History of the Iroquois Confederacy.* Norman: University of Oklahoma Press.

Fenton and Deardorff 1943
William N. Fenton and Merle H. Deardorff. The Last Passenger Pigeon Hunts of the Cornplanter Senecas. *Journal of the Washington Academy of Sciences* 33, no. 10 (October): 289–315.

Fenton and Kurath 1951
William N. Fenton and Gertrude P. Kurath. The Feast of the Dead, or Ghost Dance, at Six Nations Reserve, Canada. In *Symposium on Local Diversity in Iroquois Culture. Bureau of American Ethnology,* Bulletin no. 149, edited by

William N. Fenton. Washington, D.C.: Smithsonian Institution.

FHL
Friends Historical Library, Manuscript and Microfilms Collections, Swarthmore College, Swarthmore, PA.

Fitting 1976
James E. Fitting. Patterns of Acculturation at the Straits of Mackinac. In *Cultural Change and Continuity,* edited by Charles E. Cleland. New York: Academic Press.

Fox [1694] 1906
Percy Livingstone Parker, ed. *George Fox's Journal, Abridged.* Originally edited by Thomas Ellwood and published in London. Reprint, London: Sir Isaac Pitman and Sons.

Frazier 1992
Patrick Frazier. *The Mohicans of Stockbridge.* Lincoln: University of Nebraska Press.

Frost 1973
J. William Frost. *The Quaker Family in Colonial America: A Portrait of the Society of Friends.* New York: St. Martin's Press.

Graymont 1972
Barbara Graymont. *The Iroquois in the American Revolution.* Syracuse: Syracuse University Press.

Gunn 1903
Sarah E. Gunn. *Sarah Whitmore's Captivity in 1782: Her Life among the Mohawks and Senecas* . . . . Buffalo Historical Society Publication no. 6, edited by Frank H. Severance. Buffalo, N.Y.

Harmon 1941
George Dewey Harmon. *Sixty Years of Indian Affairs: Political, Economic, and Diplomatic, 1789–1850.* Chapel Hill: University of North Carolina Press.

Harris 1903
George H. Harris. *Life of Horatio Jones: The True Story of Hocsagowah—Prisoner, Pioneer, and Interpreter.* Buffalo Historical Society Publication no. 6, edited by Frank H. Severance. Buffalo, N.Y.

Hauptman 1986
Laurence M. Hauptman. *The Iroquois Struggle for Survival: World War II to Red Power.* Syracuse: Syracuse University Press.

Hauptman 1999
Laurence M. Hauptman. *Conspiracy of Interests: Iroquois Dispossession and the Rise of New York State.* Syracuse: Syracuse University Press.

Hertzberg 1966
Hazel W. Hertzberg. *The Great Tree and the Longhouse: The Culture of the Iroquois.* New York: Macmillan Company.

Hewitt 1892
John N. B. Hewitt. Iroquois Game of La Crosse. *American Anthropologist* 5, no. 2 (April): 189–91.

Horsman 1967
Reginald Horsman. *Expansion and American In-*

dian Policy, 1783–1812. Michigan State University Press.

Hough 1861
Franklin Benjamin Hough. *Proceedings of the Commissioners of Indian Affairs.* . . . Albany, N.Y.: Joel Munsell.

Hough 1888
Walter Hough. Games of Seneca Indians. *American Anthropologist* 1, no. 2 (April): 134.

HSP
Historical Society of Pennsylvania, Manuscript Collection, Pennsylvania Manuscripts, Indian Affairs, vol. 4, 56; letter from Cornplanter and chiefs at Jenuchshadago to David Meade at Cussawaga, n.d., ca. January 1801; letter from Munsee chiefs at Cattaraugus to David Meade at Cussawaga, dated April 11, 1801; letter from Msrs. Wallace and Baldwin, Meade's associates, at Meadville, Cussawaga, to Governor Thomas McKean at Lancaster, dated April 14, 1801. Note: the author used typewritten copies of these letters found in the Warren County Historical Society's files on chief Cornplanter.

Hultkrantz 1997
Ake Hultkrantz. *Soul and Native Americans.* Woodstock, CT: Spring Publications, Inc.

Hunt 1940
George T. Hunt. *The Wars of the Iroquois: A Study in Intertribal Trade Relations.* Madison: University of Wisconsin Press.

Jackson [1798–1800] 1952
Halliday Jackson. A Short History of My Sojourning in the Wilderness, (1798–1800). In Halliday Jackson's Journal to the Seneca Indians, 1798–1800, edited by Anthony F. C. Wallace. Parts 1 and 2. *Pennsylvania History* 19, no. 2 (April): 117–47; no. 3 (July): 325–49.

Jackson 1799 Letter Book
Halliday Jackson. Halliday Jackson's Book 1799 Genesinguhta. Book of letters, Swarthmore, PA, Swarthmore College. Jackson Manuscripts 1799–1824, folder 2.

Jackson 1800 Journal
Halliday Jackson. Some Account of My Residence among the Indians Continued. Microfilm copy of manuscript journal at Friends Historical Library, Swarthmore College, Swarthmore, PA. A partial typescript of this journal is available in the Merle H. Deardorff Collection. MG-220, box 2, State Archives of Pennsylvania, Harrisburg.

Jackson 1806 Journal
Halliday Jackson. Some Account of a Visit Paid to the Friends at Tunesassa . . . 1806. In *Halliday Jackson's Journal of a Visit Paid to the Indians of New York (1806),* ed. George F. Snyderman, *Proceedings of the American Philosophical Society* 101, no. 6 (December): 565–88.

Jackson 1830a
Halliday Jackson. *Sketch of the Manners, Cus-*

toms, Religion, and Government of the Seneca Indians in 1800. Philadelphia: Marcus T. C. Gould.

Jackson 1830b
Halliday Jackson. *Civilization of the Indian Natives*. Philadelphia: Marcus T. C. Gould.

Jacobs [1972] 1985
Wilbur R. Jacobs. *Dispossessing the American Indian: Indians and Whites on the Colonial Frontier*. Norman: University of Oklahoma Press.

James 1963
Sydney V. James. *A People among Peoples: Quaker Benevolence in Eighteenth-Century America*. Cambridge: Harvard University Press.

Jennings 1975
Francis Jennings. *The Invasion of America: Indians, Colonialism, and the Cant of Conquest*. Chapel Hill: University of North Carolina Press.

Jennings 1984
Francis Jennings. *The Ambiguous Iroquois Empire: The Covenant Chain Confederation of Indian Tribes with English Colonies from its beginnings to the Lancaster Treaty of 1744*. New York: W. W. Norton.

Jennings 1985
Francis Jennings. *The History and Culture of Iroquois Diplomacy: An Interdisciplinary Guide to the Treaties of the Six Nations and Their League*. Syracuse: Syracuse University Press.

Jesuit Relations 1896–1901
The Jesuit Relations and Allied Documents: Travels and Explorations of the Jesuit Missionaries in New France, 1610–1791, Ed. Reuben Gold Thwaites. 73 vols. Cleveland: Burrows Brothers.

Johnston 1964
Charles M. Johnston, ed. *The Valley of the Six Nations: A Collection of Documents on the Indian Lands of the Grand River*. Toronto: University of Toronto Press.

Kaufman 1964
Martin Kaufman. War Sentiment in Western Pennsylvania: 1812. *Pennsylvania History* 31, no. 4: 436–48.

Kehoe 1981
Alice B. Kehoe. Revisionist Anthropology: Aboriginal North America. *Current Anthropology* 22, no. 5 (October): 503–17.

Kelsay 1984
Isabel Thompson Kelsay. *Joseph Brant, 1743–1807: Man of Two Worlds*. Syracuse: Syracuse University Press.

Kelsey 1917
Rayner Kelsey. *Friends and the Indians, 1655–1917*. Philadelphia: Associated Executive Committee of Friends on Indian Affairs.

Kenny [1758–59 Journal] 1913
John W. Jordan, ed. James Kenny's "Journal to

ye Westward," 1758–1759. *Pennsylvania Magazine of History and Biography* 37: 395–470.

Kenny [1761–63 Journal] 1913
John W. Jordan, ed. Journal of James Kenny, 1761–1763. *Pennsylvania Magazine of History and Biography* 37, no. 1.

Kent 1974
Donald H. Kent. *Iroquois Indians I: History of Pennsylvania Purchases from the Indians*. Vol. 1. New York: Garland Publishing.

Kent and Deardorff 1960
Donald H. Kent and Merle H. Deardorff. John Adlum on the Allegheny: Memoirs for the Year 1794. *Pennsylvania Magazine of History and Biography* 84, nos. 3 and 4 (July): 265–324; (October): 435–80.

Kurath 1964
Gertrude P. Kurath. Iroquois Music and Dance: Ceremonial Arts of Two Seneca Longhouses. Bureau of American Ethnology Bulletin no. 187. Washington, D.C.: Smithsonian Institution.

Kussart 1938
Sarepta Kussart. *The Allegheny River*. Pittsburgh: Burgum Printing.

Lahontan 1735
Louis Armand Lahontan. *New Voyages to North America*. 2 vols. London: Bonwicke, Goodwin, Wotton, Tooke, and Manship, 1703. Reprint, London: J. Osborne.

Linton [1940] 1963
Ralph Linton, ed. *Acculturation in Seven American Indian Tribes*. Reprint, Gloucester, Mass.: Peter Smith.

Linton 1943
Ralph Linton. Nativistic Movements. *American Anthropologist* 45: no. 2 (April–June): 230–40.

Loskiel 1794
George Henry Loskiel. *History of the Mission of the United Brethren among the Indians in North America*. London: Brethren's Society for the Furtherance of the Gospel.

Mancall 1995
Peter C. Mancall. *Deadly Medicine: Indians and Alcohol in Early America*. Ithaca, N.Y.: Cornell University Press.

Manley 1932
Henry S. Manley. *The Treaty of Fort Stanwix 1784*. Rome, N.Y.: Rome Sentinel Company.

Marietta 1984
Jack D. Marietta. *The Reformation of American Quakerism, 1748–1783*. Philadelphia: University of Pennsylvania Press.

Marshall 1967
Peter Marshall, Sir William Johnson and the Treaty of Fort Stanwix, 1768. *Journal of American Studies* 1, no. 2 (1967): 149–79.

McConnell 1992
Michael N. McConnell. *A Country Between: The*

Upper Ohio Valley and Its Peoples. 1724–1774. Lincoln: University of Nebraska Press.

Merrell 1999
James H. Merrell. *Into the American Woods: Negotiators on the Pennsylvania Frontier.* New York: W. W. Norton.

Morgan 1851
Lewis Henry Morgan. *League of the Hodenosaunee, Iroquois.* Rochester, N.Y.: Sage & Brother.

Murdock 1934
George P. Murdock. *Our Primitive Contemporaries.* New York: Macmillan.

Nammack 1969
Georgiana C. Nammack. *Fraud, Politics, and the Dispossession of the Indians: The Iroquois Land Frontier in the Colonial Period.* Norman: University of Oklahoma Press.

Nobles 1997
Gregory H. Nobles. *American Frontiers: Cultural Encounters and Continental Conquest.* New York: Hill and Wang.

Norton [1816] 1970
Carl F. Klinck and James J. Talman, eds. *The Journal of Major John Norton.* Champlain Society Publication 46. Toronto.

Oxendine 1988
Joseph B. Oxendine. *American Indian Sports Heritage.* Champaign, Ill.: Human Kinetics Books.

PA 1855–56, 1-1, PA 1855–56, 1-3, PA 1855–56, 1-10, PA 1855–56, 1-11, PA 1855–56, 1-12
Pennsylvania Archives, ed. Samuel Hazzard. first Series, vols. 1, 3, 10, 11, and 12. Harrisburg, PA.

PA 1896, 2-4, PA 1896, 2-6
Pennsylvania Archives, ed. John B. Linn and William H. Egle. second Series, vols. 4 and 6. Harrisburg, PA.

PA 1900, 4-4, PA 1900, 4-5
Pennsylvania Archives, ed. George E. Reed. fourth Series, vols. 4 and 5, Harrisburg, PA.

PA 8-1
Pennsylvania Archives, ed. Gertrude MacKinney. eighth Series, vol. 1. Harrisburg, PA.

Parker 1909
Arthur C. Parker. Secret Medicine Societies of the Seneca. *American Anthropologist* 11, no. 2, (April–June): 161–85.

Parker 1910
Arthur C. Parker. *Iroquois Uses of Maize and Other Food Plants.* New York State Museum Bulletin 144. Albany.

Parker 1913
Arthur C. Parker. *The Code of Handsome Lake, the Seneca Prophet.* New York State Museum Bulletin 163. Albany.

Parker 1916
Arthur C. Parker. *The Constitution of the Five Nations; or, The Iroquois Book of the Great Law.*

New York State Museum Bulletin 184. Albany.

PA State Archives
State Archives of Pennsylvania, the Merle H. Deardorff Collection and the Kent-Barnard Collection, Harrisburg: Pennsylvania Historical and Museum Commission, Division of Archives and Manuscripts.

PCR
Pennsylvania Colonial Records. 16 vols. Minutes of the Supreme Executive Council. Harrisburg, PA: Theo. Fenn.

Perrot 1911
Nicolas Perrot. Memoir on the Manners, Customs, and Religion of the Savages of North America (ca. 1680–1718). Edited by Jules Tailhan. Paris: 1864. Reprint in *The Indian Tribes of the Upper Mississippi Valley and Region of the Great Lakes. . . .* Edited and translated by Emma Helen Blair. Vol. 1. Cleveland: Arthur H. Clark.

Philips [1806] 1856
John Philips. Some Account of My Journey Made to the Indians . . . 1806. In *A Nineteenth-Century Journal of a Visit to the Indians of New York,* edited by Deardorff and George F. Snyderman. *Proceedings of the American Philosophical Society* 100, no. 6 (December): 582–612.

Pierce 1798
John Pierce. Notes on a Visit to the Seneca Nation of Indians . . . (1798). Photostat of manuscript journal, MG-220, Deardorff Collection MG-220, Pennsylvania State Archives, Harrisburg; a typescript of this journal is available in the Warren Historical Transcripts, Warren Public Library, Warren, PA.

Pomedli 1991
Michael Pomedli. *Ethnophilosophical and Ethnolinguistic Perspectives on the Huron Indian Soul.* Edwin Mellin Press.

Proctor [1791] 1896
Col. Thomas Proctor. Narrative of Colonel Thomas Proctor: His Journey to the Indians of the Northwest. In *Pennsylvania Archives,* second Series, vol. 4. Harrisburg, PA.

Prucha 1990
Francis Paul Prucha, ed. *Documents of United States Indian Policy.* 2d ed. Lincoln: University of Nebraska Press.

Prucha 1994
Francis Paul Prucha. *American Indian Treaties: The History of a Political Anomaly.* Berkeley and Los Angeles: University of California Press.

PSWJ 1921–65
Papers of Sir William Johnson. Division of Archives and History, 14 vols., University of the State of New York, Albany.

PYMIC Collection
Indian Committee Collection of the Philadelphia Yearly Meeting (PYM), microfilm copy at the

American Philosophical Society Library in Philadelphia, PA. Original manuscripts at the Quaker Collection of Haverford College, Haverford, PA.

PYMIC Minutes
Indian Committee Minutes of the Philadelphia Yearly Meeting (PYM). Friends Historical Library, Swarthmore College, Swarthmore, PA.

PYMIC Proceedings 1806
Philadelphia Yearly Meeting Indian Committee, Proceedings 1795–1805: *Accounts of Two Attempts toward Civilization of Some Indian Natives.* Philadelphia: Phillips and Fardoe.

PYMMS Minutes
Minutes of the Meeting for Sufferings of the Philadelphia Yearly Meeting (PYM).

Randle 1951
Martha C. Randle. Iroquois Women Then and Now. In Symposium on Local Diversity in Iroquois Culture, edited by William Fenton. *Bureau of American Ethnology* Bulletin no. 149. Washington, D.C.: Smithsonian Institution.

Redfield, Linton, and Herskovits 1936
Robert Redfield, Ralph Linton, and Melville J. Herskovits. Memorandum for the Study of Acculturation. *American Anthropologist* 38: 149–52.

Reel, Perrusquia, and Sullivan 1995
Guy Reel, Marc Perrusquia, and Bartholomew Sullivan. *The Blood of Innocents.* New York: Kensington Publishing.

Reynolds 1938
John Earle Reynolds. *In French Creek Valley.* Meadville, PA: Crawford County Historical Society.

Ricciardelli 1963
Alex F. Ricciardelli. The Adoption of White Agriculture by the Oneida Indians. *Ethnohistory* 10, no. 4: 309–28.

Richter 1992
Daniel K. Richter. *The Ordeal of the Longhouse: The Peoples of the Iroquois League in the Era of European Colonization.* Chapel Hill: University of North Carolina Press.

Rogers and Wilson 1993
J. Daniel Rogers and Samuel M. Wilson, eds. *Ethnohistory and Archaeology: Approaches to Postcontact Change in the Americas.* New York: Plenum Press.

Rothenberg 1980
Diane Rothenberg. The Mothers of the Nation: Seneca Resistance to Quaker Intervention. In *Women and Colonization: Anthropological Perspectives,* ed. Mona Etienne, Eleanor Leacock. New York: Praeger Publishers.

Royce [1900] 1971
Charles C. Royce. *Indian Land Cessions in the United States.* Extract from the eighteenth Annual Report of the Bureau of American Ethnol-

ogy. Washington, D.C.: Government Printing Office. Reprint, Arno Press.

Rubertone 1989
Patricia E. Rubertone. Archaeology, Colonialism and Seventeenth-Century Native America: Towards an Alternative Interpretation. In *Conflict in the Archaeology of Living Traditions,* edited by Robert Layton. London: Unwin Hyman Ltd., Academic Division.

Sagard [1636] 1866
Gabriel Sagard (Theodat). *Histoire du Canada et voyages que les freres mineurs recollects. . . .* Paris: M. Edwin Tross.

SCP 1930–33
Susquehanna Company Papers. Edited by Julian P. Boyd. 6 vols. Ithaca, N.Y.: Cornell University Press.

Seaver [1824] 1982
James E. Seaver. *The Life of Mary Jemison.* New York: American Scenic and Historic Preservation Society. Originally published as *A Narrative of the Life of Mrs. Mary Jemison,* Canandaigua: J.D. Bemis.

Shafer 1990
Ann Eastlack Shafer. The Status of Iroquois Women. In *Iroquois Women: An Anthology,* edited by W. G. Spittal. Ohsweken, Ontario: Iroqrafts.

Sharpless 1798
Joshua Sharpless. *Some Account of a Journey I took into the Indian Country 1798.* Manuscript journal at Swarthmore College, Swarthmore, PA, in Friends Historical Library, Sharpless Manuscripts, series 2. Extracts published in installments in the Times-Mirror Newspaper of Warren, PA in 1930 and reprinted in a small volume titled *Record of a Quaker Mission to Cornplanter Tribe.*

Sheehan 1973
Bernard W. Sheehan. *Seeds of Extinction: Jeffersonian Philanthropy and the American Indian.* Chapel Hill: University of North Carolina Press.

Shimony [1961] 1994
Annemarie Shimony. *Conservatism among the Iroquois at Six Nations Reserve.* No. 65, Yale University Publications in Anthropology. Reprint, Syracuse: Syracuse University Press.

Shimony [1970] 1989
Annemarie Shimony. Eastern Woodlands: Iroquois of Six Nations. In *Systems of North American Witchcraft and Sorcery.* Moscow: University of Idaho Press. Reprint in *Witchcraft and Sorcery of the American Native Peoples,* edited by Deward E. Walker, Jr. Moscow: University of Idaho Press.

Simmons 1796–97 Journal
Henry Simmons, Jr. Henry Simmons, Jr., His Book (May 29, 1796, to October 16, 1797). Manuscript book of Simmons's journal of his mission to the Oneida and Stockbridge Indians includes Simmons's PYMIC certificate and some letters

from 1796 and 1797. Haverford College, Haverford, PA, Quaker Collection, 975B.

(Note: The manuscript book has come unbound and is now in a folder labeled v.1. Also laid in the folder labeled v.1 is a paper that appears, on the front side, to be Simmons's original certificate of approval, dated May 5, 1796, addressed to the PYMIC, from his monthly meeting at Middletown in Bucks County, PA. On the reverse side of the certificate is an original minute from the PYMIC, dated December 21, 1799, addressed to Middletown MM, releasing Simmons from his missionary work.)

Simmons 1797 Letter Book
Henry Simmons, Jr., Henry Simmons Jr. His Book for 1797, manuscript book of letters, treaties, and legislative acts from 1797 and earlier, Quaker Collection, 975B, Haverford College, Haverford, PA.

Simmons 1798–99 Letter Book
Henry Simmons, Jr. Henry Simmons Jr.: His Book. Manuscript book of letters from 1798 and 1799, Quaker Collection, 975B. Haverford College, Haverford, PA.

Simmons 1799 Journal
Henry Simmons, Jr. Henry Simmons Jr.: Book No. 2. Manuscript book of Simmons's 1799 journal of his mission to the Allegany Seneca, Quaker Collection, 975B. Haverford College, Haverford, PA. Extracts and excerpts from this journal have been published previously in the following: Deardorff 1951; Wallace 1952; Wallace 1972.

Sipe [1927] 1998
C. Hale Sipe, *The Indian Chiefs of Pennsylvania.* Butler: Ziegler Printing. Reprint, Lewisburg: Wennawoods Publishing.

Sloan 1902
James Sloan. Early Trade Routes: Adventures and Recollections of a Pioneer Trader. *Buffalo Historical Society,* vol. 5: 215–37.

Smith 1888
De Cost Smith. Witchcraft and Demonism of the Modern Iroquois. *Journal of American Folklore* 1, no. 3: 184–93.

Smith 1889
De Cost Smith. Additional Notes on Onondaga Witchcraft. *Journal of American Folklore* 2, no. 7: 277–81.

Snow 1994
Dean R. Snow. *The Iroquois.* Cambridge, Mass.: Blackwell Publishers.

Snyderman 1957
George S. Snyderman. Halliday Jackson's Journal of a Visit Paid to the Indians of New York. Proceedings of the American Philosophical Society 101, no. 6: 565–88.

Sosin 1961
Jack M. Sosin. *Whitehall and the Wilderness: The Middle West in British Colonial Policy,* 1760–1775. Lincoln: University of Nebraska Press.

Speck 1949
Frank G. Speck. *Midwinter Rites of the Cayuga Long House.* Philadelphia: University of Pennsylvania Press.

St. John 1989
Donald P. St. John. Iroquois. In *Native American Religions: Religion, History, and Culture Selections from The Encyclopedia of Religion,* edited by Lawrence E. Sullivan. New York: Macmillan Publishing.

Stone R 1924
Rufus B. Stone. Brodhead's Raid on the Seneca. *Western Pennsylvania Historical Magazine* 7, no. 2: 88–101.

Stone W [1838] 1864
William L. Stone. *The Life of Joseph Brant (Thayendanegea).* 2 vols. Albany, N.Y.: J. Munsell.

Stone W 1841
William L. Stone. *The Life and Times of Red Jacket (Sagoyewatha).* New York: Putnam.

Sullivan Papers [1779–95] 1930–39
Otis G. Hammond, ed. *The Letters and Papers of Major General John Sullivan.* Vol. 3. Concord: New Hampshire Historical Society.

Sword 1985
Wiley Sword. *President Washington's Indian War: The Struggle for the Old Northwest, 1790–1795.* Norman: University of Oklahoma Press.

Tiffany and Tiffany 1904
Nina Moore Tiffany and Francis Tiffany. *Harm Jan Huidekoper.* Cambridge, Mass.: Riverside Press.

Todd 1940
W. E. Clyde Todd. *Birds of Western Pennsylvania.* Pittsburgh: University of Pittsburgh Press.

Tolles 1948
Frederick B. Tolles. *Meeting House and Counting House: The Quaker Merchants of Colonial Philadelphia, 1682–1763.* Chapel Hill: University of North Carolina Press.

Tome [1854] 1928
Philip Tome. *Pioneer Life; or, Thirty Years A Hunter.* Reprint, Harrisburg, PA: Aurand Press.

Tooker 1965
Elisabeth Tooker. The Iroquois White Dog Sacrifice in the Latter Part of the Eighteenth Century. *Ethnohistory* 12, no. 2: 129–40.

Tooker 1970
Elisabeth Tooker. *The Iroquois Ceremonial of Midwinter.* Syracuse: Syracuse University Press.

Tooker 1984
Elisabeth Tooker. Women in Iroquois Society. In *Extending the Rafters: Interdisciplinary Approaches to Iroquoian Studies,* edited by Michael K. Foster, Jack Campisi, and Marianne Mithun. Albany: State University of New York Press, pp. 109–23.

Van Every 1961
    Dale Van Every. *Forth to the Wilderness: The First American Frontier, 1754–1774.* New York: New American Library.
Vennum 1994
    Thomas Vennum. *American Indian Lacrosse: Little Brother of War.* Washington, D.C.: Smithsonian Institution Press.
Voget 1956
    Fred W. Voget. The American Indian in Transition: Reformation and Accommodation. *American Anthropologist* 58, no. 2 (April): 249–63.
Wallace 1949
    Anthony F. C. Wallace. *King of the Delawares: Teedyuscung, 1700–1763.* Philadelphia: University of Pennsylvania Press.
Wallace 1952
    Anthony F. C. Wallace, ed. Halliday Jackson's Journal to the Seneca Indians, 1798–1800. In two parts in *Pennsylvania History* 19, no. 2 (April): 117–47; no. 3 (July): 325–49.
Wallace 1956
    Anthony F. C. Wallace. Revitalization Movements. *American Anthropologist* 58, no. 2 (April): 264–81.
Wallace 1958
    Anthony F. C. Wallace. Dreams and Wishes of the Soul: A Type of Psychoanalytic Theory among the Seventeenth Century Iroquois. *American Anthropologist* 60: 234–48.
Wallace 1972
    Anthony F. C. Wallace. *The Death and Rebirth of the Seneca: The History and Culture of the Great Iroquois Nation, Their Destruction and Demoralization, and Their Cultural Revival at the Hands of the Indian Visionary, Handsome Lake.* New York: Knopf, 1969. Reprint, New York: Vintage Books.
Walton [1784/1848] 1975
    William Walton. *A Narrative of the Captivity and Sufferings of Benjamin Gilbert and His Family.* New York: Garland Publishing. (Reprint of the 1784 edition published by J. Crukshank of Philadelphia bound with reprint of the 1848 edition published by John Richards of Philadelphia.)
Way 1942
    Frederick Way, Jr. *The Allegheny.* New York: Farrer & Rinehart.
Weaver 1984
    Sally M. Weaver. Seth Newhouse and the Grand River Confederacy at Mid-Nineteenth Century. In *Extending the Rafters: Interdisciplinary Approaches to Iroquoian Studies,* edited by Michael K. Foster, Jack Campisi, and Marianne Mithun. Albany: State University of New York Press.

White 1991
    Richard White. *The Middle Ground: Indians, Empires, and Republics in the Great Lakes Region, 1650–1815.* Cambridge: Cambridge University Press.
Wilkinson 1953
    Norman B. Wilkinson. Robert Morris and the Treaty of Big Tree. *The Mississippi Valley Historical Review* 40, no. 2 (September): 257–78.
Woodbury 1992
    Hanni Woodbury. *Concerning the League: The Iroquois League Tradition as Dictated in Onondaga by John Arthur Gibson.* Memoir 9. Winnipeg, Manitoba: Algonquian and Iroquoian Linguistics.
Woody [1920] 1969
    Thomas Woody. *Early Quaker Education in Pennsylvania.* New York: Teachers College of Columbia University. Reprint, New York: Arno Press and *The New York Times.*
Woolman [1794] 1909
    John Woolman. The Journal of John Woolman. In *The Autobiography of Benjamin Franklin; The Journal of John Woolman; Fruits of Solitude, by William Penn,* edited by Charles Eliot. New York: P. F. Collier and Son.
Wrenshall 1942
    Excerpts from the Journals of John Wrenshall, 1815–1821. *The Western Pennsylvania Historical Magazine:* 25, no. 1 and 2, March–June, 81–83.
Wulff 1977
    Roger L. Wulff. Lacrosse among the Seneca. *The Indian Historian* 10, no. 2 (spring): 16–22.
Zeisberger 1767 Journal
    Archer B. Hulbert and William N. Schwarze, eds. The Diaries of Zeisberger Relating to the First Missions in the Ohio Basin. *Ohio Archaeological and Historical Quarterly* 21, no. 1 (January): 8–32.
Zeisberger 1768–69 Journal
    Archer B. Hulbert and William N. Schwarze, eds. The Diaries of Zeisberger Relating to the First Missions in the Ohio Basin. *Ohio Archaeological and Historical Quarterly* 21, no. 1 (January): 32–115.
Zeisberger [1780] 1910
    David Zeisberger. Untitled manuscript notes on the history, life, manners, and customs of the Indians. In David Zeisberger's History of the North American Indians, edited by Archer B. Hulbert and William N. Schwarze. *Ohio Archaeological and Historical Quarterly* 19.

INDEX

314

reformation of, 55–56
relations with Indians, 82–86
structure of, 56–60
temperance, 68–69
testimonies, 59–60
witchcraft and, 206
Queen Anne's War, 61

Randle, Martha, 209
Red Jacket, 32–33, 104, 126, 131, 134, 139, 221, 256
  Big Tree Treaty (1797), 140, 141, 142, 143
  Canandaigua Treaty (1794), 135–37
Reformation of American Quakerism, The (Marietta), 85
Reformation of Quakerism, 55–56
Religious Society of Friends (RSF). *See* Quakers/Quakerism
Reservation system, 110
Richland, 132, 133

Sachems, role of women in nominating successors, 211–15
St. Clair, Arthur, 129, 130–31, *132*
St. Leger, Barry, 113
Sandusky, treaty of (1793), 18
Sassoonan, 162, 165–66
Savery, William, 135
Sawmill, Cornplanter's, 47–48, 239–41
Scaroyady, 165
Schuyler, Philip, 112
Seasonal round
  celebrations, 145–50
  sustenance activities, 150–57
Seaver, James, 147
Senecas
  American Revolution and, 111, 121–22
  appeal to ban/regulate alcohol, 168
  Big Tree Treaty (1797) and, 137–44
  Canandaigua Treaty (1794) and, 135–37
  dissent among, 45–51
  economic strategy, 12–15
  land ownership, 127, 129–30, 135–37
  Sullivan and Brodhead campaigns against, 8–12
  temperance movement among, 173, 174–76
  vulnerabilities, 16–20
  witchcraft, 196–207
Shafer, Ann Eastlack, 209
Shagodyoweh, 197–98
Shamans
  healing abilities, 202
  lacrosse and role of, 98–100
  witchcraft and, 200
Sharpless, Joshua, 18, 22–23, 25, 78, 84, 234, 236, 239
Shawnees, 12, 39, 105, 106, 109, 110
  American Revolution and, 111
  appeal to ban/regulate alcohol, 163–64, 165

land ownership, 122, 125, 127, 128, 129
Treaty at the Mouth of the Great Miami River (1786), 120
Shimony, Annemarie, 198
Silver Heels, 204
Simmons, Sarah Dun, 78
Simmons, Henry, 3–4, 6, 178
  among the Senecas, 27–54
  Big Tree Treaty (1797), 144
  death of, 255
  drinking problem in Indians and, 158, 173
  education of, 78
  farewell address, 232–33, 254
  feast for the dead, 193–95
  feather dance descriptions, 178, 181–86
  Green Corn Festival, 230–32
  parents of, 56, 75, 78
  as a pioneer missionary, 22, 25
  Sky Journey, 228–29
  as a teacher, 25–26, 78, 82, 234
  white-dog sacrifice, 226
  wife beating among Indians, 207
Simmons, Henry, Sr., 75, 78
Simmons, Mary Paxson, 75, 78
Simmons, Rachel Preston, 254–55
Six Nations
  See also under name of Indian community
  demise of, 110
Sky Journey, 218
  apocalyptic sights and sounds, 221
  approbation and equivocation, 228–29
  forks in the sky road, 221–22
  Great Lodge of the Punisher, 222–23
  Heaven Road, 223–25
  historical figures, 220–21
  visual parables, 219–20
Slavery, 73–74, 85
Smith, DeCost, 198, 203
Snipe clan, 88, 211
Snow snake, 102
Society of Faces, 148
Speck, Frank, 97
Stewardson, Thomas, 234
Strawberry Festival, 1, 5–6, 145–46, 149–50, 153, 179, 218
Straw game, 97
Stuart, John, 105
Sullivan, John, 9, 115–16
Sullivan's campaign, 10, 11
Susquehanna Co., 108
Susquehannock Indians, 109
Swayne, Joel, 6, 22, 25, 82, 206

Tarachiawagon, 29, 36, 178, 197–98, 226
Tawenna, 163, 164
Tawiskaron, 29, 197–98
Taylor, Jacob, 176, 206, 250
Technological innovations, 50
Teedyuscung, 17, 72, 167